Adobe Illustrator 10 allows for customized shortcuts for most tools and menu commands. Command+Option+Shift+K opens the Keyboard Shortcuts palette. Different sets of short-cuts can be saved for different users or projects. Listed below are the most important of the default keyboard shortcuts. Indented shortcuts are related to the tool or menu item directly above, but do not appear as a tool or menu item themselves.

Windows users should use **Control** instead of **Command** and **Alt** instead of **Option**.

TOOLS AND THE TOOLBOX

Selection	V
Direct Selection	A
Select Next Object Above	Command+Option+] (right bracket)
Select Next Object Below	Command+Option+[(left bracket)
Magic Wand	Y
Direct Select Lasso	Q
Pen	P
Add Anchor Point	= (equal sign)
Delete Anchor Point	- (minus sign)
Convert Anchor Point	Shift+C
Type	T
Ellipse	L
Rectangle	M
Paintbrush	B
Pencil	N
Free Transform	E
Gradient	G
Eyedropper	I
Paint Bucket	K
Hand	H
Zoom	Z
Toggle Fill & Stroke	X
Default Fill & Stroke	D
Swap Fill & Stroke	Shift+X
Color palette	, (comma)
Gradient palette	. (period)
None	/ (slash)
Toggle Screen Mode	F
Show/Hide All Palettes	Tab
Show/Hide Palettes except Toolbox	Shift+Tab

TYPE AND TEXT

Point Size Up	Command+Shift+. (period)
Point Size Down	Command+Shift+, (comma)
Font Size Step Up	Command+Option+Shift+. (period)
Font Size Step Down	Command+Option+Shift+, (comma)
Kern Looser	Command+Shift+] (right bracket)
Kern Tighter	Command+Shift+[(left bracket)
Tracking	Command+Option+K
Clear Tracking	Command+Shift+Q
Spacing	Command+Option+O
Left Align Text	Command+Shift+L
Center Text	Command+Shift+C
Right Align Text	Command+Shift+R
Justify Text	Command+Shift+J
Justify All Lines	Command+Shift+F

Menu Commands

FILE MENU

New...	Command+N
New (no dialog box)	Command+Option+N
Open	Command+O
Close	Command+W
Save	Command+S
Save As...	Command+Shift+S
Save a Copy...	Command+Option+S
Save for Web...	Command+Option+Shift+S
Document Setup...	Command+Option+P
Page Setup...	Command+Shift+P
Print	Command+P
Quit	Command+Q

EDIT MENU

Undo	Command+Z
Redo	Command+Shift+Z
Cut	Command+X
Copy	Command+C
Paste	Command+V
Paste in Front	Command+F
Paste in Back	Command+B

EDIT MENU

Select All	Command+A
Deselect All	Command+Shift+A
Keyboard Shortcuts...	Command+Option+Shift+K
General Prefs	Command+K
Units & Undo Prefs, Rotate Units	Command+Option+Shift+U

SAMS

Teach Yourself Adobe Illustrator® 10 in 24 Hours

OBJECT MENU

Transform Again	Command+D
Transform Each...	Command+Option+Shift+D
Bring to Front	Command+Shift+] (right bracket)
Bring Forward	Command+] (right bracket)
Send Backward	Command+[(left bracket)
Send to Back	Command+Shift+[(left bracket)
Group	Command+G
Ungroup	Command+Shift+G
Lock	Command+2
Unlock All	Command+Option+2
Lock Others	Command+Option+Shift+2
Hide Selection	Command+3
Hide Others	Command+Option+Shift+3
Make Blend	Command+Option+B
Release Blend	Command+Option+Shift+B
Make Clipping Mask	Command+7
Release Clipping Mask	Command+Option+7

WINDOW MENU

Show/Hide Appearance	Shift+F6
Add New Stroke	Command+Option+/ (slash)
Add New Fill	Command+/ (slash)
Show/Hide Info	F8
Show/Hide Color	F6
Show/Hide Attributes	F11
Show/Hide Transparency	Shift+F10
Show/Hide Stroke	F10
Show/Hide Gradient	F9
Show/Hide Styles	Shift+F5
Show/Hide Brushes	F5
Show/Hide Layers	F7
New Layer	Command+L
Show/Hide Transform	Shift+F8
Show/Hide Align	Shift+F7
Show/Hide Pathfinder	Shift+F9

VIEW MENU

Toggle Outline/Preview	Command+Y
Overprint Preview	Command+Option+Shift+Y
Pixel Preview	Command+Option+Y
Zoom In	Command+= (equal sign)
Zoom Out	Command+- (minus sign)
Fit in Window	Command+0 (zero)
Actual Size	Command+1
Show/Hide Edges	Command+H
Show/Hide Rulers	Command+R
Show/Hide Bounding Box	Command+Shift+B
Show/Hide Transparency Grid	Command+Shift+D
Show/Hide Guides	Command+; (semicolon)
Lock/Unlock Guides	Command+Option+; (semicolon)
Make Guides	Command+5
Release Guides	Command+Option+5
Smart Guides	Command+U
Show/Hide Grid	Command+' (apostrophe)
Snap to Grid/Pixel	Command+Shift+' (apostrophe)
Snap to Point	Command+Option+' (apostrophe)

TYPE-RELATED PALETTES

Character...	Command+T
Paragraph...	Command+M
Tab Ruler	Command+Shift+T

FILTER MENU

Apply Last Filter	Command+E
Last Filter	Command+Option+E

EFFECT MENU

Apply Last Effect	Command+Shift+E
Last Effect	Command+Option+Shift+E

Replacing the Preferences File

The Adobe Illustrator 10 Prefs file saves a record of how you want Illustrator to look and behave. It is rewritten every time you quit the program. For that reason, it is easily corruptible.

When Illustrator starts misbehaving, simply replace the preferences with a brand new set. Quit Illustrator and delete the Prefs file. The next time you start the program a set of factory-fresh defaults will be used.

For Macintosh OS X: Go to the folder called Users, and the subfolder with your name or user ID. Inside, open the Library folder, and the Preferences folder within it. You'll see a folder called Adobe Illustrator 10, which you should also open. Select the file <Adobe Illustrator 10.0 Prefs>. Delete that file.

For Macintosh OS 9.1 and earlier: Locate the Preferences file. On the hard drive that contains your active system software, look in the System folder, inside the Preferences folder, for a folder called Adobe Illustrator 10. You'll find the file named <Adobe Illustrator 10.0 Prefs>. Delete that file.

For Windows users: Locate the Preferences file at WINDOWS\Application Data\Adobe\Illustrator 10 folder. Delete that file.

SAMS

Peter Bauer

Mordy Golding

SAMS

Teach Yourself

Adobe®

Illustrator® 10

in 24 Hours

SAMS

201 West 103rd St., Indianapolis, Indiana, 46290 USA

Sams Teach Yourself Adobe® Illustrator® 10 in 24 Hours

Copyright © 2002 by Sams Publishing

All rights reserved. No part of this book shall be reproduced, stored in a retrieval system, or transmitted by any means, electronic, mechanical, photocopying, recording, or otherwise, without written permission from the publisher. No patent liability is assumed with respect to the use of the information contained herein. Although every precaution has been taken in the preparation of this book, the publisher and author assume no responsibility for errors or omissions. Nor is any liability assumed for damages resulting from the use of the information contained herein.

International Standard Book Number: 0-672-32313-3

Library of Congress Catalog Card Number: 2001096664

Printed in the United States of America

First Printing: December 2001

04   03   02   01   4   3   2   1

Trademarks

All terms mentioned in this book that are known to be trademarks or service marks have been appropriately capitalized. Sams Publishing cannot attest to the accuracy of this information. Use of a term in this book should not be regarded as affecting the validity of any trademark or service mark.

Warning and Disclaimer

Every effort has been made to make this book as complete and as accurate as possible, but no warranty or fitness is implied. The information provided is on an "as is" basis. The authors and the publisher shall have neither liability nor responsibility to any person or entity with respect to any loss or damages arising from the information contained in this book.

ACQUISITIONS EDITOR
Jennifer Kost-Barker

DEVELOPMENT EDITORS
Heather Goodell
Jon Steever

MANAGING EDITOR
Charlotte Clapp

PRODUCTION EDITOR
Chip Gardner

INDEXER
Mandie Frank

TECHNICAL EDITOR
Kate Binder

TEAM COORDINATOR
Amy Patton

INTERIOR DESIGNER
Gary Adair

COVER DESIGNER
Aren Howell

PAGE LAYOUT
D&G Limited, LLC

Contents at a Glance

Contents

About the Author

Peter Bauer is a computer graphics writer and consultant. He is the author of *Special Edition Using Adobe Illustrator 10*, and has written documentation and user guides for a variety of Illustrator-related software and plug-ins. Pete serves as the Help Desk Director for the National Association of Photoshop Professionals (NAPP), and is a Contributing Writer for *Mac Design* and *Photoshop User* magazines. He also writes a weekly column for the Web portal PlanetPhotoshop.com. He and his wife, Professor Mary Ellen O'Connell of the Moritz College of Law at The Ohio State University, live in the historic German Village area of Columbus, Ohio.

Mordy Golding is the Product Manager for Adobe Illustrator. Mordy has also written *The Web Designer's Guide to Color*. With a strong technical background, Mordy has been a designer and production artist for both print and the Web, and has been a featured panelist at Macworld.

Dedication

This book is dedicated to the innocent souls who perished on the morning of September 11, 2001. Our thoughts and prayers are with all of those who lost friends and loved ones. God Bless.

Acknowledgments

We would like to thank the fine folks at Sams Publishing who made this book a reality. Jennifer Kost-Barker, Jon Steever, Heather Goodell, Charlotte Clapp, and the entire team worked diligently to ensure that you received a quality product. They deserve a round of applause—Jennifer, take a bow!

Our Technical Editor, Kate Binder, also deserves to be singled out of the crowd. She worked relentlessly to make sure that not a single error reached print.

Our thanks also go to friends and colleagues at Adobe and the many fine folks on the forum who helped make Illustrator 10 the dynamite product that it is.

Most of all, of course, we want to acknowledge the love and understanding of our families during these way-too-busy months leading to the release of a new version of Illustrator and a new version of this book. Far too many hours at the computer, far too few around the dinner table.... Batsheva, Chayala, Simcha; Mary Ellen (and the dogs, Hugo & Stanley, too)—our thanks for your love and patience.

Tell Us What You Think!

As the reader of this book, *you* are our most important critic and commentator. We value your opinion and want to know what we're doing right, what we could do better, what areas you'd like to see us publish in, and any other words of wisdom you're willing to pass our way.

You can e-mail or write me directly to let me know what you did or didn't like about this book—as well as what we can do to make our books stronger.

Please note that I cannot help you with technical problems related to the topic of this book, and that due to the high volume of mail I receive, I might not be able to reply to every message.

When you write, please be sure to include this book's title and author as well as your name and phone or fax number. I will carefully review your comments and share them with the author and editors who worked on the book.

E-mail: graphics@samspublishing.com

Mail: Mark Taber
           Associate Publisher
           Sams Publishing
           201 West 103rd Street
           Indianapolis, IN 46290 USA

Introduction

Pencils and computers must be counted among the great improvements in the lives of illustrators over the years. The pencil allows an illustrator to erase (unlike ink), which gave him or her an easy way to change and correct artwork. The computer makes it even easier. In addition, programs such as Adobe Illustrator allow a greater degree of accuracy unachievable with manual drafting or drawing tools.

However, Adobe Illustrator is a heck of a lot more complicated than a pencil! On the flip side, when you first started using a pencil it probably took a lot more than 24 one-hour lessons to learn to write.

Who Should Read This Book?

We've designed this book for beginning Illustrator 10 users. Whether you're a Photoshop guru who has been enticed by vectors, a Freehand convert, or a complete novice looking to break into the biz, we're with you. You might think that a raw beginner and a Photoshop expert have little in common, but that's not necessarily true—in fact, the beginner has fewer preconceived notions about computer graphics.

And if you're new to Illustrator 10 (even if you're not new to Illustrator), we also had you in mind while preparing this book.

Can this Book Really Teach Illustrator 10 in 24 Hours?

You really can learn the basics of Adobe Illustrator 10 in 24 one-hour lessons. (But, trust me on this, you don't want to do the lessons in one 24-hour stretch!) Will you know everything there is to know about Illustrator? No. I don't know anyone who claims to know it all. Will this book give you a solid foundation, one that will allow you to use Illustrator confidently and productively? Yes! And that's the goal, to get you moving productively forward, with the confidence to use Illustrator, to experiment with Illustrator, and to eventually master Illustrator.

We've organized this book so that each hour builds upon the previous ones. You'll often find yourself thinking, "Yeah, that looks familiar!" We'll work to reinforce concepts, techniques, and ideas in later hours. We'll subtly build upon prior knowledge in a way that you might not even notice.

What This Book Assumes

We're not teaching basic computer skills here. You must already be fully capable of mousing to a menu and dragging to a command. On the flip side, you don't need a Master of Fine Arts degree in computer graphics. We hope that you have an interest in art, graphic production, or both, but that's not even truly necessary.

To make sure that we're on the same sheet of music, let's agree on some terminology.

- **Click:** Push down on the mouse button. If you're using the Windows OS, it's the left button.
- **Double-click:** Press-release-press-release the mouse button quickly. (The reaction time can be modified in the control panels.)
- **Drag:** Hold down the mouse button while moving the cursor on screen. This differs from just moving the cursor. When dragging, the cursor remains active. If, for example, you've got a selection tool active, you're selecting all the objects within the dragged rectangle. (Your education begins....) Consider the difference between walking through the park and trying to take a bulldog to the vet when he knows where he's going. One is simply movement, whereas the other certainly earns the title drag.
- **Click and Drag:** The mouse button goes down while the cursor is on top of a target, perhaps an object, and the button stays down while you move the cursor. This moves the object with the cursor.

Conventions Used in This Book

Sometimes we'll tell you that you should type a specific set of characters. It will look like this:

```
filename
```

You'll also see these icons in the book:

> This is a "Note." It indicates information that's related to the current discussion.

> This is a "Tip." It indicates information that can save you time or effort as you work with Illustrator.

This is a "Caution." Don't skip the Cautions. We've reserved them for information that can mean the difference between success and, um, big trouble as you work with Illustrator.

 New Term icons provide clear definitions of new, essential terms. The term appears in *italic*.

Tasks: Applying What You've Learned

As you go through the book, sections marked Task guide you in applying what you just learned.

If you're ready, it's time to start the journey. Fasten your seatbelt, 'cause we're going to move quickly though a lot of Illustrator information. We'll see you at the other end in 24 Hours! Ready, set, go!

PART I
Basic Illustrator

Hour

Hour 1

Understanding Illustrator

Adobe Illustrator 10 is part of a family of computer graphics and design programs. It is closely integrated with Adobe's Photoshop (image editing), InDesign and PageMaker (page layout), GoLive (Web design), LiveMotion (graphic animation), Acrobat (PDF file creation), AfterCast (dynamic imaging server), and the rest of the Adobe line of products.

Many of Adobe's programs share the same basic interface, using similar tools, tabbed palettes, and menu commands. Many of the tools and commands are available in several programs. Illustrator and its sister programs are also cross-platform—that is, the Macintosh and Windows versions have the same capabilities and features.

Illustrator's role in the family is vector art creation for both Web and print. To get started in this exciting field, we'll need to learn how to move around in the program. If you're familiar with Adobe Photoshop or any of the related products, you'll have a leg up and will easily adjust to the new tweaks. If not, don't worry—this tried-and-true interface has earned a merit badge for ease-of-use.

In this hour, you'll learn the following:

- The basic concepts of computer graphics
- The basic differences between vector and raster artwork
- How to get around in Illustrator
- An introduction to Illustrator's tools and palettes
- How to reset Illustrator's preferences

What Are Computer Graphics?

Images created on, or stored in, computers can be considered computer graphics. These include pictures on the Internet, digital video, and the image files used to print this book. It also can include the movies *Toy Story*, *Shrek*, and others. If you have a digital camera (or if your film-processing company includes a floppy disk or CD of your images with your prints), you already create computer graphics. If you have a scanner attached to your computer at home or office, you do, too.

Vector and Raster

The vast majority of computer artwork falls into two categories: vector and raster. Illustrator works primarily with vector images; Photoshop and its offshoots—digital cameras and scanners—work with raster images. (Photoshop's most recent release, however, does an excellent job of integrating vector-type and vector-like objects.)

NEW TERM *Vector* art consists primarily of objects in the image. Objects can be lines, circles, squares, triangles, spirals, or other shapes. Usually, they are constructed from paths (which will be fully explained in Hours 5, "Creating Paths and Compound Paths" and 6, "Editing Bézier Curves"). Paths can be open or closed. An open path has two ends, like a line or a piece of string. A closed path has no ends, like a circle or a rubber band. Paths can be *stroked* (a color or pattern applied to the path itself) and/or *filled* (a color or pattern applied to the area enclosed or partially enclosed by the path).

The objects in a vector art file are stored as mathematical descriptions. For example, an object could be recorded (very loose translation into English) as

Draw a circle, starting near the upper-left corner of the page and extending almost to the middle. The top of the circle should almost touch the top of the printed page. The left side should also be close to, but not touching, the edge. The path should be stroked with black, the width of the stroke approximately one-tenth the width of the circle. Leave the circle empty.

1

The advantage of vector art is that the specific size of the circle is never stated. Whether printed on a letter-size sheet of paper or poster six times that large, the circle will look the same relative to the other things on the page (see Figure 1.1). In addition, with printers capable of handling vector art, each line and curve will always be smooth and precise.

FIGURE 1.1

In these two examples the circle retains its appearance relative to the page, despite the difference in size.

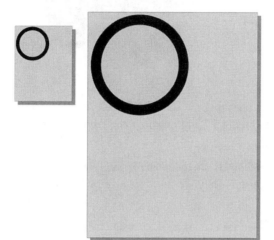

NEW TERM *Raster* art, on the other hand, consists only of tiny little colored squares, called pixels. Each pixel can be only one color. Pixels in an image can be edited individually or as groups. However, even when all the pixels in an image are changed at the same time, they remain independent of each other. Raster images get their name from the fact that these little pixels are arranged in a raster, a rectangular pattern consisting of rows.

The advantage of raster art is that it can reproduce images that don't consist of objects and it can show very subtle transitions in color. Photographs, for example, do not consist of objects. Yes, the picture might show a tree, a building, and a girl, but the actual print, of course, does not contain any physical objects. When scanned or downloaded into a computer from a digital camera, the beautiful picture consists of nothing more than pixels.

The disadvantage of raster art is that it can lose quality when resized or printed. Because an image consists of a given number of pixels, if we change the size of the picture when printed, then the size of the pixels themselves might have to change (see Figure 1.2).

FIGURE 1.2

The three figures have the same number of pixels. Notice how much larger the pixels are on the right.

The problem with changing the size of the pixels is that it can reduce the quality of the printed image. In Figure 1.2, for example, the larger pixels result in a much more jagged edge to the circle.

The lighter-colored pixels are the result of antialiasing, which is used to create an optical illusion of smoothness. They are very effective in the smallest circle, ineffective for the largest.

You can also change the size of a raster image by maintaining the size of the individual pixels and just adding more of them (see Figure 1.3). In this case, the software you're using calculates an average color of the new pixels, and inserts them among the existing pixels (this is called interpolation).

FIGURE 1.3

The pixels in the three images are the same size, but the image on the right has many more pixels.

As you can see, the curve is much smoother than it was with the larger pixels. We'll look more thoroughly at raster images in Hour 19, "Working with Raster Images and Programs."

Illustrator's Interface

For most of these 24 hours, we'll be working with vector images. To explore that arena, the first step is, of course, to open Illustrator. You should see a screen similar to the following one, making allowances for operating system interface differences (see Figure 1.4 and Figure 1.5). After the program opens, choose the menu command File, New, and after the dialog box opens, click OK to accept the default values.

FIGURE 1.4

This is the window that might greet you when opening Illustrator on a Macintosh computer running OS X.

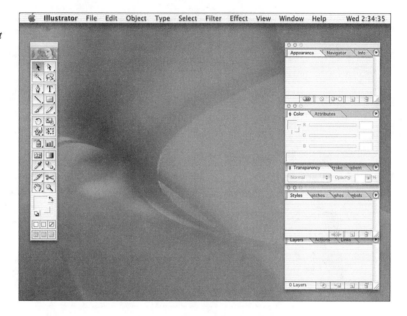

What you actually see onscreen might differ substantially from what is pictured. If the copy of Illustrator with which you're working has been used before, it might be set up for another person's individual preferences. In addition, the resolution of the monitor that you're using can affect the look. If the monitor is set for a substantially higher resolution, the palettes and things might look much smaller on your screen. That won't be a problem as we work through these 24 hours.

Other than the basic differences between Windows and Macintosh, Illustrator is virtually identical on both platforms. (This does not mean, however, that the same copy of Illustrator will run on both Windows and Macintosh. You must have the proper version for your computer's operating system.)

FIGURE 1.5

This is a window that might greet you when opening Illustrator on a Windows computer.

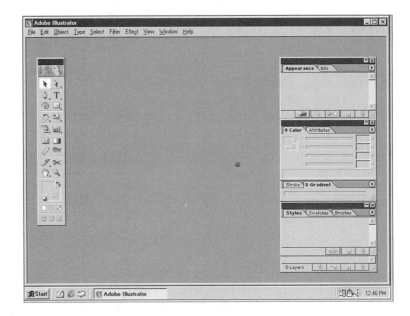

Illustrator, like most modern programs, remembers certain things every time you quit. In Illustrator, such things as tool settings and palette locations are stored in the Preferences file. If the copy of Illustrator you're using has been used before, the screen might look different. If it does, skip ahead to the section titled "Task: Resetting Illustrator's Defaults" and then restart the program and return to this point in the lesson.

Opening, Closing, Saving, and Other Standard Commands

Illustrator works like other programs on your computer in many ways. Just like a word processor, a database application, or a spreadsheet program, you use the Open, Close, Save, and Quit commands from the program's menu bar. These general commands and how they operate are normally governed by the computer's operating system (Windows or Macintosh), and should be familiar to you.

Illustrator comes with a variety of different types of files. Let's open one to see how Illustrator looks in action.

1. Use the menu command File, Open.

2. In the Open File dialog box, navigate to your Adobe Illustrator folder.

3. Inside the Illustrator folder is another folder, Sample Files, which contains a folder called Sample Art. Open that folder.

4. Click the file named Chinese Opera.ai, and then click the Open button.

Illustrator can open a variety of different file formats. This file is in Illustrator's native file format. Let's leave it open for a while.

The Illustrator Window

Illustrator will take over the majority of your monitor's screen, by default. The OS interface items will remain at the top or bottom of the screen, but you'll have just about the whole space for working with Illustrator. To the left of the screen is Illustrator's Toolbox. To the right are the floating palettes. The area in the center is usually occupied by a document window, which contains the artboard and the surrounding scratch space. At the top of the window are menus, and at the bottom is the status bar.

The Artboard and Printable Area

As you look at the open Illustrator document onscreen, notice the two rectangles surrounding it. The outer rectangle, a solid black line, represents the artboard. This is the total area of your image. When you start out with Illustrator, this is most likely to be the same size as the paper that you intend to print with.

The inner dashed-line rectangle shows the printable area of the paper/printer combination you've selected. We call this the Page Tiling. In Hour 2, "Setting Up Illustrator," we'll learn about these choices in Document Setup.

The Status Bar

At the bottom of the window is Illustrator's status bar. At the left it shows the current zoom percentage, by default. Click the number and a pop-up list will appear. Slide to any number on the list and release the mouse button. Take a look at how your document looks onscreen now. Experiment with the various zoom settings.

Next to the zoom percentage, the status bar shows the currently active tool. You can click that section and see another pop-up menu. Selecting any of the other options will change the display in the status bar. Hold down the Option key (Alt key for Windows) and open some additional possibilities (see Figure 1.6).

FIGURE 1.6

Some of the status bar's choices are more useful than others.

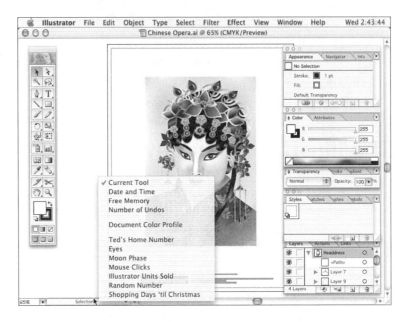

Zooming and Getting Around

There are a variety of ways to zoom in or zoom out while working. Zooming in enables you to concentrate the view on a specific part of the image, magnifying the part that you are working with at the time. Zooming out enables you to see the entire document—or more—all at once. You've already learned how to zoom using the status bar. The Zoom tool will be described later. The primary keyboard shortcuts to change the view include

- Zoom In: Command+= (Mac)/Control+= (Windows)
- Zoom Out: Command+– (Mac)/Control+– (Windows)
- Fit Page in Window: Command+0 (Mac)/Control+0 (Windows)
- Show Actual Size (100% zoom): Command+1 (Mac)/Control+1 (Windows)

Use the keyboard commands to zoom in and out a few times.

When you've zoomed in and need to see another section of the document, you can hold down the spacebar and drag. This changes any tool (unless you are entering type at the time) to the Hand tool. Holding down the mouse button grabs the image onscreen, enabling you to drag it in any direction to show another area of the document. Try it by pressing the spacebar and dragging your open artwork around the window. After you've dragged, hold down the Command key (Mac)/Control key (Windows) and press the zero key to return to the basic Fit in Window view.

Viewing the Artboard

Objects on Illustrator's artboard can be viewed in two major ways, Preview and Outline. You make the choice under Illustrator's View menu. In Preview mode, objects are shown in color, with the appropriate fills and strokes. In Outline mode, only the paths that make up the objects and lines are visible. If Illustrator is running very slowly because it's taking a long time to redraw your monitor's screen, switch to Outline and watch things fly! The difference between Preview and Outline is shown in Figure 1.7.

Preview   Outline

FIGURE 1.7

To the left are objects in Preview mode, to the right the same objects are shown in Outline mode.

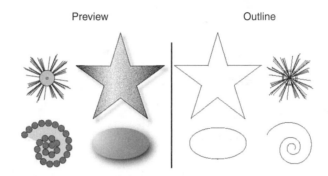

Later in this book we'll also look at some other ways that Illustrator enables you to see objects onscreen using commands under the View menu.

Illustrator's Tools

Illustrator's tools are all found in the Toolbox, a floating palette that (by default) is found along the left side of the screen. You select a tool by clicking on its icon in the Toolbox. (Don't be thrown off if the icon changes color; those colors are not the colors that will be added to your artwork.) Some tools have options that you can access by double-clicking the icon in the Toolbox.

A little triangle in the corner of a box indicates that you can click and hold to show more tools on a little flyout mini-Toolbox. (These can be torn off the Toolbox to become free-floating palettes of their own. This is very useful when switching back and forth between related tools.) If you look carefully at Figure 1.8, you'll see that the Toolbox is divided into a number of sections.

In the descriptions that follow, the default keyboard shortcut for each tool (when there is one) is shown in parentheses. (In Hour 2 you'll learn how to assign your own custom keyboard shortcuts.) Any time you're not entering text, you can press the specified key to switch to that tool.

FIGURE **1.8**
*Illustrator's Toolbox
shows 24 tools, plus
fill, stroke, and view
controls.*

Selection Tools

In Hour 4, "Making Selections," you'll learn to use these tools. They are shown in
Figure 1.9.

FIGURE **1.9**

*Illustrator's Selection
tools are shown with
the flyout palettes visi-
ble. The newest tool,
Magic Wand, is shown
as selected in the
Toolbox. (You can tell
because the icon is
darker.)*

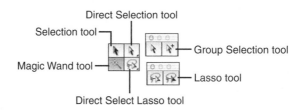

Here's a snapshot summary of each of these tools:

- Selection tool (V): Used to select and reposition objects on the artboard.

- Direct Selection tool (A): The individual parts that make up an object can be
  selected and manipulated with this tool.

- Group Selection tool: When multiple objects are combined into a group, they are normally manipulated as a single object. The Group Selection tool enables you to select
  an object within a group without having to remove it from the group (ungrouping) .

- Magic Wand: The Magic Wand tool can be used to select all objects in the illustration that have one or more characteristics in common. Double-clicking the Magic
  Wand tool's icon in the Toolbox opens a special palette that enables you to choose
  the options (see Figure 1.10) .

FIGURE 1.10

Stroke and Fill, as well as other object characteristics are discussed in later hours.

- Direct Select Lasso tool (Y): A cross between the Lasso tool and the Direct Selection tool, you drag loops to select multiple parts of one or more objects.

- Lasso tool (Q): Dragging a loop with this tool will lasso objects on the artboard to select them.

 You can see in Figure 1.10 that the palette's menu is showing. Clicking the triangle in the upper-right corner of a palette will open its menu.

Creation Tools

Illustrator is an object-based graphics program. As such, it needs objects to work with. The creation tools give you the capability of producing vector objects. They are shown in Figure 1.11.

FIGURE 1.11

Illustrator's creation tools are shown with the flyout palettes visible.

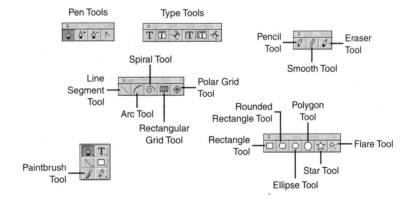

- Pen tools: In Hour 5 you'll learn to use Pen tools, which create and edit Bézier paths. These paths are the building blocks of vector art. The Pen tools (with default keyboard shortcuts) are Pen (P), Add Anchor Point (+), Delete Anchor Point (–), and Convert Anchor Point (Shift+C).

- Line Segment tool: Straight lines, with an anchor point at each end, can be created with this tool. Click, drag, release. Click it once on the artboard to open a dialog box in which you can enter dimensions numerically.

- Arc tool: The Arc tool behaves similarly to the Line Segment tool, but produces curved lines. The Shift and Option (Alt) keys can be used to constrain the curve to certain proportions, as you'll see later. Click and drag, or click to open the dialog box.

- Spiral tool: The number of winds and tightness of the spiral are both subject to your command when creating spirals.

- Rectangular Grid tool: Rows and columns of rectangles are produced with this new tool. Click to open the dialog box (see Figure 1.12), or click and drag if you know the current settings are acceptable for your needs.

FIGURE 1.12

You can control far more than just the number of rectangles in the grid.

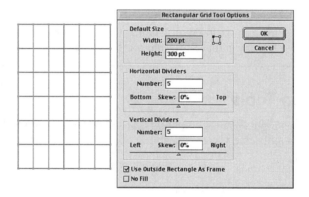

- Polar Grid tool: If you need rounded grids, use this tool. As you can see in Figure 1.13, it functions similar to the Rectangular Grid tool, but in circles.

FIGURE 1.13

The Skew sliders make the cells of the grid vary in size.

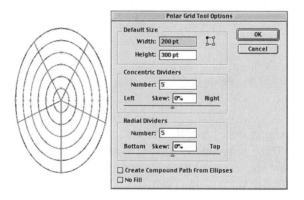

- Paintbrush tool (B): Dragging the Paintbrush enables you to create freehand. Colors and predefined artwork can be applied. (You'll learn about painting and brushes in Hour 9, "Working with Brushes.")

- The Type tools: The Type tools and their products have two full hours devoted to them, Hour 10, "Adding Text," and Hour 14, "Applying Advanced Typography Techniques." The six Type tools are Type (T), Area Type, Path Type, Vertical Type, Vertical Area Type, and Vertical Path Type.

- Rectangle tool (M): Rectangles of various sizes and squares (when the Shift key is depressed) are both available with this tool.

- Rounded Rectangle tool: This tool differs from the Rectangle tool only in a created object's corners. The Rectangle tool creates objects with sharp, square corners. This tool creates rectangular and square shapes with gently rounded corners.

- Ellipse tool (L): You can create ovals and, when Shift is depressed, circles.

- Polygon tool: This tool creates multisided objects. You control the number of sides, from 3 to 1000 (although any polygon with more than about 20 sides looks a lot like a circle).

- Star tool: You control the number of points (3 to 1000), as well as the length of the star's arms with this tool.

- Flare tool: Sort of a niche capability, the Flare tool produces a reflection, as you'd see from the sun glinting off a camera lens or window (see Figure 1.14).

FIGURE 1.14

The objects created by the Lens Flare tool can be quite complex. A single click of the tool can produce dozens of objects with complex transparency interactions.

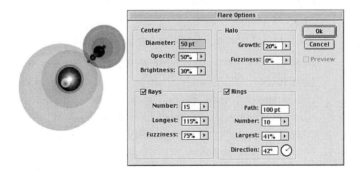

- Pencil tool (N): Similar to the Paintbrush, the Pencil enables you to create paths by dragging. There are some differences in the two tools' options, however.

- Smooth tool: The Smooth tool is used to soften the corners of paths. Dragging the tool around a rectangle, for example, can change the object into a rounded rectangle.

- Erase tool: This tool doesn't actually create, but helps you fine-tune your creations. Use it to eliminate unnecessary path segments.

Transformation Tools

This group of tools enables you to make changes in existing objects (see Figure 1.15).

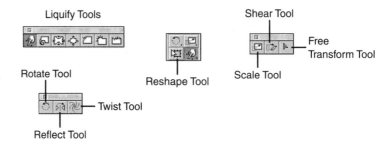

FIGURE 1.15
Illustrator's Transformation tools are shown with the fly-out palettes visible.

- Rotate tool (R): You can use this tool to rotate an object around a designated point.

- Reflect tool (O): You can flip an object over an imaginary line using this tool.

- Twist tool: The Twist tool will distort a selected object in a circular pattern around a center point.

- Free Transform tool : This tool combines the capabilities of the Rotate, Scale, Reflect, and Shear tools.

- Scale tool (S): The Scale tool enables you to resize an object, making it either larger or smaller.

- Shear tool: Shearing skews an object, enabling you to slant it in one direction.

- Reshape tool: This tool distorts an object by pushing or pulling selected points.

- Liquify tools: These seven tools will be explored in Hour 6. They use brushes to manipulate path segments and anchor points. They each have options that can be set by double-clicking the tool icon in the Toolbox, which opens a dialog box (shown in Figure 1.16). The Liquify tools are Warp, Twirl, Pucker, Bloat, Scallop, Crystallize, and Wrinkle.

The Liquify tools can create extremely complex paths very quickly. As you'll learn in later hours, these overly complex paths can create problems. Use 'em, love 'em, respect 'em. These tools are great, but be careful with them!

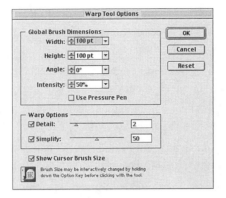

FIGURE 1.16
Variations of this dialog box are used for all seven of the Liquify tools.

Additional Tools

Illustrator's couple of dozen other tools could certainly be categorized, if you so desired. Those groupings would include just one or two groups of tools each, however. Instead, let's drop them all into one category called Additional (see Figure 1.17) .

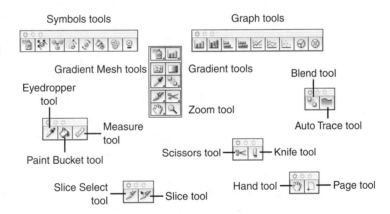

FIGURE 1.17
Illustrator's additional tools are shown with the flyout palettes visible.

- Symbol tools: There are a lot of them, used primarily with graphics for the Web, and they all live on one little flyout palette. Symbols are pieces of artwork, like patterns, that you define. When defined, you can add them with the Symbol Sprayer, and then manipulate them with the other symbol tools. We'll talk about symbols in Hour 3, "Creating Objects." The Symbol tools are Symbol Sprayer, Symbol Shifter, Symbol Scruncher, Symbol Sizer, Symbol Spinner, Symbol Stainer, Symbol Screener, and Symbol Styler.

- Gradient Mesh tool (U): A gradient mesh is an object that uses a series of blended colors as a fill. You'll learn about gradient mesh objects and gradient fills in Hour 8, "Using Strokes, Fills, and Gradients."
- Eyedropper tool (I): You can duplicate the various attributes of an object or even type using the Eyedropper tool to copy and the Paint Bucket tool to paste.
- Paint Bucket tool (K): This tool is used with the Eyedropper tool to copy and paste attributes between objects and type.
- Measure tool: You can use this tool to find both distance and angle. It is used in conjunction with Illustrator's Info palette.
- Slice tool: Slices are used to section Web graphics, creating several pieces from one whole image. This tool, which looks much like a pizza cutter, creates slices.
- Slice Select tool: To manipulate slices in a sliced image, you need to be able to select them. Here's the tool for the job.
- Hand tool (H): As you discovered earlier, the Hand tool enables you to reposition a document in the window.
- Page tool: When the artboard is larger than the page, the Page tool can be used to set which area will print on which page of a document.
- Graph tools: Considered a single tool, Illustrator actually has nine different types of graphs. Graphs are explored in Hour 15, "Inserting Graphs and Charts." We'll look at each of the Graph tools then.
- Gradient tool (G): The Gradient tool enables you to create linear and radial transitions between colors.
- Blend tool (W): Blends are transitions from one object to another. This tool enables you to create a series of intermediary objects to transition from one shape and/or color to another.
- Auto Trace tool: This tool is used to create editable paths by tracing the outlines of nonvector images.
- Scissors tools : The Scissors tool is used to split paths.
- Knife tool: The Knife tool is used to split an object into two or more independent objects.
- Zoom tool (Z): Zooming, as we discovered earlier, is changing the size (and amount) of an image seen onscreen. Illustrator offers several ways to change the view, including this tool. You can click to increase the zoom factor, centered on the place clicked. Option+click (Mac)/Alt+click (Windows) zooms out. You can also drag the tool to fill the screen with the area enclosed by the drag.

The Color and View Controls

The Toolbox also contains easy access to some of Illustrator's other capabilities (see Figure 1.18). Fills and strokes, which add color to objects, are explored fully in Part 3 of this book, in Hour 8, specifically. For now, however, it's good to know that the two swatches below the Hand and Zoom tools in the Toolbox are the fill and the stroke. The little curved arrow to the upper right swaps the colors between the two, and the white and black miniatures to the lower left can be clicked to restore them to their default values.

FIGURE 1.18

Illustrator's Toolbox also contains color and view controls.

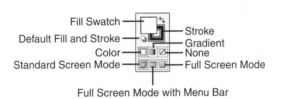

Click once on the stroke swatch (the hollow black square) to bring it to the front. That makes it the active one of the pair, so any changes to color will be applied to the stroke rather than the fill. To make the fill swatch active again, click it once. Now double-click the swatch. When the Color Picker opens, click anywhere to select a new fill color and click OK. Now press D on the keyboard. That's another way to restore the default white-and-black colors for the fill and stroke.

Below the fill and stroke swatches are three little shortcut buttons. From the left, they will

- Make the most recently used color the fill or stroke (whichever is front-most of the two swatches) and open the Color palette.
- Make the most recently used gradient the active fill (gradients cannot be used for strokes) and open the Gradient palette.
- Give the fill or stroke (whichever is active) a value of None. This makes the fill or stroke transparent.

The last three icons at the bottom of the Toolbox change the basic view in Illustrator. Click the icons in the Toolbox, or press F on the keyboard to cycle through the three views.

- Standard Screen Mode (the left-most button) is what you're seeing now in Illustrator. The Toolbox, palettes, status bar, and menus are visible. The document that you're working in is a standard resizable window, appropriate for your operating system.

- Full Screen Mode with Menu Bars hides the status bar and fills the screen with your open document. The document window is no longer resizable.
- Full Screen Mode hides the operating system interface. The menu bar disappears. If you find yourself working in Illustrator and you can't get out you might have inadvertently entered Full Screen Mode. Press F to escape to Standard Screen Mode.

> There's one other part of the Toolbox that we haven't discussed yet—the very top. Just above the Selection and Direct Selection tools you'll see a picture derived from the front of the Adobe Illustrator box, CD, splash screen, and User Guide. Clicking it opens Adobe Online. If you have an Internet connection available, Adobe Online will take you directly to the Adobe.com Web site, to an area specifically dedicated to Illustrator. You'll find the latest updates, tutorials, assistance with problems and questions, and sample galleries. The site is a great resource for both beginning and advanced Illustrator users.

Contextual Menus

You'll also find that Illustrator takes advantage of *contextual menus* in both Windows and the Macintosh OS. With any tool selected from the Toolbox, Control+click (Mac) or right-click (Windows) in the document window. Take a look at the little menu that pops up. Later on, as we work in various situations in Illustrator, we'll see how the contextual menu changes, based on the situation.

Illustrator's Palettes

In addition to the Toolbox, Illustrator uses a large number of other palettes to keep various creative capabilities at your fingertips. By default, most of the palettes are stacked along the right side of the screen, with several palette tabs visible in each palette window.

Working with Palettes

These little windows are referred to as floating palettes because they always stay in front of the illustration that you're working. However, never being hidden by the document window also means that the palettes always hide whatever is behind them. Here are the basic techniques for making sure that the palettes are a convenience and not a hindrance while you work:

1

- You can relocate palettes onscreen by dragging them. Click the palette group's title bar (across the top of the little window) and drag to a new location. Palettes will snap to the edges of the screen and to nearby palettes.

- Use Tab to hide and show the palettes.

- Shift+Tab will leave the Toolbox visible, while hiding and showing all the other palettes.

- To show a particular palette, click its tab in the palette window to move it to the front.

- You can also show and hide individual palettes using Illustrator's Window menu. You can also hide palette groups by clicking the close window box in the title bar.

- Dragging a tab from one palette window to another will move the palette into a new group. Theoretically, you can combine all the tabs into one super palette. However, this capability is designed more to enable you to make one or two windows that hold the palettes that you really need regularly. (When a tab is in position to join the new group, a thick black box will be seen all the way around the target palettes.)

- Palette windows can be docked. Drag a tab to the very bottom of another palette window and it will lock to the bottom of that window. The docked palettes can be moved and collapsed as a single unit. (When a tab is in position to dock, a thick black line will show at the bottom of the target palette.) Notice that in Illustrator's default setup, the Transparency, Stroke, and Gradient palettes are docked to the bottom of the Color and Attributes palettes.

- Some of the tabs have a little two-headed arrow to the left of the name. That indicates that the palette can be expanded to show additional options and collapsed to save space. Click the little up-down arrows to rotate through the various palette layouts. Try it on the Transparency palette.

- Even palettes without the two-headed arrow can be collapsed to make more work area visible. Double-click the palette's tab to shrink it to just its tab, double-click again to expand it.

- You can create little floating palettes of the hidden tools by mousing to the small arrow at the right side of the hidden tool flyout.

Illustrator's Primary Palettes

With over 30 palettes, it's easy to see why Adobe has chosen to combine them into groups and leave some hidden. Here are descriptions of the palettes that are visible by default in Illustrator. They are presented as shown in Figure 1.19, in their standard groups. (If you refer to Figures 1.4 and 1.5, you'll see them in their default locations.)

- Toolbox: At this point, you're quite familiar with the Toolbox. Remember that you can hide all the other palettes and leave this one visible by holding down the Shift key when you hit the Tab key.

FIGURE 1.19

Illustrator's palettes are, by default, grouped into several sets.

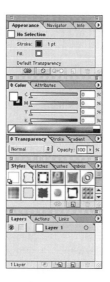

- Appearance/Navigator/Info: The first group contains three palettes. Appearance enables you to control much of how an object appears. Multiple strokes and fills can be added, or you can return an object to its basic black-and-white appearance.

  The Navigator palette enables you to get around in Illustrator. This is especially handy when you're zoomed in to see detail of an object. The red rectangle indicates what part of the artboard and scratch area is visible in the document window. The slider and buttons below give you yet another way to zoom in and out.

  The Info palette changes content based upon what is being done at the time. Bring the palette to the front by clicking on its tab, and then double-click the two-headed arrow twice to fully expand the palette. In the Toolbox, click various tools to see how the Info palette changes to meet your needs. Don't forget to activate the Type tool.

- Color/Attributes: The Color palette enables you to mix up the exact shade that you need. It can work in several different color modes. (Color and color modes are explained starting in Hour 7, "Understanding and Applying Color.")

  Attributes should not be confused with the Appearance palette. Attributes of an object that appear in this palette typically involve technical options for printing or using a graphic on the Internet, as well as how an object appears when selected

1

and possibly some object-related notes. Such notes can be useful in a production setting when trying to solve printing problems.

- Transparency/Stroke/Gradient: This set of three palettes, you'll notice, is actually docked to the bottom of the window above.

The Transparency palette enables you to regulate whether or not (and how much) an object blocks other objects behind it in the illustration. In addition to opacity, you can control the object's *blending mode*, which determines how the object's colors interact with those it overlaps.

Stroke is the color applied to a path (and is discussed fully in Hour 8). In the Stroke palette you can specify the width of the stroke, how corners and ends appear, and whether or not the line will be dashed (a dotted line).

The Gradient palette enables you to create blends of color that you can fill objects with. You can choose the colors and how they interact, and whether the fill's blending should be in a straight line (linear gradient) or in a circular pattern (radial gradient).

- Styles/Swatches/Brushes/Symbols: You'll learn how to use the Styles palette in Hour 11, "Applying Appearances and Styles." In a nutshell, it holds predefined sets of appearance and color characteristics that you can apply to objects.

The Swatches palette, discussed in Hour 7, holds little swatches of color that you can apply to objects. One of the great advantages, you'll learn, is the palette's power to change a color throughout an illustration, so that you don't have to select and change each object individually.

The Brushes palette holds artwork and patterns that can be applied to the stroke of an object or path. Hour 9 will show you how to use and create these brushes.

Symbols are pieces of artwork that you create, and can then add to your illustration and manipulate using the symbol tools. The Symbols palette stores artwork that you can use as symbols, as well as giving you control over how symbols behave in your document. (We'll talk about symbols in Hour 3.)

- Layers/Actions/Links: The Layers palette enables you to organize the pieces of your artwork on separate layers that can be rearranged and restacked in any order, and even grouped. You'll learn the power of layers in Hour 13, "Gaining Flexibility Through Layers."

The Actions palette stores and plays back little miniprograms, much like Microsoft Office macros, that can perform tasks for you. Actions are saved until the end, Hour 24, "Maximizing Efficiency with Automation."

Links enables you to manage artwork that you've added to your document from elsewhere. (These links should not be confused with those used on the Internet. Web links are controlled through the Attributes palette.)

Illustrator's Additional Palettes

The palettes shown in Figure 1.20 are also useful, but they're not as readily available as those described previously.

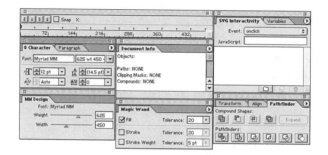

- Tab Ruler: Tabs and indents of blocks of text can be adjusted using this floating palette.

- Character/Paragraph: Used exclusively with text, these two palettes are now activated through the Window menu.

  Character controls the appearance of letters and groups of letters.

  Paragraph helps you regulate blocks of text. You'll learn about these palettes in Hour 14, "Applying Advanced Typography Techniques."

- MM Design: This palette is used to control the appearance of certain fonts, called multiple master fonts. Such fonts, identified by MM in their names, can be adjusted for a variety of appearance characteristics. We'll look at it also in Hour 14.

- Document Info: This handy floating palette contains a wealth of information about your document, or about individual objects in the document. (The palette's menu enables you to switch between the two capabilities.)

- Magic Wand: This palette contains the options for the new Magic Wand tool. The tool is used to select objects with ranges specified in the palette. You can open the palette using the Window menu or by simply double-clicking the Magic Wand icon in the Illustrator Toolbox.

- SVG Interactivity/Variables: You can make the SVG Interactivity palette available by using the menu command Window, Show SVG Interactivity. It is used to control Java scripts used in Scalable Vector Graphic (SVG) files. SVG is a specialized file format designed primarily for use on the Web. (Hour 22, "Creating Web Graphics," and Hour 23, "Animating the Web," discuss the format.)

  The Variables palette is used to designate which items are dynamic. Dynamic images, text strings, and graph data can be updated automatically. We'll talk about dynamic data-driven graphics in Hour 24.

- Transform/Align/Pathfinder: These three palettes, normally seen grouped, are also made available through Illustrator's Window menu.

  Transform enables you to manipulate the appearance of objects. You'll learn about transforming objects in Hour 12, "Utilizing Transformations and Blends."

  The Align palette enables you to position objects in relation to each other or to the artboard. It is very useful for precisely placing objects.

  The Pathfinder palette is capable of taking several overlapping objects and combining, dividing, intersecting, merging, and cropping them.

Task: Resetting Illustrator's Defaults

Now that we've taken a look at Illustrator's interface, it's time to quit. End the Illustrator session by using the menu command File, Quit. When asked to save the open file, click Don't Save.

Regularly throughout these lessons, we'll be restoring Illustrator to its factory-default settings. We do this by quitting Illustrator and deleting the Preferences file. The next time you start the program, a new Preferences file will be created, using the default settings.

For Macintosh OS X

1. Quit Illustrator.
2. Go to the folder called Users, and the subfolder with your name or user ID.
3. Inside, open the Library folder, and the Preferences folder within it.
4. You'll see a folder called Adobe Illustrator 10, which you should also open. (This path is shown in Figure 1.21.)
5. Select the file Adobe Illustrator 10.0 Prefs.
6. Drag the file to the Trash.
7. Restart Illustrator (if you'll be continuing to work with the program, otherwise just leave it shut down until you need it again) .

FIGURE 1.21

Mac OS X stores separate preferences for each user.

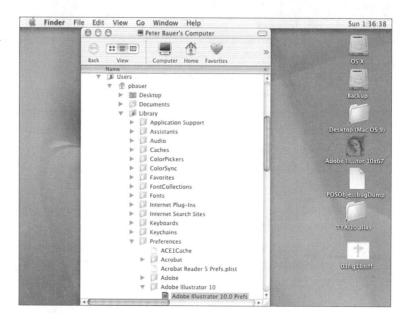

For Macintosh OS 9.1 and earlier

1. Quit Illustrator.

2. Locate the Preferences file. On the hard drive that contains your active system software, look in the System folder, and then inside the Preferences folder, for a folder called Adobe Illustrator 10. You'll find the file named Adobe Illustrator 10.0 Prefs.

3. Command+click the file to send it to the Trash.

4. Restart Illustrator (if you'll be continuing to work with the program, otherwise just leave it shut down until you need it again).

For Windows users

1. Quit Illustrator.

2. Locate the Preferences file at C:\Windows\Application_Data\Adobe\Illustrator 10.

3. Send the file named AIPrefs (shown in figure 1.22) to the Recycle Bin by right-clicking and choosing the appropriate command from the contextual menu.

4. Restart Illustrator (if you'll be continuing to work with the program, otherwise just leave it shut down until you need it again).

FIGURE **1.22**

*Delete the AIPrefs file
in Windows*

 If Illustrator starts misbehaving, and you see symptoms such as disappearing icons, blank palettes, and tools that don't work, don't panic! The first thought for many is to reinstall the program. There's an easier fix most of the time—simply replace the Preferences file.

Summary

The first hour is just about done! You've discovered what Illustrator does and a little about what Illustrator provides you with to do it. You now know the difference between vector and raster artwork. You've learned your way around the Illustrator computer screen and picked up some handy info about tools and palettes. In addition, you've learned how to replace Illustrator's Preferences file, one of the handiest troubleshooting techniques you can know.

Workshop

As you can tell, there's a lot to learn about Illustrator. For everything you learn a dozen questions come up. Most will be answered in time, but let's look at a couple of important questions now, then we've got a little quiz, and we'll end the hour with some learn-by-doing exercises.

Q&A

Q How many types of paths are there?

A There are two basic categories of paths, open and closed. Open paths are straight and curved lines, and the defining characteristic is that each open path has two ends. Closed paths have no ends, being formed from a continuous path. Both open and closed paths can have both strokes and fills.

Q What is the difference between an object and a path?

A The term object includes each distinct item in your illustration. Vector and raster artwork are both objects. Paths, on the other hand, refer only to vector art.

Q If Illustrator can work with raster art as well as vector, is there any need for me to buy Photoshop as well?

A When it comes to raster art, Photoshop remains far more sophisticated than Illustrator. As a dedicated image editor, it has capabilities far beyond those of Illustrator for working with pixels.

Q If an object has no stroke or fill, does it disappear?

A Yes. An object with no stroke or fill is indeed invisible on the artboard. However, the object is still there and can still be selected and manipulated.

Quiz

1. What is the size of a pixel?
   a. Exactly one second long.
   b. One centimeter on a side.
   c. It depends upon the resolution of a printed image.
   d. Tinkerbell was considered slightly undersized for a pixel.

2. Can pixels and paths exist in the same image?
   a. Yes
   b. No
   c. Only when separated by United Nations Peacekeepers

3. Illustrator's preferences are stored in a floating palette.
   a. True. You can open the palette and make changes to your preferences.
   b. False. Illustrator's preferences are stored in a computer file.

4. A small triangle in the corner of an icon in the Toolbox indicates what?
   a. The tool is active.
   b. There are hidden tools also stored in that Toolbox slot.

c. The tool is currently not available.

d. That is the Triangle tool, used to make three-sided polygons.

e. Radiation Warning! That tool has been exposed to plutonium and can explode at any moment!

5. Which of the following does not exist in Illustrator 10?

a. A direct link to the Adobe Web site

b. Guidelines

c. Measure tool

d. A three-eyed, mouth-open, drunken lizard flying through space on a seahorse

Quiz Answers

1. c. On the printed page, resolution will determine the size of the pixel. For example, at 300 pixels per inch (ppi), each pixel is 1/300th of an inch square. (Pixel size on the computer's monitor is dependent upon monitor resolution.)

2. a. Yes, both Illustrator and Photoshop enable you to work with vector and raster art together.

3. b. False. And you'll learn how to change those preferences in the next hour.

4. b. To expose the hidden tools, click and hold on the icon. The additional tools will appear on a flyout palette. To detach the flyout, move the mouse to the triangle at the right end of the little window and release the mouse button.

5. d. …until you draw it, that is!

Exercises

1. Open a new document in Illustrator by using the menu command File, New. When the dialog box opens, click OK to accept the default values. Click the Selection tool in the Toolbox to make it active. Now poke around on the keyboard, looking for those one-key shortcuts that switch tools, V for Selection, A for Direct Select, T for Type, and so on.

2. How many ways do you remember to zoom? There's the Zoom Tool, of course, and the status bar. Let's not forget the Navigator palette. How about those keyboard shortcuts? Work with each of them until you find the one that seems most natural for you. And now, just to add to the list, mouse up and click the View menu. See that? Yet another set of techniques for zooming around in Illustrator!

3. Palette Time! Grab the tab of the Info palette and drag it right into the middle of your screen. Now get the Stroke palette by the tab. Drag it to the bottom of the Info palette. Move it up and down until you recognize the thick black line that indicates docking. Remember that you want to see the line at the bottom of the Info palette, not all the way around it. After you've docked the Stroke palette, get the Actions palette and dock it to the bottom of Stroke. Now add Navigator to the bottom. At this point, you should have four palettes all docked together, stretching from the middle of the screen downward. In Mac OS X, click the second button in the window bar above the Info palette to collapse the palettes. For earlier versions of the Mac OS and for Windows, double-click the window bar at the top (Info) palette to collapse them all. Do it again to make them all visible again. When you're done, quit Illustrator and delete your preferences file to get ready for the next hour.

Hour **2**

Setting Up Illustrator

Adobe Illustrator 10 gives you several ways to personalize your work environment. Although it's very early in your Illustrator career, we'll take the time now to explore these options. A basic understanding now will lead to full comprehension later.

The various ways that you can adapt Illustrator to your needs can be grouped into two categories: global, the settings that affect Illustrator each and every time you use it, and document-specific, the options that affect only one particular file.

In this hour, you'll learn about the following:

- Setting Illustrator's preferences
- Customizing the keyboard shortcuts
- Document Setup options
- Rulers, guides, and grids
- The two startup files

Setting Illustrator's Preferences

If Illustrator has been used since the end of the last hour, reset the preferences file to its default settings. (If you've forgotten how, or are the least bit uncertain, instructions can be found on the back of the reference card in the front of this book.) By deleting the existing file, you force Illustrator to create a new preferences file when the program is next started. The new file uses the default settings. It's important to know what the preferences file is and a little bit about how it works.

The Prefs, as we can refer to the file, is a recording of a variety of settings that you determine. How you want the palettes arranged, whether you prefer to work in points or inches or centimeters or pixels, what hard drive Illustrator should use to support its memory, how to name files when you save them, and dozens of other choices are saved for you. The file is updated every time you quit the program. The next time you start Illustrator, the Prefs file is read and things get set up the way you last left them, saving you the trouble of making each of those changes again. The preferences are global—they affect every Illustrator document opened in the program.

> For Windows and Mac OS 9, you'll find Preferences under the Edit menu. Mac OS X, however, lists the command under the Illustrator menu.

Throughout these hours, we'll be resetting the Prefs to the defaults. But you'll get a look at some of the choices right now, so that you can consider them as we work with Illustrator. At the end of Hour 24, "Maximizing Efficiency with Automation," you'll probably have a pretty good idea of how you want to set your preferences, and what options make most sense for you. You'll even get a few suggestions during the coming hours. The menu command Edit, Preferences, General is the place to start exploring the Prefs. (Mac OS X uses the command Illustrator, Preferences, General.)

Looking at the Prefs

Rather than go through each checkbox of the ten preference windows individually, we'll look at the specific preferences that are important for beginners and intermediates. The majority of the terms would make little or no sense at this point in your Illustrator education, so we'll bypass the techno-jargon. However, toward the end of this hour, we'll present some specific settings that you should know.

Don't make any changes to the Prefs at this point, unless you want to experiment, because we'll be resetting them at the start of most hours. (That ensures that your version of Illustrator is working the same as ours.)

You might see some terms that aren't familiar in the following discussion. Keep them in mind, you'll see them again—in context—and they'll seem familiar.

Remember that the default preferences are not chosen at random. They are the defaults because they work for most people, most of the time. You can survive pretty well with the defaults, but tweaking a few to suit your purposes will probably be advantageous sometime down the road. Read, learn, and remember. Later, when you've got a better idea of your specific requirements for Illustrator, you'll be able to change the Preferences to suit your needs.

Task: Review the Preferences Panels

Let's take a moment to review the various options to be found in Illustrator's Preferences Window.

1. Open the General preferences window (see Figure 2.1) by selecting it in the appropriate menu or by pressing Command+K (Mac)/Control+K (Windows). It is the first of nine panels for the Preferences dialog box. For now, keep the preferences as the defaults show. Take note, however, of the button Reset All Warning Dialogs. If you ever click the Don't Show Again box when you get a warning message, this button can make the warnings appear again.

FIGURE 2.1

Illustrator's General Preferences can also be opened with the default keyboard shortcut Command+K (Mac)/Control+K (Windows).

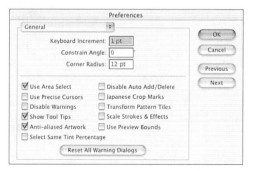

2. Click the Next button to take us to the Type & Auto Trace preferences panel. You'll learn about these options in Hour 14, "Applying Advanced Typography Techniques." Until then, the defaults are perfect.

▼ 3. Click Next again to open Units & Undo, a very important set of preferences (see
       Figure 2.2). As you work with Illustrator, you'll likely find that points is not your
       favorite unit of measure. Here, you can change the General unit of measure to
       inches, centimeters, pixels, and others. This affects rulers, dialog boxes, tools, and
       more. If your computer has a lot of memory available, you might also want to
       adjust the minimum number of Undo levels.

FIGURE 2.2

The Units & Undo Preferences govern the units of measure for Illustrator.

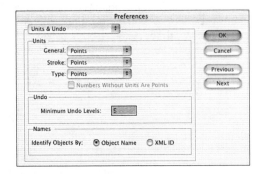

4. Guides & Grid is a preference panel that we'll visit now and then during the coming hours. Select it from the pop-up menu or click the Next button. Primarily, we'll
   be looking at the grid spacing (see Figure 2.3). Sometimes the default colors might
   inconveniently match the colors that you're working with. Here is where we can
   change them.

FIGURE 2.3

*Remember that, even though you see pt (points) as the unit of measure for Grid Spacing, Illustrator enables you to input your choice. For exam-ple, simply type **1** in to get one-inch spacing.*

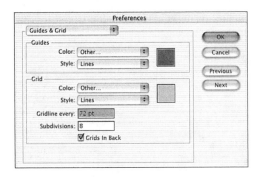

5. Click Next again to move along. The options for Smart Guides & Slices are combined for purposes of alliteration, perhaps, because the two capabilities have nothing in common. Smart Guides, which we'll discuss later in this hour, can be helpful
   or annoying. Making changes here can often determine which Slices are used for
▼ Web images. They will be explored in Hour 22, "Creating Web Graphics."

6. Open the Hyphenation window of the Prefs, which is used only with text. Again, you can ignore these preferences until Hour 14.

7. The preferences for Plug-ins & Scratch Disks affect some of the commands and capabilities available to you in Illustrator, as well as the program's overall performance. Open that window. Plug-ins are add-ons for Illustrator, things such as filters, effects, and extra tools produced by some outside companies. This is where you tell Illustrator where to look for them. The program uses scratch disks to back up the memory. If you have multiple hard drives, assign them in order here. For best performance, a fast hard drive with nothing else on it is perfect. Do not use removable media, such as Zip disks, or network drives for scratch disks.

8. Select the Files & Clipboard preferences window from the pop-up menu. It has some very important options, as shown in Figure 2.4. If you work with Windows, or if your files might be sent to a Windows computer or get posted on the Web, you need to append the two- or three-character file extension that indicates the file's format. Rather than doing this manually every time you save a new file, you can have Illustrator do it automatically. Select Lower Case to ensure that the extension will be readable by all computers. Even if you are strictly a Macintosh operation, being able to identify the file type from the extension can be handy. There is no practical reason not to append the file extension. In contrast, having Illustrator ask whether to update a linked file (rather than doing it automatically) is usually the best idea. The Clipboard is where Illustrator stores data, and objects that you cut or copy. PDF can preserve transparency, but AICB retains the appearance of objects better under some circumstances. AICB should be your choice if you're working with Photoshop. With AICB, you can specify that the accuracy of the paths takes precedence, or that the overall appearance of the image is more important.

FIGURE 2.4

The option you choose for the Clipboard affects Illustrator's capability to transfer artwork and paths to other programs.

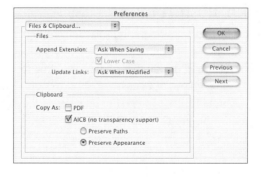

▼   9.   The Next button will now take you to the Workflow panel. We'll look at managed
            documents in Hour 24. In a nutshell, these preferences are used with documents
            that are stored on network servers and can be accessed by more than one person at
            the same time.

     10.   The final set of preferences cannot be accessed with the Next button or the pop-up
            menu. Close the Preferences dialog box. Now, from the Preferences submenu,
            select Online Settings. (Remember that you'll find the Preferences submenu under
            Edit for Windows and Mac OS 9, but it's under the Illustrator menu for Mac OS
            X.) These preferences govern the behavior of the accessory that enables you to
            connect directly to the Adobe Web site to view Illustrator-related subjects, materi-
            als, downloads, and tutorials. The default values are usually okay. However, you
            can set Adobe Online to automatically check for updates according to a schedule,
▲   and to automatically install updates when found.

Preferences and Illustrator's Bad Behavior

If Illustrator should start misbehaving, acting funny, or not responding, it's a good idea to
try replacing the Preferences file. Simply using a clean Prefs file often eliminates these
problems. After you delete the existing preferences file, the next time you start Illustrator
it generates a new one, using the factory presets.

> The Prefs are rewritten every time you quit Illustrator. Those frequent
> changes can lead to corruption in the file. In addition, any time Illustrator
> crashes, the file doesn't get updated.

Preferences for Intermediate Users

After you're familiar with Illustrator's capabilities and can find your way around, let's
say in about another 22-and-a-half hours, you'll be better prepared to make some decisions about preferences. (Again, during these hours, we'll be resetting the Prefs regularly.) When you know how you want to customize Illustrator, here's a way to save
yourself some time and trouble. Quit Illustrator, then delete the Prefs file. Restart
Illustrator and customize your preferences. Quit Illustrator without doing anything other
than setting the Prefs. Copy the new preference file and save it elsewhere. If Illustrator
should ever start acting up, you can delete the corrupt Prefs and substitute a copy of this
new file. This step saves you the trouble of resetting the Prefs every time you delete the
file.

Custom Keyboard Shortcuts

Illustrator enables you to create your own keyboard shortcuts for most tools and commands. The default shortcuts conform to those used by other Adobe products, so if you also work with Photoshop, LiveMotion, or GoLive, you might not want to change them. However, there's absolutely no reason not to add to the list.

Assigning Keyboard Shortcuts

There are dozens and dozens of commands and tools with no assigned shortcuts. If you use a command without a shortcut, even occasionally, it makes sense to assign one. The dialog box itself even has a shortcut. Let's use it now: Command+Option+Shift+K (Mac)/Control+Alt+Shift+K (Windows). (They don't get much longer than that.) The dialog box is shown in Figure 2.5.

FIGURE 2.5

The Keyboard Shortcuts dialog box has two panels, Tools and Menu Commands.

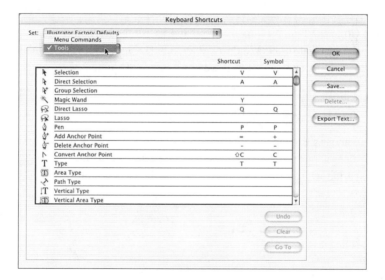

To change or assign a particular shortcut, click the name in the Shortcut column. Type the desired command. If the keystroke combination is already in use, Illustrator will warn you at the bottom of the dialog box.

Saving Keyboard Shortcuts

After you've made your changes, don't forget to click the Save button to store your settings. You can also create a text file of your shortcuts by clicking the Export Text button.

Creating and printing a text file of your shortcuts can serve as a handy reference while you're adjusting to the changes. A card with the default shortcuts can be torn from the front of this book.

Customizing Document Setup

Unlike the Prefs, which affect every document opened in Illustrator, these settings pertain only to a specific document. They are saved with that file and when the file is reopened, they are applied. The Document Setup dialog box has three separate (but related) panels. To the right in each of the panels are five buttons. OK and Cancel, respectively, will either accept or ignore the changes you've made and close the dialog box. Prev and Next take you to the additional panels of Document Setup. Page Setup opens that dialog box for you. It's just a shortcut so you don't have to leave Document Setup to make a change.

Go to the File, New menu command or use the keyboard shortcut Command+N (Mac)/Control+N (Windows) and click OK in the New Document dialog box. We can't look at Document Setup if we don't have a document with which to affiliate these "setups."

Artboard Options

Choose the menu command File, Document Setup (which is not available unless a document is open) or use the keyboard shortcut Command+Option+P (Mac)/Control+Alt+P (Windows) . You'll see the dialog box shown in Figure 2.6.

FIGURE 2.6

The Mac OS X version of the dialog box is shown. Yours might vary in appearance, but the options are the same.

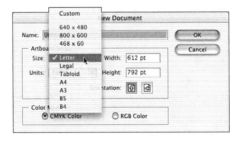

The top half of the dialog box pertains primarily to the overall size of your illustration, not the actual physical page on which you'll be printing your image.

- Size: The pop-up menu has both U.S. and European page sizes, and the option for Custom. Click and hold on the menu to see the choices.

- Units: Open this pop-up menu, which enables you to choose among inches, millimeters, centimeters, points, pixels, and picas. This setting will not change the page size, but will affect the unit of measure in the rulers and dialog boxes. Your choice here overrides the Preferences setting for this particular document only.

- Width: If you choose a paper size from the Size pop-up menu, this field (and Height) will be entered automatically, and will be shown in the unit of measure specified in Unit. You can enter a value here and Size will be automatically adjusted. If you enter a non-standard size, Custom will be selected.

- Height: See Width.

- Use Page Setup: This option makes the dialog box fields automatically conform to the settings in the Page Setup dialog box (File, Page Setup). Check this box and your illustration size will match your page size.

- Orientation: Illustrator is pretty smart. It can determine whether you've got a larger number in Width or in Height, and will select either Landscape or Portrait to match (see Figure 2.7). If you'd like to swap the numbers, click the unselected orientation and Illustrator adjusts the dimensions accordingly.

FIGURE 2.7

To the left is portrait orientation; to the right is landscape. Think about your last trip to the art museum and you'll see where the terms originate.

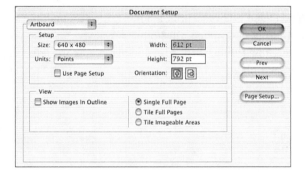

The lower part of the dialog box determines how things will be shown in the document window.

- Show Images in Outline: When you are in Outline mode (under the View menu), any raster images that you have placed into your illustration normally appear just as empty rectangles. If you check this box, you'll see a low-resolution black and white version of the images. This affects only raster images and has no effect on Preview mode. Figure 2.8 shows the difference.

FIGURE 2.8

On the left is the default view of a raster image in Outline view. On the right, you can see how it looks if you choose the Show Images in Outline option.

- Single Full Page: Select this option when your artboard size and your page size match.

- Tile Full Pages: When your illustration (artboard size) is substantially larger than the page size, this option will show you what will be printed on each individual sheet of paper. This option places the pages side-by-side, ignoring their margins. Only those pages that fit completely within the artboard are tiled, as shown in Figure 2.8.

- Tile Imageable Areas: If your artboard is larger than the size specified in Page Setup, and you'll have to print the illustration on multiple sheets of paper, this might be your best option. Illustrator shows you only the printable area of each sheet, aligning (tiling) them edge-to-edge across the artboard, as shown in Figure 2.9.

FIGURE 2.9

The artboard is 17 inches by 22 inches on both side and Page Setup is set for letter-sized paper. On the left you see Tile Full Pages, on the right is Tile Imageable Areas.

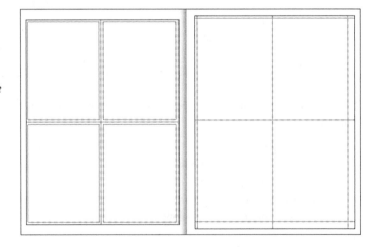

Printing & Export Options

You can get to the next bunch of Document Setup options by clicking the Next button or using the pop-up menu in the upper-left corner of the dialog box, as shown in Figure 2.10. In this case, use the Next button now.

FIGURE 2.10

These options help determine the quality of your printed output.

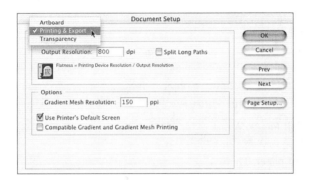

- Output Resolution: As will be discussed in Hour 21, "Printing Your Illustrations," resolution determines the fineness of the printed output. The capability of a printer to produce detail is measured in dpi (dots per inch). Here, you help determine the roundness of your curves when the image is printed. Normally, the default value is fine.

- Split Long Paths: As you'll learn in the coming hours, paths determine the shape and size of lines and objects for Illustrator's vector artwork. Extremely complex paths can cause problems for printing devices. If you're having trouble with a PostScript printer or imagesetter, checking this box might solve the problem.

If you're not having problems with a laser printer or imagesetter, don't split paths or change the output resolution.

- Use Printer's Default Screen: Checked as the default, this option let's your printer do its job to the best of its capability. Screen refers to the *lines per inch* (lpi) setting for the printer, which measures a printer's capability to produce detail.

- Compatible Gradient and Gradient Mesh Printing: Check this box only if your laser printer or imagesetter has only PostScript Level 1 capability.

- Rasterization Resolution: As you'll see in Hour 19, "Working with Raster Images and Programs," the quality of a raster image is measured in pixels per inch (ppi), and is directly related to the quality of the image. 300 ppi is fine for most printed output.

- Mesh: Gradient Mesh objects, which you'll learn about in Hour 8, "Using Strokes, Fills, and Gradients," contain very complex blends of color. This setting, usually 150 ppi, determines their output resolution.

Transparency

The third Document Setup panel involves both the appearance of partially transparent objects on the artboard (top half) and how they are reproduced when printed (bottom half). In addition to see-through objects, these settings affect such special effects as drop shadows and glows (with which you'll work in Hour 18, "Working with Filters and Live Effects"). Open this panel with either the Next button or the pop-up menu. Some examples of objects with transparency are seen in Figure 2.11.

FIGURE 2.11

Semi-opaque objects, shadows, and glows are some of the transparency capabilities of Illustrator.

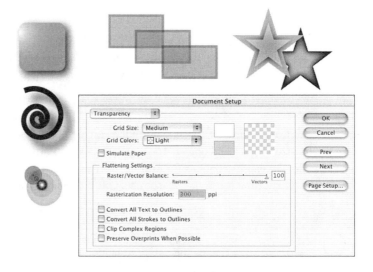

- Grid Size: The transparency grid, which you can show and hide through the View menu, enables you to better see which objects have reduced opacity on the artboard. As you can see in Figure 2.12, the plain white background of the artboard and surrounding area is replaced with a checkerboard pattern. This option determines the size of the checkerboard squares. (Remember that the grid is for on-screen use only, it never prints.)

FIGURE 2.12

Shown are the medium-sized (default) squares. Notice how they appear behind the semi-transparent objects. Observe, too, that where these partially opaque objects overlap, the transparency grid is less visible.

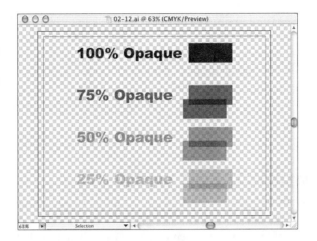

- Grid Colors: In addition to light, medium, and dark gray, Illustrator enables you to show the grid in various colors. This is convenient when the grid's default, gray, is too close to one or more colors in your image. Open the pop-up menu to see your preset choices.

- Color Swatches: Located just to the right of Grid Size and Grid Color are a pair of swatches. Click each to specify the exact colors you want to use for the grid. The top swatch is the background; the lower is the grid.

- Simulate Colored Paper: If your illustration will be printed on colored paper, you can use this option. Check the box, and then click the upper color swatch to select the paper color. This color won't print, but it will give you an opportunity to see how your artwork will look (and interact) with the color that it will be printed. You can use this option even if you don't show the transparency grid.

- Quality/Speed: This slider enables you to choose one of five levels of printing quality. The first setting (left-most) rasterizes the entire image. It is good for very complex illustrations, those with a lot of transparency, and for low-resolution images. High-resolution images might take a long time to print and might generate very large files. The second setting keeps simple objects as vector, but rasterizes objects with transparency. The middle setting rasterizes only areas of very complex transparency. The fourth setting rasterizes only the most complex areas, and might take considerable time to process. The right-most setting maintains all vector artwork as vector, except when impossible to do so. Although producing the best possible resolution-independent printing, this setting can be both time and memory intensive. It is not appropriate for low-memory systems.

- Preserve Overprints When Possible: Overprinting occurs when two inks will be placed on the same area of the printed page. When two opaque objects overlap, typically only the color of the top-most object is printed (knocking out the lower color). When the top object is not totally opaque, overprinting of two translucent inks can produce a third color.

Close the Document Setup dialog box by clicking Cancel. (This closes without recording any changes.) Leave the document itself open.

Rulers, Guides, and Grids

When preparing an image in Illustrator, exact placement and relationships among objects can be very important. Illustrator offers you a number of aids. Rulers appear at the top and left edges of the window. When they are visible, you can click a ruler, and drag a guide onto your window. The guide can be positioned anywhere in the window, on or off the artboard. The grid is a series of lines, both vertical and horizontal, at intervals you specify in Illustrator's Preferences.

Use these keyboard shortcuts to take a look at each.

- Show/Hide Rulers: Command+R (Mac)/Control+R (Windows)
- Show/Hide Grid: Command+` (Mac)/Control+` (Windows)
- Show/Hide Guides: Command+; (Mac)/Control+; (Windows)

Task: Setting Up the Rulers

1. Use the keyboard shortcut Command+R (Mac)/Control+R (Windows) to toggle the rulers on and off. Now try the menu command View, Show/Hide Rulers. By default, the Illustrator rulers have their point of origin (the place from which they measure, the zero-zero point) in the lower-left corner of the artboard.

2. With the rulers visible, click once in the upper-left corner, where the horizontal and vertical rulers meet. That changes the zero-zero point to the upper-left corner of the window, where you just clicked. This is true regardless of the zoom factor at the time; it will always be where you clicked.

3. Double-clicking at that point restores zero-zero to the lower-left corner of the artboard. Try it now.

4. You can also click and drag from that intersection to place the point of origin anywhere you'd like. Click in the ruler intersection and drag to the upper-left corner of the artboard. When you're designing for the Web, this is the most logical place for the point of origin, because Web pages start from the upper left.

5. To change the unit of measure for the rulers, you can go to Preferences, Units & Undo, or you can use the Units pop-up menu in the Artboard section of Document Setup. However, the easiest way to change the rulers' unit of measure is to Control+click (Mac)/right-click (Windows) on the ruler and select from the contextual menu. Try it now, setting the rulers to inches, as shown in Figure 2.13.

FIGURE 2.13

Control+click (Mac)/right-click (Windows) on the ruler to show the menu, and then mouse to the desired unit of measure and release the mouse button.

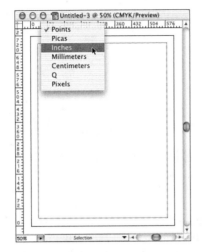

Task: Using Guides

Guides are very helpful for aligning things on the artboard. They are horizontal and vertical lines that can be placed anywhere in the image. They will not print, nor will they be visible in an image on the Web.

1. With the rulers visible, move your cursor to the top of the window.

2. With the pointer over the ruler, click and drag downward onto the middle of your artboard. A thin-blue line should appear.

3. Now drag a guide from the left-side ruler to the middle of the artboard. You can drag guides with any tool selected from the Toolbox. (You can't usually drag guides when a dialog box is open, however.)

4. Move the cursor up to the View menu. Click and drag down to the Guides submenu. You should see the commands shown in Figure 2.14.

FIGURE **2.14**

Remember that the keyboard shortcuts in the menu will change if you assign your own custom key combinations.

By default, the guides are locked into place as soon as you release the mouse button. That prevents you from accidentally moving or selecting them. If you need to relocate or remove a guide, you'll need to come to this menu first and uncheck the Lock command (or use the keyboard shortcut). Guides can then be dragged back on to the rulers to put them away.

Task: Working with Guides

Let's practice with guides a bit.

1. Select Unlock Guides from the View, Guides submenu.

2. Press V on the keyboard to activate the Move tool. (This is the tool required to reposition guides.)

3. Position the cursor directly on top of the vertical guide. You'll see the cursor change from the usual arrow to just the arrowhead.

4. Click and drag the guide to the 4-inch mark on the ruler, and then release the mouse button. You need not be exact.

5. Move the horizontal guide to the 10-inch mark on the ruler.

6. The commands Hide/Show Guides and Clear Guides apply to all guides in the document at that time. Select the command View, Guides, Clear Guides.

▼ 7. From the Toolbox, select the Rectangle tool. Drag a rectangle, any size, anywhere on the artboard. Go to the menu command View, Guides, Make Guides. The rectangle is transformed to a four-sided guide.

▲ 8. Go back to the menu and choose Release Guides. The rectangle is restored to its original condition. Any Illustrator object or line can become a guide.

Setting Up the Grid

You can think of the grid as a series of vertical and horizontal guides that work together, as shown in Figure 2.15. However, the grid has another feature that makes it truly wonderful. When moving objects on the artboard, you can have them *snap* to the grid. When the edge of an object gets within a couple of pixels of a grid line, it will jump to the line. That's your cue that it's aligned. Very handy for making sure that several objects are all aligned vertically or horizontally—just snap them all to the grid. Don't forget that at an intersection of a pair of lines, objects can snap both vertically and horizontally at the same time.

FIGURE 2.15

The objects snapped to the grid, so they're perfectly aligned with each other.

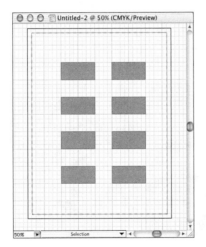

Choose the menu command View, Show Grid, or use the keyboard shortcut Command+" (Mac)/Control+" (Windows). The artboard and surrounding area will be covered with the grid, making it appear to be graph paper. Adding the Shift key to the keyboard shortcut gives you Snap to Grid (View, Snap to Grid) .

Remember that the spacing of the grid lines is controlled in the Prefs. And that's where you can adjust the color of the grid's lines as well.

By default, Illustrator's grid appears behind all objects on the artboard. (You can move the grid to the front in the Preferences.) With the grid behind, you'll easily be able to tell whether an object is filled with white or with nothing, and the grid can serve as an easy-to-access alternative to the transparency grid.

Working with Smart Guides

The menu command View, Smart Guides activates another type of Illustrator guide. Smart guides are more versatile and flexible that normal guides. When they're activated, they appear and disappear as you drag an object on the artboard. Depending upon what settings you've selected in the Preferences, the guides show up when the object that is being dragged is in various positions in relation to other objects on the artboard. For example, using the defaults, if one object is dragged to a position 45° from another object, the smart guide would appear.

Smart guides are very handy when establishing relationships among items on the artboard. However, when the illustration contains many objects, the smart guides might be more of a distraction than help (see Figure 2.16).

FIGURE 2.16
With all the objects on the artboard, it's hard to tell which corner or center is being used as a reference point by the smart guide.

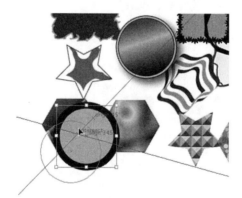

Illustrator's Startup Files

When you start Illustrator, the program reads the Preferences file to get certain settings. The Prefs hold things such as the position of palettes, grid settings, the location of the plug-ins folder, and more. Quite a few other settings are found in Illustrator's startup files.

There's one startup file for RGB documents and another for CMYK files. When you start the program, the Prefs are read. When you start a new document, the startup file is consulted. Page size and orientation, preferred font for type, colors, swatches, patterns, and more are stored in the startup file.

Task: Creating Custom Startup Files

Later, when you're more comfortable with Illustrator, you'll have a good idea about what type of files you're likely to create. For example, if your CMYK files are usually letter size and use portrait orientation, perhaps the default CMYK startup file is fine. If, however, whenever you work in RGB you're producing Web graphics, you might want a different RGB startup file. Let's see how to create a new RGB startup file.

1. Open a new document and specify the size and make sure to check RGB as the color mode.

2. Change the document settings, ruler and point of origin, font, colors, and other options. The Startup file determines the contents of the Swatches, Styles, Brushes, and Symbols palettes, as well. (You'll learn about the content of those palettes in later hours.)

3. Name the file Adobe Illustrator Startup_RGB and save it in your Adobe Illustrator folder. (Do not include the .ai file extension.)

4. Quit Illustrator.

5. Locate the original Adobe Illustrator Startup_RGB file inside Illustrator's Plug-ins folder.

6. Rename the original, adding old or some such modifier to the filename.

7. Move the newly created Adobe Illustrator Startup_RGB file into the Plug-ins folder.

The next time that you create an RGB document, your preferred settings will be used. The page size and orientation are not taken from the startup file, but rather reflect the last settings you used.

If you'll be doing a series of files that all require a certain piece of artwork, add it to the startup file. It will then appear in the same place in every document of that color mode that you create.

Ten Preferences and Settings You Need to Know

As promised earlier, here are some settings that you should be aware of. After you've completed Hour 24 and have become a full-fledged Illustrator user, consider these suggestions.

- Preferences, General, Use Area Select: When this option is checked, you can select (make active) any object by clicking its stroke (the outer path) or its fill (the color inside). When it's not checked, you can only click directly on the path to select an object. Generally, leave Area Select activated.

- Preferences, General, Show Tool Tips: Some folks find these little labels to be an annoyance. Other folks never even notice that they're on, because their cursors never stay in one place long enough for the Tool Tips to pop up! Down the road you might need to look up some rarely used tool in this book or Illustrator's Help. Tool Tips will show you the proper name for the tool (see Figure 2.17). Generally, leave it checked.

FIGURE 2.17

Tool Tips, when activated, appear after your cursor has remained stationary on an icon in the Toolbox. They disappear when you move the mouse.

- Preferences, General, Disable Auto Add/Delete: When checked, the Pen tool will not automatically switch to the Add Anchor point or Delete Anchor Point tools. Check the box when creating a lot of paths in a very small space, otherwise leave it unchecked. This is one of the preferences that might be turned on and off several times in the course of one creative afternoon. Feel free to adjust your Prefs to meet the specific situation, even if that situation changes from one minute to the next.

- Preferences, General, Transform Pattern Tiles: When unchecked, a pattern that fills an object will remain oriented toward the top of the page when you rotate or otherwise transform the object. When checked, the pattern fill rotates with the object, as shown in Figure 2.18.

FIGURE 2.18

To the left is the original object. In the middle, the object has been rotated, but the pattern is still oriented vertically. On the right, the Transform Pattern Tiles option was checked, and both the object and the pattern are rotated.

- Preferences, General, Scale Strokes & Effects: If you need to change the size of something, but you need it to look the same, this box should be checked. Take a look at Figure 2.19 for a visual comparison. Remember that you can also control this in the dialog box for Object, Transform, Scale, and by double-clicking the Scale tool's icon in the Toolbox. Keep track of whether you generally need to scale strokes and effects or not, and then decide which way you want it to work as a default. Check or uncheck the option in the Preferences.

FIGURE 2.19

When the object on the left is scaled to 50%, its appearance varies considerably depending upon whether or not the stroke is also scaled.

- Preferences, Type & Auto Tracing, Type Area Select: Like Area Select for objects, this enables you to click anywhere on the type to select it. When unchecked, you'll need to be very precise and click directly on the type's baseline to select it. Remember that the selection tool cursors will change to let you know when you're in the right spot. The little black square will appear to the lower right of the arrow.

- Preferences, Guides & Grid, Grids in Back: Compare the difference shown in Figure 2.20. Notice how having the grid in back also enables you to view transparency. Check out how having the grid in front can hide rectangles that have snapped to it. Keep the grid in back.

FIGURE 2.20

The same set of objects is shown with the grid in back (left) and in front (right).

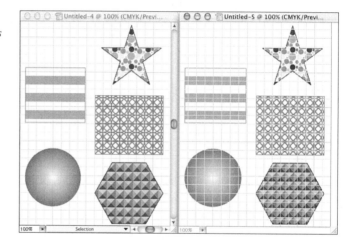

- Window, Document Info: This palette, shown in Figure 2.21, is a wealth of information about your illustration. As you can see in the top of the palette's menu, you can choose to display information about the currently selected object(s) or about the document as a whole. Uncheck the Selection Only option so that you can get the full scoop on your document. Check the option and you can do things such as checking a complex path to see how many points it has.

FIGURE 2.21

The palette's menu enables you to choose what information you want to display, either about a selection or about the document as a whole.

- File, Document Setup, Split Long Paths: In the Printing & Export panel of the Document Setup window, you'll find this checkbox. If (and only if) you're having trouble outputting your illustration to a laser printer or an imagesetter, try this: Open a copy of the file, check this box, save, and close the document. When you reopen it, complex paths will be divided into smaller paths (and objects). It will ease output trouble, but will make editing the illustration problematic. (That's why we say do this to a *copy* of the image.)
- File, Document Setup, Use Page Setup: In the Artboard panel of the Document Setup dialog box, you'll see Use Page Setup. Checking this box automatically sets your artboard to match the dimensions and margins of the current printer options. Unless you're working on a piece of artwork that has to be printed on several sheets, use this option.

2

Summary

You've learned a lot about how to customize Illustrator in this hour. Much of it is just vague theory and strange terminology right now. However, as we progress through the remaining hours, all will become clear, Young Grasshopper! Later, you'll see these terms again, you'll learn the techniques behind the concepts, and you'll think "Ah-ha! I can set *that* in the Preferences!"

You've also learned about Document Setup; rulers, grids, guides; shortcuts; and even startup files. More than any other hour in this book, these are sections that you'll want to return to. When you're comfortable in Illustrator, remember where you need to come to figure out how to set Preferences, change document settings, assign keyboard shortcuts, and create startup files.

Workshop

Let's reinforce some of this hour's customization concepts with a couple of questions with answers, some questions with several possible answers, and some hands-on exercises.

Q&A

Q Are there any preferences that I shouldn't change?

A Actually, you shouldn't change any preferences until you understand them. Every option in the Preferences can be changed for a reason, but changing without purpose or understanding can create serious problems.

Q Let's say that I *accidentally* changed some preferences that I shouldn't have messed with. What can I do?

A Simply quit Illustrator and delete the preferences file. The next time you start the program, the default settings will be restored.

Q Are startup files important?

A Without a startup file, Illustrator can still create a new document of the given color mode using the factory-set defaults. However, you should make sure that you always have a valid startup file for both RGB and CMYK in the Plug-ins folder. (And don't delete the original files until you're sure that your replacements work.)

Quiz

1. Changes made to Illustrator's preferences...

    a. ...don't take effect until you restart Illustrator.

    b. ...are in effect until you restart Illustrator.

    c. ...apply to all documents opened in Illustrator.

    d. ...apply to only the document open at the time.

2. Changes made to the Document Setup...

    a. ...don't take effect until you restart Illustrator.

    b. ...are in effect until you restart Illustrator.

    c. ...apply to all documents opened in Illustrator.

    d. ...apply to only the document open at the time.

3. Illustrator enables you to assign which keyboard shortcuts?

    a. Any that are not already assigned

    b. Most tools and menu commands

    c. Only tools

    d. Only menu commands

4. Changing the ruler's unit of measure will automatically change the grid spacing.

    a. True

    b. False

Quiz Answers

1. c. All documents opened from that point onward reflect the new Preferences settings.

2. d. Document Setup is for only that one document.

3. b. You can change existing shortcuts or add new ones.

4. b. False. The two units are independently set.

Exercises

1. Open a new file. Show the rulers. Drag guides—a lot of guides—onto the artboard from the rulers. Unlock the guides using the menu command View, Guides, Unlock Guides. Practice using the Move tool to rearrange the guides. When done, close the document without saving.

2. Open a new file. Show the grid using the keyboard shortcut. (If you've forgotten it, you'll find it next to the menu command View, Show Grid.) Use the Preferences to change the spacing of the grid. Don't just change the "Gridline every" setting, experiment with "Subdivisions" as well. Hide the grid and turn off Snap to Grid, and leave the document open for the next exercise.

3. Press M to activate the Rectangle tool. Create a few rectangles around the artboard by clicking and dragging with the Rectangle tool. (You'll learn more about creating objects next hour.) Now press V on the keyboard to activate the Move tool. Select the menu command View, Smart Guides. Click any rectangle near the center of the artboard and drag it around. Get a feel for how the smart guides work, when they show, and what they indicate.

HOUR 3

Creating Objects

Adobe Illustrator, as you already know, is a vector art program. The basic building block of vector art is the path. Paths can be used to create objects and lines. When a path has definable starting and ending points, it is called an open path. Think about a piece of string. When a path has no identifiable end points, it is a closed path. Think about a rubber band. This is the difference between a line and an object. (We'll get into the nitty-gritty of paths in Hour 5, "Creating Paths and Compound Paths," and in Hour 6, "Editing Bézier Curves.") Fasten your seatbelt, because this is going to be a real hands-on hour!

In this hour, you'll learn about the following:

- Creating basic objects, such as rectangles, squares, ellipses, and circles
- Creating line segments and curves
- Creating more complex objects, such as polygons, stars, spirals, and grids
- Using symbols in your artwork
- Saving your work

Creating Rectangles, Squares, Ellipses, and Circles

These basic shapes are among the easiest to create in Illustrator and are among the most common. From the walls of a phone booth to the eyes of a squirrel, you'll find these shapes everywhere in illustration. In addition to being common and easy to create, they are also the shapes that you'll start creating in Illustrator.

Getting Ready to Create

If Illustrator has been used since the last time you replaced the Prefs, go ahead and return them to their default settings. If you have any doubts about the procedure, see the instructions on the back of the reference card in the front of this book.

Use the menu command File, New, or the keyboard shortcut Command+N (Mac)/Control+N (Windows). In the New Document dialog box, accept the default values by clicking OK.

▼ TASK

Task: Making Rectangles and Squares

Among the most basic of objects are those ever-useful rectangles and squares. These are some of the building blocks of illustration, and are also used for such things as crop marks and trim marks (which will come later in your Illustrator education). This is a great place to start creating.

1. In the Toolbox, click on the Rectangle tool to select it (see Figure 3.1).

FIGURE 3.1

Most of the tools we'll use in the first part of this hour are located either under the Rectangle tool or under the Line Segment tool, immediately to the left.

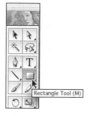

2. Move the cursor onto the artboard. Notice how it becomes a crosshair.

3. Simply click at a point near the upper-left corner of the artboard and drag down and to the right, near the center of the page. When the rectangle is of the proper size, release the mouse button. Your artboard should look similar to Figure 3.2.

FIGURE 3.2

*Don't worry if
your rectangle is
different...as long as
you actually have a
rectangle on your
artboard, that is.*

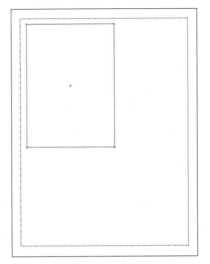

3

4. In another part of the artboard, click and drag from a point toward the upper-right corner.

5. Now click and drag toward the upper-left corner. Release the mouse button.

6. Hold down the Shift key and drag another rectangle. Notice that it remains a perfect square rather than following the cursor. Release the mouse button.

7. Start dragging a rectangle and, without releasing the mouse button, press Shift. Observe how the outline of the rectangle jumps to a perfect square. Keeping the mouse button down, release Shift. Press Shift. Release Shift. Press Shift. You see how it works. Release the mouse button.

8. Position the cursor in the middle of the artboard. It doesn't matter if it is on top of an existing rectangle or not.

9. Click and begin dragging. Without releasing the mouse button, press and hold the Option (Mac)/Alt (Windows) key. Continue dragging. Notice that Illustrator is creating the rectangle from the center outward. Release Option (Mac)/Alt (Windows). Press Option (Mac)/Alt (Windows). Release the mouse button.

10. Once more from the center, press both Shift and Option (Mac)/Alt (Windows) and begin dragging a rectangle. Experiment with releasing one or the other or both keys. Release the mouse button.

11. Click on the artboard and begin dragging a rectangle. Without releasing the mouse button, press the spacebar and move the cursor. This allows you to reposition the object while you're drawing. Release the spacebar and then the mouse button.

12. Drag a few more rectangles and squares.

You've successfully created several rectangles. There are several points to note:

- When you released the mouse button, the Rectangle tool stayed selected, ready to draw another object.
- When you released the mouse button, the object you just drew stayed selected until you started drawing again.
- You can drag in any direction; objects don't have to start from the upper-left corner.
- The Shift key constrains the dimensions so that the height and width are equal. With the Rectangle tool, this produces a square. With the Ellipse tool, it produces a circle.
- The Option (Mac)/Alt (Windows) key forces the tool to create from the center.
- Shift and Option (Mac)/Alt (Windows) can be used together.
- The spacebar allows you to reposition an object while you are dragging to create it.
- Objects can overlap.

Starting Over

Your artboard probably looks like some kind of a mess. Rectangles and squares, overlapping each other with corners poking out. No sense of order. No sense of symmetry. Wow! I think in some circles they call that "art."

Now, let us suffer for our art and destroy these works of genius! Hold down the Command (Mac)/Control (Windows) key and press the letter A on the keyboard. Command+A (Mac)/Control+A (Windows) is the shortcut for Select All. You'll see that each object on the artboard is highlighted, even those that are hidden. You should see something similar to Figure 3.3.

That distinctive look that tells you an object is selected is called the *bounding box*. No matter the shape of the object or the number of objects selected, the bounding box will, by default, be a rectangle. We'll learn more about bounding boxes in Hour 4, "Making Selections."

Now press the Delete (Mac)/Backspace (Windows) key or use the menu command Edit, Clear. That removes all of the selected objects from your artboard. Hold down the Command (Mac)/ Control (Windows) key and press Z. Command+Z (Mac)/Control+Z (Windows) is the keyboard shortcut for Undo. Memorize this one! Everything reappears. Delete everything again, so that your artboard is clean and clear for the next learning experience.

FIGURE 3.3

Your artboard should show a variety of rectangles and squares, all selected. There's a large rectangle surrounding them all, called the bounding box.

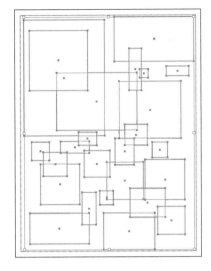

TASK ▼

Task: Making Rounded Rectangles

Like regular rectangles, rounded rectangles have four straight sides. However, these objects don't have pointy, 90° angle corners, they have gentle curves where two sides meet.

1. Click and hold on the Rectangle tool icon in the Toolbox.

2. When the hidden (flyout) palette appears, continue to hold down the mouse button and move the cursor onto the second icon, the Rounded Rectangle tool.

3. Release the mouse button.

4. Click anywhere on the artboard and drag. Release the mouse button.

5. You've just created a rounded rectangle. Take a look at the curves that create the corners. Now, with the object still selected, press Delete (Mac)/Backspace (Windows) to get rid of it.

6. With the Rounded Rectangle tool still selected, click once near the upper-left corner of the artboard. The dialog box shown in Figure 3.4 should open.

7. Enter Width 200 pt, Height 150 pt, Corner Radius 10 pt, and click OK. (The default unit of measure is points, so the pt doesn't really need to be added. But if the Prefs didn't get reset recently…) Your artboard should look like Figure 3.5.

▼

▼

FIGURE 3.4

A comparable dialog box opens when you click once with most of the creation tools. The options vary according to the tool.

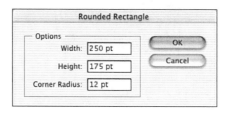

FIGURE 3.5

A single rounded rectangle should be on the page, located in the upper-left quadrant of the page.

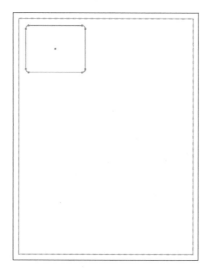

8. Move the cursor to the top middle of the artboard and click again. This time, hit the Tab key a couple of times to highlight the Corner Radius field in the dialog box. Enter 25 and click OK.

9. Position the cursor somewhat below the lower-left corner of the first object and click. In the dialog box, enter 200, 200, and 50, and then click OK.

10. Move to below the second object and click. In the dialog box, enter 200, 200, and 100. Click OK. Theoretically, this object is indeed a rounded rectangle, although it looks like a circle. (See Figure 3.6.)

▲

You've just learned how to create rounded rectangles both numerically (using the dialog box) and by dragging. A single click with most creation tools will open a dialog box into which you can enter precise values. You also learned that appearances can be deceiving—a rounded rectangle might look like a circle, and a circle might actually be something else. But in fact, to Illustrator, it's just an object. Objects are defined by their paths, strokes, and fills, and don't rely on such limiting labels as circle or rectangle. Quite a refreshing attitude, I think.

FIGURE 3.6

Your four objects should look like these, although the placement might be slightly different.

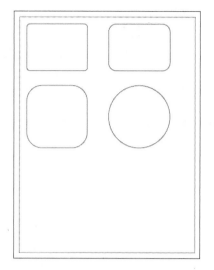

3

Creating Ellipses and Circles

Let's apply what you've learned about the Rectangle and Rounded Rectangle tools to the Ellipse tool. You can select the Ellipse tool in the Toolbox (it's just to the right of the Rounded Rectangle tool), or you can simply press L on the keyboard. (No modifiers are necessary. No Shift, no Control, no Command, no Option, no Alt. Just the L key.)

With the Ellipse tool selected, repeat the Select All, Delete procedure to clear your artboard. Now click and drag to create ellipses (also called ovals). Shift+drag to create circles. Option+drag (Mac)/Alt+drag (Windows) to create ellipses from the center. Shift+Option+drag (Mac)/Shift+Alt+drag (Windows) to create circles from the center. See how this tool parallels the Rectangle tool. The same techniques, the same modifier keys, the same results. Except, of course, for the shapes produced.

Click once in the artboard to open the Ellipse dialog box. You'll see that the only options are width and height. Keep in mind that if the width and height are equal you're creating a circle. Enter 250 and 250, and then click OK. Instant circle, exact dimensions.

Creating Complex Objects

Both rectangles and ellipses have four path segments and four anchor points. (You'll learn more about them in Hour 5.) Illustrator also has tools that can create objects with different numbers of sides. Like the Rectangle and Ellipse tools, the Polygon and Star tools can be dragged or clicked. However, they always create from the center of the object.

Using the Polygon Tool

The Polygon tool creates closed paths with multiple sides. Your object can range from three sides, producing an equilateral triangle to as many as 1,000 sides. To give you an idea of what a 1,000-sided polygon looks like, even at an incredibly huge size, see Figure 3.7.

FIGURE 3.7

Illustrator's maximum document size is a little over 227 inches by 227 inches. This 1,000-sided polygon is about 200 inches across, and still looks like a circle. For reference, in the upper-left corner you can see the page-tiling indicator for a single letter-sized sheet of paper.

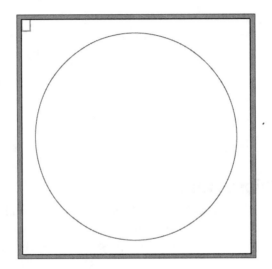

Task: Working with Polygons

▼ TASK

Unlike the Rectangle, Rounded Rectangle, and Ellipse tools, you always drag polygons from the center. Let's give it a try.

1. Select the Polygon tool in the Toolbox.

2. Determine where on your artboard you want the center of the object.

3. Click and drag straight toward the top or bottom of the page.

4. Continue to hold down the mouse button and drag the cursor in a circle around your object. Observe how the object rotates with the cursor.

5. Still holding the mouse button, press the Shift key. You'll see the polygon snap into a specific orientation. When Shift is pressed, the polygon will always have a flat side on the bottom. Release Shift, and then press it again. Release Shift, but keep the mouse button down.

6. Press the up arrow key on your keyboard several times. Every press of the up arrow adds one more side to the polygon.

▼

▼   7. Press the down arrow key several times. This subtracts sides from the object. Keep the mouse button down.

8. Press the spacebar and drag. You can also reposition polygons while creating them.

9. Release the mouse button. Click once more in the center of the artboard and release. Give your clicking finger a break while we look at the Polygon dialog box
▲   (see Figure 3.8).

FIGURE 3.8

You can create numerically with any of the object creation tools. Simply click once on the artboard to open the appropriate dialog box.

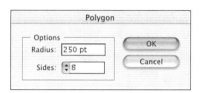

You can input the radius (from the center to any one of the points) and the number of sides.

Using the Star Tool

The Star tool is very similar to the Polygon tool. And, as you'll see right now, it has a lot of similar behavior.

- Click or drag to create stars
- Stars are created from the center
- Pressing the Spacebar lets you move the star while continuing to hold down the mouse button
- The Shift key orients the star so that a point is always toward the top of the page
- The Option (Mac)/Alt (Windows) key will align the path segments on either side of a point. (You'll see an example later, in Figure 3.10.)
- The up and down arrow keys add points to the star, rather than sides
- The number of points can range from 3 to 1,000

There are a couple of additional concepts to consider when creating stars. To understand them, let's first look at the Star dialog box (Figure 3.9).

FIGURE 3.9

The numbers you'll see
in the Star dialog box
are those of the last
star created, whether
numerically or by
dragging.

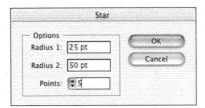

Task: Working with the Star Tool

Stars have two radii. Radius 1 is the distance from the center of the star to the end of a point. Radius 2 is the distance from the center of the star to the angle at the base of two points. Let's see how they work.

1. First, use the command Select, All or the keyboard shortcut Command+A (Mac)/Control+A (Windows) and delete all of the clutter.

2. Click somewhere to the left of the center of your artboard. In the Star dialog box, enter Radius 1: 100 pt, Radius 2: 45 pt, Points: 5, and click OK.

3. Move the cursor to the right of the new star and click again.

4. Leave Radius 1 set to 100 pt, and leave the number of points at 5. Change Radius 2 to 60 pt. Click OK.

The only difference between the two stars is the length of the second radius, the distance from the center of the star to the base of the points.

Task: Mastering the Star Tool

The Star tool has a couple of other little tricks up its sleeve as you drag it on the artboard.

1. In the empty area near the top of the artboard, click with the Star tool and begin dragging.

2. While continuing to drag, press the Shift key and continue to hold down both it and the mouse button. This, you will recall, orients the star to the top of the page. (If you need to reposition the star, remember the spacebar.)

3. Now press the Option (Mac)/Alt (Windows) key. This makes the shoulders of the star square to each other, as in Figure 3.10. (The Shift key is not required, but it makes it easier to see.) Release and press the Option (Alt) key several times. Each point is constructed of two straight path segments. With Option (Mac) or Alt (Windows) depressed, the segments on either side of a point's segments will be parallel.

FIGURE 3.10

To the left, a star with Radius 1 set to 100 and Radius 2 set to 55. On the right, dragging a star with Radius 1 at 100 and the Option (Alt) key depressed to automatically adjust Radius 2.

3

4. Press the up arrow key four times to give the star nine points. (Release the Shift and Option (Mac)/Alt (Windows) keys momentarily, if necessary, but continue to hold down the mouse button.)

5. Once again, press and release the Option (Mac)/Alt (Windows) key several times. Release the Shift key and do it again. Press the Shift and Option (Mac)/Alt (Windows) keys.

6. Release the mouse button.

7. Start dragging to create another star in another part of the artboard. Don't drag very far—keep the star small for the moment.

8. With the mouse button still down, press and hold the Command (Mac)/Control (Windows) key. Now drag the cursor farther from the center of the new star. At this point, Radius 2 is not changing, but you are dragging the points of the stars (Radius 1) farther from the center. Release the mouse button and the Command (Mac)/Control (Windows) key.

The Flare Tool

While we're working with this group of tools, let's take a quick look at the Flare tool. The flare in Flare tool signifies lens flare; those pesky reflections on a camera's lens that cause unwanted highlights. Photographers have spent thousands of hours trying to discover easy ways to remove these flares from negatives. And Adobe is giving us an easy way to add them. Cool, eh?

Task: Working with the Flare Tool

TASK

The Flare tool creates rather complex objects, and it works somewhat differently than the other tools with which you've just worked. Keep in mind that you'll always need a click-drag and another click to complete a flare.

▼   1. Select all and delete to clear your artboard.

      2. In the Toolbox, click on the Star tool (or which ever of the object tools is currently showing) and drag the cursor to the right to select the Flare tool.

      3. With the Flare tool active, click in the center of the artboard and drag a short way toward the upper-left corner of the artboard. When the paths that you're creating stretch almost to the edges of the artboard, release the mouse button as shown in Figure 3.11.

FIGURE 3.11

When the artboard looks something like this, release the mouse button.

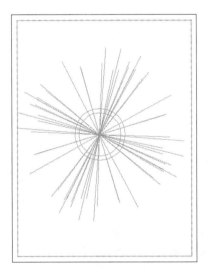

      4. With the cursor a short distance to the up and right of the center of your flare, click the mouse button once. This completes the flare, as shown in Figure 3.12.

      5. Hit the Delete (Backspace) button. That was just a practice flare.

      6. Click in the center of the artboard again, and drag as you did before.

      7. Before you release the mouse button, experiment with the Shift key and the Command (Mac) Control (Windows) key. Press them both and continue dragging. Notice that Shift stops the flare from rotating as you drag. The Command (Mac)/Control (Windows) key allows you to resize the flare in relation to its inner circle.

      8. Again, release the mouse button, move the cursor a short distance and click once. This completes the flare. It should still be selected on the artboard.

▼   9. In the Toolbox, double-click the Flare tool's icon to open the Flare dialog box, as shown in Figure 3.13.

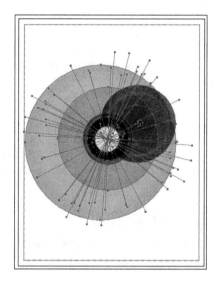

FIGURE 3.12
The flare is completed and it remains selected on the artboard.

3

FIGURE 3.13
It's a complicated dialog box, with many cryptic sliders. Thankfully, it has a Preview option.

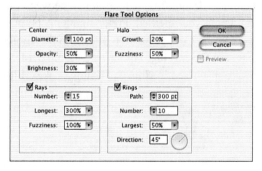

10. Rather than attempt to explain what each variable is and what it does, just click on the checkbox next to Preview and we'll look at some basics. Move the dialog box out of the way if necessary by dragging its title bar.

11. The first thing to do, perhaps, is to uncheck the Rings box and then recheck it. That shows you the two major parts, the flare and its rings.

12. Change the amount in Diameter to 50 pt, and then press the Tab key (which moves you to the next field and tells Illustrator to accept the value you just entered). The Preview will update the look on the artboard. Click back in the Diameter field, enter 150 pt, and hit Tab again.

13. You get the idea. Experiment. Have fun. See if you can figure out what each control does to the flare.

▼   14. When you're done experimenting, hold down the Option (Mac)/Alt (Windows) key
        and look at the upper-right corner of the dialog box. The Cancel button has
        changed to Reset. Click reset and see what Illustrator's programmers have decided
        a flare should look like. Click OK.

    15. Press Delete to send your flare to that place where professional photographers try
▲   to send real lens flares.

Creating Lines

So far you've created objects—closed paths—in the shape of rectangles, squares,
ellipses, and circles. Now we'll take a look at some of the open paths that you can create
by dragging or clicking a tool.

Using the Line Segment Tool

The Line Segment tool, like the Flare tool, does one thing and one thing only.
Thankfully, this tool does it much more simply than Flare does.

Click, drag, and release. A straight line will be drawn between the point where you
clicked and the point where you released. Pretty simple. A point at each end, with a path
in between. Double-click the Line Segment tool icon in the Toolbox to open its dialog
box. Length and angle are the two big options (see Figure 3.14). There's also an option
to fill the line. (Fills are discussed in Hour 8, "Using Strokes, Fills, and Gradients.")

FIGURE 3.14

*The Line Segment tool
is a good antidote for
the very-complex Flare
tool.*

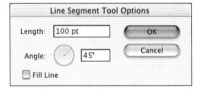

Be aware that adding a fill to a straight path segment changes nothing on the artboard.
However, if you combine this path with another at some later date, a fill might be appropriate.

Pressing the Shift key while dragging constrains the Line Segment tool to 45° angles.
The Option (Mac)/Alt (Windows) key allows you to create lines from the midpoint.

Using the Arc Tool

The Rectangle tool is to the Ellipse tool as the Line Segment tool is to the _____. If
you answered "Arc tool," go to the head of the class! Similar to the Line Segment tool,

the Arc tool produces a single path segment with an anchor point at each end. Similar to the Ellipse tool, it uses curved segments.

Double-click the Arc tool's icon in the Toolbox to open the Arc dialog box. As you can see in Figure 3.15, it is substantially more complicated than the Line Segment dialog box. This tool, however, offers a preview window in the dialog box.

FIGURE 3.15

The Arc tool has a variety of options.

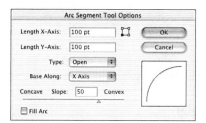

When you double-click the Arc tool's icon in the dialog box and adjust the settings, you don't actually create an arc. Rather, you're setting the tool for the next time it's clicked in the artboard. When you next click it, the dialog box will again open (without a preview), but you can just click OK and create the arc.

Don't overlook the little four-point grid (called a proxy) in the upper middle of the dialog box. Click on any of the four corners to establish the arc's point of origin. Think of the selected point as being where you just clicked, and the small square of the proxy representing the bounding box of the arc.

If you double-click the Arc tool's icon in the Toolbox and the preview window looks broken or empty, close the dialog box by clicking Cancel. Now change the foreground color to black and the background color to white by pressing D on the keyboard. Reopen the dialog box and you'll see the preview. (This preview uses the current foreground and background colors. If the foreground color is white or None, the arc won't be visible in the preview window.)

Task: Working with the Arc Tool

Here's a quick way to get a handle on all of the Arc dialog box options.

1. If the dialog box is not open already, double-click the Arc tool icon in the Toolbox.

2. Set Length X-Axis and Length Y-Axis to the same value, any value. (Well, any value between 1 and 1000 points.)

▼   3. Change Type from Open to Closed.

4. Drag the Concave/Convex slider all the way to the right.

5. Take a look at the preview. Start making changes to the various options and creating arcs by clicking the tool on the artboard. You'll soon recognize what each does.

6. Practice creating curves with different points of origin. After creating an arc, press V to switch to the Selection tool so that you can see the bounding box. Compare the bounding box to the proxy square in the dialog box. You can then switch back to the Arc tool.

▲   7. When done, click the Cancel button, select all, and delete to clear your artboard and get ready for the next step in your journey.

Using the Spiral Tool

Spirals are constructed of a series of linked arcs. Select the Spiral tool from the Toolbox and click once on the artboard to open the Spiral dialog box, as shown in Figure 3.16.

FIGURE 3.16

Shown are Illustrator's default values for the Spiral tool.

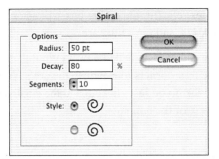

 When Decay is at 100%, the segments of the spiral will be placed atop each other, simulating a circle. Remember, however, that this is an open path, not a closed path like an actual circle.

The Spiral tool is easy to work with if you know the basic terms and functions.

• The radius is the distance from where you first click (the center of the spiral) to the start point of the spiral.

• Decay is the change in distance between the winds (segments) of the spiral.

- The number of segments is measured in quarter turns. Each segment (also called a wind) is one-fourth of a circle.
- The style of the spiral refers simply to the direction in which it goes.

When you drag the Spiral tool, you control the number of winds with the up and down arrow keys. Holding down the Option (Mac)/Alt (Windows) key while dragging controls the radius. The Command (Mac)/Control (Windows) key is used while dragging to adjust the amount of decay. If you press Shift while dragging a spiral, your movement will be constrained to 45° angles. Practice dragging a few spirals. Use the modifier keys Shift, Option (Mac)/ Alt (Windows), and Command (Mac)/Control (Windows) while dragging. When you've got a good understanding of how the modifier keys work, select all and delete to clear the artboard.

Creating Grids

Illustrator's grid tools create objects that are actually made from a series of intersecting or connected lines. There are two types of grids, rectangular and polar. Rectangular grids use straight-line segments to produce boxes arranged in rows and columns. Polar grids use arcs to produce concentric circles that are divided by the radius. Figure 3.17 shows the difference.

FIGURE 3.17
To the left is a rectangular grid, created from straight-line segments. On the right, arcs and radial segments are aligned to create a polar grid.

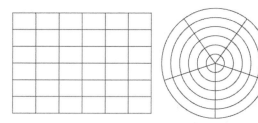

Creating with the Rectangular Grid Tool

Double-click the Rectangular Grid tool icon in the Toolbox. That opens the dialog box shown in Figure 3.18.

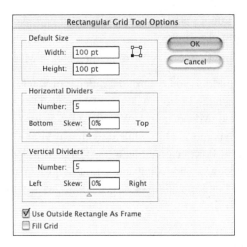

Creating a grid numerically requires a bit of information and a bit of practice.

- The width and height are for the grid as a whole, and the numbers you enter are the dimensions of the rectangle that will be created.

- The proxy to the right of Width allows you to select the point of origin for the grid. For example, if you click the top-left corner, the grid will be created down and to the right of the point where the tool was clicked on the artboard.

- The number of horizontal dividers does not include the top and bottom of the rectangle. Rather, it counts just the number of dividing lines. (Add one to the number of dividers to determine the number of rows.)

- Horizontal skew creates a uniform change in the size of the rows. Use the slider to determine where the larger rows will be, either at the bottom (drag the slider to the left) or at the top of the grid (drag the slider to the right). Figure 3.19 shows some examples of skewed grids.

- The number of vertical dividers does not include the left and right sides of the rectangle. Rather, it counts just the number of dividing lines. (Add one to the number of dividers to determine the number of columns.)

- The vertical skew changes the size of the columns, with larger columns created either to the left or right. (See Figure 3.19.)

- Using the outer rectangle as a frame enables you to include the all-encompassing rectangle as part of the grid. When checked, the outer box of the grid will be a rectangle. When unchecked, the outer box will be four separate paths. (Use the Group Select tool to choose the frame of a grid and adjust its stroke and color.)

- The fill option allows you to use the current fill color, gradient, or pattern in the grid. (The grid tools automatically use the current stroke color and width to create the lines.) If the option Use Outer Rectangle As Frame is not selected, the grid cannot be filled.

FIGURE 3.19

The upper-left grid is unskewed. The upper-right grid is skewed 50% horizontally. The lower-left grid is skewed 50% vertically. The fourth grid is skewed 50% in both directions.

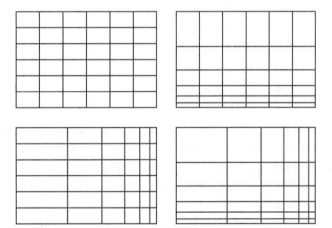

3

Task: Creating with the Polar Grid Tool

The Polar Grid tool creates concentric circles with radial dividers. You can set the options in the dialog box shown in Figure 3.20. To open the box, double-click the Polar Grid tool icon in the Toolbox.

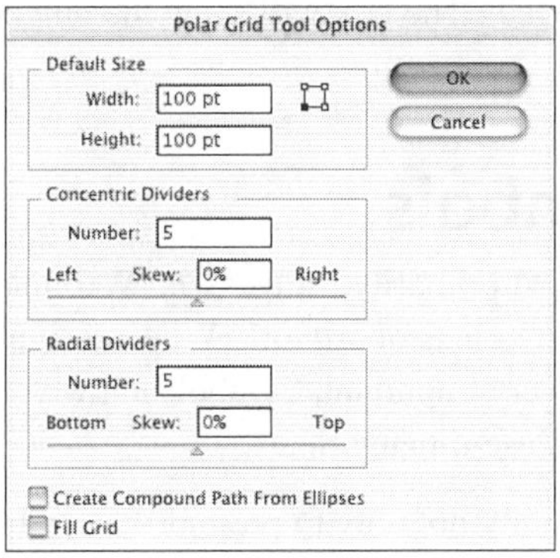

FIGURE 3.20

The Polar Grid Tool Options dialog box is comparable to Figure 3.18 for the Rectangular Grid tool.

▼ Concentric dividers are the circles, while radial dividers are the lines extending from the center.

1. With the Polar Grid Tool Options dialog box open, set the width and height to 250 pt.

2. Use 5 concentric dividers and 15 radial dividers, both skew sliders set to zero.

3. Ignore the two checkboxes at the bottom of the dialog box.

4. Click OK.

5. Select all and delete.

6. Click the Polar Grid tool in the center of the artboard and begin dragging toward the lower-right corner.

7. Press the Shift key. The grid's proportions will be constrained to a perfect circle. Release Shift, but keep the mouse button down.

8. Press the Option (Mac)/Alt (Windows) key. The grid will be created from the center. Release the Option (Mac)/Alt (Windows) key, but continue to hold down the mouse button.

9. Press the up arrow key several times to increase the number of concentric dividers. Press the down key to decrease the number of concentric dividers.

10. Press the right arrow key to increase the number of radial dividers, and the left arrow to decrease.

▲ 11. Release the mouse button.

If you'd like to see the specifications of the grid you just created, open the Polar Grid Tool Options dialog box once again. The box will show the numbers for the most recently created grid.

Working with Symbols

The symbolism tools are designed primarily for use with Web images, but they have tremendous possibilities for many kinds of artwork. When designing graphics for the Web, keeping file size small is very important. Symbols allow you to record only a single copy of an image in the file, yet use it many times.

We're going to take this opportunity not only to present the symbolism tools, but also to give you a head start on a variety of other Illustrator concepts. We'll be introducing such concepts as fill color, transparency, tinting, and more. Each of the more advanced concepts will be explained in later hours. For now, just enjoy the creative possibilities.

Adding Symbols

Illustrator comes with a variety of artwork already designated as symbols. You'll find it in the Symbols palette. Click on the tab for the Symbols palette to bring it to the front, and then drag it by the tab to the upper-right corner of the work area. Click on the Symbol Sprayer tool icon in the Toolbox and hold the mouse button down until the fly-out palette appears. Without releasing the mouse button, move the cursor to the right end of the mini-palette and position it on the little arrow symbol. Release the mouse button. That should turn the strip of Symbolism tools into a small floating palette. Move it to the upper-left corner of the work area. Your screen should now look similar to Figure 3.21.

FIGURE 3.21

For the next little while, we'll be working with these symbols and tools. (The contents of your Symbols palette might vary.)

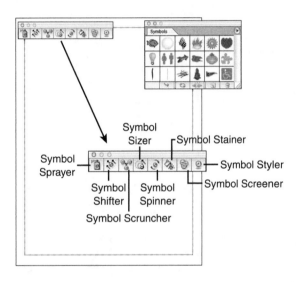

Creating symbols can take a lot of horsepower! Be patient when working with symbols. The screen might take a few seconds to redraw, and the tools might not be as responsive as you expect.

Task: Using Symbols

Let's get creative!

1. Pick a symbol, any symbol, from the Symbols palette by clicking on it. Feeling fishy? Light (bulb) headed? On fire? Puzzled? There's a little something for everyone. The individual little pieces of artwork in the Symbols palette are called symbol instances. Think of an instance as a particular symbol.

2. With the Symbol Sprayer selected, click on the left side of the artboard, just below your floating palette of symbolism tools, and drag slowly to the bottom of the page. Release the mouse button.

3. Move the cursor back up to just under the symbolism tools, and a little to the right of the path you just drew.

4. Click and drag *quickly* to the bottom of the page. Compare the two sets of symbols. Press V on the keyboard to switch to the Selection tool. Notice that the bounding box (the rectangle that indicates a selection) now encompasses both lines of symbols (see Figure 3.22).

FIGURE 3.22

The bounding box is the blue rectangle that surrounds the objects currently active (selected) on the artboard.

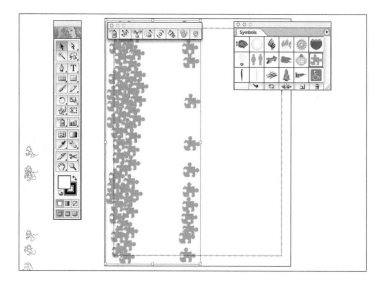

5. In the lower-right corner of the artboard, press the mouse button and leave it down for a couple of seconds without moving the mouse. Watch how the symbols continue to be created for as long as the button is down.

6. Select all and delete to clear your artboard.

7. Select a symbol and drag a long lazy arc or two to spread some symbols around. Switch to a different symbol instance and drag some more, overlapping the first set in a few places.

As you recall, the term instance refers to the actual symbol in the Symbols palette. When talking about a bunch of symbols on the artboard, all of a particular instance, we'll use the term *set*.

▼ 8. Hold down the Command (Mac)/Control (Windows) key and click somewhere on the artboard that isn't covered with symbols. This deselects the symbols and gets you ready to start another set.

9. Double-click the Symbol Sprayer icon in the tool palette that you tore from the Toolbox. In the Symbolism Tool Options dialog box, change the diameter to 100 and increase both the Intensity and Symbol Set Density to 10 (see Figure 3.23).

FIGURE 3.23

You can use the sliders to make changes or simply type a value in the numeric field.

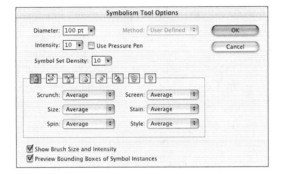

10. Switch back to the Symbol Sprayer. Choose another symbol from the Symbols palette and add a lot more artwork to the artboard. You should have something that looks vaguely like Figure 3.24.

FIGURE 3.24

If your artboard doesn't compare to this masterpiece, don't despair—it was created by a trained professional!

 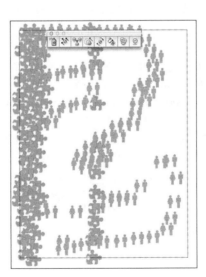

▲

Task: Basic Symbol Manipulation

Now that we've got some symbols with which to experiment, let's do just that.

1. From the symbolism tool palette, choose the Symbol Shifter.

2. In the Symbols palette, click once on the type of symbol that you first added to the artboard in the previous exercise. You must select the type of symbol that you want to move before using the Symbol Shifter.

3. Hold down Command (Mac)/Control (Windows) to temporarily switch to the Selection tool and click on your first set of symbols. The symbol set must be selected on the artboard for the tool to work. (You'll find that manipulating symbols with any of the symbolism tools requires that the set be selected on the artboard.) Release the Command (Mac)/Control (Windows) key.

4. Now click and drag with the Symbol Shifter in an area of your image where these symbols are overlapped by another type of symbol. Note that only the first type of symbol moves. Release the mouse button.

5. Press the Shift key and drag again. The symbols that you're shifting are moved on top of (in front of) the other symbols. Option+Shift (Mac)/Alt+Shift (Windows) can send them back behind.

6. Switch to the Symbol Scruncher. Click and hold on an area of the artboard containing the currently selected symbols. The symbols within the cursor will move closer together. Using the Option (Mac)/Alt (Windows) key moves the symbols farther apart.

7. The fourth tool in the symbolism tool palette is the Symbol Sizer. As you've probably guessed, you can scale symbols with this tool. As you've also probably guessed, the symbol set needs to be selected on the artboard and the target symbol should be selected in the Symbols palette. Try it out by positioning the cursor over a bunch of symbols and holding down the mouse button for a few seconds. Notice that the symbols in the center of the cursor are affected more than those toward the edge (see Figure 3.25). Try the Symbol Sizer with the Option (Mac)/Alt (Windows) key. Indeed, the targeted symbols are reduced in size.

8. Next on the agenda is the Symbol Spinner. Aptly named, it will rotate targeted symbols. Give it a shot. Pay attention to what happens when you drag the cursor in a tight circle several times. Drag figure 8's over a group of targeted symbols.

9. Select all and delete. It's time to analyze what we've done and refresh the artboard for the next round.

FIGURE 3.25

To the left are the original symbols. To the right you can see the result of using the Symbol Sizer. The symbols in the center are enlarged much more than the symbols toward the edge of the cursor.

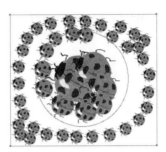

The true value in these symbol manipulation tools is in randomizing your set of symbols. When you created them with the Symbol Sprayer, all of the symbol instances (the individual pieces of artwork) were the same size, pointed in the same direction, and were generally uniform except for location. These tools help you create more natural-looking groupings.

Task: Advanced Symbol Manipulation

▼ TASK

Let's get set up before we actually start this project. In the Symbols palette, grab a colorful symbol and use the Symbol Sprayer to add some to the lower half of the artboard. Now select a very plain symbol, perhaps one that is a single color. Be quick with the Symbol Sprayer, adding a light spread of symbols over much of the artboard (see Figure 3.26).

FIGURE 3.26

Your choice of symbols might vary, as might the distribution across the page.

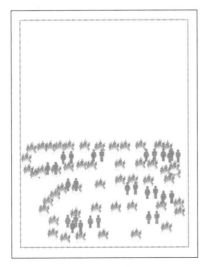

▼

▼   1. Select the Symbol Stainer. In the Swatches palette, click on a color that is substantially different than your second symbol.

2. Click and hold for one second on some of your symbols. (Make sure that the symbol is selected in the Symbols palette and that the symbol set is selected on the artboard.)

3. Move the tool to another area and hold down the mouse button for two seconds. The longer the button is down, the more the color changes. It adopts a tint of the selected color or swatch.

4. Switch to the Symbol Screener tool. In an area where the two types of symbols overlap, click and hold down the mouse button for a second or so. Check the result. Experiment with longer and shorter times. Try Option+clicking (Mac)/Alt+clicking (Windows) with the Symbol screener. Just as the previous tool changes color, so this tool changes opacity.

5. The final symbolism tool is the Symbol Styler. In the Styles palette, choose Scribbly Fawn (the first style in the second row). Click and hold on your targeted symbols. The longer you hold the mouse button down, the more the style is applied.

6. Select all and delete to clear the artboard. Select a symbol, activate the Symbol Sprayer, and add just a few of the symbol instance to your artboard. Too many symbols in your set could result in a long wait.

7. Use the Symbol Stainer, Symbol Styler, and Symbol Screener to customize your symbol set. Rotate and resize a few, too.

8. In the Symbols palette, choose another symbol instance by clicking on it once. Then, from the palette's menu (the small triangle in the upper-right corner), choose the menu command Replace Symbol. Give Illustrator a little while to do its stuff and the symbol on the artboard should be replaced. All of the twisting, turning, resizing, staining, screening, and styling should all remain unchanged. Figure 3.27
▲   shows a simplified example.

Congratulations! You've just been exposed to the concept of "live" in Illustrator. Basically, what the term means is that you can change the appearance of an object without changing the object itself. In this case, we used the various tools to alter the appearance of the symbols, but the symbols themselves remained unchanged. When we replaced the first symbol instance, the second instance assumed all of the live appearance changes. You'll learn more about how this works in Hour 18, "Working with Filters and Live Effects."

FIGURE 3.27

On the left are the original symbols. In the center, they've been fine-tuned with the symbolism tools. On the right, the symbol instance has been replaced, and the changes applied to the symbols remain.

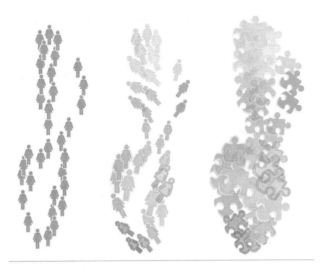

Defining a Symbol

You can easily create your own symbols. Create a vector object, color it, even apply a style to it (which you'll learn about later), and use the Symbols palette menu command, New Symbol. Try it using the basic creation tools you learned at the beginning of this hour. Create a spiral symbol, a circle symbol, and a five-pointed star symbol. Test them using the Symbol Sprayer.

Saving Your Work

If you really like the results of your efforts, you can save the illustration and perhaps later print it to hang on the refrigerator. The command File, Save is the basic method.

Choosing a File Format

For now, you'll want to save your files in the native Adobe Illustrator file format (.ai). (The pop-up menu in the Save dialog box offers a couple of other formats, as shown in Figure 3.28.) The native Illustrator format is the only one that is sure to preserve all the features of your document.

If your work will be printed on a commercial printing press, using the Export command to create a TIFF (.tif) file or saving as an Encapsulated PostScript (.eps) file might make more sense. For the World Wide Web, you'll need .gif, .jpg, or.png (all of which are available through the Save for Web command), or SVG from the Save dialog box. We'll look at file formats more closely in Hour 20, "Understanding File Formats and Platform Issues." The various print and Web formats will also be discussed in Hours 21, "Printing Your Illustrations," 22, "Creating Web Graphics," and 23, "Animating the Web."

FIGURE 3.28

*PDF can be opened
with Adobe Acrobat
Reader. EPS is used
for print. SVG
(Scalable Vector
Graphics) is designed
for the Web.*

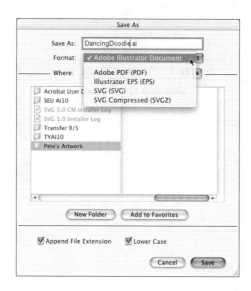

Picking a Location, a Name, and Some Options

Where you choose to save your file is up to you. Perhaps in the My Documents folder in
Windows, in your Documents folder in Mac OS X, on the Mac OS 9 Desktop, or perhaps
even on a removable disk.

Most modern computer systems recognize long file names, so you can basically choose
any name you want. Some characters shouldn't be used (and will be listed in Hour 20). It
is a good idea, even for Macintosh-based operations, to use the filename extension. (You
can have Illustrator automatically add the extension by selecting that option in the
Preferences, Files & Clipboard window.)

After you click OK, you're presented with the dialog box in Figure 3.29.

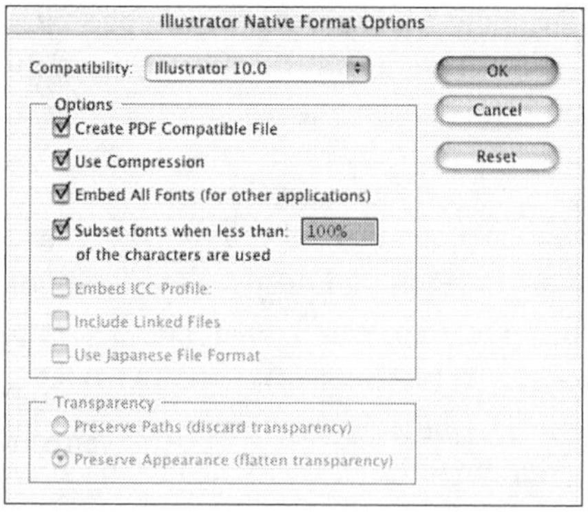

FIGURE 3.29

*The second dialog box
allows you to choose
what data to include in
the file.*

Choosing Illustrator 10 for compatibility ensures that everything will be editable later. For now, as a general rule of thumb, if a box isn't grayed out, check it. The file might be somewhat larger, but you'll be retaining all of the information.

Summary

We've covered a lot of ground this hour. If it hasn't all sunk in, don't worry. We'll be reinforcing the basics throughout the rest of the book. Some of the more advanced concepts to which you were introduced while learning about symbols will be reintroduced later.

The highlight of this hour was learning to use the various object creation tools. You've created shapes, such as rectangles, circles, spirals, grids, and the list goes on. You've created advanced designs using symbols. And to top that off, you've started using some of Illustrator's palettes, including Swatches and Styles. Quite a list of accomplishments for a single hour!

Workshop

Now that you've got basic creation skills and some more advanced concepts, let's get in a little practice time.

Q&A

Q Can two objects be created on top of each other?

A Sure! Multiple objects can overlap in Illustrator without any problem. In a later hour, you'll learn all about the Layers palette, but for now just think of objects being stacked on the artboard.

Q What is the difference between a rectangle and a rounded rectangle?

A There are a couple of ways of looking at the difference. For right now, let's just say that one object has square corners and the other has curved corners. In Hour 6, when you learn about editing paths, you'll recognize the difference in the paths and anchor points that make up the objects.

Q A spiral is an open path. Is it an object or a line?

A Because it's an open path, a spiral is a line, just like an arc.

Q Why is my computer so slow when working with symbols?

A A set of symbols is a whole lot of little vector objects, some of them rather complex. (Think about all of the little pieces that are required to construct an American flag.) Making changes to each of those little collections of objects takes a lot of computational power. Patience!

Quiz

1. Which of the following is a line, rather than an object?

    a. Circle

    b. Rounded rectangle

    c. Arc

    d. Star

2. When working with spirals, a wind is how big?

    a. One quarter of a turn

    b. One quarter of a circle

    c. Ninety degrees

    d. All of the above

3. How many of the eight symbolism tools can place symbols on the artboard?

    a. One

    b. Two

    c. Three

    d. Eight

4. Which file format retains all of Illustrator's features?

    a. .eps

    b. .ai

    c. .tif

    d. .png

Quiz Answers

1. c. Arcs are lines rather than objects because they have end points.

2. d. All of the above. These are several ways to say the same thing.

3. a. Only the Symbol Sprayer actually adds symbols to the artboard. The rest of the symbolism tools are used to edit the appearance of the symbol sets.

4. b. The Adobe Illustrator (.ai) file format is the only one of *these* formats that supports all of the program's features. (PDF, EPS, and SVG can also produce files that retain all Illustrator information.

Exercises

1. Practice using the modifier keys with the object creation tools. Try to remember what Shift does for each tool. Don't forget Option (Mac)/Alt (Windows), either.

2. Create a number of grids. Use the dialog box to skew them horizontally, vertically, or both. Try to determine the highest skew percentage that results in a useable grid. Also see if you can create some 3D effects with skewed grids.

3. Double-click on each of the symbolism tool icons in the Toolbox. Take a look at each tool's options. Experiment with the settings to see how they work.

3

HOUR 4

Making Selections

Illustrator has far more to offer than simply the capability to create objects; you can also do things with those objects. In later hours, you'll learn about adding color, styles, and patterns, and about applying special effects and filters. Before we start doing fancy things like that, however, we need to learn how to tell Illustrator what we want to change, and how to identify the objects with which we want to work. For example, let's say fifteen circles are on the artboard, and we want to make one of them red. We need to tell Illustrator which one. Or, suppose we have fifteen circles and a half-dozen rectangles, with a few triangles and stars scattered around. If we need to move just the squares, we've got to let Illustrator know our intentions are limited to those objects. After they've been created, we identify those objects for change by selecting them on the artboard.

In this hour, you'll learn how to select objects, including the following:

- Basic selections and the bounding box
- Using the selection tools
- Grouping and ungrouping objects
- The Selection commands

- The Magic Wand tool
- Arranging objects

The Selection Tools

The most basic way of selecting an object for change on the artboard is with the selection tools. The six selection tools are the Selection tool, the Direct Selection tool, the Group Selection tool, the Direct Select Lasso tool, the Lasso tool, and the Magic Wand, a new addition to the Toolbox in Illustrator 10 (see Figure 4.1). The first three in the list can also be used to drag objects around on the artboard, moving them to new positions.

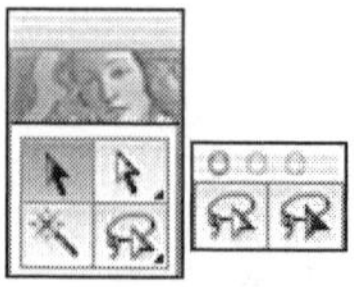

FIGURE 4.1

Illustrator's selection tools are found in the top part of the Toolbox.

Task: Preparing to Select

Before we can practice selecting objects, we need some objects to select. Let's put a variety of things on the artboard.

1. Open a new document in Illustrator by pressing Command+N (Mac)/Control+N (Windows) and clicking OK. (The default values will be fine.)
2. Choose the Rectangle tool from the Toolbox.
3. Drag a few rectangles on the artboard, spacing them so that they don't overlap.
4. Switch to the Ellipse tool and drag a few ovals and circles.
5. Add some stars and polygons. These can overlap with both rectangles and ellipses. Your artboard should look something like Figure 4.2.

The Basics of Selection and the Bounding Box

To use the Selection tool, you must, of course choose it from the Toolbox by clicking its icon or by using the keyboard shortcut V.

FIGURE **4.2**

You don't need to re-create this image, but you'll need something similar to work with.

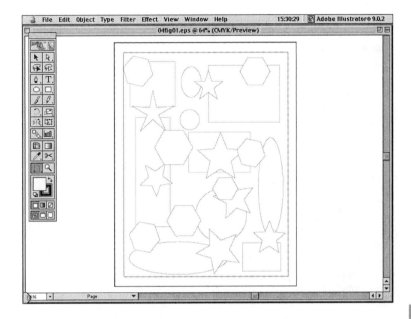

You can select an object by clicking it with the Selection tool. To select multiple objects, hold down the Shift key and click them. You can also select multiple objects by holding down the mouse button and dragging across them on the artboard. Let's practice.

Task: Using the Selection Tool

1. Move the Selection tool around the artboard. When it is above a shape, the cursor will show a small black box to the lower left. If you see a hollow box, the cursor is directly over one of an object's anchor points. (Anchor points will be explained in the next two hours.)

2. Click once on any rectangle. You can click either on the black outline (stroke) or the white interior (fill) of the object. You'll see by the change in appearance that the rectangle is now active, as shown in Figure 4.3.

3. Now click any circle. The circle becomes the selected object and the rectangle is deselected.

4. Hold down the Shift key and click a star somewhere in the lower right of the artboard. Both the circle and the star are selected, as shown in Figure 4.4.

FIGURE 4.3

The currently selected rectangle is obvious on the artboard.

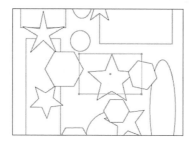

FIGURE 4.4

The circle and the star are both selected. Each shows its path and anchor points, and a large bounding box is also visible around both.

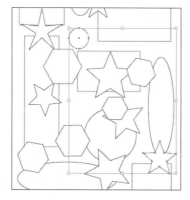

5. Use the menu command Edit, Clear. The two selected objects disappear from the artboard. Observe that none of the unselected objects are affected at all.

6. Use the menu command Edit, Undo Clear. The objects are not only returned to the artboard, but they are in exactly the same place and are still selected.

7. Position the cursor over the middle of the star, hold down the mouse button, and drag the star to the left. As you drag, an image of a new location is shown for both the star and the circle, while the original objects appear in their original places, As shown in Figure 4.5.

8. Keep dragging the star until it is near the bottom of the artboard in the middle. Press the Shift key and the objects will be restricted to exactly horizontal while you drag. (Actually, Shift+dragging restricts you to any 45-degree angle. It so happens that the closest multiple of 45 degrees, right now, is horizontal.) Release the mouse button, then the Shift key.

Using the Bounding Box

The large box that surrounds both the circle and the star is called a bounding box. Notice that it has hollow squares in each corner and in the middle of each side. These squares are called handles. Let's see what they do.

FIGURE 4.5

While the star and the circle are being moved, both the original position and the new are visible.

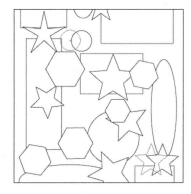

▲

Task: Practicing with the Bounding Box

1. With the circle and star still selected, use the menu command Edit, Copy or Command+C (Mac)/Control+C (Windows).

2. Now use the menu command File, New or Command+N (Mac)/Control+N (Windows) and click OK. This starts a second document without closing our first document.

3. The menu command Edit, Paste or Command+V (Mac)/Control+V (Windows) puts copies of the circle and star in the new document. Rather than being pasted into their original positions, they are centered (as a pair) in the new document, as shown in Figure 4.6.

4

FIGURE 4.6

The circle and the star are both still selected, and the bounding box still surrounds them.

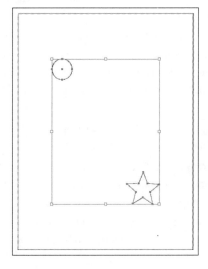

▼

▼   4. Position the cursor over the bounding box handle in the middle of the right side. Notice that the cursor changes to a two-headed arrow. Click and drag inward until the cursor is near the middle of the page (see Figure 4.7). Don't release the mouse button.

FIGURE **4.7**

Changing the bounding box alters the selected objects within it.

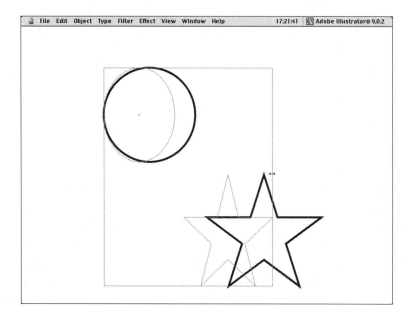

5. Move the cursor back outward to somewhere near its original position before releasing the mouse button.

6. Position the cursor over the handle in the upper-right corner of the bounding box. The two-headed arrow is pointed at an angle. Click and drag inward, and move the cursor both horizontally and vertically. Unlike the side handles, corner handles enable you to resize the bounding box in two dimensions. Don't release the mouse button yet.

7. While still dragging, press the Shift key. Illustrator constrains the drag in such a way that the original shapes are not distorted.

8. Continue dragging the upper-right corner until you go well past the lower-left corner. Release the mouse button. You've just flipped the circle and star, both horizontally and vertically.

▼   9. Close this window using either the box or button in the corner of the window or the menu command File, Close, or Command+W (Mac)/Control+W (Windows).

▼ When prompted, choose Don't Save. You should now see your original collection of rectangles, circles, stars, and polygons again.

10. Go to the View menu and select Hide Bounding Box. We will not need it for a while and hiding it makes the artboard a little less confusing.

▲

The Direct Selection Tool

The Direct Selection tool can be found next to the Selection tool in the Toolbox. It is identifiable by the white arrow icon. (If the icon has a small plus sign to the upper right, you've got the Group Selection tool. Click and hold on its icon in the Toolbox to show the Direct Selection tool.) This tool is used to select individual points and path segments. It will be explored fully in Hour 6, "Editing Bézier Curves." Right now, however, let's give it a quick test drive.

TASK ▼

Task: Using the Direct Selection Tool

1. Select the Direct Selection tool from the Toolbox.

2. On the artboard, click once directly on the outside line (stroke) of any rectangle.

3. Do you see the tiny squares in the corners? If they aren't hollow, and appear as solid black boxes, you missed the stroke. Try again, and make sure that the very tip of the Direct Selection tool's arrow is on the line.

4. When you have hollow squares in each of the corners, click and drag one corner outward (see Figure 4.8). Unlike the bounding box, which changed the object as a whole, the Direct Selection tool changes only the selected point.

FIGURE 4.8

The Direct Selection tool alters the shape of the object by manipulating individual points.

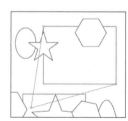

▲

Don't worry too much about this capability just yet—we'll be working with it more in later hours.

Working with Groups and the Group Selection Tool

For now, let's think of groups as two or more objects or paths that have been linked together so that they can be moved as a unit. (Hour 13, "Gaining Flexibility Through Layers," presents the concept of targeting. You'll learn then that groups have other powerful features.)

4

Task: Selecting Multiple Objects and Groups

Let's create a group.

1. Press V to activate the Selection tool.
2. Click whatever object is in the upper-left corner of your artboard.
3. Hold down the Shift key to add to the selection. Shift+click any four other objects in the image.
4. With those objects still selected, and the Shift key still depressed, click again on any selected item. That removes it from the selection.

> Memorize this shortcut: Shift+click to add objects to a selection, Shift+click to subtract objects from a selection.

5. We've now got a total of four objects selected on the artboard. Mouse to the Object menu at the top of the screen and choose the menu command Group, or Command+G (Mac)/Control+G (Windows) .
6. Click outside the artboard to deselect your group (but remember that the object in the upper-left corner is part of the group).
7. Click that upper-left object. The entire group of four objects should be selected (see Figure 4.9).

FIGURE 4.9

The object in the upper-left corner of your artboard should be selected, along with the three randomly selected objects you added to your group.

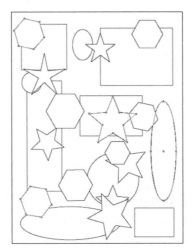

8. Drag slightly down and to the right. The four objects should all move the same distance and direction (shown in Figure 4.10).

FIGURE 4.10

The grouped objects move as a unit.

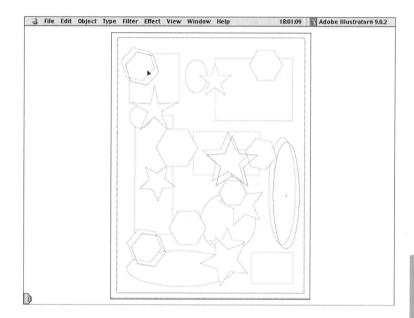

9. Click outside the artboard to deselect the group.

10 Switch to the Group Selection tool. Click and hold on the Direct Selection tool's icon in the Toolbox until you can see the Group Selection tool. Mouse over and grab it before releasing the button.

11. Now click once on the object in the upper-left corner. Only the one object is selected, although it remains part of the group.

12. You can drag the object without moving other members of the group, as shown in Figure 4.11).

13. Click outside the artboard to deselect.

14. Using the Group Selection tool, click twice on the object in the upper-left corner. The first click selects the object itself, and the second click selects the rest of the group. Cool, eh?

4

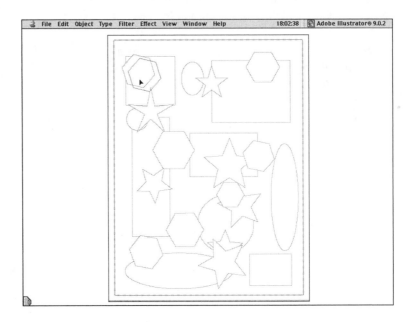

FIGURE 4.11

A single click of the Group Selection tool selects a single member of a group.

You can ungroup objects with the Object, Ungroup command or Shift+Command+G (Mac)/Shift+Control+G (Windows). The individual objects will again function independently.

Drag Selecting

In addition to Shift+clicking, you can drag with the selection tools to select multiple objects and paths. When dragging with the Selection tool, any object over which it passes will be selected. You don't need to enclose the entire object (see Figure 4.12). Likewise, when using the Selection tool, if you drag over even a single corner of an object that is part of a group, the entire group will be selected. Dragging with the Direct Selection tool selects anchor points over which you drag. With the Group Selection tool, only the object itself will be selected, not the entire group.

The Lasso and Direct Select Lasso Tools

As I'm sure you've noticed, the Selection tool (and its cohorts) allow you to drag only rectangular selections. Those might not always suit your needs. Sure, you can drag a rectangle and then Shift+click those objects that you didn't intend to select. (Sort of like casting a net and then throwing some of the fish back into the ocean.) There's an easier way.

Figure 4.12

The dashed line repre-
sents the rectangle
dragged with the
Selection tool. You can
see that all objects
even partially within
are now selected.

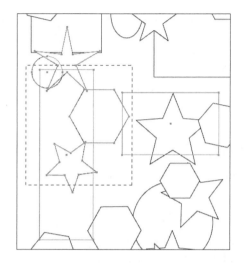

The Lasso tool is sort of a free-form version of the Selection tool. You can drag any way you please, zigging and zagging, hither and yon, and select whatever you want. Any object that falls even partially within the loop you drag will be selected (see Figure 4.13).

Figure 4.13

The dashed lines rep-
resent the path of the
Lasso tool.

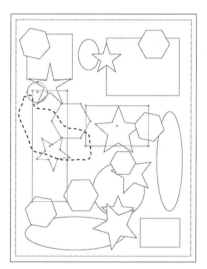

The Direct Select Lasso tool also enables you to drag a selection in any shape. However, like the Direct Selection tool, it will also activate anchor points in the objects and paths that are enclosed by the selection. Keep in mind that the lasso tools, unlike the other selection tools, cannot be used to move objects, only to select them. To add to a selection, Shift+drag. To subtract from a selection Option+drag (Mac)/Alt+drag (Windows).

The Select Menu

Illustrator has a variety of commands that can help you make selections. Let's look at the commands available.

- All: All objects and paths on the artboard will become part of the selection.
- Deselect: Everything will be deselected. There will be no active selection after using this command. It is comparable to clicking outside the artboard with a selection tool, which you've done a couple of times in this hour.
- Reselect: If you choose Deselect or inadvertently click somewhere and you lose your selection, use this command to restore it. This is especially handy when you accidentally deselect a very complex set of objects.
- Inverse: Let's say that you've got a hundred objects on the artboard and need to select all but two of them. Simply Shift+click those two objects and use this command. Those objects that were selected are then deselected, and those that were not selected become selected.
- Next Object Above: When objects overlap, this command might be easier to use than a selection tool.
- Next Object Below: When objects are stacked on top of each other, this command enables you to access even those that you can't see because they're hidden by other objects.
- Same: Take a look at Figure 4.14 to see the list of Select, Same commands. You select one object that has the common characteristic, then use the appropriate command to add to the selection to all objects on the artboard with that particular characteristic. These are very powerful commands, which you'll come to appreciate a bit later. (In Hour 8, "Using Strokes, Fills, and Gradients," you'll get an understanding for fill and stroke color and stroke weight, and such transparency issues as blending mode and opacity. You'll then have a better grasp of how to use these characteristics as selection criteria.)

FIGURE 4.14

The Select, Same commands enable you to select all objects with similar characteristics.

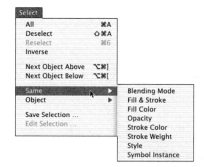

• Object: Figure 4.15 shows the various Select, Object commands. Similar in nature to the Select, Same commands, these enable you to select based on a common characteristic. Unlike the Select, Same commands, you don't need to select an example object first.

FIGURE 4.15

These commands enable you to select all objects based on a specific characteristic.

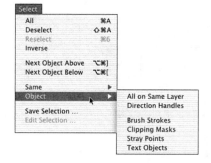

Use the menu command Select, Object, Stray Points followed by the menu command Edit, Clear every time you finish an illustration. This deletes any random points that might have been inadvertently added to the artboard.

• Save Selection: This command enables you to save and later recall a selection. Make a selection of one or more objects (just one is kind of a waste). Use the command Select, Save Selection. Give the selection a name and click OK. The saved selections appear at the bottom of the Select menu. To reselect all the objects in the saved selection, simply choose the saved selection from the list (see Figure 4.16).

FIGURE 4.16

When this saved selection is chosen, all the objects that had been selected will be reselected.

- Edit Selection: This command opens a dialog box that enables you to do some housekeeping on your saved selections (shown in Figure 4.17). You can delete saved selections, which only removed the selection from the list in the Select menu; it does not delete the objects themselves. You can also rename a saved selection.

FIGURE 4.17

In this case, four separate selections have been saved with the command Select, Save Selection.

The Magic Wand

Although the Magic Wand is a selection tool, we thought it best to save it until now to discuss. The Magic Wand is sort of a cross between a selection tool and a selection command; it selects all objects with specified characteristics. What makes the Magic Wand exceptionally cool is that you can specify a *range* of characteristics. Rather than exactly match, for example, a fill color, as you would with the command Select, Same, Fill Color; the Magic Wand can choose a variety of similar fill colors.

Figure 4.18 shows the options for the Magic Wand. Double-click the Magic Wand in the Toolbox to open the palette or choose the menu command Window, Magic Wand. (Note that you might need to use the palette menu commands, Show Stroke Options and Show Transparency Options, to see the entire palette.)

FIGURE **4.18**

*The palette menu com-
mands are accessed by
clicking the small tri-
angle in the upper-
right corner of the
palette.*

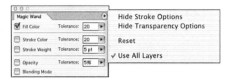

To use the Magic Wand, click an object on the artboard. All objects with characteristics
similar to the options you've chosen are also selected. Before using the tool, however,
you need to specify which characteristics you want to use as selection criteria. You also
determine how closely you want that characteristic to match the object you click.

Let's say, for example, that we checked the box to the left of Stroke Weight in the Magic
Wand options, and then clicked with the tool on an object that had a stroke weight of 9
points. With a tolerance of 4 points, the Magic Wand would add to the selection every
object on the artboard with a stroke weight between 5 and 13 points. (See Figure 4.19.)

FIGURE **4.19**

*The Magic Wand was
clicked on one object
and all objects within
the tolerance were
selected.*

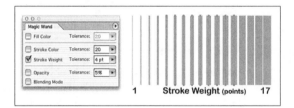

You can Shift+click with the Magic Wand to add to a selection and you can
Option+click (Mac)/Alt+click (Windows) to subtract from a selection. However, you
cannot drag with the Magic Wand to make a selection.

Arranging Objects on the Artboard

As you know, objects can overlap on the artboard. In fact, objects can be completely hidden by other objects. (That's a good reason to have the menu command Select, Next
Object Below.) If you plan very, very efficiently, you can draw your objects in their order
of appearance, from bottom to top. If you're like me, you're far more likely to change
your mind and add objects later, delete objects, or simply rearrange the way the existing
objects overlap. Illustrator helps you change your mind (and fix mistakes) with some
very handy commands.

With one or more objects selected on the artboard, Illustrator provides you with the Arrange commands (shown in Figure 4.20). Located under the Object menu (most naturally), they include Bring to Front, Bring Forward, Send Backward, and Send to Back.

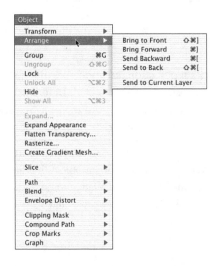

FIGURE 4.20

The Arrange commands are only available when one or more objects are selected on the artboard.

 You might see or hear or use several different terms in relation to arranging objects on the artboard. Forward, up, and on top all refer to the same concept. These are the objects that will be blocking or hiding those objects that are behind, down, or below.

Figure 4.21 illustrates the differences among the four commands. The original objects are on the left. The commands were executed one at a time, from left to right: Bring to Front, Bring Forward, Send Backward, and Send to Back.

These concepts of above and below, in front and in back, will also be addressed in Hour 13, "Gaining Flexibility Through Layers."

FIGURE **4.21**

The dashed rectangles show the areas where you can see whether an object was moved on top of or behind a neighboring object or all objects.

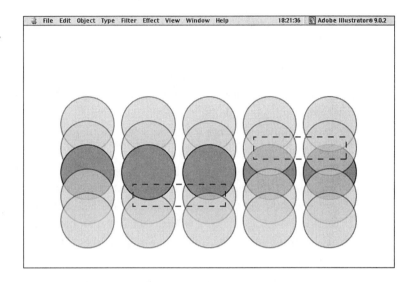

Summary

In this hour you've learned how to identify the objects you want to move or change. You've learned quite a range of selection techniques, using tools and commands. We've even looked at rearranging the order of objects on the artboard, a very handy thing to know! The concept of selecting will play a part in most of the remaining hours. After all, if you don't tell Illustrator what objects to change, you won't get any change at all.

Workshop

Because selection is such an important part of editing and manipulating objects on the artboard, we've put together a variety of questions and exercises to help reinforce the concepts and techniques.

Q&A

Q Do I have to make a selection to move an object on the artboard?

A Yes, you do. Without a selection, Illustrator won't know which object(s) you want to move.

Q What is the difference between the Selection tool and the Direct Selection tool?

A The Selection tool selects objects in their entirety, the whole object. The Direct Selection tool, on the other hand, selects anchor points of one or more objects. The anchor points are used to change the shape of the object. (This is discussed in Hour 6.)

Q Does it matter whether I use the Selection tool or the Lasso tool to drag a selection?

A Nope! The only difference is that the Selection tool always drags a rectangle, while the Lasso tool enables you to drag however you want, avoiding or including whichever objects you choose. However, the Selection tool can also be used to move the selected objects, whereas the Lasso tool cannot.

Q Doesn't the Group Selection tool do everything that the Selection tool does— and more?

A Yes, the Selection and Group Selection tools do the same things. In fact, the Direct Selection tool, which can select individual points, can be converted temporarily to the Group Selection tool by holding down the Option (Mac) or Alt (Windows) key. For that reason, many Illustrator users rarely if ever use the Selection tool. They prefer the Direct Selection tool, converting to the Group Selection tool when required.

Quiz

1. To select and move objects on the artboard you can use the _____ tool.

    a. Selection

    b. Direct Selection

    c. Group Selection

    d. Direct Select Lasso

    e. All of the above, except d

2. Which of the following enables you to deselect one of several selected objects?

    a. Shift+click the object with the Selection tool

    b. Option+click (Mac)/Alt+click (Windows) the object with the Selection tool

    c. Use the menu command Select, Deselect, All But *That* One

    d. Use the menu command Select, Deselect, Only *That* One

3. You have five objects stacked atop each other on the artboard. The object in the middle (and only that object) is selected. You choose the menu command Object, Arrange, Bring Forward. The object moves from the third position (the middle of five) to what position?

    a. Position One, on top of all other objects

    b. Position Two, second from the top

    c. Position Three, it doesn't move

    d. Position Four, second from the bottom

    e. Position Five, at the bottom

4. Which tool enables you to select and move one object of a group of several objects without moving the other objects?

    a. The Group Selection Lasso tool

    b. The Group Move tool

    c. The Group Selection tool

    d. None of the above

Quiz Answers

1. e. The Lasso and Direct Select Lasso tools can make selections, but cannot move objects.

2. b. Shift+clicking with the Selection tool subtracts from and adds to a selection. The Select, Deselect command has no subcommands and always deselects everything.

3. b. Position Two, it moves forward (up) one spot.

4. c. The Group Selection tool can be used to select and move one member of a group without disturbing the others.

Exercises

1. Draw a variety of objects, overlapping them. Use the Selection tool to select individual objects and then use the Arrange commands to restack the objects. Get a feel for the difference between moving forward and moving to the front.

2. Draw a bunch of objects, at least ten. Shift+click with the Selection tool or drag with the Lasso tool to select several of them. Control+click (Mac)/right-click (Windows) on one of the selected objects. Choose Group from the contextual menu. Use the Selection tool to drag these grouped objects around on the artboard. Watch how the stacking affects whether they move in front of, or behind other

objects. Use the command Object, Arrange, Bring to Front. Continue dragging and notice how the grouped objects always pass in front of other objects now.

3. Use the same document and objects as Exercise 2 and Deselect. Use the Group Selection tool to select only one of the grouped objects and move it. (Click only once.) Now click twice on that object to select the entire group. Despite the change in location, the object you moved remains part of the group.

4. Keep using the same document and objects. Deselect. Select several objects that are *not* part of the group. Group them using the menu command Object, Group. Deselect. Select whatever objects remain that are not part of either group, and group *them*. With that group still selected, use the Selection tool to Shift+click an object from another group (the entire group should be selected). With both groups selected, choose Object, Group. That forms one group from the two groups. Shift+click an object from the other group, and again use the Group command. At this point you have one group, which consists of three groups. Deselect. Get the Group Selection tool from the Toolbox. Pick an object, any object. Click it once and it is selected. Click it a second time and its original group is selected. Click it a third time and all the members of the largest group get selected. Nesting groups, groups within groups. Cool, eh? And the Group Selection tool lets you choose an object, or a subgroup, or a group. Very, very cool!

Hour **5**

Creating Paths and Compound Paths

Adobe Illustrator, as you have seen, works primarily with objects and lines. You've already learned how to use tools to create paths in the shape of certain objects, such as squares, rectangles, circles, ellipses, stars, and spirals. Illustrator also has the capability to create custom shapes and lines using the Pen and Pencil tools. It can also help you make more complex objects, like circles with holes in them.

In this hour, you'll learn the following:

- The anatomy of a path
- The three types of anchor points
- The difference between open and closed paths
- Creating with the Pen tool
- Drawing with the Pencil tool
- Creating compound paths

Creating Paths with the Pen Tool

 NEW TERM Objects and lines in Illustrator are actually *paths*. Think of a path as a mathematical definition of a relationship between two points on your artboard. This doesn't mean we need to understand mathematics to draw. As a matter of fact, Illustrator does the calculations for us.

Paths are actually created by selecting a starting and an ending point. The shape of the path between is determined by vectors. A vector, in this sense, is a direction and a distance from the point. Recall the difference between vector art and raster art. We discussed it briefly in Hour 1, "Understanding Illustrator," and, you'll see in Hour 6, "Editing Bézier Curves," that when we start editing paths, you can manipulate the vectors by moving control points.

 If Illustrator has been used since you last reset the preferences file, delete that file now. It's best to start this hour with a clean slate, using Illustrator's factory-default settings. (If you've forgotten how or are the least uncertain, refer to the reference card that came in the front of this book.)

TASK ▼

Task: Learn About the Parts of a Path

Let's look at the parts of a path by creating as we go.

1. Use the menu command File, New or the keyboard shortcut Command+N (Mac)/Control+N (Windows) to open a new document. You can accept the default settings.

2. Now select the Pen tool from Illustrator's Toolbox or press P to activate it.

    NEW TERM 3. Click near the upper-left corner of the artboard. You've just created an *anchor point*. You don't have a path yet, but you're on the way.

4. Click to the right of the first anchor point on the artboard, about two-thirds of the way across. You've just placed a second anchor point. And, as you can see, Illustrator has connected the two anchor points with a thin line. That line is the path (see Figure 5.1).

    NEW TERM You've just created a straight path. We'll use the term *line* for a straight path. Other paths will be referred to as *curves*.

 ▼

FIGURE 5.1

The path has a black line drawn on it, by default, but the actual path is visible on your screen as the thin line between the anchor points.

NEW TERM   Notice that the first anchor point is indicated by a hollow square, whereas the second is shown as a filled square. The filled square indicates that the anchor point is *selected* or *active*.

5. Move the cursor straight down toward the middle of the artboard and click again. Another path segment is created.

6. Now move the cursor halfway to the left edge of the artboard. Click and drag the cursor a short distance toward the upper-left corner of the artboard. Before you release the mouse button, you should see a situation similar to that shown in Figure 5.2.

FIGURE 5.2

The parts of the path are shown here. Control points and direction lines show only when a path segment or its anchor point is selected. They do not print or appear in Web graphics.

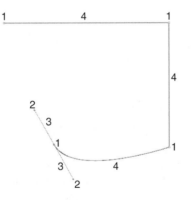

1. Anchor Point
2. Control Point
3. Direction Line
4. Path

7. Release the mouse button, and move the cursor straight to the left until it is directly under the first anchor point.

8. Click and drag, moving the cursor straight up, about halfway to the first anchor point. Release the mouse button. Let's take a look at what you have created so far, which should be similar to Figure 5.3.

5

▼

FIGURE 5.3
*The parts of the path
are shown here.*

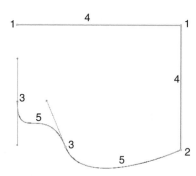

1. Corner Point
2. Combination Point
3. Smooth Point
4. Line
5. Curve

 NEW TERM
- The top two anchor points are *corner points*; they have only straight path segments connected to them. The first point has only one segment at this point. It can be referred to as an endpoint.

- The point in the lower-right corner is a *combination point*; it has a straight path segment and a curved segment.

- The fourth anchor point is a *smooth point*; there are curved path segments on either side.

- The final anchor point is also a smooth point, although it has only one path segment adjoining. Like the first point, it is also an endpoint.

Remember, too, that we refer to straight path segments as lines, whereas others are curves. A true line will have a corner anchor point at either end, or a corner and a combination point. Take another look at Figure 5.3, and determine which path segments are lines and which are curves. (The first two path segments, which comprise the top and right side, are lines. The last pair of segments, along the bottom, are curves.)

9. Let's finish off the object we've been drawing. Position the cursor's tip directly over the first anchor point. Notice that now a small circle is to the lower right of the cursor (as shown in Figure 5.4). That indicates that you are going to close the path. With the small circle visible, click once to draw the final path segment.

▲

NEW TERM Up to this point, you've been working with an *open path*. Open paths have two endpoints. When you clicked again on the first anchor point, you created a *closed path*. Closed paths are objects, whereas open paths are lines.

When you closed the path, of course, you changed the status of the first and fifth anchor points—they are no longer endpoints. However, the first is still a corner point, and the fifth remains a smooth point.

FIGURE 5.4

The Pen tool's cursor changes to indicate when it will be completing a closed path.

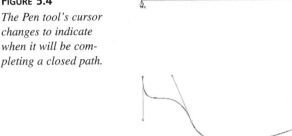

Drawing Precise Straight Paths

The true value of the Pen tool is the precision with which you can draw paths. Straight paths are relatively easy—you click in one spot, then click in another. (You can also use the Line Segment tool, which you read about in Hour 3, "Creating Objects," to create a single path segment.) If you want to add more segments, just keep clicking. When you're done, you can click the first anchor point, creating a closed path. Sometimes, however, you'll want an open path. You tell Illustrator that your open path is finished in any number of ways. The two most basic options are

- Hold down the Command (Mac)/Control (Windows) key and click away from the path with the Pen tool. That ends the path and keeps the Pen tool active.

- Select any other tool by clicking on it in the Toolbox or pressing its keyboard shortcut.

If you have a free finger, one of the fastest ways to end an open path and still have the Pen tool ready to go is to quickly type O, then P. The two keys are next to each other on the keyboard, so it's lightning fast. What you are actually doing is changing to the Reflect tool (O), then switching back to the Pen tool (P).

You can draw straight path segments that are perfectly horizontal or vertical very easily.

1. Click where you want the beginning of the path segment to be with the Pen tool.

2. Hold down the Shift key.

3. Click where you want the other end of the segment to be.

The Shift key can also be used to constrain path segments to 45° angles.

5

Dragging to Produce Curves

Straight path segments are all well and good, but they don't take full advantage of the Pen tool's power. Creating custom curves—now that's a key to creative freedom! Let's practice.

Task: Choppy Seas

Use Figure 5.5 as a guide. Don't worry about being precise.

FIGURE 5.5

The relationship among the points you click should be similar to the distances and directions shown here.

1. Select everything on your artboard and delete it. The keyboard shortcut for Select All is Command+A (Mac)/Control+A (Windows). You can use the Delete or Backspace key.

2. Click at a location near the left edge of your artboard. Consider this to be the point labeled 1 in Figure 5.5.

3. Click at point 2, and drag to point 2a.

4. Click at point 3.

5. Click at point 4, and drag to point 4a.

6. Continue in this pattern until you reach the right edge of the artboard or click the 11th point. The result should be similar to Figure 5.6.

FIGURE 5.6

The combination of curves and straight path segments creates waves or scallops.

Dragging to Create Curves

Let's look at how the direction that you drag affects the shape of a curve. In Figure 5.7, you'll see several templates. Use the Pen tool to create the paths shown.

Remember that you can end a path by Command+clicking (Mac)/ Control+clicking (Windows) with the Pen tool. When you hold down the Command (Mac)/Control (Windows) key and click away from a path, that path is finished. The Pen tool is then ready to start the next path.

FIGURE 5.7

Click on the numbered squares, and drag as shown by the dashed lines. Each path consists of only two points. Command+ click (Mac)/Control+ click (Windows) before starting another path.

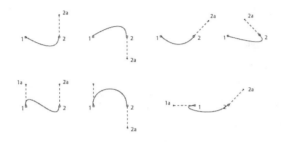

Notice that when you drag in opposite directions, you get a simple curve. When you drag in the same direction, you get a compound curve, as shown in Figure 5.8.

FIGURE 5.8

On the left, the Pen tool was dragged upward for the first point, downward for the second point. On the right, the Pen tool was dragged upward for both points.

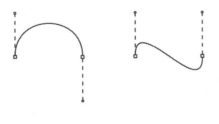

5

TASK

While Illustrator provides you with a perfectly good tool for creating circles and ovals (the Ellipse tool), it's handy to know how to create them manually. This is also a fine time to introduce Snap to Grid as a technique for ensuring curve precision. We'll create the three ellipses shown in Figure 5.9.

FIGURE 5.9

The figures to the left and right are ovals (ellipses), and the one in the center is a circle.

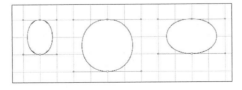

1. From the View menu, select Show Grid or use the keyboard shortcut Command+"
   (Mac)/Control+" (Windows). (That's the double-quotation key.)

2. Also from the View menu, select Snap to Grid, or add the Shift key and repeat the
   keyboard shortcut shown previously. That would be Shift+Command+"
   (Mac)/Shift+Control+ " (Windows).

3. By default, Illustrator is set to show a gridline every inch (72 pts) and eight subdivisions between. Go to the Edit menu and select Preferences, Guides & Grid.
   Change that to Gridline every: 36 pt and Subdivisions: 1. Click OK.

4. Press P to select the Pen tool.

5. Pick an intersection of gridlines and click. Before you release the mouse button,
   drag the cursor one square to the right. Release the mouse button.

6. Click exactly two gridlines below the first anchor point (not control point), and
   drag one square to the left.

7. Click again on the first anchor point, and again drag one square to the right. The
   resulting closed path should be an oval, comparable to the left object shown in
   Figure 5.9.

8. Move to another area of your artboard and click the mouse on the intersection of
   two gridlines. Before releasing the mouse, drag two squares to the right. (Notice
   that the first path, a closed path, was automatically deselected when you started the
   next path.)

9. Move the cursor three squares below the first anchor point, click, and drag two
   squares to the left.

10. Click on the first anchor point and drag to the right two squares. The resulting cir-
    cle should look like the middle object in Figure 5.9.

11. In another area of the artboard, click and drag two squares to the right.

12. Move the cursor two squares below the first anchor point, and click and drag two
    squares to the left.

13. Click on the first anchor point and drag two squares to the right. The object you've
    created should look like the object on the right in Figure 5.9.

If you noticed, to get an arc of consistent radius, like a circle, you need to
drag the control points a distance one-third longer than the radius. Look
again at the middle ellipse in Figure 5.9. The control points are two squares
from the anchor points, and the radius of the circle is 1.5 squares.

The Pencil Tool

When you click the Pen tool, you place an anchor point. You must place each anchor point individually with a click or a click and drag. With the Pencil tool, on the other hand, you simply drag. Illustrator sets the anchor points while you draw the path.

Task: Drawing with the Pencil

1. Select all and delete to clear your artboard.

2. Click on the Pencil tool in the Toolbox to select it, or use the keyboard shortcut N.

3. Click and drag in the artboard, making an S shape. Before you release the mouse button, you'll see a trail of dots, like those visible to the left in Figure 5.10. After you release the button, you'll see a path complete with anchor points, as shown in Figure 5.10.

FIGURE 5.10

While dragging, the Pencil tool leaves behind a trail of crumbs to show you where it's been (left). Once done, that trail becomes a path (right).

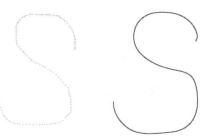

The Pencil tool is exempt from Snap to Grid! Even if you have activated Snap to Grid from the View menu, the Pencil tool will go where you drag it, leaving a trail of anchor points behind. If you need the precision offered by Snap to Grid, use the Pen tool.

4. When you release the mouse button, the path you've drawn will be selected. Position the Pencil tool away from the path, but don't click the button. Look at the small X to the lower-right of the cursor. That indicates that the Pencil tool is set to start a new path.

5. Move the Pencil tool to the top of the S shape you've just drawn. Notice that the X has disappeared. That indicates that the Pencil tool is ready to edit the path that appears below it.

6. With the Pencil tool on the top of the S-shaped path, click and drag a smaller S, as shown in Figure 5.11.

FIGURE 5.11

The Pencil tool can quickly and easily edit existing paths.

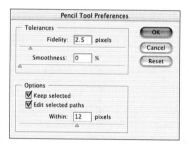

7. When you release the mouse button, Illustrator will redraw the path from the point at which you clicked.

Pencil Tool Options

In the Toolbox, double-click the Pencil tool to open its preferences (see Figure 5.12).

FIGURE 5.12

The Pencil tool has its own set of preferences.

Fidelity, which ranges from 0.5 to 20 pixels, determines how closely the path created follows the path that you dragged the Pencil tool. In Figure 5.13, the path on the left was created with Fidelity set to 0.5. The path on the right was created with Fidelity set to 20. The path that was traced is shown in the middle. Note the difference in the number of points in the two paths.

Smoothness, like Fidelity, affects the relationship between where the cursor went and where the path is drawn. In Figure 5.14, you can see the difference between low and high Smoothness settings.

FIGURE 5.13

Fidelity can be considered to be how precisely your path will follow your motion. (For optimal accuracy, this image was created using a Wacom Intuos tablet).

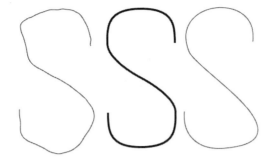

FIGURE 5.14

On the left, Smoothness was set to 10%. On the right, the setting was 90%. (For optimal accuracy, this image was created using a Wacom Intuos tablet).

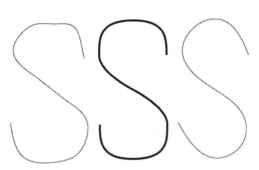

To get the most from the Pencil tool, it is important to understand how Fidelity and Smoothness work together. Think of Fidelity as the number of anchor points, and Smoothness as the roundness of the curves. You can have a lot of points on round curves, a few points on round curves, a lot of points on sharp curves, or few points on sharp curves. When trying to create smoothly rounded paths, fewer points and rounder curves should work best (low Fidelity, high Smoothness). If you need to produce something angular, perhaps you need low Fidelity and low Smoothness. If the adjective jagged comes to mind, we're likely to be best off with high Fidelity, low Smoothness. Examples of the three are shown in Figure 5.15.

5

FIGURE 5.15

The top path is low Fidelity/high Smoothness; the middle path is low Fidelity/low Smoothness; the bottom path is high Fidelity/low Smoothness.

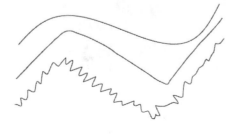

You'll also see a couple of checkboxes at the bottom, in the Pencil tool's options. When Keep Selected is checked, the path you just drew is active and you can edit it without having to use a selection tool. As you saw previously, simply dragging the Pencil tool over a selected path will redraw the path.

The second checkbox, and its accompanying slider, determine how far the Pencil tool must be from a selected path to edit it. With a range from 2 to 20 pixels, you can adjust for a crowded artboard.

Compound Paths

Compound paths enable you to create objects that have holes in them. For example, think of the difference between a hamburger bun and a donut. They're both round, made from flour (more or less), yet they differ not only in taste, but also in shape. Being able to see through the middle of your hamburger bun is not generally considered to be a good thing.

In illustrations, compound paths enable you to make areas of an object transparent. For example (an example with fewer calories), consider constructing an image of a window frame. You could draw all the parts individually, or you could draw a rectangle and punch out holes for the window panes, as shown in Figure 5.16.

FIGURE 5.16

The outside lines and the inner bars could be created individually, but here a rectangle was created and the smaller rectangles were subtracted.

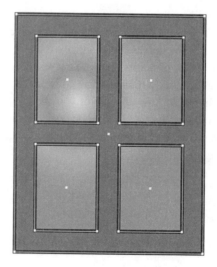

In Figure 5.16, you can see that there are five rectangles, one large and four small. Each rectangle's corners and center point are visible.

Creating Compound Paths

Basically, you create the shapes and combine them using the Pathfinder palette. The shapes that are on top are used like cookie cutters to punch holes in the lower object. New in Illustrator 10, these compound paths are live. In other words, you can create them, then come back later and change them. Figure 5.17 shows the same image as Figure 5.16, but with a couple of little changes made to the window panes.

FIGURE 5.17

The objects that were used to cut out the windows have been edited, yet the compound path remains intact. (You'll learn how to edit objects and paths in the next hour.)

The Pathfinder palette, shown in Figure 5.18, offers several ways to combine paths. Generally speaking, you need to create the objects or paths before using the Pathfinder palette. The options are

- Add to Shape Area: Create two shapes. When you click this button, the two objects will be joined as one.

- Subtract from Shape Area: As shown in Figure 5.16 and 5.17, an object or objects is/are subtracted from the original object.

- Intersect Shape Areas: Areas where two objects overlap are retained, the rest are deleted.

- Exclude Overlapping Shape Areas: Areas where two objects overlap are deleted, the rest are retained. When the top object is completely within the lower object, like Figures 5.16 and 5.17, this command is similar to Subtract from Shape Area.

- Divide: An object on top is used to cut one or more objects below.

- Trim: Deletes hidden parts of the object below.

- Merge: Deletes hidden objects, removes the strokes from paths, and merges objects of the same color.

5

- Crop: Anything beyond the bounds of the top-most object is deleted.

- Outline: Unfilled open paths are created, using overlapping objects to define places where paths end.

- Minus Back: The front-most object is retained, but areas that overlap the object behind are deleted.

Remember that multiple objects must be selected on the artboard for the Pathfinder palette to work. Also keep in mind that the order in which the objects are drawn makes a big difference. (In Hour 13, "Gaining Flexibility Through Layers," you'll learn the fine points of restacking objects on the artboard.

Task: Merging Paths

Drawing one long path to create a complex object isn't always possible. And with the tools Illustrator offers you, it's not even necessary most of the time! You can use shapes and paths in combination to create complex objects. Here's the basic training you'll need to carry out these missions.

1. Open the New dialog box by pressing Command+N (Mac)/Control+N (Windows). Accept the defaults by clicking OK.

2. Use the Rectangle tool to drag an object near the upper-left corner of the screen. Make it rather large.

3. Switch to the Ellipse tool, and drag an oval that overlaps the rectangle.

4. Use the menu command Window, Pathfinder. Position it to the upper right of your objects.

5. Press Command+A (Mac)/Control+A (Windows) to select all. Your artboard should look similar to Figure 5.18.

6. Open the Styles palette and, with both objects still selected, click the second Style in the top row, Bermuda, as shown in Figure 5.19). We'll learn about Styles in Hour 11, "Applying Appearances and Styles." We'll use a Style now to make the results of the Pathfinder functions more recognizable.

7. Click the first of the buttons in the Pathfinder palette. Take a look at how it affected the objects. Press Command+Z (Mac)/Control+Z (Windows) to undo.

8. Click the next button in the Pathfinder palette, take a look, undo.

9. Continue through all the buttons in both rows, skipping the Expand button, and look at the results.

10. To truly understand the Divide button, you should take things apart. After you've made it through the list, click Divide.

FIGURE 5.18

Each object has four anchor points and its center point is visible. Notice that the rectangle's path is visible where the oval is on top of the rectangle, but the stroke is not.

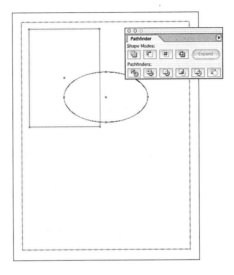

FIGURE 5.19

The Styles palette is normally nested to the right of your screen with the Swatches, Brushes, and Symbols palettes.

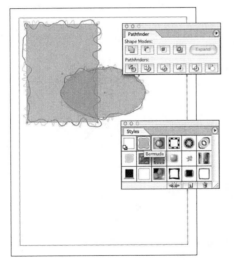

5

11. Get the Group Selection tool from the Toolbox (under the Direct Selection tool).

12. Click once, away from your objects, to deselect them.

13. Click the lower-right corner of the oval and drag it away from the rectangle.

14. Click the lower-right corner of the part of the oval left behind, and drag it away. You can now see how the Divide button created three objects, one from the area where the rectangle and oval overlapped, and one each from the remaining pieces. You can now select all and delete, leaving the document open.

Task: Using the Compound Paths Commands

Under Illustrator's Object menu, you'll find the commands Compound Path, Make, and Compound Path, Release. (Release is the opposite of Make—it restores the objects to their original states.) When two or more objects are combined with the Compound Path command, they are grouped.

1. Select the Ellipse tool from the Toolbox.
2. Click once near the upper-left corner of the artboard.
3. In the dialog box, input 300 pt for each of the fields and click OK. A circle will appear, with the Bermuda style applied. (If Bermuda does not appear, perhaps due to an interruption in your Illustrator education, click on it in the Styles palette to apply it to your circle.)
4. Move the cursor just inside the upper-left edge of the circle, and click once more.
5. In the dialog box, enter 150 pt and 150 pt, and then click OK. Another circle will appear in front of the first.
6. Press V on the keyboard to select the Move tool.
7. With the smaller circle still selected, Shift+click the larger circle. They should both be selected.
8. Choose the menu command Object, Compound Path, Make. The smaller circle is used as a cookie cutter to create a hole in the larger circle.
9. From the Toolbox, get the Group Select tool.
10. Click away from the objects to deselect them.
11. Click and drag in the smaller circle. See how it can be repositioned. You must click directly on the smaller circle's path. If you see anchor points for the outer circle, you missed. Hint: Click directly on the edge where the green of the outer circle meets the white of the cutout portion, as shown in Figure 5.20.

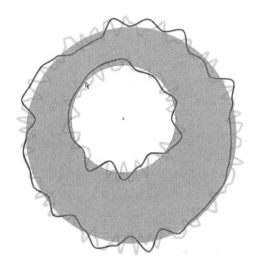

FIGURE 5.20

Click right on the dividing line between the green and the inner white areas. That ensures that you'll select only the inner circle.

Summary

Some consider the Pen tool and creating paths to be the toughest part of Illustrator. And you've already got these topics well in hand! You've learned how objects and lines are created, and you understand the basic building blocks, those anchor points and control points. You can create paths with both the Pen and Pencil tools, and you can create compound paths. You can even work with overlapping objects to create other objects. In the next hour, you'll learn how to fine-tune your creations by editing paths.

Workshop

You can now create any shape, any object, any line, or any path that you want to create. That's all there is to it! Well, that and a bit of accuracy. In the next hour we'll teach you about editing paths, for those occasions when the curve doesn't go exactly where you told it to go.

The Pen tool is considered by many to be the most powerful capability that Illustrator (or any graphics program) can have. Becoming proficient at creating paths gives you not only precision, but also speed. It is often far faster to create an object with the Pen tool than it is to cobble it together from other objects. To help you down that path of proficiency, here are some questions, some answers, and some exercises.

5

Q&A

Q **How can I predict what a curve will look like while dragging the Pen tool?**

A Illustrator will show you a preview as you drag.

Q **When I edit an existing path with the Pencil tool, it sometimes picks the wrong end to save. What am I doing wrong?**

A Illustrator guesses which part of a path you want to replace by the direction in which you drag. Grab your Pencil tool and make a path. Now, somewhere in the middle of the path, click and drag in the general direction of one end. From that same spot, click and drag in the opposite direction. See how it works.

Q **What is the difference between using the command Compound Path, Make and clicking the Exclude button in the Pathfinder palette?**

A The Compound Shape buttons in the Pathfinder palette are live effects—meaning that they don't permanently alter objects and can be reversed. The Compound Path, Make command can also be reversed, of course. Compound shapes, however, can be imported into Photoshop as shape layers. The two capabilities also differ in how they determine visibility.

Quiz

1. You're making a path with the Pen tool. You want to end that path and start another. You…

    a. …click once on the first anchor point, creating a closed path.

    b. …Command+click (Mac)/Control+click(Windows) away from the path.

    c. …change tools in the Toolbox and then reselect the Pen tool.

    d. Any of the above.

2. Double-clicking the Pencil tool icon in the Toolbox does what?

    a. Switches to the Pen tool

    b. Opens the Pencil Tool Options dialog box

    c. Switches to the Eraser tool

    d. Opens the Illustrator Preferences dialog box

3. The three types of anchor points are

    a. Corner, Line, and Curve

    b. Line, Path, and Smooth

    c. Smooth, Corner, and Combination

    d. Combination, Pepperoni, and Veggie Supreme

4. A compound path…

    a. …is an object with holes cut into it by another object.

    b. …is called compound because it has both smooth and straight path segments.

    c. …is always an open path.

    d. …must contain two verbs.

5. You can use the Pathfinder palette with a single path.

    a. True

    b. False

Quiz Answers

1. d. Those are all ways that you can terminate a path and have the Pen tool ready to start another path.

2. b. That's where you set such things as Fidelity and Smoothness.

3. c. Corner anchor points have straight path segments on either side. Smooth anchor points have curved path segments on either side. Combination points have one of each. Of course, if the point is an endpoint, it has only one path segment adjoining, either straight (making it a corner point) or curved (making it a smooth point).

4. a. A compound path is made of two or more paths, which are combined into a single group. One or more paths define areas of transparency in the object behind.

5. b. False. You need at least two paths to tango with the Pathfinder, baby!

Exercises

1. With Snap to Grid active, click and drag a few smooth anchor points with the Pen tool. Take a look at how using Snap to Grid can help you produce symmetrical curves.

2. With Snap to Grid still active, create some zigzag lines by clicking to place a number of anchor points at angles to each other. Turn off Snap to Grid by using the View menu of the keyboard shortcut Shift+Command+" (Mac)/Shift+Control+" (Windows). Just below your path, try to replicate the zigzags.

3. Attempt to draw a circle with the Pencil tool. Have a good laugh. Attempt to create the circle with the Pen tool. Have another laugh. Turn on Snap to Grid and make a *real* circle. Pat yourself on the back!

4. Experiment with various Fidelity and Smoothness settings of the Pencil tool. Draw a couple of S shapes, change the settings, then draw a few more S's. Get comfortable with how the two settings affect the paths that you draw.

5

5. Create compound paths that consist of circles within circles, squares within squares, and circles within squares. Use two, three, even four closed paths within each other. Use a combination of tools, including the Ellipse and Rectangle tools, the Star tool, and the Pen tool.

Hour **6**

Editing Bézier Curves

As you already know, paths can be either closed, with no endpoints (objects) or open, with two endpoints (lines). They are constructed of one or more path segments, with each segment bordered by two anchor points. With the exception of endpoints on lines, each anchor point has a segment on either side. The anchor points can be smooth points, with curved segments on either side, or corner points, which have one or two straight segments adjoining. Corner points with one straight segment and one corner segment can be considered combination points, at which curved path segments can form a corner.

In the last hour you learned how to create paths and compound paths to produce custom lines and shapes. In this hour we'll talk about how to fine-tune Illustrator objects and lines by manipulating anchor points and editing the path segments. And, in the spirit of learn-by-doing, you'll be working with the most important tools as we discuss their capabilities.

In this hour, you'll learn about the following:

- Adding and deleting anchor points
- Moving and converting anchor points on a path

- Simplifying paths to prevent output problems
- Using Illustrator's new Liquify tools
- The Smooth, Erase, Reshape, Scissors, and Knife tools
- Combining paths with the Join and Average commands

Changing Objects and Lines

The paths with which an object is created define its shape. The anchor points define those paths. Therefore, if we want to change the shape of a line or an object, we change its anchor points. Among the most basic changes are adding and deleting anchor points.

Task: Creating a Path

Let's start by creating a path to manipulate. If Illustrator has been used since you last reset the preferences file, delete that file now. It's best to start this hour with a clean slate, using Illustrator's factory-default settings. (If you've forgotten how or are the least bit uncertain, refer to the reference card that came in the front of this book for instructions.)

1. Open a new document in Illustrator. Use the keyboard shortcut Command+N (Mac)/Control+N (Windows) and accept the default settings.
2. From the Toolbox, select the Pen tool and create a closed path similar to the one shown in Figure 6.1.
3. Click with the Pen tool near the upper-left corner of the artboard. Move the cursor to the upper-middle of the artboard and click again. Mouse downward to the center of the artboard and click, then drag about halfway to the lower-left corner of the artboard. Click to the left of the previous point near the edge of the artboard and drag up and slightly to the left. Click the first point to close the path.

Task: Adding Anchor Points

The more anchor points a path has, the more precisely you can control its shape. Too many points, however, can ruin the flow of a curve or even create problems with printing.

1. In the Illustrator Toolbox, click and hold the Pen icon. The additional Pen tools will appear on the flyout menu.
2. Continue to hold down the mouse button and slide to the far-right edge of the hidden tools. When the cursor is over the small sideways-pointing arrow, release the mouse button. That enables the hidden tool to appear on a floating palette.
3. Position the palette to the upper right of your path, where you can conveniently change tools (see Figure 6.2) .

FIGURE 6.1

Click and click+drag as shown to create the test object. This path is just for practice; you don't need to be overly precise.

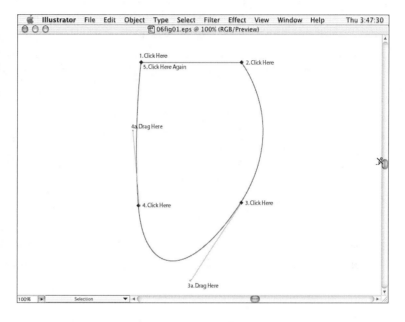

FIGURE 6.2

The tear-off palette gives you convenient access to the various pen tools.

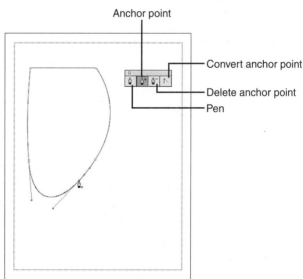

4. In the new floating palette, you'll see (from the left) the Pen tool, the Add Anchor Point tool, the Delete Anchor Point tool, and the Convert Anchor Point tool. Select the Add Anchor Point tool by clicking it in the tear-off palette.

5. Click once on the path near the location shown in Figure 6.3. Notice that the anchor point you just added has direction lines and control points. To maintain the current shape of the path, the new point must be a smooth anchor point.

6. Now click once with the Add Anchor Point tool in the middle of the top segment of the path. Because that is a straight segment, bounded by two corner anchor points, this new anchor point is also a corner point and has no direction lines or control points.

FIGURE 6.3

If the cursor is not over a path when you click, you'll get an error message.

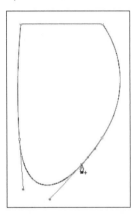

▲

Task: Deleting Anchor Points

Deleting an individual anchor point is simple with the Delete Anchor Point tool.

1. Slide the cursor over to the tear-off palette and switch to the Delete Anchor Point tool.

2. Click once on the anchor point in the upper-right corner of your path. Notice how the path is reshaped to compensate for the loss of the anchor point. (See Figure 6.4.)

3. Use the Undo command or the keyboard shortcut Command+Z (Mac)/Control+Z (Windows). The anchor point, and therefore the path's shape, should be restored.

4. Click once on the anchor point in the middle of the top segment (which you added just moments ago with the Add Anchor Point tool). Notice that the point is removed but the path is unchanged. That's because the corner point was added to a straight segment and had no effect on the shape of the path. It was an unnecessary point and, because of that, an excellent candidate for removal.

▲

As you modify objects and lines, it's a good idea to delete unnecessary anchor points, such as the one removed in Step 4. Not only are they not needed, they can affect later modification of the object, especially when you

use the Liquify tools, some of the Transform commands and tools, and when
you apply Effects. (Transformations are covered in Hour 12, "Utilizing
Transformations and Blends." Effects are discussed in Hour 18, "Working
with Filters and Live Effects.")

FIGURE 6.4

*The cursor indicates
the spot where the
anchor point was
deleted.*

Task: Using Auto Add/Delete

Now that you've learned how to use the Add Anchor Point and Delete Anchor Point tools
you'll never need them again. Really! Try this:

1. Mouse to the tear-off tool palette and select the Pen tool, or simply press P on the
   keyboard.

2. Position the Pen tool directly over the middle of the top segment of your path. That's
   where you just deleted an anchor point. Don't click, just mouse on to the path. Look
   closely at the cursor. Notice how it has changed from the Pen tool to the Add Anchor
   Point tool? There's now a small plus sign (+) to the lower right of the cursor.

3. Move the cursor slightly below the path segment. The plus sign changes to a small
   X. That change indicates that if you click the mouse button, you'll be starting a
   new path.

4. Move the cursor back over the path. The X changes back to a plus sign.

5. Move the cursor directly over any of the existing anchor points. Notice the minus
   sign (–) next to the cursor? The tool has automatically changed from the Pen tool
   to the Delete Anchor Point tool.

This behavior can be turned off in the General preferences. Look for the check box
Disable Auto Add/Delete. However, when it is active, you never need to mouse to the
Toolbox or use a keyboard shortcut to select either the Add Anchor Point tool or the
Delete Anchor Point tool. Just press P to get the Pen tool and position it where you want

to add or delete a point. Illustrator will know which tool you need based on whether you are over a path segment or an anchor point.

You can now dismiss the tear-off tool palette by clicking the palette's Close button.

Task: Moving Anchor Points

The Direct Selection tool (keyboard shortcut A) is found in the upper-right corner of the Toolbox. It can be used to select and move individual points in a path.

1. Select the Direct Selection tool by clicking on its icon in the Toolbox or by pressing A on the keyboard.

2. Click once in the artboard, away from your path, to make sure that the path is not active (selected).

3. Position the tip of the arrow on the top path segment of your object. Notice the small black square to the lower right of the cursor (see Figure 6.5). The black square indicates that the Direct Selection tool is above a path segment. (If the black square is not visible, the cursor is not close enough to the path. Move it slightly up and down on the artboard until the black square is visible.)

FIGURE 6.5

In this image, the Direct Selection tool is over a path. When the cursor is not over a path, the black box will not be shown.

4. Now move the cursor to the right until the tip of the arrow is directly over the corner of the object, where the horizontal and vertical paths meet. The little square will become hollow (see Figure 6.6). This indicates that the Direct Selection tool is above an anchor point.

5. Carefully move the cursor clockwise along the path and watch the small black square. Between the upper-right corner and the bottom of the object, the cursor should change twice to indicate that it is over an anchor point.

6. Move the cursor directly over the path segment at the bottom of the object (watch for the black square) and click once. That makes the path active (selected) and the anchor points will be visible. Notice that the control points and direction lines for the path segment you clicked on are also visible. Only one direction line for each of the two bordering anchor points is visible. They are the direction lines that

▼   affect the segment of the path on which you clicked. Also note that all the anchor points are visible, and all are indicated by hollow squares. (See Figure 6.7.)

FIGURE 6.6

The cursor's hollow square indicator is only visible when the Direct Selection tool is over an anchor point, corner or smooth.

FIGURE 6.7

All five anchor points are visible, and all are indicated by hollow squares. The control points at the ends of the two visible direction lines are indicated by solid diamonds.

7. Click the anchor point at the lower right of the object. The anchor point will now be indicated by a filled square, showing that it has been selected (and is active). Notice, too, that the two control points for the segment to the right of the anchor point are now also visible. (The direction lines might not be visible, since they fall along the path itself, but the control points are indicated by solid diamonds. See Figure 6.8.)

8. Click that anchor point again and drag it straight up until it's approximately even (horizontally) with the neighboring anchor points (see Figure 6.9) .

9. Click once on the anchor point in the upper-left corner. Now Shift+click the point in the upper-right corner. Both anchor points will show as selected (filled squares). Continue to hold the mouse button down, release the Shift key, and drag upward. Both anchor points move (see Figure 6.10). Before you release the mouse button, press the Shift key once again. That constrains the movement to straight lines, either vertical, horizontal, or 45° angles. Release the mouse button and then the Shift key.

6

FIGURE 6.8

Four control points are now visible, two for the segment to the left of the active anchor point, and two for the segment to the right. Two direction lines belong to the active anchor point, and there's one each from the neighboring points.

FIGURE 6.9

The path segment changes to conform to the new location of the anchor point. The length and angle of direction lines and control points do not change as the anchor point is moved.

FIGURE 6.10

Shift+clicking enables you to select multiple anchor points or path segments when editing an object or line. You can also Shift+click to select a combination of anchor points and path segments.

Editing Path Segments

Just as objects and lines can be altered by adding, deleting, and moving anchor points, the path segments that make up the objects and lines can be manipulated by working with the anchor points.

As you learned last hour, each path segment is bordered by two anchor points. The three types of anchor points are corner, smooth, and combination. When you drag to create a smooth anchor point, you determine the shape of the adjoining path segments. Now we'll look at ways that you can change paths using existing anchor points.

▼ TASK

Task: Adjusting Smooth Anchor Points

Just as you use the Direct Selection tool to move anchor points, you also use it to move control points. As you remember, the distance and direction of a control point from its anchor point affect the shape of the path segment. For this discussion, we can pretty much ignore the direction lines—they are simply lines that show which control point belongs to which anchor point. The control points themselves are what we will manipulate to edit path segments.

1. With the Direct Selection tool, click the middle of the three lowest anchor points (see Figure 6.11).

FIGURE 6.11

With that anchor point selected, its two control points and the control points for the neighboring anchor points are available. Notice that the only control points that can be selected are those for the two path segments that connect to the active anchor point.

6

2. Click the active anchor point's lower control point and drag it until it is directly below the anchor point. The control point should be approximately even with the control point to the left (see Figure 6.12). Release the mouse button. Notice that the anchor point's other control point also moved.

▼

FIGURE 6.12

*The Shift key will help
you make sure that the
control point is directly
below its anchor point,
although such preci-
sion isn't necessary
for this exercise.*

3. Hold down the Option key (Mac)/Alt key (Windows) and click the anchor point's higher control point. The Option (Mac)/Alt (Windows) key enables the control point to be moved independently of the anchor point's other control point. Drag the control point until it is at a 45° angle from the anchor point, and near the path (see Figure 6.13). Release the mouse button. The active anchor point has now been converted to a combination point.

FIGURE 6.13

*Again, the Shift key
can be depressed after
you begin dragging to
make sure that the
angle is precisely 45°.*

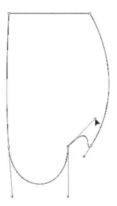

4. Option+click (Mac)/Alt+click (Windows) on the visible control point for the anchor point to the right of the active point. Drag that control point until its direction line is parallel to the one you just modified (see Figure 6.14). Release the mouse button.

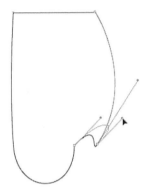

FIGURE 6.14
Notice that the other control point for the point you are editing is now visible. When you release the mouse button, it is hidden again.

5. Click the anchor point of the control point you just moved. That makes it the active anchor point. You'll see that its two control points are active, as is the other control point for the path segment you just changed. However, the anchor point in the upper-right corner of the object has no visible control point. It is a corner anchor point and therefore has no control points.

6. Use the Direct Selection tool to grab the control point at the end of the longer direction line and drag it until it's directly to the right of its anchor point, and near the right edge of the artboard. (See Figure 6.15.)

FIGURE 6.15
Notice that you didn't have to use the Option (Mac)/Alt (Windows) key? Once the control points become unaffiliated, they stay that way.

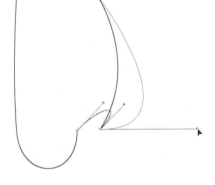

6

The Shift key will not allow you to select multiple control points for editing. Unlike anchor points, you can manipulate only one control point at a time.

Task: Converting Corner Anchor Points

When editing an object or a line, it might be advantageous to have a corner point where you currently have a smooth anchor point, or vice versa. It's easy to convert one type of point to another.

1. From the Toolbox, choose the Convert Anchor Point tool. You'll find it on the same hidden flyout palette as the Add Anchor Point and Delete Anchor Point tools. (It's the one that looks like a flying angle.)

2. Click the anchor point in the upper-left corner of your object and drag up and to the right, as shown in Figure 6.16. The anchor point, which had been a corner point with no control points, is now a smooth anchor point with two control points.

FIGURE 6.16

The tear-off palette shows the Convert Anchor Point tool selected.

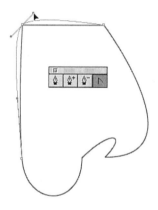

3. With the Convert Anchor Point tool still active, you can move control points. Click the lower of the two visible control points and drag it to the center of the object, as shown in Figure 6.17. Notice that when you're using the Convert Anchor Point tool, you don't need to hold down the Option (Mac)/Alt (Windows) key to move one control point without moving its companion. This, too, produces a combination point.

4. Click once (don't drag) on the anchor point in the lower-left corner of your object (see Figure 6.18). That converts the smooth anchor point to a corner point.

FIGURE 6.17

*The Convert Anchor
Point tool can be used
to reposition control
points independently of
each other.*

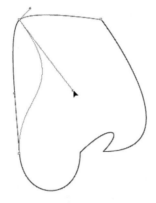

FIGURE 6.18

*While the point is now
a corner anchor point,
the segments bordering
it remain curved.
That's because the
points at the other end
of both segments are
smooth points.*

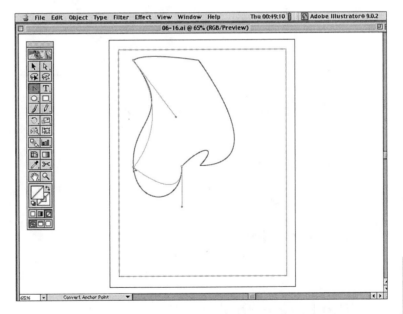

If you'd like, go ahead and save this image now for use with an exercise at the end of
this chapter.

The Liquify Tools

Illustrator 10 contains a group of tools that might feel familiar to users of recent versions of Photoshop, SuperGoo, and similar image editors. The Liquify tools (shown in Figure 6.19) enable you to push and pull, swirl and scallop, expand and contract, and generally distort (and have fun with) shapes.

FIGURE 6.19

The original object is shown in the upper left. Each Liquify tool was applied to one copy of the object. A description follows in order, from left to right.

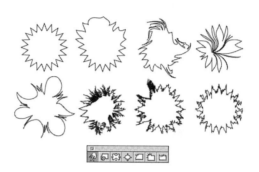

 The Liquify tools have preferences (including brush size) that can be specified by double-clicking the tool's icon in Illustrator's Toolbox.

The Warp Tool

Pull on the object, moving the anchor points with the Warp tool. (See Figure 6.19, top row, second object.)

The Twirl Tool

Dragging the tool twists and swirls the anchor points and segments. (See Figure 6.19, top row, third object.)

The Pucker Tool

As you drag, the control points of the anchor points are moved inward toward the center of the cursor. Adobe calls this deflating an object. (See Figure 6.19, top row, fourth object.)

The Bloat Tool

The opposite of the preceding tool, this one inflates an object by moving control points away from the cursor. (See Figure 6.19, second row, first object.)

The Scallop Tool

Anchor points are added, producing scallop-like details along the paths as the tool is dragged. (See Figure 6.19, second row, second object.)

The Crystallize Tool

Like the preceding tool, this one adds points to create effects along path segments. These details are described as crystal-like.(See Figure 6.19, second row, third object.)

The Wrinkle Tool

Jagged lines are added to provide detail with this tool. (See Figure 6.19, second row, fourth object.)

> After using a Liquify tool, consider using the command Object, Path, Simplify (discussed below). All the tools can add points to a path, and Simplify can get rid of the extra ones without changing the path's shape. In Figure 6.19, the original object has 41 anchor points. The Liquify tools add anywhere from a few new anchor points (Warp) to more than 750 new anchor points (Scallop). Simplifying paths can help reduce the chance of output errors.

You'll learn more about the Liquify tools in Hour 17, "Distorting, Warping, and Liquifying Your Artwork."

Additional Path Editing Tools

Illustrator also has some tools dedicated to fulfilling certain tasks with paths. Some of the tools work with points on a path, whereas others work with the paths themselves. They all make changing objects and lines easier in certain respects.

Task: Using the Smooth Tool

The Smooth tool, which lives under the Pencil tool, can be used to round off corners and to simplify paths.

1. Use the Polygon tool to create a hexagon or an octagon on the artboard.

2. Select the Smooth tool.

3. Drag it around the top part of the polygon, making sure to cross the existing anchor points.

4. Release the mouse button. Observe not only the change in the shape, but also the change in the anchor points (see Figure 6.20).

5. Drag the Smooth tool repeatedly around the object, trying to stay directly on the path as much as possible. Take a look at your results.

The Erase Tool

Last hour you learned how to use the Pencil tool. As a wise man once said, "What's a pencil without an eraser?" Just as the Pencil tool creates points as you drag it, the Erase tool removes points.

Drag the Erase tool over any part of an active path and the anchor points and path segments will be deleted. If you start dragging in the middle of a segment, rather than at an existing anchor point, Illustrator will create an anchor point at that spot. Likewise, you can stop erasing in the middle of a segment, too, and create an anchor point.

The Reshape Tool

The Reshape tool enables you to push or pull selected anchor points. The three kinds of points when you're using the Reshape tool are unselected, selected, and focal. Focal points maintain their relationship when moved, and move as a group. Selected (nonfocal) points will move, too, but the distances among them (and between the selected, unselected, and focal points) will change. Unselected points are unaffected by the Reshape tool. Figure 6.21 shows how it works.

The Scissors Tool

The Scissors tool cuts paths. To be cut, the path doesn't need to be selected. Click the tool to cut a path, and endpoints are created. If you divide a path at an anchor point, a new endpoint will be created directly on top of the existing point.

The Knife Tool

The Knife tool is used to divide closed paths (objects). New segments will be created where an object becomes divided, creating two closed paths. Attributes of the original object are retained.

FIGURE 6.21

The left image is the original. The difference between the middle and right objects are the number of selected focal points (squares in boxes) versus the selected points (squares). The unselected points are identical.

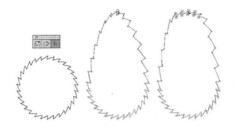

> To divide one or more objects along a straight line, Press Option (Mac)/Alt (Windows) before you start dragging the knife tool, and leave it down until you've finish.

Path Editing Menu Commands

Illustrator has several menu commands dedicated to helping you work with paths. They are both creative and, let us say, administrative in nature. Some help you produce artwork, some help make sure that you *can* produce your artwork. You'll find these commands under the Object menu, in the submenu Path.

Joining Paths

You can join the two endpoints of an open path to form a closed path, or you can join ends of two open paths. Use the Direct Selection tool to select a pair of endpoints and then choose Object, Path, Join. A straight path segment will be created between the two anchor points. If the points are located on top of each other, a single point will remain. You'll have the option of it being a corner or smooth anchor point.

Averaging Points

This command (Object, Path, Average) enables you to reposition two or more selected anchor points toward each other. You'll have the option of averaging their positions horizontally, vertically, or both. If you select both, the pair of points will be placed on top of each other, in a spot midway between their original positions.

6

When you use the Average command on a pair of points to colocate them, you can then combine them into a single point with the Join command.

Offsetting Paths

The Offset path command creates a replica of the selected path, a specified size and distance from the original. The new path can be offset both positive and negative distances, moving it outside or inside the original. The paths will have the same center point, making Offset Path perfect for creating concentric circles, parallel lines, and a variety of other precise elements for your artwork. In Figure 6.22, the original path is selected. You can see that a pair of replicas have been created with negative offset values, and four have been created with positive offset values.

FIGURE 6.22

To the left of the paths, the corner point is preserved in the replicas, maintaining the sharpness. To the right, however, the curve formed by the two smooth points gets rounder (outward) and sharper (inward).

Simplifying Paths

The Simplify command can be your best friend when complex artwork doesn't seem to want to output properly. Too many points on too many paths can choke a printer or an imagesetter. The Simplify dialog box offers you a slider to determine the fidelity of the changes (Curve Precision) and another to regulate corners (Angle Threshold). Check the Preview box and you can see not only how accurately the path will be reproduced, but also the reduction in the number of anchor points. Dragging the top slider to 90% can result in substantial reductions in the number of points, with virtually no change in the path's appearance.

Adding Anchor Points

Sometimes a path needs a few more anchor points to make an effect or transformation really zing. Without anchor points with which to work, some commands and tools don't work very well. The Add Anchor Points command will put a new anchor point between every pair of existing points. On straight path segments, the new point will be placed directly in the middle. On curved points, Illustrator takes care to place the added anchor point where it will best maintain the shape of the path segment. To calculate how many anchor points you'll have after using this command, multiply the number of original anchor points by two and subtract one.

The Divide Objects Below Command

The Divide Objects Below command enables you to use one path (open or closed) as a stencil to cut overlapping objects and lines. Objects and lines beneath the selected path are separated wherever the object crosses them (similar to the Knife tool) .

Summary

In this hour, you've learned a lot of great ways to alter objects and lines. Some give you incredible control but might take some time, whereas some are easy but not as precise. Whether you edit your paths with the Direct Selection tool or the Liquify tools, keep in mind that they are all Bézier paths, constructed of anchor points and path segments, and shaped by control points and direction lines.

Workshop

You've had quite a workout this hour! But the fun's not over yet—we've prepared some additional hands-on exercises and the usual questions and quizzes to reinforce what you've learned about editing paths.

Q&A

Q Is everything in my image created from Bézier paths?

A Objects, Lines, and even text are Bézier paths at heart. However, raster images that have been added using the Place or Paste or Open commands are constructed from pixels rather than paths, as are vector objects that have been rasterized and some filters and effects.

Q Where do we get the term "Bézier"?

A Pronounced "beh-zyay" or "behz-YAY," Pierre Etienne Bézier (1910–1999) was an engineer who spent much of his career with the French auto manufacturer Renault. He developed a workable system of defining curves based on the control points and direction lines we use today in Illustrator. Dr. Bézier's work paved the way for the desktop publishing revolution. Even the fonts with which this book is printed rely on Bézier curves to define the letter shapes.

6

Q Can the Direct Selection tool work with multiple control points?

A No. Only one control point can be edited at a time.

Q I have a rather complex path that I want to edit, but I'm afraid of losing my work-to-date. Other than making a back-up copy of the file, what can I do?

A Rather than copying the file, why not copy the path? You'll learn more about the Layers palette in Hour 13, "Gaining Flexibility Through Layers," but for now you can protect your work by dragging the path to the Create New Layer button at the bottom of the Layers palette. Hide the path and save it for emergencies by clicking the eye icon in the left column of the Layers palette.

Quiz

1. Which tool can be used to move an anchor point?

    a. The Direct Selection tool

    b. The Reshape tool

    c. The Twirl tool

    d. All of the above

2. When moving a control point with the Direct Selection tool, the Shift key does what?

    a. Enables you to select another control point for movement

    b. Constrains the movement to 45° angles

    c. Switches to the complementary control point

    d. Maintains the integrity of the path segment shape

3. When using the Liquify tools…

    a. …shapes automatically become rectangles.

    b. …all objects are converted to open paths.

    c. …the number of anchor points is likely to increase.

    d. …the number of anchor points is likely to decrease.

4. The Simplify command is found in which Illustrator menu?

    a. The Object menu

    b. The View menu

    c. The Help menu

    d. The Assistant menu

Quiz Answers

1. d. Most of the tools mentioned in this hour can move anchor points.

2. b. When you are in the process of dragging, Shift invariably restricts the movement to the angle specified in the Preferences (by default, 45°).

3. c. The number of anchor points along a path can easily get out of hand when we experiment with the Liquify tools. Remember the Simplify command!

4. a. Object, Path, Simplify.

Exercises

1. Open the image that you saved earlier in this hour. Use the various tools and commands to produce something similar to that shown in Figure 6.23.

FIGURE 6.23

Just adding and editing a couple of paths can drastically change the appearance of an object.

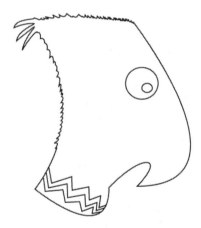

2. Use the command File, New or the keyboard shortcut Command+N (Mac)/Control+N (Windows). Select the Pen tool from the Toolbox. Click and click-and-drag around randomly for a minute or so until you have a rather complex piece of abstract art. Make both corner and smooth anchor points. With the path selected and active on the artboard, choose the menu command Object, Path, Simplify. Check the Preview box. Look at the number of points in your original object. Slide the upper slider to the right, to 100%. Compare Original and Current. Is the Current number perhaps higher than Original? Click in the check box to activate Show Original. Drag that slider to 95%. Then to 90%. Then to 75%. And now to 50%. See the difference in the number of points? Also notice the amount of change in the path itself (or lack thereof). You might need to move the dialog box to see what's happening with the path. When you're satisfied with the settings, click OK.

6

3. Select the Star tool from the Toolbox. (You'll find it under the Rectangle tool.) Click it once on the artboard and in the dialog box, input these values: 50/40/20. Click OK. Use the various Liquify tools to alter this 20-point star in various ways.

4. Select All. Delete. Grab the Pen tool. Click once near the top-left corner of the artboard and again near the top-right corner. Command+click (Mac)/Control+click (Windows) anywhere. Click with the Pen tool in the lower-left corner and again in the lower-right corner. You should now have a simple line across the top and another across the bottom. Press A on the keyboard to activate the Direct Selection Tool. Shift+click the upper-left point to select it (the lower-right anchor point should still be selected, too). Now go to the menu command Object, Path, Average. Try averaging the paths horizontally. Type Command+Z (Mac)/Control+Z (Windows) to Undo. Use the Direct Selection tool and Shift+click to reselect the two anchor points. Average them vertically. Again, undo and reselect, and this time average them using the Both setting.

PART II
Creative Illustrator

Hour

Hour 7

Understanding and Applying Color

Now you're ready to add some color. Illustrator has a lot of options when it comes to coloring objects, such as creating your own colors, choosing from preset custom colors such as PANTONE, Trumatch, and Web-safe colors, and applying transparent and blending effects. Throughout this hour, you'll learn how to apply these colors, using the following:

- The Color palette
- The Swatches palette
- The Transparency palette
- The Eyedropper tool
- The Paint Bucket tool

Fill and Stroke

In Illustrator, each object has two attributes: a fill and a stroke (see Figure 7.1). As you'll soon see, Illustrator has several kinds of fills and strokes. You can give a fill and a stroke to just about any object (with the exception of a mask) even one that is an open path (see Figure 7.2).

FIGURE 7.1

Each object has a fill and a stroke.

FIGURE 7.2

Illustrator fills an open path by using the two open points as a boundary.

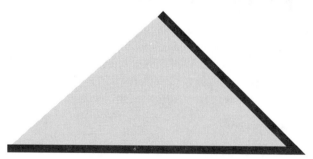

At the bottom of the Toolbox are the Fill and Stroke indicators (see Figure 7.3). They are very similar to Photoshop's Foreground and Background color indicators. The box to the upper left is the Fill indicator, and the one to the lower-right is the Stroke indicator. You can click either one to make it active, or you can press X on the keyboard to switch the active one. When the Fill box is selected, any changes you make in the Color, Style, or Swatch palette are applied to the fill of a selected object, and the same is true for the Stroke.

FIGURE 7.3

Illustrator's Fill and Stroke indicators.

You can find two more icons there: a curved arrow (upper right) and a pair of little boxes (lower left). Clicking the arrow swaps the fill and stroke, meaning that if the fill is currently white and the stroke is black, clicking the arrows makes the fill black and the stroke white. Clicking the little boxes sets the fill and stroke to Illustrator's default setting (as does pressing D), which is a white fill and a one-point black stroke.

Fill and Stroke indicators also appear in the Color palette, which I'll discuss next.

When you're changing the color of the fill or stroke, any object that is selected during the change will take on the new color attributes. If no object is selected, the next object you create will take on the new color attributes you just set.

The Color Palette

Illustrator's Color palette, shown in Figure 7.4, consists of the Fill and Stroke indicators, a color slider (or sliders) with percentage boxes, and a color bar, which, depending on what colors are selected, is either a color spectrum or a grayscale/tint ramp. If all you see is the color bar, select Show Options from the palette menu (see Figure 7.5) or click twice on the arrows in the tab.

FIGURE 7.4

Illustrator's Color palette.

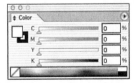

FIGURE 7.5
*Select Show Options in
the Color palette.*

CMYK and RGB

As mentioned briefly in Hour 1, "Understanding Illustrator," Illustrator works within either of two different color modes: CMYK (used for commercial printing presses) and RGB (used with inkjet printers, monitor displays, and for the Web). When you create a new document in Illustrator, you can choose to work in either CMYK or RGB. An Illustrator file cannot contain both CMYK and RGB objects. To switch color modes after a file is created, you can choose File, Document Color Mode and select either CMYK Color or RGB Color (see Figure 7.6).

FIGURE 7.6
*Switch the Document
Color mode.*

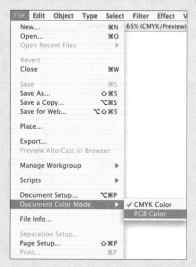

Because CMYK and RGB are very different, when you switch documents from RGB to CMYK or vice versa, color shifts can occur. To maintain color integrity, it is best not to switch constantly back and forth between color modes because it will result in unpredictable color output.

Illustrator does enable you to select colors from any of its supported color models in the Color palette, but any chosen colors will be converted on-the-fly to whatever the document color mode is set to. For example, if your document is set to CMYK and you choose an RGB Web-safe color from the Color palette, Illustrator will convert that color to CMYK when you use that color within the document.

To quickly cycle through each of the color modes in the Color palette, hold down the Shift key, and click the color bar.

In case you aren't sure, you can always check whether a document is in CMYK or RGB mode by looking in the title bar of the document window. Illustrator lists the name of the document, the zoom percentage, and then color and preview mode.

Selecting a Color

To select a color, either click anywhere in the color spectrum or tint ramp, or adjust the sliders manually by clicking the little triangles and dragging them to the left and right. You can also enter numeric values manually by clicking in the field, entering a number, and pressing the Tab key to advance to the next field or pressing Shift+Tab to go back to the previous field.

After you put the focus into the Color palette, you can quickly move through all the fields by pressing the Tab key. Remember, however, that if you're not entering information in a palette, the Tab key hides and shows your palettes. If you have other palettes docked to the palette where your focus is, such as the Gradient or Stroke palette, you can also cycle through those fields with the Tab key. To put Illustrator's focus into the last used palette, press Command+~ (Macintosh)/Control+~ (Windows): Note that this only works with palettes that contain text entry fields.

Illustrator's Color palette slider bars are very intuitive and change color as you drag to approximate other colors. You can also hold down the Shift key while dragging any one slider, and all sliders move proportionately, making it easy to get lighter or darker shades of colors.

Color Models

7

NEW TERM   Although all Illustrator documents are either RGB or CMYK, Illustrator enables you to select colors from several different palettes or *color models*. These are (in order of appearance) Grayscale, RGB, HSB, CMYK, and Web Safe RGB. I know, that's a lot of acronyms, but I'll explain them all.

Grayscale

For black-and-white work, use Grayscale, which supports 256 levels of gray. In this mode, the Color palette has a grayscale ramp to choose different percentages of black (see Figure 7.7). There are also buttons to quickly access the colors of None and white and black to the left and right of the ramp.

FIGURE 7.7

The grayscale ramp in the Color palette.

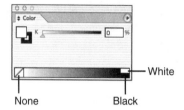

RGB

NEW TERM The RGB color model (Red, Green, and Blue) is the standard used for today's televisions and computer monitors. If you are designing work for multimedia applications, for the Web, or for output to an inkjet printer, use the RGB Color palette. RGB colors have a much wider range, or *gamut*, and have more colors that are brighter than CMYK.

HSB

The HSB color model (Hue, Saturation, and Brightness) is not as widely used and is based on the human perception of color. The Hue value determines which color you get, whereas Saturation determines how intense that color is. Brightness determines how light or dark it is.

CMYK

NEW TERM The CMYK color model (Cyan, Magenta, Yellow, and Black) is the standard for most of today's offset printing and is also known as *four-color process*. If your color artwork will be printed on paper, you're probably going to create it in CMYK. One of the shortcomings of CMYK is that its gamut is significantly smaller than RGB and many bright colors, such as oranges and blues, cannot be achieved in CMYK. Use CMYK only when the artwork will be printed commercially on four-color printing presses.

Web-Safe RGB

Not really a color model in itself, Web-Safe RGB is a small collection of RGB colors (216 to be exact) that can safely be viewed without dithering on the World Wide Web.

(Because most surfers on the Web have monitors set to more than 8-bit color, the Web-safe palette is not an important as it once was.) Color values appear in hexadecimal format (for use in HTML coding) when in this color mode (see Figure 7.8). For more information on dithering (mixing colors to make it appear that they blend) and Web colors, see Hour 22, "Creating Web Graphics."

FIGURE 7.8

The little lines in the color bar represent the predesignated stops for Web-safe colors.

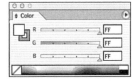

Custom Colors

NEW TERM   Though not a color model, another kind of color is supported within Illustrator: custom colors. A *custom color* is a predefined color that you can either create or choose from a list such as PANTONE, FOCOLTONE, Toyo, or Trumatch. Custom colors are also called *spot colors*. They are standard colors that have been designated to ensure color accuracy. Spot colors are used primarily with CMYK in commercial printing.

The PANTONE system, for example, was created so that when a designer wanted to print red, he or she could specify a PANTONE number that a printer could match exactly by using a red ink, instead of producing the color with a combination of cyan, magenta, yellow, and black inks. Custom colors have much in common with the way we use black. Just as you can reduce the darkness of black to create shades of gray, you can also reduce a custom color to produce lighter shades, called tints.

Loading Custom Color Palettes

Included with Illustrator are several useful custom color libraries. They include Diccolor, FOCOLTONE, HKS, PANTONE (Coated, Process and Matte, Uncoated), Toyo, and Trumatch, plus system palettes for both Macintosh and Windows for multimedia work and a few more specialized libraries that you're unlikely to need. Illustrator also has a wonderful color-safe Web palette for use when you're creating art for the World Wide Web.

To load any of these palettes, choose Swatch Libraries from the Window menu (see Figure 7.9) and choose one of the libraries. But suppose you went through all the trouble of creating your own custom colors in one document, and you want to use them in another one. At that point, you select Other Library from the submenu (see Figure 7.10), after which Illustrator asks you to locate another Illustrator file and import its custom colors in a palette of their own.

7

FIGURE 7.9

Choose a custom color library.

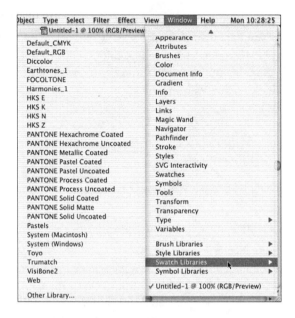

FIGURE 7.10

Import custom colors from another Illustrator file.

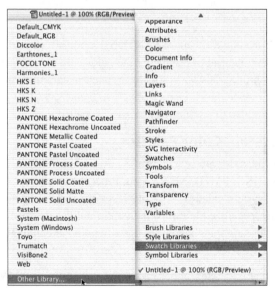

The Swatches Palette

NEW TERM Imagine that if every time you wanted to apply a color, you had to enter the values for that color in the Color palette. Besides being a pain, it would also be a big waste of time. Use the Swatches palette instead, to save time and trouble. A *swatch* is a color that you define. It can be a process color, a spot color, or even a gradient or pattern, as you'll soon see. After you define a swatch, you can apply it to any object. You can also edit and modify an existing swatch.

Now take a look at the Swatches palette (see Figure 7.11). If the palette is not already open, choose Show Swatches from the Window menu.

FIGURE 7.11

The Swatches palette.

First, notice the little buttons across the bottom of the palette. From the left, the first one is Show All Swatches. The next three are for Color, Gradient, and Pattern swatches, respectively. At first glance, the palette might look too messy, and it might be difficult to determine what's what. By clicking the Color, Gradient, or Pattern button, you can choose to view only those swatches, making it easier to choose a swatch (see Figure 7.12).

FIGURE 7.12

Here are the buttons on the bottom of the Swatches palette. Notice that only the Gradient swatches are shown.

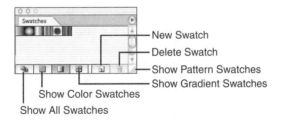

New Swatch
Delete Swatch
Show Pattern Swatches
Show Gradient Swatches
Show Color Swatches
Show All Swatches

Next are the New Swatch and Delete Swatch buttons. Clicking the New Swatch icon creates a new swatch with whatever color is currently selected. (Selected swatches have a white border.) Clicking the Delete Swatch button deletes any selected swatch. To select a swatch, simply click it. You can select several contiguous swatches by holding down the Shift key, or you can select noncontiguous swatches by holding the Command (Mac)/Control (Windows) key when selecting the swatches (see Figure 7.13) .

FIGURE 7.13

You can select multiple swatches with the Command (Mac)/ Control (Windows) key.

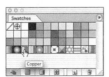

7

Task: Creating a New Color Swatch

Perform the following steps to create a new color swatch:

1. Open the Color palette and, using the sliders, choose a color.

2. Open the Swatches palette and click once on the New Swatch icon (it's the one just to the left of the Delete Swatch button icon).

3. You'll notice a new swatch pop up in the Swatches palette. Double-click it to open the Swatch Option dialog box.

4. Give the swatch a name and choose the color type (Spot or Process).

▲ 5. Click OK. You've just created a new color swatch!

> Illustrator has drag-and-drop capabilities. You can delete swatches by dragging them onto the Delete Swatch button, and you can also create a duplicate swatch by dragging an existing swatch on top of the New Swatch icon. You can drag colors between the Fill and Stroke indicators, the Color palette, and even between custom color and Swatches palettes.

Double-clicking a swatch opens the Swatch Options dialog box (see Figure 7.14). You can then edit the name of the swatch, determine whether it should be a spot or process color, and choose which color model to use. You also should see a box marked Global. With this box checked, you can edit the swatch at any time, and all objects colored with that swatch will update to reflect those changes. By unchecking this box, each object you color with this swatch is independent.

FIGURE 7.14

The Swatch Options dialog box.

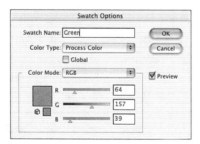

Task: Editing a Color Swatch

Perform the following steps to edit an existing color swatch:

1. Open the Swatches palette and double-click the swatch you want to edit.

2. Adjust the color sliders in the Swatch Options dialog box. You can also change the color model by selecting one from the pop-up menu.

3. When you're done editing the color, press OK to update the swatch with the new setting.

Notice that some swatches have a white triangle in the lower-right corner. The triangle indicates that the color is global. Other swatches might also have a small dot in the lower-right corner. This dot indicates that the swatch is a spot color. You can also change the order of the swatches simply by dragging and moving them around.

Viewing the Swatches Palette

Illustrator also gives you three ways to view the Swatches palette: Small Thumbnail View, Large Thumbnail View, or List View (by name) (see Figure 7.15). To choose a viewing mode, select a choice from the palette menu. You can also select the functions I mentioned earlier, such as Duplicate Swatch and Delete Swatch, as well as sort the swatches by kind or name (see Figure 7.16). When you view swatches by name, an icon on the far right of the swatch name indicates whether the swatch is Spot or Process. Finally, there is an option to Show Find Field, which is cool because it adds a find field at the top of the Swatches palette that enables you to find colors by name simply by typing a few letters.

FIGURE 7.15

The three viewing modes of the Swatches palette.

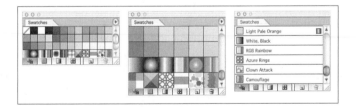

FIGURE 7.16

Sorting the swatches through the palette menu.

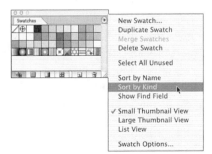

7

> Remember that a keyboard shortcut is available for the None attribute. To quickly fill an object or stroke with None, press the slash (/) key. Whether the fill or stroke of the selected object is changed to None depends on the focus of the Fill and Stroke icons on the Toolbox.

The Transparency Palette

Illustrator has the capability to make just about anything transparent, and that's just the tip of the iceberg, my friend, as you'll see throughout the book. What you are about to read is way cool.

Opacity and Blending Modes

Transparency in Illustrator consists of two basic functions. The most basic is opacity, which determines how see-through an object appears, and is controlled by the Opacity setting, found in the upper-right corner of the Transparency palette (see Figure 7.17). At 100% opacity, an object appears opaque, or completely solid, meaning that any object underneath it is completely hidden. As you drag the slider to a lower setting, the object becomes more transparent and the objects beneath begin to show through (see Figure 7.18).

FIGURE 7.17
The Opacity setting in the Transparency palette.

FIGURE 7.18
Overlapping objects with varying opacity.

NEW TERM   The other function of transparency in Illustrator is the *blending mode*. If you are familiar with Photoshop, you know what blending modes are. They enable objects to interact with objects underneath to achieve certain effects. You choose a blending mode by selecting from the pop-up menu at the upper left of the Transparency palette (see Figure 7.19). For example, if an object has the Multiply blending mode applied to it, the object will interact with any objects that it might overlap by multiplying their color values by its own values. Try experimenting with the different blending modes—it can be fun!

FIGURE 7.19

Choose a blending mode option.

Task: Working with Transparency

Creating cool effects with transparency is really easy, as you're about to find out.

1. Draw any shape and apply a color to it.

2. Open the Transparency palette and, with the object selected, set the opacity of the object to 75%.

3. Draw another shape that overlaps the first one you've drawn and give it an opacity of 50%.

4. With the second object still selected, apply the Multiply blending mode. Notice how the second object interacts with the first one where they overlap.

Transparency Options

Three options are at the bottom of the Transparency palette: Isolate Blending, Knockout Group, and Opacity & Mask Define Knockout Shape. The first two enable you to specify whether blending or transparency effects apply to just a group or to all objects that the group overlaps, and the third option enables the effects of knockout groups to be determined by their mask's opacity setting. We will discuss the Invert Mask button found in the middle of the Transparency palette later in Hour 16, "Showing and Hiding with Masks."

The Eyedropper Tool

The Eyedropper tool, as shown in Figure 7.20, is used to sample colors and attributes for use in applying those colors and attributes to other objects. Say you have a shape with one color, for example, and you want it to be the color of another shape. Without dese-lecting your shape, you can switch to the Eyedropper tool and click the other object. This operation colors your selected object the same as the one on which you clicked.

You can also press and hold down the mouse button while using the Eyedropper tool, and then drag anywhere to sample the pixel color of anything on your screen. (In real-time—I might add—watching the colors zip through the Fill indicator is cool.)

To control exactly which attributes the Eyedropper (and Paint Bucket) picks up, double-click the Eyedropper tool in the Toolbox. Illustrator presents you with a comprehensive dialog box in which you can specify settings for picking up strokes and fills and even font and text attributes (see Figure 7.21). To see all the attributes, use the scrollbars to scroll down, and click the little triangles to access each section.

FIGURE **7.21**

Specify options for the Eyedropper and Paint Bucket tools.

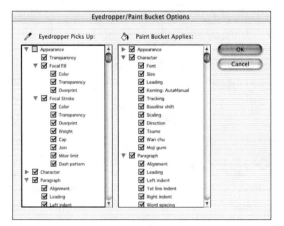

The Paint Bucket Tool

Working in tandem with the Eyedropper tool, the Paint Bucket tool (see Figure 7.22) applies colors and attributes to unselected objects. You just click an object, and Illustrator fills that object with whatever colors and attributes are selected.

FIGURE 7.22

The Paint Bucket tool.

If you press the Option (Mac)/Alt (Windows) key with the Paint Bucket tool selected, it toggles to the Eyedropper tool, and vice versa. With this simple operation, you can quickly sample a color and apply it to other objects.

Summary

What a colorful hour! You learned all about the different kinds of colors Illustrator uses, and you learned how to create and edit swatches of colors. You also learned about three new palettes: Color, Swatches, and Transparency. Speaking of Transparency, you learned how to make some *really* cool effects. Next hour, you'll learn what you can do with all these wonderful colors.

Workshop

I imagine that you already have plans for using your newfound knowledge of color. First we'll expand that knowledge a bit more with a few questions and answers. Then we'll test that knowledge. Finally, we'll end this hour with a couple of exercises to get you started in this bright new world.

7

Q&A

Q **Is there a limit to how many color swatches I can have in a document?**

A No. You can create and use as many swatches as your heart desires (although at some point when you hit a couple million, you might need to add some more RAM to your computer).

Q **I'm trying to fill an object with a color I made, but it isn't working. What's wrong?**

A You might have your focus on the stroke and not the fill. Make sure you have the fill selected (remember the X key toggles the focus between the fill and stroke).

Q **Can I apply both opacity and blending modes to a single object?**

A Yes. You can apply an opacity setting in addition to specifying a blending mode. You can only select one blending mode per object, however.

Q **Will the Eyedropper tool sample transparency settings as well as color settings?**

A Certainly! If you sample an object that's colored with blue at 45% opacity and apply that to another object, the object will take on the blue color and the 45% opacity setting.

Quiz

1. Which is not an attribute of a shape in Illustrator?

   a. Fill

   b. Stroke

   c. Color

2. What is the keyboard shortcut for setting colors to the default white fill and black stroke?

   a. Command+D (Mac)/Control+D (Windows)

   b. D

   c. W

3. Which of these color models is not supported in Illustrator?

   a. CMYK

   b. CIE LAB

   c. HSB

4. The Eyedropper tool can sample what point size a font is.

    a. True

    b. False

Quiz Answers

1. c. Color is actually a characteristic of the fill and/or the stroke, not the shape itself.

2. b. This is one of the most useful shortcuts, as you'll see in coming hours.

3. b. The L*a*b color mode is used in Photoshop, but not supported directly in Illustrator.

4. a. That's just one of many characteristics that Illustrator's Eyedropper can sample.

Exercises

1. Select all three view options for the Swatches palette, and see which one is most comfortable for you. Then get used to using the buttons on the bottom of the palette to view only certain kinds of swatches.

2. With no objects selected, practice using the Eyedropper to sample attributes and colors, and then press the Option (Mac)/Alt (Windows) key to toggle to the Paint Bucket tool so you can quickly apply those attributes to other objects without having to select them.

7

HOUR **8**

Using Strokes, Fills, and Gradients

As mentioned before, a vector object in Illustrator has two attributes: a fill and a stroke. Remember how, when you were little, you used crayons on coloring books and were careful not to go out of the lines? Well, that's what a fill in Illustrator does—colors an object, up to the boundary of the path. The good thing about Illustrator is that it never colors out of the lines—it's perfect every time—and you don't have to worry about sharpening the crayon. You'll also learn about strokes, the outlines of objects.

In this hour, you'll learn about the following:

- Applying a fill to an object
- Making gradient fills
- Creating gradient mesh objects
- Making pattern fills
- Using the Stroke palette

Solid Color Fills

A solid color fill is rather simple. Using the same crayon example as earlier, a solid color fill is akin to using one particular crayon for the interior of the object. In the preceding hour, you learned how to define new colors in Illustrator, as well as how to apply them to objects.

The two other kinds of fills in Illustrator are gradients and patterns. In this hour, you'll learn how to define and apply these kinds of fills.

Gradients

NEW TERM   *Gradients* are a powerful feature in Illustrator that enables you to specify a fill of different colors, blending with each other. Illustrator can create a gradient between just two colors or up to 32 colors. Gradients can be used to achieve cool shading effects or to add dimension to objects, and they are also a great design element (see Figure 8.1).

FIGURE 8.1

Gradients are used for shading and adding dimension.

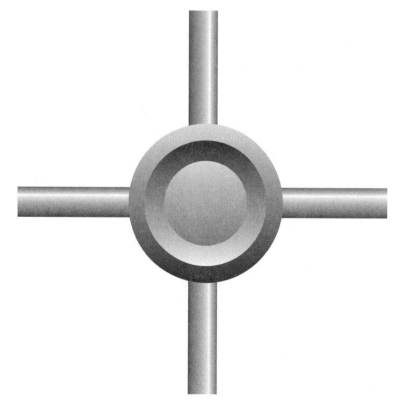

The Gradient Palette

You can apply a gradient by simply selecting a gradient swatch from the Swatches palette. To create or edit a gradient, however, you need to open the Gradient palette (F9). There you will find a gradient swatch, an option to make the gradient Linear or Radial, fields for Angle and Location, and a gradient bar (see Figure 8.2).

FIGURE 8.2

The Gradient palette.

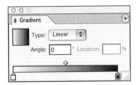

Defining a Gradient

You create a gradient in much the same way you create a color. First, you define the gradient, and then you click the New Swatch icon in the Swatches palette. After you create the new swatch, you should double-click it and give it a name. Illustrator names your creations New Gradient Swatch 1, New Gradient Swatch 2, and so on. You might be able to track them more easily with names, such as Vertical Reflection, Rivet Head, and the like (be creative, but not so creative that you forget what "Bob's Favorite Gradient" is).

NEW TERM Notice that underneath the gradient bar are icons that look like little houses. They are *color stops*, indicating the points at which a color is used in the gradient. To create a new color stop, click anywhere underneath the gradient bar. When a new house appears, you can drag it to the left or right. You can also drag any color from the Swatches or Color palette onto the gradient bar to create a color stop in that color. To change an existing color stop, either drag a new color directly on top of it, or click the icon to select it and change the color in the Color or Swatches palette.

Also, notice that little diamond-shaped icons appear on top of the gradient bar. They indicate the midpoint of the gradation. In other words, wherever the diamond is, that's the place where 50% of each color appears (see Figure 8.3). You can drag the midpoint indicator left or right to adjust the midpoint location.

FIGURE 8.3

Notice the color stops and midpoint indicators.

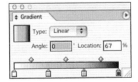

Task: Defining a Gradient

Now you're ready to define a gradient:

1. Open the Gradient palette (F9), the Color palette (F6), and the Swatches palette (F5).

2. In the Gradient palette, click the gradient swatch (it's the large square in the upper-left of the palette). Notice that the gradient bar below becomes active, and the color stops and midpoint indicators become visible.

3. Click a color stop. Now a color stop is visible underneath the color swatch in the Color palette.

4. Use the sliders in the Color palette, or the spectrum at the bottom of the Color palette to select a color for the selected color stop. Alternatively, you can drag a color from the Swatches palette directly onto the color stop in the Gradient palette.

5. Create a new color stop. Click anywhere directly underneath the gradient bar in the Gradient palette. Notice that another color stop appears. Apply a color to it the same way you did in step 4. Alternatively, you can drag a color from the Swatches palette directly onto the gradient bar. When you let go of the mouse, a color stop of the color you dragged appears.

6. Delete a color stop. You need at least three color stops to delete one (a minimum of two color stops is required). Click and drag downward on the color stop you want to delete. When the color stop disappears, release the mouse button.

7. Make your final adjustments by moving the color stops and the midpoint indicators.

8. After your gradient is complete, click on the gradient swatch and drag it into the Swatches palette, where it appears highlighted with a white outline.

9. Double-click the new swatch, and give it an appropriate name. Then click OK.

Editing a Gradient

To edit an existing gradient, modify the gradient in the Gradient palette, and then drag the gradient swatch from the Gradient palette on top of the swatch you want to update in the Swatches palette, while holding down the Option (Mac)/Alt (Windows) key.

You can change the angle of the gradient in the Angle field of the Gradient palette. The angle does not affect the object in any way; it affects only the gradient that fills the object. In Figure 8.1, for example, 3D effects were achieved just by flipping the gradient 180°.

Using the Gradient Tool

The Gradient tool is used to control the direction and placement of a gradient in an object or over several objects (see Figure 8.4). After you fill an object with a gradient, select the Gradient tool (G) and, with the object still selected, click and drag across the object in the direction you want the gradient to go. The place you begin dragging is the position the gradient starts, and the place you let go is the position the gradient ends. If you stopped dragging before the end of the object, Illustrator continues to fill the object with the color at the end of the gradient. This tool is perfect for specifying where the center of a *radial blend* should be when you're making 3D spheres (see Figure 8.5). (A radial blend has concentric rings of the blended colors. A linear gradient has stripes.)

8

FIGURE 8.4

The Gradient tool.

FIGURE 8.5

Using the Gradient tool, you can make realistic-looking 3D spheres.

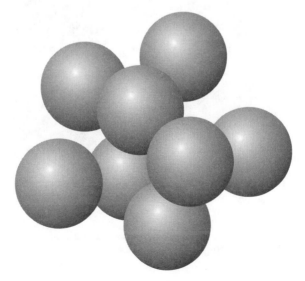

The Mesh Tool

Gradients are pretty cool, but all colors in a gradient fill work in a predictable way, and they must all be in the same direction. As mentioned in Hour 1, "Understanding Illustrator," an advantage of working with raster programs is the capability to create very subtle transitions in color. Illustrator addresses that exact issue with the amazing Mesh tool (see Figure 8.6), which creates gradient mesh objects (see Figure 8.7).

FIGURE 8.6

The Mesh tool.

FIGURE 8.7

An object with a fill created using the Mesh tool.

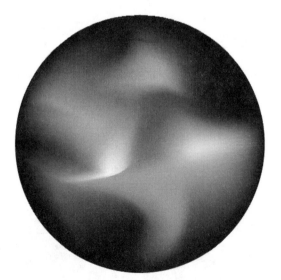

Use the Mesh tool with any filled path to create a gradient mesh object. Every time you click in an empty space, Illustrator will add a pair of mesh lines. When you click on an existing mesh line, a perpendicular line will be added. The mesh points at the intersections of mesh lines (or at the intersection of a mesh line and the object's path) control the appearance of the gradient, as shown in Figure 8.8. You assign a color to the mesh point and use direction lines to control the spread of that color. (Working with the direction lines is basically the same as editing a path with the control lines of anchor points.) Colors can also be applied to the areas within mesh lines, known as mesh patches. Using this tool might sound difficult, but as soon as you try it, you'll understand—which brings you to the next Task.

FIGURE **8.8**

The object selected, with the mesh lines visible.

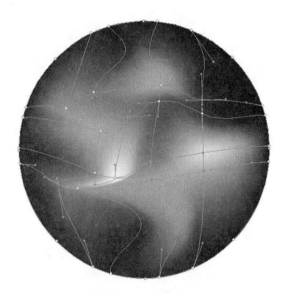

Task: Using the Mesh tool

Creating a gradient mesh isn't hard at all. Just follow these easy steps.

1. Draw a shape. Start with a rectangle to make your job easier.

2. Press the U key to select the Mesh tool. Without pressing the mouse button, move the cursor into the rectangle, and then move it out. Notice how the cursor changes to indicate where you can use the tool (see Figure 8.9) .

3. With the cursor inside the rectangle, click once. A mesh then appears (see Figure 8.10).

▼

FIGURE 8.9

*The cursor on the left
indicates that
Illustrator is ready to
add a mesh to the
object. The cursor on
the right indicates that
you cannot place a
mesh at the current
spot.*

FIGURE 8.10

*After you click inside
the shape, a mesh is
applied to the shape.*

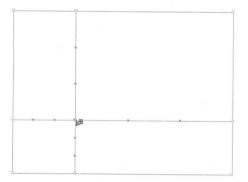

4. Apply a color to this mesh point. Go ahead and select a red color from the
   Swatches palette, or create your own color in the Color palette. The color then
   appears in the mesh (see Figure 8.11). You can tell right away how the gradient
   mesh is unique. Notice how the center, or highest concentration of color, is the
   place where the mesh point is located, where you clicked. More important, notice
   how the gradient stretches and fades out based on the positions of the control
   points and the angles of the mesh lines.

FIGURE 8.11

*The first color applied
to the mesh.*

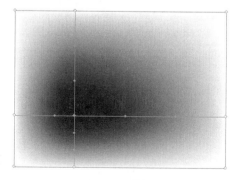

▼

5. Edit the mesh to your liking. Grab a control point or a mesh point, and drag it to a different location. See how the gradient now follows the new path (see Figure 8.12).

FIGURE 8.12

Note how the gradient follows the shape of the mesh.

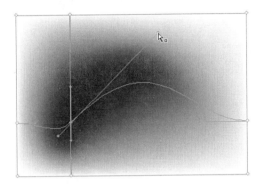

6. Add another mesh point. To do so, find an open area in the same shape and click. More mesh lines are then added to the shape (see Figure 8.13).

FIGURE 8.13

The rectangle with another mesh added.

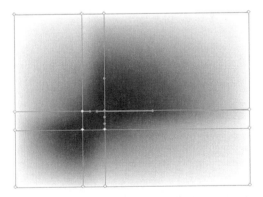

7. Select a new color for the new mesh point you just made. You can add as many mesh points as you like and each one can represent a different color.

8. Delete any single mesh point by pressing and holding the Option (Mac)/Alt (Windows) key while clicking the point with the Mesh tool.

You can use the Mesh tool much like the Pen tool to add mesh points. It will also function like the Direct Selection tool when positioned over a mesh point or control point, enabling you to reposition and distort the gradient.

You can create a gradient mesh in yet another way. With an object selected, in the menu you can choose Object, Create Gradient Mesh (see Figure 8.14). Illustrator prompts you with a dialog box asking how many rows and columns you want in the mesh, how intense the highlight should be, and whether the gradient should face inward or outward (see Figure 8.15) .

FIGURE 8.14

Select the Create Gradient Mesh option from the Object menu.

FIGURE 8.15

The Create Gradient Mesh dialog box.

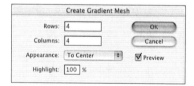

If you want to add or delete anchor points in an object with a gradient, you can use the Pen tool as you would on any Illustrator path. However, you cannot add or delete mesh points with the Pen tool. You can delete only the anchor points that define the shape of the object. You can also use the Convert Anchor Point tool for fine control over control points.

A few comments about the Mesh tool before we move on. The Mesh tool takes advantage of certain technologies, mainly the PostScript Level 3 page description language. The Mesh tool also requires a lot of computer power because each mesh point that you add slows down the system, as well as the screen redraw.

Patterns

NEW TERM Patterns can be real timesavers. A pattern is a defined piece of art, or *tile*, created in Illustrator that, as a Fill or Stroke attribute, is repeated over and over again, much like wallpaper (see Figure 8.16).

FIGURE 8.16

Here are several pattern tiles and what they look like when used to fill an object.

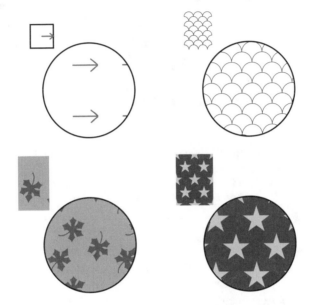

Defining a Pattern

Defining a pattern is a little different from defining gradients or colors. Instead of clicking the New Swatch icon, you drag your objects directly into the Swatches palette to define the pattern. Again, after you create the swatch, you need to give it a unique name so that you can find and edit it quickly.

When you're creating a pattern design, remember that your object will be repeated over and over again, so be careful how you set it up. If you need extra space around your art, create a box with a fill and stroke of None, and send it to the back of your artwork. Then select your art, along with the background box, and define the pattern. Illustrator treats that empty box as the boundary for the pattern tile (see Figure 8.17).

FIGURE 8.17

The patterns with their bounding boxes (top) and the way they appear in a filled object (bottom).

A pattern tile cannot contain another pattern or a gradient. If you want to have a gradient effect or use a pattern within your pattern, use the Expand command to convert the gradient or pattern into individual filled objects. The Expand command is covered later in this hour.

To edit a pattern, drag the new artwork on top of the swatch you want to change while pressing the Option (Mac)/Alt (Windows) key. Also, if you lose the artwork for your pattern, don't worry. When you drag a pattern swatch out of the Swatches palette and onto the page, the objects that make up the pattern are placed onto the page as new objects, just as if you had drawn them there.

To move the pattern around within the object, select the object with the Selection tool, and then click and drag the object's fill or stroke (whichever has the pattern) while holding down the tilde (~) key. When you let go, only the pattern is repositioned; the object does not move.

Using the Expand Command

NEW TERM *Gradients* can sometimes pose printing problems. They are very complex. There are also some effects and filters that can't be applied to gradients. You can get around both of these problems with Illustrator's Expand command. Expanding converts the gradient fill to a series of blended objects. To expand a gradient, select the object on the artboard and choose Expand from the Object menu (see Figure 8.18). You'll be able to specify how many steps Illustrator uses in the blend.

FIGURE 8.18

Choose Expand.

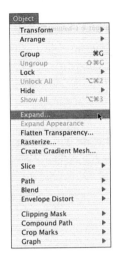

8

You might also find yourself in a situation where a file must be compatible with early version of Illustrator, version 5 or earlier. Gradients didn't exist in Illustrator back then, so make sure that you expand any gradients before saving the file.

You can also expand an object filled or stroked with a pattern. By doing so, the fill or stroke that until now has not been editable becomes editable and ceases being a pattern. The shape also becomes a mask that blocks out parts of the pattern tiles that should not be visible (see Figure 8.19). See Hour 16, "Showing and Hiding with Masks," for more information on masks.

FIGURE 8.19

From the top, a pattern and gradient as viewed in Preview mode, the same pattern and gradient viewed in Artwork mode, and on the bottom, the same pattern and gradient viewed in Artwork mode after being expanded.

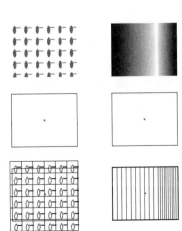

Strokes

A stroke is the line around an object. You can give an object's stroke a different color than its fill. You also have several stroke options, which actually make for some very interesting and useful implementations, as we'll soon find out.

The Stroke Palette

The Stroke palette (F10) can be set either to show only the stroke weight or all the stroke attributes including Miter Limit, Line Caps and Joins, and Dashed Lines (see Figure 8.20). You can choose either setting by selecting Show Options from the palette menu.

FIGURE 8.20

A view of the entire Stroke palette.

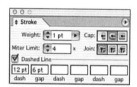

Weight and Miter Limit

NEW TERM   The most-used option in the Stroke palette is the *stroke weight*. It determines how thick or thin the stroke is. Illustrator's default is 1 point. For hairline rules, most people use .25 point. You can enter any amount from 0 to 1,000 points. You can even enter numbers in different measurements (such as 2.5 in.), and Illustrator converts them to points for you.

NEW TERM   The *Miter Limit* option determines how far the stroke sticks out on a sharp corner. A thick line, for example, needs more room to complete a sharp point than a thin one does (see Figure 8.21).

Line Caps and Joins

NEW TERM   *Line caps* determine the ends of a stroked path. This setting in the Stroke palette is used only for open-ended paths. By choosing different caps, you can make the ends either flat or rounded or have the stroke width enclose the end of the path as well (see Figure 8.22).

FIGURE 8.21

From the left, a 2-point stroke with a miter limit of 2, a 20-point stroke with a miter limit of 2, and a 20-point stroke with a miter limit of 4.

8

FIGURE 8.22

The three types of line caps. Notice how the last two actually protrude one-half the stroke weight from the actual anchor point.

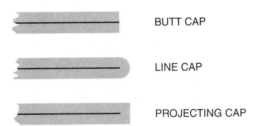

BUTT CAP

LINE CAP

PROJECTING CAP

Line joins control how the stroke appears at each corner on the path. You can choose Mitered, Round, or Beveled joins (see Figure 8.23) .

FIGURE 8.23

A star with (from left) mitered, round, and beveled joins.

Dashed Lines

New Term The last option in the Stroke palette, Dashed Lines, can be one of the most powerful. Here, you can specify dashed or dotted lines. Depending on what settings you have set for weight, line caps, and joins, you can create a *stitched line*, a *skip line*, or almost anything. You control the *dash* and *gap* (the space between each dash) by entering numbers into the Dash and Gap fields at the bottom of the palette. If you're only using one sequence, you can enter just the first two fields. Alternatively, you can enter up to three different Dash and Gap settings to achieve complex dash patterns (see Figure 8.24) .

Figure 8.24

Here are a variety of strokes with different Dash and Gap settings. The last stroke uses round caps to achieve the dotted line effect.

(1, 6, 6, 1)

(2, 10, 10, 10)

(2, 8,8)

(12, 2)

(4, 2, 4, 20)

(1, 6 — Round Cap)

Offset Path and Outline Path

For outlining and special effects, Offset Path is a great function. Offset Path creates an object that perfectly outlines, or traces, a selected path at a distance that you specify. To use it, select one or more objects, and choose Object, Path, Offset Path (see Figure 8.25). The Offset Path dialog box then appears (see Figure 8.26). Enter an amount to offset and click OK. Positive numbers move the copy outside the original, and you can use negative numbers to create a smaller copy inside the original. Note that Offset Path always makes a copy of your selection and does not affect the original (see Figure 8.27) .

> You might notice that the Offset Path command produces what look like extra lines in each object (see Figure 8.27). To clean up these lines use the Pathfinder Unite function (it's the first button on the upper left of the Pathfinder palette). Running this function right after you use Offset Path is best because your selection is still active. (You can find more details on the Unite and Pathfinder commands in Hour 12, "Using Transformations, Compound Shapes, and Blends.")

FIGURE 8.25

Choose Offset Path from the Object menu.

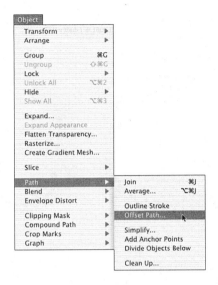

FIGURE 8.26

You can select one of three Join options: Round, Bevel, and Miter.

FIGURE 8.27

The result of using Offset Path.

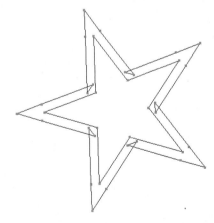

Outline Stroke is another great feature that converts strokes into filled objects (see Figure 8.28). Found in the same location as the Offset Path command, the Outline Stroke command works by taking the stroke width and creating a filled shape the size of the stroke width (see Figure 8.29). This feature can be a real timesaver when troubleshooting in a production environment. It also enables workarounds, such as filling an outlined stroke with a gradient (a gradient cannot be applied to a stroke).

FIGURE 8.28
On the left, a stroked path. On the right, the path converted to an outline.

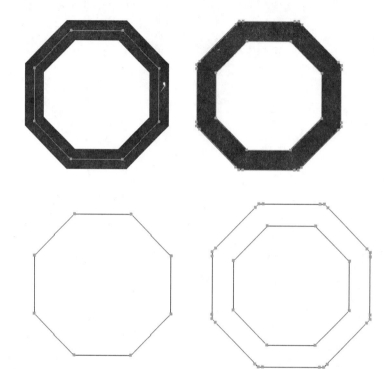

FIGURE 8.29
With the same images viewed in Artwork mode, you can see how the stroke has been outlined.

Unfortunately, Outline Stroke does not use dash information when converting a path to an outline. When you use this option, the path (actually the object) becomes solid.

Summary

Are you all filled up? In this hour, you learned how to fill your shapes not only with flat solid colors, but also with interesting multicolor gradients and patterns. You also learned that strokes are a good thing (at least in Illustrator). You learned about stroke weight and how different joins and caps can change a stroke's appearance. In the next hour, we'll take this concept further and apply it using the Paintbrush, too.

Workshop

In the previous hour you learned about color in Illustrator. In this hour, we showed you how to apply that color to objects in productive and creative ways. We're going to run a few questions past you, then we'll turn you lose to complete some fun exercises.

Q&A

Q Can I apply opacity settings to gradients or patterns?

A Yes, you can make gradients or patterns overlap each other and apply opacity settings to them via the Transparency palette. Be forewarned, however, that transparency effects applied to complex patterns can lead to large files and long print times.

Q Can a single object have more than one gradient applied to it?

A Yes, it can, but you'll have to wait until you get to Hour 11, "Applying Appearances and Styles," to learn how.

Q Will the Outline Stroke function work accurately when the Round or Projecting cap feature is used?

A Yes, Outline Stroke will correctly convert a path to outlines taking into account the Cap setting.

Q After I expand a gradient or pattern, can I still edit it?

A No, you cannot edit it as a gradient or a pattern anymore. However, you can edit each individual object as you would any other object.

Quiz

1. The diamond-shaped icon above the gradient bar is called the

    a. Color stop

    b. Midpoint indicator

    c. Swatch

2. To define a pattern, you drag your artwork where?

    a. Into the Swatches palette

    b. Into the Pattern palette

    c. Into the Color palette

3. The Expand command is used for gradients only.

    a. True

    b. False

4. Stroke weight is

    a. A heart condition

    b. The thickness of a line

    c. Another term for how long a line is

5. Illustrator offers three Join options for strokes. The first is Miter, the second is Round, and the third is

    a. Square

    b. Oval

    c. Bevel

Quiz Answers

1. b. It controls the midpoint between the colors, not necessarily between the color stops on the gradient bar. It doesn't have to be at the 50% point, and can be as close as the 13% mark to either color stop.

2. a. Patterns are stored in the Swatches palette, along with color and gradient swatches.

3. b. Nope! You can use it on patterns, too.

4. b. By default, the weight of a stroke (its thickness) is measured in points (1 pt = 1/72 inch). However, the Preferences allow you to change that to pixels or inches or centimeters or any of Illustrator's other units of measure.

5. c. You'll find this option when you expand the Stroke palette, and in the Offset Path dialog box.

Exercises

1. Try creating gradients and then adjusting the gradient angle and midpoint location. Also try achieving the same effects using the Gradient tool.

2. Use the Offset Path function to quickly create outlines and borders around grouped objects. Use positive numbers to create an outline that is larger than the original, and use negative numbers to create an inner line that is smaller than the original.

3. Create a large rectangle on the artboard. Grab the Mesh tool and start clicking. When you have a dozen or more mesh lines running here and there, start assigning colors to the mesh points. Drag points to rearrange them. Work with the direction lines to reshape the mesh.

4. Create a circle. Fill it with the Honeycomb pattern. Use the Expand command to expand the fill. Get the Direct Selection tool from the Toolbox. Click once, away from the circle to deselect, and then click on individual components of the pattern. Try it with other patterns in the Swatches palette. Get a feel for how many individual objects are used to create a pattern.

8

HOUR 9

The Paintbrush Tool

Now it's time to put a little pizzazz and spunk into your drawings. The Paintbrush tool in Illustrator is very powerful, allowing for some really cool drawing possibilities. Actually, this tool is made up of four different kinds of brushes. These brushes are called *live* brushes because you can edit the strokes they create even after you've drawn them, and Illustrator recalculates and redraws them as necessary.

In this hour, you will learn about the following:

- The Brushes palette
- The Calligraphic brush
- The Scatter brush
- The Art brush
- The Pattern brush

The Brushes Palette

Before you learn about the different kinds of brushes themselves, you first need to meet the Paintbrush tool's partner-in-crime, the Brushes palette.

Remember as a child when you played with the Play-Doh Fun Factory? You would squeeze the Play-Doh through one end, and you could put different attachments on the other end that would determine the shape the Play-Doh came out. Well, the Paintbrush tool is like the Play-Doh factory, and the Brushes palette is your set of attachments; only your hands don't smell like Play-Doh when you're finished.

Open the Brushes palette now, and take a look at what it has to offer. You open this palette by choosing Brushes from the Window menu (see Figure 9.1). Illustrator has a default collection of brushes that are already loaded into the Brushes palette (see Figure 9.2). You can easily tell which brush is selected by the double outline, as evident in Figure 9.2, where the Banana Leaf brush is selected.

FIGURE 9.1

Open the Brushes palette.

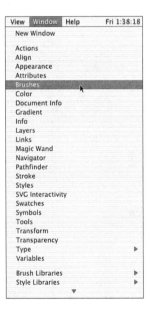

Illustrator comes with many preset brushes. To load other Brush palettes, choose Window, Brush Libraries, and choose from the list of other brush sets.

While you are looking at the Brushes palette, take note of the two buttons on the bottom right of the palette. (Two other buttons to the left are grayed out, totaling four; I'll get to those in a little bit.) They are the New Brush and the Delete Brush buttons. You can create a new brush by clicking the New Brush button, and you can duplicate an existing brush by dragging an existing brush shape onto the New Brush button. You can delete brushes either by selecting them and clicking the Delete Brush button, or you can drag selected brush shapes directly on top of the Delete Brush button and release the mouse button. Illustrator then asks you to verify that you want to delete the brush shape.

FIGURE 9.2

This is the Brushes palette. Notice the double outline, indicating that the Banana Leaf brush is selected.

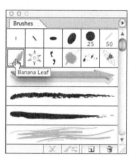

Drawing with the Paintbrush Tool

I can tell that you're already itching to use the Paintbrush tool, so take the time now to draw a couple of items before visiting the four kinds of brushes Illustrator has to offer. Drawing with the Paintbrush tool is easy. Just select the Paintbrush tool, shown in Figure 9.3, press the mouse button, and drag. Release the mouse button as you complete each stroke in your drawing.

FIGURE 9.3

The Paintbrush tool.

When you're using the Paintbrush tool, several options can change the way the paintbrush works. Double-click the Paintbrush tool in the Toolbox, and Illustrator presents you with the Paintbrush Tool Preferences dialog box, as shown in Figure 9.4. The Fidelity and Smoothness options affect how smooth and clean your paintbrush strokes appear. Of course, drawing with the mouse is difficult, so Illustrator smoothes your paths as you draw them. Lower Fidelity and Smoothness settings result in more ragged strokes, and higher settings result in smoother, less-jerky strokes. Note that there are three other options here: Fill New Brush Strokes, which determines whether you want your paint-brush strokes to have a Fill attribute (covered previously in Hour 8, "Using Fills, Strokes, and Gradients"); Keep Selected, which tells Illustrator whether you want a paintbrush stroke to stay selected immediately after you draw it (you learned all about selections in Hour 4, "Making Selections"); and Edit Selected Paths, which, if enabled, enables you to simply draw over an existing path to change it.

FIGURE 9.4

The different options available with the Paintbrush tool.

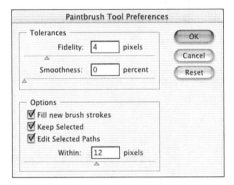

Now take a look at each of the four kinds of brushes the Paintbrush tool offers.

The Calligraphic Brush

A calligraphy pen has an angled tip, or *nib*, which, when used to draw or write, creates a tapered line that gets thicker or thinner, depending on the angle and direction of the stroke (see Figure 9.5). The Calligraphic brush simulates this effect. Illustrator has many options for controlling the Calligraphic brush, and they're worth a look.

FIGURE 9.5

A stroke drawn with the Calligraphic brush.

Task: Setting Up a Calligraphic Brush

▼ TASK

To get started with this tool, do the following:

1. If the Brushes palette isn't already open, open it by choosing Brushes from the Window menu.

2. In the upper-right corner of the Brushes palette is a little right-facing triangle. By clicking and holding the mouse button down on it, you are presented with the Brushes palette pop-up menu. In the middle of the menu are four options: Show Calligraphic Brushes, Show Scatter Brushes, Show Art Brushes, and Show Pattern Brushes. A check mark next to each one means those kinds of brushes are visible in the Brushes palette (see Figure 9.6). Hide all brushes except for the Calligraphic ones for now. You should see only the Calligraphic brushes in the palette now (see Figure 9.7).

FIGURE 9.6

View of the Brushes palette pop-up menu.

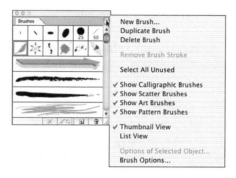

FIGURE 9.7

The Brushes palette with only the Calligraphic brushes visible.

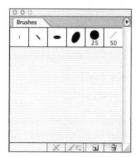

3. Double-click any of the Calligraphic brushes in the Brushes palette to open the Calligraphic Brush Options dialog box, as shown in Figure 9.8.

FIGURE 9.8

The Calligraphic Brush Options dialog box.

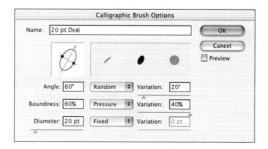

In the Calligraphic Brush Options dialog box, you can specify exactly how the tip of the brush should function. I'll go through each of the options with you:

- At the top of the box, you can specify a name for the brush.
- Directly underneath the name is a white box with a picture of an ellipse with an arrow going through it and two black dots on either side. This is the Brush Shape Editor. Simply click and drag on the arrow to rotate the brush shape and adjust its angle. Click and drag inward or outward on the black dots to adjust the roundness of the brush shape.
- To the immediate right of the Brush Shape Editor is a window that shows you a preview of your brush shape. Notice the three shapes. The outer two are grayed out, and the center one is black. If you have variations set (which I'll get to in a minute), the gray shapes illustrate the minimum and maximum values for the brush shape.
- The next three options are numerical values that you can enter for the brush shape. They are Angle, Roundness, and Diameter. These values are automatically adjusted when you edit the brush shape by using the Brush Shape Editor you just learned about. Each of these options can also have three attributes:
    - Random: Illustrator randomly changes the setting.
    - Pressure: Uses information collected from a pressure-sensitive tablet to calculate how the brush changes as you draw.
    - Fixed: The number you have specified remains constant.

  For each of these attributes, you can specify how much of a variation is allowed by using the Variation sliders that follow each option.

Before going on to the next kind of brush, I'd like to introduce you to two other buttons at the bottom of the Brushes palette. You need to have a stroke selected for these buttons to work, so if you haven't already drawn one, do so now. The first button on the left is Remove Brush Stroke. Clicking this button removes the Paintbrush attribute from the path and turns it into an ordinary Bézier path. The one on the right controls the options of the selected object. In this way, you can edit the brush properties of just the selected stroke, without having it affect any other strokes in your document that use that brush.

The Scatter Brush

Imagine if you could dip your paintbrush into a bucket of nice fall leaves, and, when you painted, each stroke left a trail of the autumn icons. Well, wake up and smell the flowers because that's exactly what the Scatter brush does—well, not with real leaves, silly (see Figure 9.9). The Scatter brush takes predefined art and distributes it along the stroke you draw with the Paintbrush tool.

FIGURE 9.9

*A stroke drawn with
the Scatter brush.*

Task: Setting Up a Scatter Brush

Perform the following steps to use the Scatter brush:

1. If the Brushes palette isn't already open, open it by choosing Brushes from the
   Window menu.

2. In the preceding exercise, remember that you hid all brushes except for the
   Calligraphic ones. Show the Scatter brushes by selecting Show Scatter Brushes
   from the Brushes palette pop-up menu. You should now see the previous
   Calligraphic brushes and the Scatter brushes below them, as shown in Figure 9.10.

FIGURE 9.10

*The Brushes palette
with both the
Calligraphic and
Scatter brushes visible.*

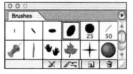

3. Double-click any of the Scatter brushes in the Brushes palette to open the Scatter
   Brush Options dialog box (see Figure 9.11).

Figure 9.11

*The Scatter Brush
Options dialog box.*

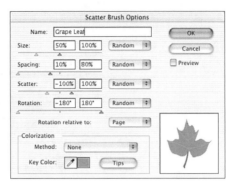

In the Scatter Brush Options dialog box, you can specify exactly how the tip of the brush should function. I'll go through each of the options with you:

- At the top of the box, you can specify a name for the brush.

- Directly underneath are four options in which you can enter numerical values to specify the size of the art when it's drawn on the path; the spacing between the art as it appears on the stroke; the scatter, which defines how far from the path the art can stray; and finally, the rotation, which specifies the rotation of each individual piece of art on the path. You can set the Rotation value to be relative to the page or to the actual path itself. For each of these four settings, you can specify fixed values, random, or pressure, just as you could in the Calligraphic brushes. The Pressure option works only if you are using a pressure-sensitive tablet, such as a Wacom tablet.

- The final option for the Scatter brush is Colorization. This option enables you to make color changes to the art that appears on your painted strokes. Choosing None keeps the color consistent with the original color defined with the brush you have selected. To use the Hue Shift option, click the Eyedropper box, and click to choose a color from the art that appears in the box to the right. This procedure works on colored images only, not black-and-white images. Clicking the Tips button can help you see how the color changes are applied.

To create a Scatter brush of your own, simply drag your art into the Brushes palette. When Illustrator asks you which kind of brush you want to create, select Scatter Brush and click OK. After you name your new Scatter brush and make any necessary adjustments, click OK and it will appear in the Brushes palette with the other brushes.

The Art Brush

The Art brush differs from the Scatter brush in that the Art brush stretches a single piece of predefined art along a stroke (see Figure 9.12), whereas the Scatter brush litters the stroke with many copies of the art.

FIGURE 9.12
*A stroke drawn with
the Art brush.*

9

Task: Setting Up an Art Brush

You can use the Art brush as follows:

1. If the Brushes palette isn't already open, open it by choosing Brushes from the Window menu.

2. As you did in the preceding exercise, you need to show the Art brushes, which you hid earlier. Select Show Art Brushes from the Brushes palette pop-up menu, and scroll down to the bottom of the palette. You should now see the Art brushes (see Figure 9.13).

FIGURE 9.13
*View of the Art brushes
in the Brushes palette.*

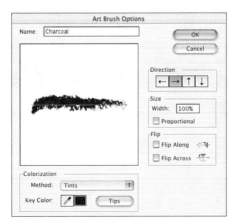

3. Double-click any of the Art brushes in the Brushes palette to open the Art Brush Options dialog box (see Figure 9.14) .

FIGURE 9.14
*The Art Brush Options
dialog box.*

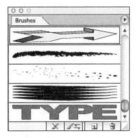

▲

In the Art Brush Options dialog box, you can specify exactly how the tip of the brush should function. I'll go through each of the options with you:

- At the top of the box, you can specify a name for the brush.
- Directly underneath the name is a white box with the art in it. Notice that an arrow goes through the art. This arrow indicates the direction the art is drawn on the stroke; you can edit it by clicking any of the arrows that appear to the right of the white box.
- Below the Direction option is the Size option, in which you can specify what size the art appears on the painted stroke. If you click the Proportional button, the artwork will retain its height-to-width relationship for the length of the stroke. You can also specify whether the art should be flipped along or across the painted stroke.
- The final option for the Art brush is Colorization. This option enables you to make color changes to the art that appears on your painted strokes. Choosing None keeps the color consistent with the original color defined with the brush you have selected. To use the Hue Shift option, click the Eyedropper box, and click to choose a color from the art that appears in the white box above. Clicking the Tips button can help you see how the color changes are applied.

To create an Art brush of your own, simply drag your art into the Brushes palette. When Illustrator asks you which kind of brush you want to create, select Art Brush and click OK. After you name your new Art brush and make any necessary adjustments, click OK and it will appear in the Brushes palette with the other brushes.

The Pattern Brush

You have to give Adobe credit. Just when you think it has given you every kind of brush you could possibly dream of, it throws in one more. The Pattern brush takes patterns and applies them across a painted stroke. What makes this different from any brush you've encountered previously is that you can define patterns with different attributes for corners and ends, as shown in Figure 9.15. We covered patterns in detail in Hour 8, so I'll just touch on the subject here.

FIGURE 9.15

A stroke drawn with the Pattern brush. Notice how the corners line up perfectly.

Task: Setting Up a Pattern Brush

To use the Pattern brush, do the following:

1. If the Brushes palette isn't already open, open it by choosing Brushes from the Window menu.

2. Select Show Pattern Brushes from the Brushes palette pop-up menu, and scroll down to the bottom of the palette. You should now see the Pattern brushes (see Figure 9.16) .

FIGURE 9.16

View of the Pattern brushes in the Brushes palette.

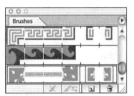

3. Double-click any of the Pattern brushes in the Brushes palette to open the Pattern Brush Options dialog box (see Figure 9.17).

FIGURE 9.17

The Pattern Brush Options dialog box.

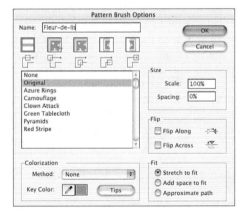

In the Pattern Brush Options dialog box, you can specify exactly how the tip of the brush should function. As before, let me go through each of the options with you:

- At the top of the box, you can specify a name for the brush.

- Directly underneath the name are five boxes, each representing a different tile of the pattern: Side, Outer Corner, Inner Corner, Start, and End. You do not need to define all five parts, and Illustrator uses the parts only when necessary. With a tile section selected, choose a pattern from the list that appears directly under the tiles.

- As with the previous brushes, you can specify Size and Spacing, as well as specify if the pattern should be flipped along or across.

- With the Pattern brush, you can decide how Illustrator fits the pattern to the path. Obviously, not every pattern will fit every path length perfectly. If you select Stretch to Fit, Illustrator stretches the pattern tiles to make the pattern fit seamlessly across the entire painted stroke. If you select Add Space to Fit, Illustrator does not adjust the size of the pattern tiles, but spaces them evenly across the painted stroke. Finally, the Approximate Path option adjusts the size of the stroke to fit the size of the pattern tiles, without changing the path itself (which means the stroke doesn't necessarily sit along the path at all points).

- The final option for the Pattern brush is Colorization. This option enables you to make color changes to the art that appears on your painted strokes. Choosing None keeps the color consistent with the original defined with the brush you have selected. To use the Hue Shift option, click the Eyedropper box, and click to choose a color from the art that appears in the white box above. Clicking the Tips button can help you see how the color changes are applied.

To create a Pattern brush of your own, simply drag your art into the Brushes palette. When Illustrator asks you which kind of brush you want to create, select Pattern Brush and click OK. After you name your new Pattern brush and make any necessary adjustments, click OK and it will appear in the Brushes palette with the other brushes. For detailed information on creating pattern tiles, refer back to Hour 8.

In closing, if you find it hard to tell what type each brush is just by looking at the Brushes palette, you can opt to view the brushes by name. Choose List View from the Brushes palette pop-up menu. Notice that on the far right of each line is an icon that indicates what kind of brush each one is (see Figure 9.18) .

FIGURE 9.18

When viewing your brushes by name, you can quickly tell what kind of brush each one is from the icon that appears to the right of each name.

You can apply a paintbrush stroke to any shape that you learned to draw earlier in Hour 3, "Creating Objects." Apply Art or Scatter brushes to spirals and stars for some really interesting effects. To remove a paintbrush stroke from these shapes, just click the Remove Brush Stroke button at the bottom of the Brushes palette.

9

Task: Creating a Complex Pattern Brush

Many people overlook the sheer power of the Pattern Brush. The following is a really cool example that will give you just a glimpse of that power—drawing a treasure map.

1. First, you will create all the elements you will be using in your brush and define them as patterns. We will use simple shapes for this exercise, although you are free to use your imagination. To start, draw a square and fill it with any color you'd like. This will be your starting point.

2. Drag the square into the Swatches palette to define it as a pattern. Double-click the swatch you just created and name it Start, as shown in Figure 9.19.

FIGURE 9.19

Name the new pattern swatch Start.

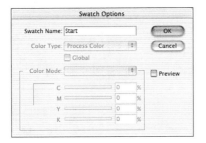

3. Next, draw a narrow rectangle and fill it with another color. This will become the steps or dashes on your map (see Figure 9.20) .

FIGURE 9.20

The steps for your treasure map.

4. Drag the rectangle into the Swatches palette to define it as a pattern. Double-click the swatch you just created and name it Dash.

5. Now you'll draw some landmarks. Make a star and a polygon and define them each as patterns as you've done before. To make things easy, call them Star and Polygon, respectively.

6. Now draw a circle and define it as a pattern called Treasure.

7. OK, it's time to define your new Pattern Brush. In the Brushes palette, click the New Brush button, select New Pattern Brush, and click OK.

8. For the first tile (Side Tile), select Dash (see Figure 9.21) .

FIGURE 9.21

Define the Dash pattern as the Side Tile.

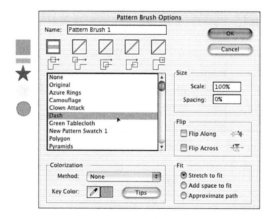

9. Select the Outer Corner Tile icon and select Star (see Figure 9.22).

FIGURE 9.22

Define the Star pattern as the Outer Corner Tile.

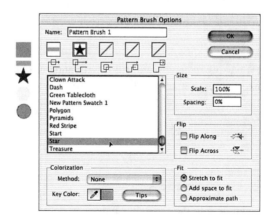

10. For the Inner Corner Tile, use the Polygon pattern (see Figure 9.23).

FIGURE 9.23

Define the Polygon pattern as the Inner Corner tile.

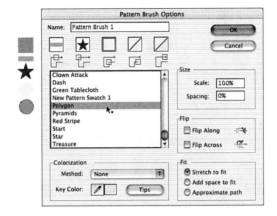

11. For the Start Tile, use the Start pattern and specify the Treasure pattern for the End Tile.

12. You'll want some space between each of the objects when the pattern brush is drawn, so set the size spacing to 20%. Also, because you want the path to be filled from end to end, choose the Add space to fit option (see Figure 9.24) .

FIGURE 9.24

Adjusting the Size and Fit options.

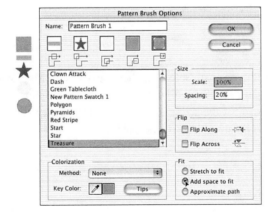

13. Finally, name the Pattern Brush Treasure Map and click OK to define it (see Figure 9.25).

14. Now comes the really fun part! Draw a path for your treasure map. Be sure to include a few corner points so all the tiles you defined will be used (see Figure 9.26).

▼

FIGURE 9.25

Name the new Pattern Brush.

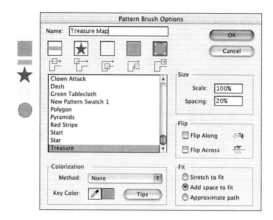

FIGURE 9.26

Draw a path for the map.

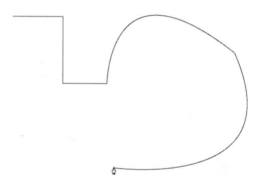

15. Ready? With your path selected, click the Treasure Map pattern brush in the Brushes palette. Pretty cool, don't you think (see Figure 9.27)? Remember that you can always adjust the sizing and spacing of the pattern brush simply by double-clicking the brush in the Brushes palette.

FIGURE 9.27

The finished Treasure map.

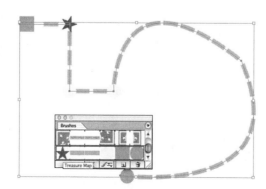

▲

Summary

Isn't the Paintbrush tool cool? This hour, you learned how to use the Paintbrush tool to create all different kinds of art. In addition to learning how to use the Calligraphic, Scatter, Art, and Pattern brushes, you now know how to create and edit the brush shapes and brush art themselves, as well as load brush libraries. (There are plenty on the Adobe Illustrator CD-ROM.) But just when you thought the Paintbrush tool was the coolest thing you have ever seen—look out. In Hour 11, you'll learn about Object Styles and that will change *everything*.

9

Workshop

The Paintbrush and the Brushes palette give you an incredible amount of creative freedom in Illustrator. The following questions and exercises will help you refine that power.

Q&A

Q **If I edit a brush after I've already drawn several objects with that brush, will my edits apply to the objects I've already drawn?**

A If you edit a brush that's currently applied to an object already in your document, Illustrator will ask you if you want the edits to apply to new objects only, or those that already exist as well.

Q **Can I define a brush stroke with an object that uses gradients?**

A No, gradient-filled objects cannot be used to define brushes, but if you expand the gradient and then define the brush, Illustrator will accept that.

Q **If I don't have a pressure-sensitive tablet, is there any way to use the variable settings?**

A Not really. While you can use the Random setting, it does the opposite of using a pressure-sensitive palette. Rather than increasing your control, Random lessens it. It can be fun, however.

Q **Can I send custom brushes I've created to friends?**

A Certainly. Simply save your Illustrator file and send it to your friend. He or she can either open your file directly, or choose Other Library from the Window, Brush Libraries submenu.

Quiz

1. How many brush types are available in the Paintbrush tool?

   a. 3

   b. 4

   c. 5

2. What affects the smoothness of a painted stroke?

   a. Spacing

   b. Colorization

   c. Fidelity

3. You can't change the brush options of one path without affecting all other paths with the same brush attribute.

   a. True

   b. False

4. The Brush Shape Editor is used with which type of brush?

   a. Art

   b. Pattern

   c. Calligraphic

Quiz Answers

1. b. The four types of brushes are Calligraphic, Scatter, Art, and Pattern.

2. c. Fidelity controls how closely the brush stroke will follow the cursor's path.

3. b. When you change a brush, Illustrator will ask you if you want to apply the change to existing brush strokes. You can always Just Say No.

4. c. The Brush Shape Editor is that cool interactive preview to the left in the Calligraphic Brush Options dialog box.

Exercises

1. Using the Paintbrush tool, draw several strokes. Now using the Selection tool, change the paths to use different kinds of brushes.

2. Remember that brushes are live, meaning that if you change the path itself, the brushstroke artwork will reconfigure to the path. Try using the Pen tool to edit the same paths you drew in the preceding exercise, and watch what happens.

3. Create your own brushes by dragging artwork right onto the Brushes palette. Also, load some of the brush libraries that came on the Adobe Illustrator CD-ROM. See if you can reverse engineer them to see how they work.

HOUR 10

Adding Text

Illustrator would be incomplete without text capabilities. Whether you're designing a logo, creating a headline and body copy for an ad, or creating a caption for a technical illustration, Illustrator can handle it. Text alone can also be a powerful way of graphic expression. Illustrator works with type in a variety of ways and, as you go through this hour, you'll learn where and when to use each one.

Topics covered in this hour include the following:

- Point text
- Area text
- Text on a path

Using the Type Tool

Illustrator has three types of text: point text, area text, and text on a path. To create text in Illustrator, you use one of the many type tools found in the Toolbox (see Figure 10.1).

FIGURE 10.1

Type tools for every occasion.

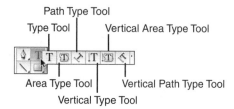

Path Type Tool
Type Tool   Vertical Area Type Tool
Area Type Tool   Vertical Path Type Tool
Vertical Type Tool

Point Text

NEW TERM The most popular kind of text in Illustrator is point text. Also called headline text, *point text* takes its position and orientation from a single point, meaning that justification (such as left, right, or centered) is based on that one point (see Figure 10.2). Creating point text is also very easy. With the Type tool (T) selected, just click a blank area anywhere on the page and start typing.

FIGURE 10.2

Although the points are aligned vertically, the type can be aligned to the right, center, or left of the point.

Left

Center

Right

Editing Text

After you create the text, you can edit it by simply using the Type tool to click and drag over letters. This action highlights the text, as shown in Figure 10.3, and typing something new replaces the highlighted text. To simply add text to an existing block of type, click where you want the type to begin, and a blinking cursor appears; ready for you to add text. (In this respect, Illustrator functions much like any modern word processing program.)

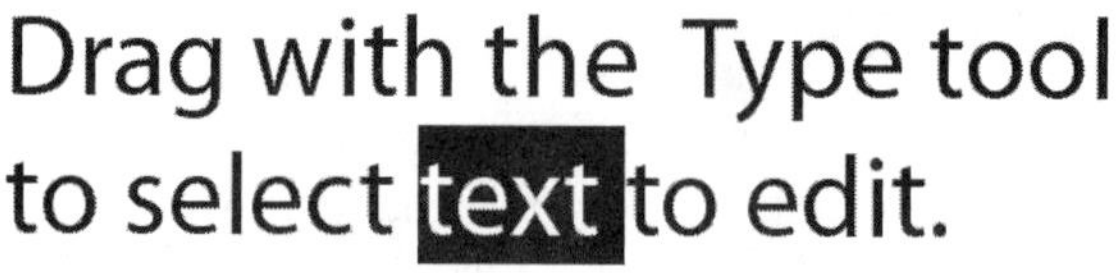

FIGURE 10.3

The text is selected.

Drag with the Type tool
to select text to edit.

Before you begin using the Type tool, let me remind you that your Preferences dialog box contains an option on how to select text blocks: Type Area Select (under File, Preferences, Type & Auto Tracing). With Type Area Select activated, you can select a text block by clicking anywhere within the type's bounding box with the Selection or Direct Selection tool. With Type Area Select turned off, you must click the baseline to select the text block. If you have trouble selecting text blocks because other objects get in the way, lock or hide those objects first, and then you can select and edit your type easily.

Creating Area Text

 Area text, also called body text, is defined by a shape—much like QuarkXPress, in which all type must be within a text box (see Figure 10.4).

10

FIGURE 10.4

Type within a circle.

Text can be contained within an object. The object can then be called, quite naturally, a "container." The type uses the object's path as its boundaries, never straying outside. The paragraph will automatically "wrap" from the end of one line to the beginning of the next as it reaches the side of the object. In Illustrator, we call this type "area text."

You can create area text in several ways:

- With the Area Type tool selected, as in Figure 10.5, click an existing path (an object or a line). Any type you enter fills the interior of the path.

FIGURE 10.5

Selecting the Area Type tool from the Toolbox.

- With the Type tool selected, click and drag diagonally to draw a box (see Figure 10.6). Any type you enter fills the interior of the path.

FIGURE 10.6

*Draw a text box with
the Type tool.*

- With the Type tool selected, click an existing path. As you drag your cursor over a path, it changes to the Area Type tool cursor, as shown in Figure 10.7. Any type you enter fills the interior of the path.

FIGURE 10.7

*Dragging the Type tool
cursor over a path
turns it into the Area
Type tool cursor.*

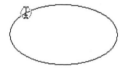

Linking Text Blocks

If you have more type than can fit into the selected shape, a small plus sign in a box appears at the lower right of the shape (see Figure 10.8). The symbol indicates that more text overflows from the shape.

FIGURE 10.8

*The cursor is pointing
to the little plus sign
symbol that indicates a
text overflow.*

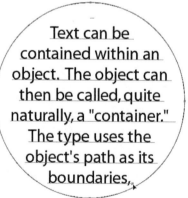

Illustrator enables you to link shapes so that overflow type from the first shape flows into the next shape. You can do so by selecting the object with the overflowing type, along with the object that you want to link it with. Then choose Type, Blocks, Link (see Figure 10.9).

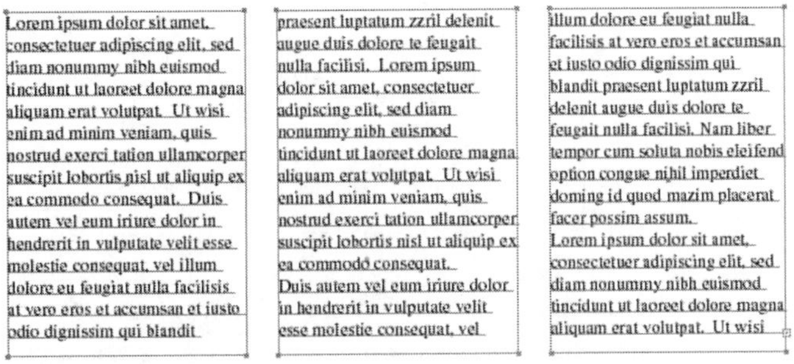

FIGURE 10.9

Linked text blocks.

Lorem ipsum dolor sit amet, consectetuer adipiscing elit, sed diam nonummy nibh euismod tincidunt ut laoreet dolore magna aliquam erat volutpat. Ut wisi enim ad minim veniam, quis nostrud exerci tation ullamcorper suscipit lobortis nisl ut aliquip ex ea commodo consequat. Duis autem vel eum iriure dolor in hendrerit in vulputate velit esse molestie consequat, vel illum dolore eu feugiat nulla facilisis at vero eros et accumsan et iusto odio dignissim qui blandit

praesent luptatum zzril delenit augue duis dolore te feugait nulla facilisi. Lorem ipsum dolor sit amet, consectetuer adipiscing elit, sed diam nonummy nibh euismod tincidunt ut laoreet dolore magna aliquam erat volutpat. Ut wisi enim ad minim veniam, quis nostrud exerci tation ullamcorper suscipit lobortis nisl ut aliquip ex ea commodo consequat. Duis autem vel eum iriure dolor in hendrerit in vulputate velit esse molestie consequat, vel

illum dolore eu feugiat nulla facilisis at vero eros et accumsan et iusto odio dignissim qui blandit praesent luptatum zzril delenit augue duis dolore te feugait nulla facilisi. Nam liber tempor cum soluta nobis eleifend option congue nihil imperdiet doming id quod mazim placerat facer possim assum. Lorem ipsum dolor sit amet, consectetuer adipiscing elit, sed diam nonummy nibh euismod tincidunt ut laoreet dolore magna aliquam erat volutpat. Ut wisi

Setting up Rows and Columns

All this talk about linking text blocks reminds me about a wonderful feature in Illustrator called Rows & Columns. Although you can't create columns of text within one text block, you can create several blocks of type and link them. This handy feature makes it easy to create rows and columns of type.

▼ TASK

Task: Creating Rows and Columns of Type

Here's how to get started:

1. Draw an ordinary box. It should be large enough to contain all the rows or columns you want to create.

2. Select Rows & Columns from the Type menu (see Figure 10.10). You are presented with the Rows & Columns dialog box (see Figure 10.11) .

FIGURE 10.10

Choose Rows & Columns from the Type menu.

▼

▼

FIGURE **10.11**

The Rows & Columns dialog box.

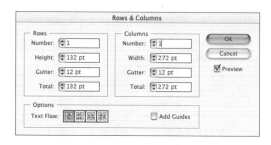

3. Enter the number of rows (horizontal) and columns (vertical) and the gutter (the space between each row and column). The height and width are adjusted automatically. If you have the Preview button checked, you can see the rows and columns changing in real-time as you enter the numbers (see Figure 10.12).

FIGURE **10.12**

The box before and after the Rows & Columns feature has been applied.

▲

To make life even easier, the Rows & Columns feature even links the boxes for you, so that type automatically runs from one to the next, as shown in Figure 10.13. By choosing from the Text Flow icons, you can specify the direction the type should flow (see Figure 10.14). You can also choose to add guides, which is a great timesaving feature in itself because Illustrator automatically draws guides to help you align objects to your rows and columns.

Figure 10.13

After the columns are created, the text is placed in the first box and runs through the linked boxes.

Lorem ipsum dolor sit amet, consectetuer adipiscing elit, sed diam nonummy nibh euismod tincidunt ut laoreet dolore magna aliquam erat volutpat. Ut wisi enim ad minim veniam, quis nostrud exerci tation ullamcorper suscipit

lobortis nisl ut aliquip ex ea commodo consequat. Duis autem vel eum iriure dolor in hendrerit in vulputate velit esse molestie consequat, vel illum dolore eu feugiat nulla facilisis at vero eros et accumsan et iusto odio dignissim qui blandit

praesent luptatum zzril delenit augue duis dolore te feugait nulla facilisi. Lorem ipsum dolor sit amet, consectetuer adipiscing elit, sed diam nonummy nibh euismod tincidunt ut laoreet dolore magna aliquam erat volutpat.

Ut wisi enim ad minim veniam, quis nostrud exerci tation ullamcorper suscipit lobortis nisl ut aliquip ex ea commodo consequat. Duis autem vel eum iriure dolor in hendrerit in vulputate velit esse molestie consequat, vel

illum dolore eu feugiat nulla facilisis at vero eros et accumsan et iusto odio dignissim qui blandit praesent luptatum zzril delenit augue duis dolore te feugait nulla facilisi. Nam liber tempor cum soluta nobis eleifend option congue nihil

imperdiet doming id quod mazim placerat facer possim assum. Lorem ipsum dolor sit amet, consectetuer adipiscing elit, sed diam nonummy nibh euismod tincidunt ut laoreet dolore magna aliquam erat volutpat. Ut wisi enim ad minim

Figure 10.14

These icons specify which way the text should link from box to box.

Task: Creating a Grid with Rows and Columns

I'll tell you a little secret—you don't have to use Rows & Columns only for text blocks. This feature is great for making quick grids, or rows of even-sized boxes, as well. Ready for a little bit o' fun?

1. Draw a large square.

2. Select Rows & Columns from the Type menu.

3. For the number of rows, enter 3, and for the number of columns, enter 3. Set the gutter for each to 0.25 inch, and click OK, the result is shown in Figure 10.15.

Now you can play tic-tac-toe, design the Ralston logo, or, even better, make believe you are on *The Brady Bunch*!

FIGURE **10.15**
The completed 3×3 grid.

FIGURE **10.15**
The completed 3×3 grid.

Placing Type on a Path

One of Illustrator's most popular type features is its capability to place text along a path, as shown in Figure 10.16. You can place text along any path in Illustrator, whether it's an open or closed path.

FIGURE **10.16**
Type on a path.

To place text on a path, do one of the following:

- With the Path Type tool selected (see Figure 10.17), click any path and begin typing.

FIGURE 10.17

Choosing the Path Type tool.

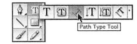

- With the Type tool selected, click any open path and begin typing.
- With the Type tool or the Area Type tool selected, press and hold the Option (Mac)/Alt (Windows) key while clicking any closed path, and begin typing. Notice that the cursor changes to the Path Type tool cursor when you press the Option (Mac)/Alt (Windows) key (see Figure 10.18).

FIGURE 10.18

With the Type tool selected, the cursor, when placed over a closed path, changes to the Path Type tool cursor when the Option (Mac)/Alt (Windows) key is pressed.

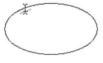

Task: Moving Text Along a Path

When text is on a path, you can move its position as well as flip it to the other side of the path. To see how, do the following:

1. Select the type or the path by using the Selection tool (the Direct Selection tool or Group Selection tool does not help here). Notice that the path is highlighted as well as the I-beam insertion point for the type.

2. To edit where the type lies on the path, click the I-beam and drag in the direction you want to move the type.

3. To flip the type to the other side of the path, double-click directly on the I-beam, or drag the I-beam toward the opposite side of the path (see Figure 10.19).

FIGURE 10.19

By double-clicking the I-beam, you can flip the type to the inside of the circle.

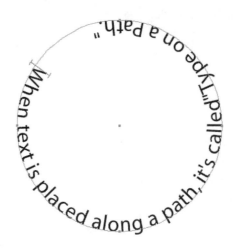

Vertical Type

Illustrator also supports vertical type (see Figure 10.20), as well as complicated alphabets such as Kanji (Japanese). The Vertical Type tool, Vertical Area Type tool, and Vertical Path Type tool all work the same as their horizontal counterparts.

FIGURE 10.20

Samples of type created with the vertical type tools.

Task: Creating Vertical Type

To see how to work with vertical type, perform the following steps:

1. Draw an open path that goes from north to south.

2. Select the Vertical Path Type tool, and click the path.

3. Type the words Vertical Type on a Path.

Summary

Now you've explored most of the creative tools in Illustrator. (We'll talk about the last in Hour 15, "Inserting Graphs and Charts.") This hour, you've seen one of the most important tools in the program. You've learned about the three types of text, you've learned how to use objects to determine the shape of text, and you've discovered rows and columns. Hour 14, "Applying Advanced Typography Techniques," will build on this hour and show you how to get the most from your type. In the intervening hours, we'll move our focus from creating to using some of Illustrator's more complex and powerful capabilities.

Workshop

A picture may be worth a thousand words, but sometimes words are critical. We'll use a few more of them for some questions and answers about type, a little quiz, and a couple of exercises to firmly implant this powerful new knowledge.

Q&A

Q Can I convert point text into area text or vice versa?

A No. But you can select point text, cut it, and then click a shape and paste the text as area text. You can also cut and paste area or point text and paste it onto a path using the Path Type tool.

Q Is there any way to edit text that overflows from a text box (indicated by a plus sign)?

A Technically, no, you cannot. Illustrator is not a word processor, and whatever text overflows from a box is not visible onscreen. However, if you're the daring kind, continue typing, even after the text block has been filled and, and although you can't see the type, it's there. Then, if you select all the type in that block and reduce the point size temporarily, you might be able to see more of the text.

Q Can I place text along a path on the top and bottom of a circle?

A Illustrator only enables you to place one text block on a single path. So how do you create those emblem logos where they have text along the top and bottom of a circle? Use two circles. Draw your first circle, add the text for the top, duplicate your circle, move the text down to the bottom of the circle (dragging the I-beam with the Direct Selection tool) and then place both circles directly on top of each other.

Quiz

1. Which of these is not a Type tool in Illustrator?

    a. Area Type tool

    b. Straight Type tool

    c. Vertical Path Type tool

2. Area text is also called

    a. Body text

    b. Wide text

    c. Headline text

3. Point text is also called

    a. Small text

    b. Sharp text

    c. Headline text

4. A small plus sign at the bottom of a text block indicates that

    a. There is additional text

    b. The text in the block is the truth

    c. Something is wrong with your screen

5. The Rows & Columns feature can be used only to create text blocks.

    a. True

    b. False

Quiz Answers

1. b. If you want straight text, you're probably looking for the good-old Type tool, which creates point type.

2. a. Body text generally is used to refer to the main text flow in a document, such as the articles in a newspaper (as opposed to the headlines and photo captions).

3. c. This type is placed at a specific point, such as above the body text.

4. a. The additional text can flow to a linked container.

5. b. You can use Rows & Columns to create objects that have no relationship to text.

Exercises

1. Draw three shapes, and link two of them. Add text so that the text flows from one shape to the next. Now unlink the two shapes, and link the first shape to the third.

2. Create a path, and flow text along the path. Now practice moving the text around on the path, as well as flipping the text from inside to outside the path.

3. Practice editing, copying, and pasting text by highlighting it with the Type tool.

10

Hour **11**

Applying Appearances and Styles

As you've learned, without color or a pattern or a gradient, an object is nothing more than an invisible path. Applying color gives a path an appearance. You have a great deal of control over the appearance of an object, and can create some very complex looks. In addition, just as you are able to save custom colors as swatches, you can save appearances as styles. In this hour, you'll learn the following:

- Working with the Appearance palette
- The anatomy of the Appearance palette
- Using multiple fills and strokes
- Rearranging appearance characteristics
- Using the Styles palette
- Expanding an appearance

Working with Appearances

Any time you create an object or a path that has any stroke or fill, you're applying an appearance. The only time that an object or path has no appearance is when there is no stroke, no fill, and no effects are applied.

Introducing the Appearance Palette

All appearance characteristics for an object or path are listed in the Appearance palette (see Figure 11.1).

FIGURE 11.1

The Appearance palette is shown with its menu open.

At the top of the palette, you see No Selection. That indicates that no object or path has been selected on the artboard. The stroke is shown as the default 1-point black, and the fill is white. Any object created now would have these characteristics.

> You might see the term attributes applied to those items listed in the Appearance palette. To avoid confusion, we'll call the individual lines in the Appearance palette characteristics. The fill, stroke, and transparency are just three possible characteristics. Do not confuse the Appearance palette with the Attributes palette. That's a whole different set of object characteristics.

As you can see in Figure 11.2, the Appearance palette can become quite full with a complex object.

Notice in Figure 11.2 that some effects are applied to the object in general, and some are applied to a specific characteristic. Let's look at each characteristic in the Appearance palette, starting at the top:

- The uppermost fill is a gradient fill, and an opacity of 35% has been applied to it. That opacity characteristic affects only the fill. (It is offset to the right, under the fill.)
- The uppermost stroke is a plain black stroke of 5 points.

- The next stroke down, which appears below the 5-point black stroke, is a plain white stroke of 10 points. However, the blending mode has been changed from Normal to Screen. (If no blending mode is shown, you can assume that it's Normal.)

- The next attribute is a 20-point black stroke with opacity of 75%.

- Below that is another white stroke, this one 25-points wide, with no special characteristics.

- The lowest stroke is a black stroke, 30-points wide. It, too, has no special identifying characteristics.

- The Appearance palette next lists the pattern fill. The fill's opacity is 70% and its blending mode is Multiply.

- The lowest fill is another radial gradient.

- Below the strokes and fills are the appearance characteristics that apply to the object as a whole. First is the drop shadow.

- Another characteristic that affects the entire star is an inner glow. (Similar to the drop shadow, this is a live effect applied through the Effects menu. You'll learn more about shadows and glows in Hour 18, "Working with Filters and Live Effects.")

- The lowermost entry in the Appearance palette is the object's overall opacity of 80%.

FIGURE 11.2

The Appearance palette reflects the object to the left.

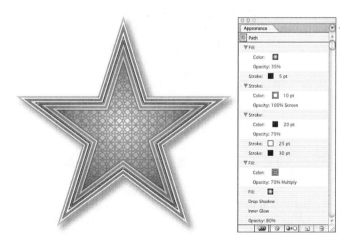

11

The order in which characteristics appear in the palette affects how they appear on the artboard. In Hour 4, "Making Selections," you saw how objects can be selected based upon whether they are above or below other objects. You've also seen several times how the order that objects are drawn determines which are shown and which are hidden. The same basic concept applies to strokes and fills in the Appearance palette.

▼TASK

Task: Rearranging Characteristics in the Appearance Palette

Let's work with a couple of simple appearance characteristics. It's a good idea to replace your Preferences file before we get started. If you've forgotten how, or have any question, refer to the reference card that came in the front of this book.

1. Open a new Illustrator document, using the default values in the New dialog box. (If you haven't replaced your Preferences, press D on the keyboard to restore the default stroke and fill values.)

2. Grab the Ellipse tool from the Toolbox and click once near the upper-left corner of your artboard.

3. In the Ellipse dialog box, enter 400 pt for both Width and Height. Click OK. You should have a nice big circle, as shown in Figure 11.3.

FIGURE 11.3

The circle remains selected by default.

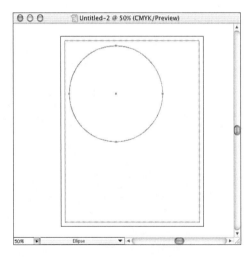

4. Hit Tab to hide your palettes, and then use the Window menu to show Appearance, Stroke, and Transparency. Arrange these three palettes conveniently.

5. In the Appearance palette, click Stroke.

6. In the Stroke palette, make the weight 40 points. You can either type the number or select it from the pop-up menu. Notice that the path is in the center of the stroke, as shown in Figure 11.4.

FIGURE **11.4**

Don't be too concerned with the location of your circle. For this exercise, it's fine if the stroke extends outside of the page tiling and artboard boundaries.

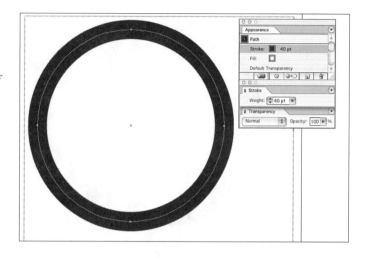

7. In the Appearance palette, click and drag the Fill characteristic above the Stroke characteristic (see Figure 11.5). The Fill, which extends to the path itself, now hides the part of the stroke that was inside the path.

11

FIGURE **11.5**

Compare this image with Figure 11.4. Look at the relative difference in the width of the stroke.

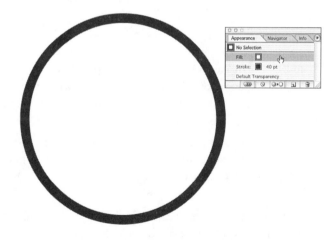

8. With the fill still selected (highlighted) in the Appearance palette, click the Transparency slider and drag it to 50%, as shown in Figure 11.6. You should now see the inner part of the stroke showing through the fill.

9. From the Appearance palette menu, choose Add New Stroke, as shown in Figure 11.7.

FIGURE 11.6

The change in transparency is applied to the selected characteristic.

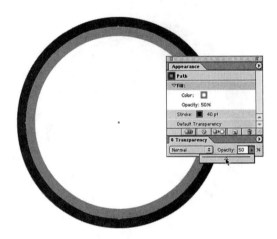

FIGURE 11.7

By default, the new stroke will have the characteristics of the most recent stroke. In this case, we'll get another 40-point black stroke.

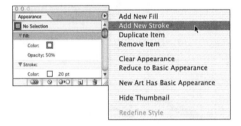

10. With the new stroke still selected in the Appearance palette, change the weight to 20 points in the Stroke palette. The new stroke will be centered on the path, as is the first stroke. It will cover half of the original stroke (although because both are black you'll only see it on the inside).

11. Because the new stroke is above the fill in the Appearance palette, it is not partially hidden like the original stroke. But we can change that. In the Appearance palette, drag the new stroke downward below the fill (but above the original stroke). Figure 11.8, shows the change in progress.

12. Because both strokes are black, the 20-point stroke is invisible against its wider brother. In the Appearance palette, double-click the stroke's color swatch to open the Color palette. Position the cursor over the white swatch at the right end of the color ramp and click.

FIGURE 11.8

The thick black line shows that the 20-point stroke is being dragged to a new position between the fill and the 40-point stroke.

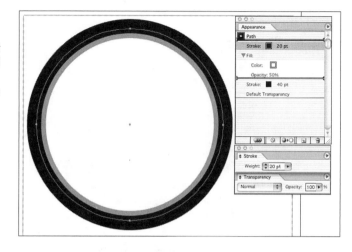

FIGURE 11.9

Because the 20-point stroke is the only characteristic selected in the Appearance palette, the change in color is applied only to it. It is now visible above the 40-point stroke.

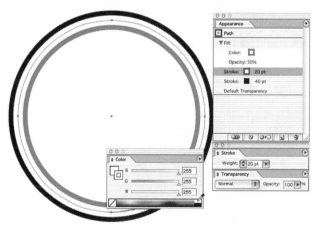

11

13. You can hide the Color palette now by reselecting it in the Windows menu. With the 20-point stroke still selected in the Appearance palette, lower the opacity to 50% in the Transparency palette. You now have four concentric strokes around the white fill, using only two actual strokes, as shown in Figure 11.10.

FIGURE **11.10**

The outermost stroke is the unaltered 40-point black stroke. Next is the 50% opaque 20-point black stroke. The 50% transparent white fill covers the two inner circles.

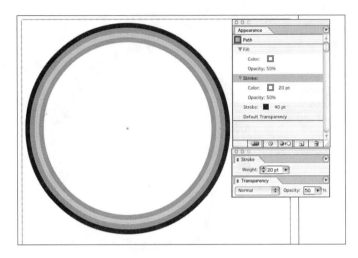

A Closer Look at the Appearance Palette

You've been looking at the Appearance palette throughout this hour. Now let's take a closer look (see Figure 11.11).

FIGURE **11.11**

If your Appearance palette doesn't show all of the characteristics, drag the lower-right corner to expand it.

This figure shows the Appearance palette as it stands at the end of the previous task, with the addition of the palette menu.

- At the top of the palette you see Path. When appropriate, this can also say Group or Layer. (You'll learn about applying appearance characteristics to layers in Hour 13, "Gaining Flexibility Through Layers.")

- Just below, you see Fill: with a downward-pointing triangle to the left. By clicking on the triangle you can hide the color and other characteristics of that particular item. Clicking a second time will expand the information. (This comes in handy when the Appearance palette gets full.) A swatch shows the fill's color, white. Note that the swatch has a double box around it. That indicates that it's the currently selected fill color. The fill's opacity (50%) is shown, too.

You can double-click the color swatch for a fill or stroke to open the Color palette.

- Similar to the fill, the uppermost stroke is shown with its specific characteristics. In this case, that includes color, width, and opacity. You can see that this stroke's color is the selected subcharacteristic (not a technical term) because it is highlighted.

- The lower stroke has no triangle next to it because it has only color and width. (That's easy to fit on one line.)

- Next is the only other characteristic applied to the entire object—the Default Transparency (which is, of course, 100% opaque) .

Notice that the default transparency, the fill, and the strokes are slightly shaded or lined, whereas the Color: and Opacity: lines for the fill and the upper stroke are not. We can consider that the difference between an object's characteristics and the subcharacteristics of a characteristic.

Now let's turn our attention to the palette buttons.

- The first of five buttons across the bottom of the palette is New Art Maintains Appearance. When this option is not selected, the next object you draw automatically has all of the characteristics shown in the Appearance palette. When you click this button to make the option active, only the stroke color and width, and the fill color, pattern, or gradient are transferred to the new object. (Notice the double box around the 20-point stroke's color. That indicates that it is the stroke color that will be assumed by the next object drawn with this option selected.)

- The second button is Clear Appearance. When clicked, any objects or paths selected on the artboard will be reduced to a stroke and fill of None and the default opacity. If no objects are selected, it simply clears the Appearance palette.

- The middle button is Reduce to Basic Appearance. The currently selected fill and stroke colors (in the bottom of the Toolbox and in the Color palette) and the current stroke width (in the Stroke palette) will be retained.

- The fourth button, Duplicate Selected Item, is available when a stroke, fill, or effect is selected in the Appearance palette. (This does not include the subcharacteristics.) Clicking the button is an easy way to duplicate a stroke or fill.

- The button on the right, which looks like a trash can, is called the Delete Selected Item button. It deletes the highlighted characteristic from the Appearance palette and removes it from the selected object(s) or path(s). You can drag an item to the Trash or click the Trash button to delete the currently selected item.

The Appearance palette menu also deserves attention.

- Add New Fill will do exactly that, and the new fill will use the color, pattern, or gradient currently selected. The new characteristic will be placed at the top of the Appearance palette's list, or if a characteristic is selected in the palette, directly above it.

- Add New Stroke uses the current stroke color and width. The new characteristic is, like a new fill, added at the top or immediately above the active characteristic.

- If a characteristic is selected in the Appearance palette, it can be copied with the Duplicate Item command. (Note that this doesn't work for subcharacteristics.)

- Remove Item will, like the Delete Selected Item button, delete a selected characteristic.

- Clear Appearance does the same as the button of the same name.

- Likewise, Reduce to Basic Appearance duplicates the button.

- Not surprisingly, New Art Has Basic Appearance will toggle that option, just like the palette's button.

- Hide/Show Thumbnail affects only the little preview that appears directly to the left of Path (or Group or Layer) at the top of the palette.

- Redefine Style is used with the Styles palette, which will be discussed later in this hour.

Working with Styles

In Hour 8, "Using Strokes, Fills, and Gradients," you learned about the Swatches palette. In Hour 9, "Working with Brushes," you learned how to create complex art that can be applied to your illustration quickly and easily by using brushes. Styles enable you to do comparable things with appearances. You can create complex combinations of fills, strokes, and effects, and save them to be used over and over. You will be able to apply these styles to virtually any path or object, and can even transfer them from file to file, using style libraries.

The Styles Palette

Think of the Styles palette as a close relative of the Swatches palette. Instead of storing colors, gradients, and patterns, it stores collections of appearance characteristics. Illustrator comes with a variety of styles preloaded in the palette, which you can see in Figure 11.12.

FIGURE 11.12

Your palette's default styles might vary.

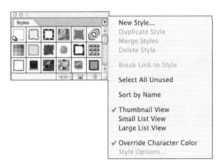

In the upper-left corner is the default black-stroke-and-white-fill combination. Applying that style is the equivalent of using the Reduce to Basic Button in the Appearance palette. You can see that the Styles palette menu offers a variety of housekeeping commands, such as duplicating, merging, and deleting styles. You can also choose how you want to view them. By default, Illustrator shows you only thumbnail views of each style. If you want, you can also see the names, with large or small thumbnails by selecting a different view from the palette menu.

To apply a style to a path or object, select the item on the artboard and click the thumbnail or the name of the style. You can Shift+click to select multiple objects and paths and apply a style to them all at once.

If you create several styles that are similar in appearance, it might be easier to find the one you need by name, rather than by thumbnail.

When you create a new style, you can give it a descriptive name. You can also change the name of any style by using the Style Options command at the bottom of the Styles palette menu.

Across the bottom of the Styles palette you'll see three buttons. The familiar icons for New and Delete are there, along with a button on the left called Break Link to Style. That button leads us to our next big discovery about the power of styles.

11

Task: Editing Styles

When a style is applied to one or more objects on the artboard, it stays linked to the objects. If you change the style, the objects will be updated to match. As you've just read, you can use the left-most button at the bottom of the palette to break the connection between a style and the objects to which it has been applied, should you so desire. (You might want to do this to leave some objects with the original style while creating a variation of the style for other objects.) Let's see how it works.

1. Open a new document in Illustrator. To practice our skills, let's make this one letter sized and use the Landscape orientation. Don't forget to change your Page Setup settings to match. Your artboard should look similar to Figure 11.13.

FIGURE 11.13

Notice that the Page Tiling (inner-dashed line) and the artboard (outer-solid line) are oriented the same way. If yours are not, go to File, Document Setup and adjust either the artboard or the Page Setup.

2. Press D on the keyboard to reset your foreground and background colors, the stroke weight, and the opacity.

3. Create the following objects, each with a width and height of 125 points, by clicking with the appropriate tool: A rectangle, a circle, a polygon (Radius=62.5, 6 sides), and a star (Radius 1=62.5, Radius 2=24, 5 points). (Because the polygon and star are created from the center, you'll work with the object's radius instead of its diameter.) Line up the objects across the top of your artboard and move the Styles palette directly below them (see Figure 11.14).

4. Press V on the keyboard to activate the Selection tool, and then click the square to select it. Click the first style in the second row of the Styles palette (Scribbly Fawn) to apply it.

5. Use the Selection tool to select the circle and apply the next style in the second row (Honeycomb Silk).

6. Apply the third style in the second row (Powder Puff) to the polygon, and the fourth style (Blue Goo) to the star. Don't deselect. Your artboard should now look similar to Figure 11.15.

FIGURE 11.14

By default, each object will have a 1-point black stroke and a white fill.

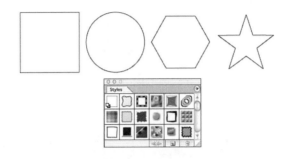

FIGURE 11.15

If your Styles palette shows different styles, that's okay, try to find these four. If not, choose any other styles that catch your eye.

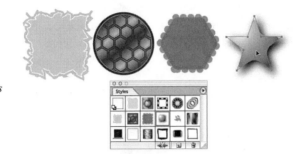

11

7. With the star still selected, click various other styles in the Styles palette and watch the star's appearance update automatically.

8. Shift+click the polygon so that both it and the star are selected. Apply various styles to both objects. When you're done, apply the style Caution Tape to both objects (see Figure 11.16) .

FIGURE 11.16

Your palette may be arranged differently, but the specific styles should be easy to spot.

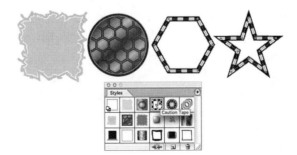

9. Open the Appearance palette. If necessary, drag the lower-right corner downward so that you can see all of the characteristics applied to the two objects.

10. Double-click the color swatch for fill (it shows the None symbol) to open the Color palette (see Figure 11.17).

FIGURE 11.17
You probably have a few other palettes nested with those visible. We hid them just to keep things tidy.

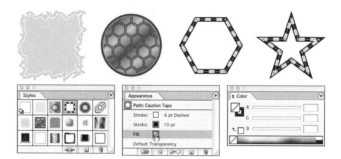

11. Click once in the Color Ramp at the bottom of the Color palette, somewhere in the cyan area. The two objects on the artboard will change, the Appearance palette will be updated, but the style in the Styles palette will not change, as shown in Figure 11.18.

FIGURE 11.18
This changes the look of the objects without affecting the style itself.

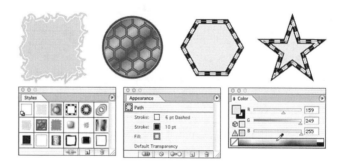

12. Use Command+Z (Mac)/Control+Z (Windows) to Undo. With the Selection tool, click somewhere in the artboard away from all objects to deselect.

13. Once again click Fill in the Appearance palette and this time choose a purplish color from the Color Ramp.

14. The style in the Styles palette remains unchanged. No objects are selected on the artboard, so none of them are changed. If you look at the Appearance palette, not only is the Fill color updated, but the palette menu now offers you the option of redefining the style in the Styles palette. Let's take that option. The results should be similar to those shown in Figure 11.19.

15. Press Command+Z (Mac)/Control+Z (Windows) to undo. You really don't need to have a purple fill in the middle of Caution Tape—sort of ruins the effect.

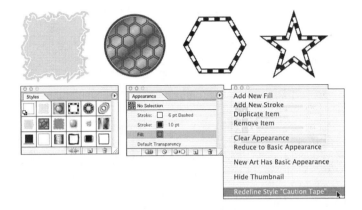

FIGURE 11.19

The style in the Styles palette adopts the new fill, and that redefined style is applied to the objects on the artboard that had the original Caution Tape style.

Unless you need to change the appearance of objects already created, consider making a new style rather than redefining an existing style. Click the original style and make your changes in the Appearance palette. Then, instead of Redefine Style from the Appearance palette menu, use New Style from the Styles palette menu. You'll still have the original style for use later.

▼ TASK

Task: Combining Appearance Characteristics Creatively

In the previous task, we placed four objects on the artboard but only used two. Let's work with the others for a few moments. One great way to learn how to execute your artistic vision in Illustrator is to dissect existing artwork. You can learn a lot about how Illustrator works by examining the default styles.

1. Click the square to select it. The Appearance palette should now show the characteristics of the Scribbly Fawn style. You'll see there is a pair of effects applied (Roughen and Scribble & Tweak). The style also uses a pair of strokes and a single fill.

2. Try dragging the lower stroke above the upper in the Appearance palette. The 7-point white stroke hides the smaller 4-point stroke.

3. Undo. Open the Transparency palette. With the white stroke still selected in the Appearance palette, drag the slider to 50%. Undo. Change the opacity of the upper stroke to 50%. Undo.

4. Select the circle on the artboard. In the Appearance palette, drag the top fill (the pattern fill) to the trash icon to delete it. You can see that the lower fill is a linear gradient applied at an angle. Undo.

▼

▼ 5. With the pattern fill still selected in the Appearance palette, go back to the
      Transparency palette and change the blending mode from Darken to Normal. The
      transparency information below the fill in the Appearance palette disappears
      because the opacity and blending mode are the defaults, as shown in Figure 11.20.

FIGURE 11.20

*The Honeycomb Silk
style is unchanged,
but the appearance
of the object and the
characteristics in the
Appearance palette
are different.*

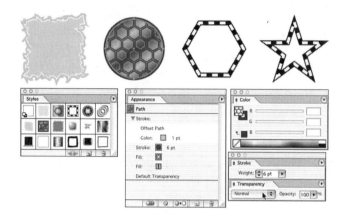

▲

The Honeycomb Silk effect relies on layered fills. You can also layer strokes to create an
appearance or style. If you check the Caution Tape style, you'll find that it uses a dashed
line to create its effect. There are two strokes; a solid black stroke and a smaller-dashed
yellow stroke. Later, during the exercises at the end of this hour, you'll have an opportunity to look at the rest of the styles in the Styles palette. We're sure that you'll come up
with quite a few creative ideas of your own.

Creating New Styles

As you work with Illustrator, you're likely to create a set of appearances that you'd like
to reuse. Or, perhaps, you'll develop artwork that might have to be changed later. If you
use the Styles palette to store your collection of appearance characteristics, you'll be
able to easily retrieve or edit one or more objects in an illustration.

Virtually any set of appearances can be saved as a style, including strokes, fills, and
effects. Create the look using the Appearance palette as your base and working with
other palettes as necessary. You can work with one or more objects if you'd like, but you
can also create a style with no object or path selected (or even on the artboard at all).
When ready, use the Styles palette menu command, New Style. You can give the new
style a name and it will be added to the Styles palette.

> Styles are saved with a specific document. To make custom styles available to other documents, you need to use style libraries, which will be discussed later in the hour.

▼TASK

Task: The Road to Style

One of the classic examples of the power of appearances is a four-lane freeway that you can apply to any path. By simply layering strokes we can (and will) create a road.

1. Rather than open a new document, simply select and delete everything on the artboard. Use Command+A (Mac)/Control+A (Windows) for Select All, and then use the Delete (Backspace) key to toss it all away.

2. The only floating palettes we'll need for now are the Toolbox, Appearance, Stroke, and Color. If you think back to the early hours, you'll remember that we can dock palettes. Click its tab and drag the Stroke palette to the bottom of the Appearance palette. Release the mouse button when you see a heavy black line at the very bottom of the Appearance palette. Dock the Color palette to the bottom of the Stroke palette. The advantage of docked palettes is that we can minimize them all at once to enable us to see our work area better. Your artboard should look similar to Figure 11.21 at this point.

FIGURE 11.21

Observe how the three palettes are all part of one window. There is only one title bar for all three.

3. Using the Pen tool, create an open path that has a gentle S-shape, such as the one shown in Figure 11.22.

FIGURE **11.22**

*Your path can vary
considerably, but try to
keep the curves
smooth.*

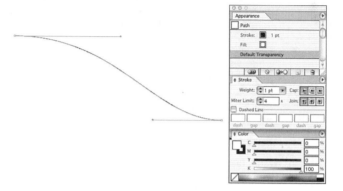

4. With the path active, change the stroke weight to 200 points and the color to a
   grassy green. (The exact color doesn't matter.) This stroke, at the bottom, represents the grassy shoulder.

5. In the Appearance palette, use the menu command Add New Stroke. Make the
   stroke weight 160 points, and the color a dark gray. CMYK values of 0/0/0/80 are
   perfect. (RGB 50/50/50 is fine, too.) This is our pavement.

6. Add another stroke, this one white and 154 points. This will be the pavement's
   edge lines.

7. The next stroke should be your same dark gray and a width of 150 points. It should
   match the pavement stroke perfectly so that it looks like the white lines are painted
   on a single gray stroke. At this point our path (and Appearance palette) should look
   similar to Figure 11.23.

FIGURE **11.23**

*Remember that you
can expand the
Appearance palette by
dragging the lower-
right corner. Because
the palettes are
docked, the Stroke
and Color palettes
automatically move
downward, too.*

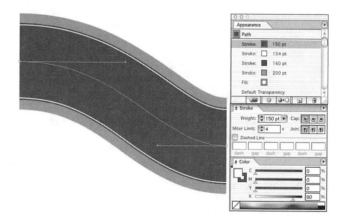

8. Now we want to add the white lane lines. To do so, we'll need a dashed line. Add a new stroke, make it white, and give it a width of 80 points. In the Stroke palette, check the Dashed Line box and input 20 pt in the first box and 10 pt in the second. Leave the rest empty.

9. Our next stroke, which will cover the dashed white line except for the narrow edge we need to see, will again be dark gray. Make the width 76 points and don't forget to uncheck the Dashed Line box in the Stroke palette.

10. Let's add the middle lines now, using just two strokes. A 6-point, bright-yellow stroke is needed to create the No Passing lines.

11. Divide that yellow stroke into a pair of lines by adding the final piece to the puzzle, a 2-point, dark-gray stroke.

12. Just to keep things clean, in the Appearance palette, click the Fill color swatch and then click the delete icon at the bottom of the palette. That changes the fill from the default white to None. Your path and Appearance palette (shown alone this time) should look similar to Figure 11.24. When done, hold down the Command (Mac)/Control (Windows) key and click away from your path to deselect.

FIGURE 11.24

The Appearance palette conveniently shows you the color and width of each stroke.

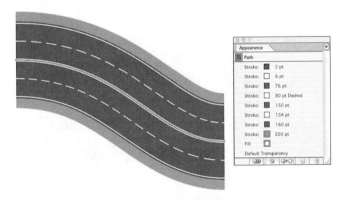

13. The original path should be deselected on the artboard, but its characteristics should still be visible in the Appearance palette. Select the Pen tool from the Toolbox and create a path. Your road appearance is automatically applied, without having to go through the previous 12 steps!

To create this road without the Appearance palette would involve putting 15 separate paths next to each other—and keeping them properly aligned! The 15 component parts are shown in Figure 11.25.

FIGURE 11.25

*To re-create our road
with individual paths
would require all 15 of
the paths shown here.
And they would have
to be perfectly aligned,
including around
curves.*

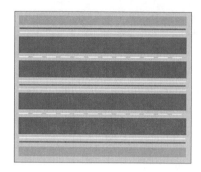

Saving a Style

So far the road you've created isn't a style, but rather an appearance. Sure, we can draw additional paths right now using that appearance, but if we want to come back to it later or use it in another document, we need to save it as a style in the Styles palette.

You don't need to have the path selected on the artboard, but make sure that your series of strokes are still visible in the Appearance palette. Use the Window menu to show the Styles palette and click the New Style button at the bottom (see Figure 11.26).

FIGURE 11.26

*The new style will
appear at the bottom
of the palette.*

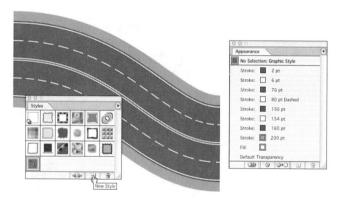

Double-click your newest style in the Styles palette—it will be the last one. This opens the Style Options dialog box, which enables you to rename your style (see Figure 11.27).

The style name is used in both the Styles palette list view and in the Appearance palette (see Figure 11.28) .

FIGURE 11.27

You can choose any name that you'd like for your style.

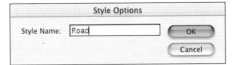

You can skip a step by holding down the Option (Mac)/Alt (Windows) key when you click the New Style button. That opens the Style Options dialog box automatically.

FIGURE 11.28

You'll see a thumbnail of your style along with the name. Sometimes the thumbnail isn't very accurate because it tries to create a tiny square sample from the style.

Editing an Existing Style

To edit existing styles deselect all objects and paths on the artboard. Click once on the style in the Styles palette to select it. Make the changes in the Appearance palette. You can then either click the New Style button at the bottom of the Style palette, or use the Appearance palette menu command Redefine Style. Here's the difference; creating a new style leaves the original style untouched, and doesn't change any objects or paths to which that style has been applied. Redefining a style, on the other hand, changes the style in the Styles palette and updates all objects using that style in the document. (You can redefine a style and not update existing objects by using the Break Link to Style button at the bottom of the Styles palette before redefining. Select the objects whose appearance you want to preserve, then click the button.)

Style Libraries

Illustrator has a number of predefined style libraries, and you can create your own. To load one of Illustrator's supplied style libraries, pop over to the Window menu. You'll find a list of available libraries in the Style Libraries submenu (see Figure 11.29). Also note the Other Library option at the bottom of the list enables you to load styles from any Adobe Illustrator document.

FIGURE 11.29

Your list of libraries might differ.

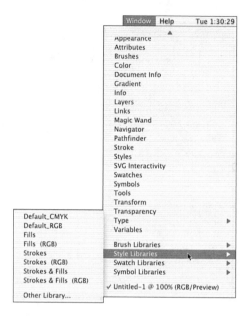

Any custom style can be saved in any Illustrator document. To use that style in another document, use the Other Library command and navigate to the document in the dialog box.

You can save a series of Illustrator documents with various sets of styles in them. Give the documents descriptive names and save them in a designated folder. That makes it easy to load related styles into any Illustrator document.

If you want to transfer a single style from one document to another, create a path or object, apply the style, and then copy and paste it into the destination document. The style will be added to the Styles palette. You can delete the object or path and the style will remain.

Remember that each document stores the contents of the Styles palette in the file. To reduce the file size a bit, you can use the Styles palette menu command Select All Unused. You can then remove the unnecessary styles from the palette by clicking the delete icon. When you save the file it will be slightly smaller and somewhat less complex to output.

Expanding Styles and Appearances

When exchanging files with people who use early versions of Illustrator, or who need to place Illustrator files in other programs, you might need to expand a style. Expanding a style simply means creating individual objects from each of the strokes and fills. Select the object(s) on the artboard and use the menu command Object, Expand Appearance. Figures 11.30 and 11.31 show a comparison of the Appearance and Layer palettes before and after expansion.

FIGURE 11.30

Before expanding an appearance, the Layers palette will show the object or path, whereas the strokes, fills, and effects will be shown in the Appearance palette.

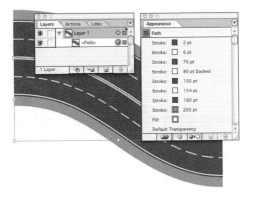

FIGURE 11.31

After expanding an effect or appearance, each of the strokes, fills, and effects become a separate object within a group.

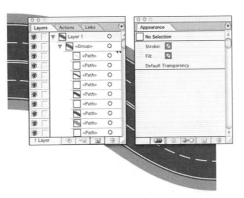

As you can see in Figure 11.32, when we expand the style we just created, each stroke becomes a separate path. The paths remain in the order that we created them, so the appearance of the path remains the same. Effects such as drop shadows can also be successfully expanded.

Summary

In this hour you've learned a lot about one of Illustrator's most powerful features. You now know how to create complex appearances and save them for use at your convenience. You can layer and rearrange strokes and fills, change the transparency of individual characteristics of an appearance, and even expand an appearance to create individual objects and paths from each characteristic.

Workshop

With a solid understanding of the Appearance and Styles palettes, you can now experiment and develop your creative skills. We'll start with a few refresher questions and then get into a few exciting exercises.

Q&A

Q What is the difference between an appearance and a style?

A An appearance is a collection of one or more strokes, fills, and/or effects applied to a path or an object. A style is an appearance that has been saved in the Styles palette.

Q How do I apply my new style to an object?

A Select the object on the artboard and click the style in the Styles palette.

Q What happens if I apply a style to an object that already has a style applied?

A The new style will replace the original style and the object's appearance will change to match the new style.

Quiz

1. Fills must always be below strokes in the Appearance palette.

    a. True

    b. False

2. Reducing the opacity of a characteristic applied to an object...

    a. ...makes objects behind partially or completely visible.

    b. ...changes the Appearance palette to show a subcharacteristic for that particular characteristic.

    c. Neither a nor b.

    d. Both a and b.

3. How do you access a style that you created in another document?

   a. It automatically appears in the Styles palette—just click it

   b. Use the menu command Window, Style Libraries, Other Library and load the styles from the original document

   c. Drag the style from the Styles palette of one open document to the Styles palette of another open document

   d. All of the above

4. A style can have a maximum of three strokes.

   a. True

   b. False

Quiz Answers

1. b. False. You can mix the strokes and fills in the Appearance palette to suit your needs.

2. d. The Appearance palette will show the transparency value for the characteristic below the characteristic, and the reduced opacity enables other objects to show through.

3. b. When you load a document's styles library, all of the styles saved with the document are added to the current image's Styles palette.

4. b. False. Our road, for example, has eight strokes.

Exercises

1. In a new document, practice layering strokes and fills on a variety of objects. This is a good opportunity to experiment with colors and opacity. Use very low opacity percentages if you plan on layering a lot of characteristics.

2. Create a new document in Illustrator. Open the Styles palette and the Appearance palette. One at a time, click each of the styles. Look in the Appearance palette and see how they were constructed. You'll find a variety of interesting interactions among multiple strokes and fills. Rearrange the various characteristics in the Appearance palette to see how they interact. Change colors, stroke weights, opacities, blending modes, and other subcharacteristics. Don't bother using Undo because these styles won't be saved with the document. When you're done, simply close the illustration without saving.

11

3. Use the menu command Window, Style Libraries to load each of Illustrator's pre-
    prepared style sets. Look at each style set. Don't forget to look at both the CMYK
    (unmarked) and RGB versions—they differ. Learn the names of some interesting
    styles.

4. Pick an interesting style from one of the style libraries. Using the Appearance
    palette as a guide, try to re-create the style from scratch. Compare your results to
    another object that you have applied to the original style.

HOUR 12

Using Transformations, Compound Shapes, and Blends

As we mentioned in the Introduction, computers give you the capability to change your artwork in a way unmatched by manual drafting and drawing techniques. You can quickly update or alter any illustration to meet your needs. In addition, Illustrator offers you numerous features to streamline your initial production of art. The transform capabilities enable you to manipulate one or more objects in creative (and precise) ways. Compound shapes enable you to make complex objects from simple ones. Blends, an extremely powerful capability, actually create objects for you. In this hour, you'll learn:

- How to use the transformation tools to manipulate objects
- How to work with the Transform palette
- How to create compound shapes
- How to use the Pathfinder palette to combine shapes

- How to align objects precisely to each other and to the artboard
- How to work with blends

Illustrator's Transformation Tools

Theoretically, any time we edit a path or manipulate an object, we're applying a transformation. Illustrator gives us a supply of tools and commands specifically for these tasks.

Working with the Tools and Commands

Illustrator's Toolbox includes seven tools that enable you to resize, rotate, shear, twist, flip, and reshape objects (see Figure 12.1).

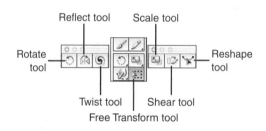

FIGURE 12.1

By default your Toolbox shows the Rotate, Scale, and Free Transform tools. Two hidden palettes contain the additional transform tools.

Like any good collection of superheroes, each of these has its own special powers. Several of the Transform tools are duplicated by Transform commands. The exceptions are the Twist tool, which is duplicated by a filter and an effect, and the Reshape and Free Transform tools, which cannot be duplicated by a command. Conversely, the menu command Object, Transform, Move is not associated with a specific tool, but rather is somewhat of a numeric dialog box equivalent of the Selection tool's capability to reposition objects on the artboard. The other Transform tools are

- Rotate tool
- Reflect tool
- Twist tool
- Scale tool
- Shear tool
- Reshape tool
- Free Transform tool

In general, you select one or more objects on the artboard, select the tool you want to use in the Toolbox, and drag to transform. Four of the tools (Rotate, Reflect, Scale, and

Shear) enable you to transform numerically by double-clicking the tool's icon in the Toolbox. These are the four Transform tools that use a point of origin.

One of the key concepts for using the Transform tools is the point of origin (also known as the origin point or the key point). This is the spot that the tool will use as an anchor, the point around which the transformation will take place.

Double-clicking the tool in the Toolbox is comparable to opening the dialog box using the Object, Transform menu. The transformation will occur around the center point of the object(s). You can also Option+Click (Mac)/Alt+click (Windows) these tools to establish a different point of origin and open the dialog box.

Rotate Tool

Let's experiment with the Rotate tool and learn how the point of origin works at the same time. In Figure 12.2, you see four formerly identical objects. All four had been aligned on the dashed line. The first remains unrotated. The second was rotated 45° with the point of origin in the default center of the object. The second was rotated with the point of origin moved to the lower-left corner. And, to show that the point of origin need not remain within an object, the fourth was rotated with the point moved below the base of the rectangle. (For ease of viewing, the points of origin are indicated with dashed circles.)

FIGURE 12.2

Think of the point of origin as the pivot around which you rotate or otherwise transform an object.

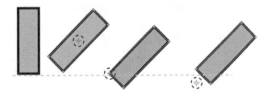

12

The easiest way to move the point of origin for an object selected on the artboard is not dragging. Rather, position the cursor where you want the point of origin, hold down the Option (Mac)/Alt (Windows) key and click once.

Another handy trick is to start dragging with your Transform tool and then press the Option (Mac)/Alt (Windows) key. (You must have the mouse button down first or you'll simply move the point of origin.) When you release the mouse button, you'll create a copy of the original object transformed, as you desired. In Figure 12.3, the single star at the top was Option+dragged with the Rotate tool around the point of origin shown. Seven copies were made using this technique, which produced the pattern shown.

FIGURE 12.3

FIGURE 12.3

The last star created is still selected on the artboard.

The Rotate tool can, of course, be used to rotate in a variety of ways. The most common is perhaps shown in the second object in Figure 12.2, a rotation around the object's own center point. (Remember that you can double-click the tool's icon in the Toolbox or use the menu command Object, Transform, Rotate to rotate numerically around the center point.) The Rotate tool's dialog box is seen in Figure 12.4.

FIGURE 12.4

Checking the Preview box enables you to see the effect of the rotation on all selected objects. When the object(s) selected on the artboard have a pattern fill, you have the option of rotating the object, the pattern, or both.

With the Info palette open and the Rotate tool in use, you will be able to see the angle of rotation. However, the palette is not live as you drag—it only updates the angle when you release the mouse button.

Reflect Tool

The Reflect tool flips an object across a line you determine. Select the object on the artboard, click once to set the point of origin, and then move the cursor to form a line across which the object will be flipped and click a second time.

The Reflect tool can be a great time saver. In many cases you can create half of a symmetrical image and copy-reflect to create the other half. Figure 12.5 shows the original line art on the left and the reflected art on the right.

FIGURE 12.5

Creating one half of a symmetrical object not only saves time, it increases accuracy. Note the vertical guide used to ensure alignment.

Although the Reflect tool doesn't show the line of reflection, it will preview for you. Click at the first point to place the point of origin. Then click and drag. Illustrator will show you where the reflected object will be placed. This also works in conjunction with the Option (Mac)/Alt (Windows) key to create a copy.

Using the menu command Object, Transform, Reflect, double-clicking the tool's icon in the Toolbox, or Option+clicking (Mac)/Alt+clicking (Windows) with the Reflect tool opens the dialog box. The dialog box allows precision reflections, using numeric input. The Copy button leaves the original unchanged and produces a reflected copy.

Twist Tool

Also known by the older name Twirl, this tool differs from the other Transform tools in one major respect. This tool actually creates new anchor points on the paths. The other transform tools work only with existing anchor points.

The Twist tool creates and manipulates anchor points and path segments to, well, twist the object or path on the artboard. Examples are shown in Figure 12.6.

The point at which the Twist tool is clicked determines the point around which the object will be twisted. As you can see in Figure 12.6, the appearance of the twisted object can vary considerably. In each case (other than the original object, of course), the Twist tool was Option+clicked (Mac)/Alt+clicked (Windows) at the X and a twist of 45° was applied. (The X for the object to the right of the original is in the middle of the star.)

Because the Twist tool creates additional anchor points, it's possible to produce overly complex paths that might not print correctly. A single revolution of the Twist tool on a fancy path can easily triple or quadruple the number of points. Several revolutions can create paths with several hundred anchor points.

The Twist tool can be Option+clicked (Mac)/Alt+clicked (Windows) to open the Twist dialog box.

Scale Tool

The Scale tool resizes the selected object(s). The point from which the object is scaled (the point of origin) can be within or outside the object. Option+clicking (Mac)/Alt+clicking (Windows) establishes the point of origin and opens the Scale dialog box (see Figure 12.7).

FIGURE 12.7

The original is at the top. The middle object was scaled without scaling stroke or effects. The bottom object was scaled with the Scale Strokes & Effects box checked.

Shear Tool

The Shear tool and Shear command can skew or angle the selected object(s). You can drag with the tool to shear around the object's center, or you can click to establish a new point of origin, and then drag. Shift+dragging constrains the shear to vertical or horizontal. The Shear dialog box is shown in Figure 12.8.

FIGURE 12.8

The original object is shown to the left; the object on the right is being previewed as a sheared object.

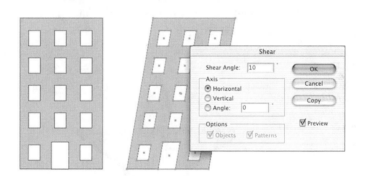

12

Task: Shearing for Shadows

One of the nifty uses for the Shear tool is creating cast shadows. In Illustrator, there are two types of shadows, a drop shadow and a cast shadow. A drop shadow, which you'll learn about when we discuss filters and effects in Hour 18, "Working with Filters and Live Effects," is what you see around the edges when an object is on or just above a parallel surface. A cast shadow, on the other hand, is what you see when an object is standing or perpendicular to a surface. See Figure 12.9 for the difference.

FIGURE 12.9

A drop shadow is shown on the left and a cast shadow on the right. The object on the left appears to be in front of and parallel to the background, whereas the object on the right appears to be standing on the surface.

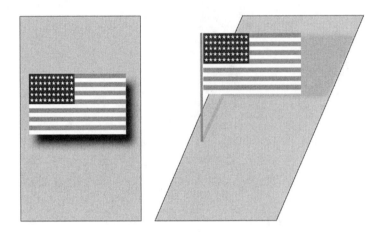

Let's create a simple cast shadow using the Shear tool.

1. Open a new document in Illustrator. The default settings are fine.

2. Drag a star, similar to the one shown in Figure 12.10. Hold down the Shift and Option (Mac)/Alt (Windows) keys while dragging, give it a stroke of 10 points, and use a radial gradient fill. In the Appearance palette (which you mastered last hour), we reduced the opacity of the fill to 90%.

FIGURE 12.10

Your star can vary considerably from this, but remember to hold down the Shift key so that it's pointed upward.

3. With the star still selected on the artboard, pick the Shear tool from the Toolbox.

4. Click the bottom-right anchor point to set your point of origin, and then Shift+drag to the right until the star's upper arms don't overlap with those of the original star. Don't release the mouse button.

5. Hold down the Option (Mac)/Alt (Windows) key and continue to hold the Shift key. Now release the mouse button and then the modifier keys. You'll get a second star at the angle that was showing when you released the mouse button. It should look similar to Figure 12.11.

FIGURE 12.11

The new star copy, sheared to perfection!

6. With the copy still selected on the artboard, move it behind the original using the menu command Object, Arrange, Send Backward or use the keyboard shortcut, Command+[(Mac)/Control+[(Windows) .

7. With the copy still selected, change the stroke to None and grab the Gradient tool. In the Gradient palette, change to a linear gradient, with a light gray on the left and a very dark gray on the right.

8. Drag a gradient from the top of the copy to about where the two lower arms of the star meet. In Figure 12.12 the points are labeled A and B.

FIGURE 12.12

The gradient simulates the way that a real shadow fades with distance.

12

9. Deselect and hide all palettes by pressing Tab, enjoy your work!

Reshape Tool

The Reshape tool is used to create controlled deformations of an object. It works by moving anchor points. However, unlike the Direct Selection tool, the Reshape tool enables you to use focal points to control how the object will be deformed.

When you work with the Reshape tool, an object's anchor points fall into one of three categories: unselected (the anchor points will not move), selected (the anchor points will move when the tool is dragged), and focal points (all focal points move as a group when dragged). Boxes around the anchor points, as shown in Figure 12.13, identify focal points.

FIGURE 12.13

On the left are three unselected anchor points. In the middle are two selected anchor points. On the right are three focal points.

You select anchor points with the Selection tools. You select focal points by clicking or dragging with the Reshape tool. You can Shift+click to designate multiple focal points.

In Figure 12.14, there were once four identical objects, which had been aligned to the left along the dashed line. The top object, which retains the original shape, shows the unselected, selected, and focal points. The focal points of the second object were dragged directly to the right. The third object's focal points were dragged left and downward. The focal points for the bottom object were pushed backward through the object itself.

FIGURE 12.14

The three lower objects were once identical to the top object, with the same selected points and focal points.

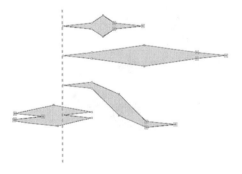

Notice how, in each case, the focal points have maintained their relationship among themselves and how the unselected points have not moved. The selected points (which are not focal points) are where the Reshape tool has made its changes.

Task: Using the Free Transform Tool

▼ TASK

The Free Transform tool combines the capabilities of several other transform tools and the Selection tool into one handy package. It rotates, it scales, it shears, it moves, and it even distorts! With all these capabilities rolled into one tool, the others might seem superfluous. However, the Free Transform tool doesn't allow you to do two important things. You cannot change the point of origin and you cannot create a copy. The Free Transform tool transforms only from the center of an object, and because the Option (Mac)/Alt (Windows) key has other responsibilities, it cannot be used to copy while transforming.

Let's see how the Free Transform tool works.

1. If you have a document still open, select all and delete. If not, open a new document and accept the defaults.

2. On your blank artboard, drag a rectangle using the default black stroke and white fill. (Remember that you can restore the fill and stroke to the basic appearance by pressing D on the keyboard.) Keep the rectangle selected throughout the following steps.

3. Select the Free Transform tool from the toolbox.

4. Position the cursor outside the rectangle. It changes to a curved, two-headed arrow that indicates that it is functioning as the Rotate tool. Click and drag to rotate the rectangle, and then release the mouse button. Undo.

5. Position the cursor inside the rectangle. Click and drag to reposition the object. The Free Transform tool is functioning as the Selection tool. Release the mouse button. Undo.

6. The Free Transform tool can duplicate other Selection tool behaviors, too, sparing you the trouble of switching tools constantly. Position the cursor on the upper-left handle of the rectangle's bounding box. Click and drag outward. Don't release the mouse button.

7. Press the Shift key. The rectangle automatically constrains its proportions, retaining the original height-width ratio. Don't release the mouse button or the Shift key.

8. Press the Option (Mac)/Alt (Windows) key. The rectangle is now being resized from the center. Continue to hold the Option (Mac)/Alt (Windows) key and the mouse button and release the Shift key. Press the Shift key. Release the Shift key. Don't get dizzy! Release all keys and buttons. Undo.

▼

12

▼
9. Position the cursor over the handle in the middle of the right side of the rectangle. Click and drag. While dragging, press and release the Option (Mac)/Alt (Windows) key a couple of times. Again the tool is resizing from the center. Release the key while keeping the mouse button down. Press and release the Shift key a couple of times. Observe that it has no effect. Continue to hold the mouse button down.

10. While dragging the right side of the rectangle, press and hold the Command (Mac)/Control (Windows) key. Move the mouse up and down. The Free Transform tool is now serving as the Shear tool. Keep the mouse button and the Command (Mac)/Control (Windows) key down and press the Option (Mac)/Alt (Windows) key. The shearing is now centered on the rectangle, with both the left and right
▲   sides being skewed.

That about covers the capabilities of the Free Transform tool. When you consider the capabilities, this tool is either (a) worthless because it doesn't do anything a different tool can't do, or (b) golden because it duplicates the capabilities of a lot of tools, eliminating the need to constantly switch tools. I'll pick (b). To summarize:

- Positioned outside a selected object, you can rotate.
- Positioned within a selected object, you can move.
- Positioned on a corner handle of the bounding box, you can resize in any direction.
- Positioned on a side handle, you can resize in and out from that side.
- Hold down the Shift key while resizing and you can constrain the proportions of the object.
- Hold down the Option (Mac)/Alt (Windows) key while resizing and you can resize from the object's center.
- You can hold down both the Shift and Option keys to resize from the center while constraining proportions.
- Positioned on a side handle of the bounding box, with the Command (Mac)/Control (Windows) key depressed, you can shear an object.
- Adding the Option (Mac)/Alt (Windows) key while shearing skews from the center.

Special Considerations

A couple of Illustrator's preferences have a major impact on what you do with the Transform tools. When rotating an object filled with a pattern, you can rotate the object and leave the pattern with the original orientation, or you can rotate the pattern along with the object, as shown in Figure 12.15. This behavior can be controlled through the General Preferences. Check or uncheck the box for Transform Pattern Tiles.

FIGURE 12.15

On the left is the original object. In the middle, the object has been rotated but the pattern has not. On the right, both object and pattern have been rotated.

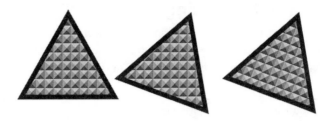

Another check box in the General Preferences determines whether strokes and effects will be scaled with an object or not. As you saw in Hour 2, "Setting Up Illustrator," the Scale Strokes and Effects option can have a major impact on the results of a transformation.

The Tilde Key

The tilde key (~) can be used to transform a pattern fill without changing the object that contains it. It works with the Rotate, Reflect, Scale, and Shear tools. Hold down the key (located in the upper-left corner of your keyboard) and drag. By the way, although you need the Shift key to produce the ~ symbol, you can just hold down the key itself when dragging, Shift isn't necessary.

In Figure 12.16 you can see some samples of how transforming a pattern works.

FIGURE 12.16

From the left, the original object, pattern rotated, pattern reflected, pattern scaled, and pattern sheared.

12

Transform Again

Any time that you want to repeat the last completed transformation, use the menu command Object, Transform, Transform Again or the keyboard shortcut Command+D (Mac)/Control+D (Windows). That last transformation, with the last settings, whether executed with a menu command or with a tool, will be repeated on whatever object(s) you've selected. For example, you can select an object, rotate it precisely, and then select a different object and apply exactly the same rotation quickly and easily with the keyboard shortcut.

Task: Reset Bounding Box

When you transform artwork by rotating or reflecting, the object's bounding box is also transformed. To reorient the bounding box to the artboard (without undoing the transformation), use the menu command Object, Transform, Reset Bounding Box. Try it yourself.

1. Add any object to the artboard.
2. Use the Rotate tool to swing the object in a short arc.
3. Switch to the Selection tool and look at the bounding box.
4. Use the menu command Object, Transform, Reset Bounding Box and take another look.

The Transform Palette

The Transform palette folds several transform dialog boxes into one handy palette (see Figure 12.17). You can move (the X and Y fields), scale (the W and H fields), rotate (the lower-left field with the angle symbol), and shear (the lower-right field with the shear symbol). In addition, the palette's menu gives you some reflect capability (Flip Horizontal and Flip Vertical) and the capability to control the scaling of strokes and effects and the transformation of patterns.

FIGURE 12.17

The Transform palette is opened through the Windows menu.

Note that the 3×3 grid (called a proxy) to the left of the X and Y fields enables you to choose, within certain limitations, the point of origin for the transformation. You can choose the center (which is the default) or any of the eight bounding box handles.

Transform Each

Another powerful transformation tool is the menu command Object, Transform, Transform Each. It opens the dialog box shown in Figure 12.18.

What sets Transform Each apart is its capability to apply the transformation to each object of a selection individually. Figure 12.19 shows the difference between applying a rotate transformation to a number of objects together and to the same objects individually.

FIGURE 12.18

With Transform Each you can scale, move, rotate, and reflect (horizontal and vertical only), as well as make the same point-of-origin choices as the Transform palette offers.

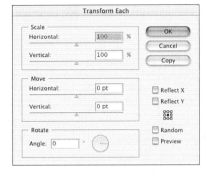

FIGURE 12.19

The original set of objects is on the left. In the middle, the command Object, Transform, Rotate has been applied to them. On the right, the same rotation transformation has been applied through Transform Each.

Another great feature of Transform Each is its capability to provide a more natural look to a group of objects with the Random option. Checking this box applies the transformation within a positive and negative range of the value you specify. In Figure 12.20, each of the three groups you just saw were rotated 45° using Transform Each with Random checked. The individual objects within each of the three groups are rotated randomly between –45° and +45°. None of the three groups match.

FIGURE 12.20

Each of the three groups was rotated individually with the Random option engaged.

12

Compound Shapes and the Pathfinder Palette

Compound shapes are an evolution in the way Illustrator works with compound paths. (You learned about compound paths in Hour 5, "Creating Paths and Compound Paths.") Using compound shapes, you can create complex objects made of multiple paths and yet edit each of the original paths at any time. (This is another of Illustrator's live capabilities, such as styles, symbols, and effects.) In practice, Illustrator simply hides the parts of the objects that you don't want to use. They receive a stroke and fill of None, but are still there. As you'll see, you can edit those original paths to make changes to the compound shape.

Compound shapes are created using the top row of buttons in the Pathfinder palette, as shown in Figure 12.21.

The Shape Mode buttons create compound shapes. We'll use the two shapes shown to experiment.

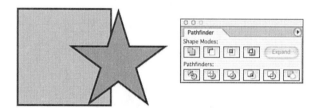

The four ways to combine a pair of objects to create a compound shape are

- Add the two shapes together
- Subtract the top shape from the shape behind
- Intersect the two shapes, saving the area where they overlap and deleting the rest
- Delete the area where the objects overlap, saving the rest

Task: Creating Compound Shapes

▼ TASK

Let's see how the various commands work.

1. Open a new document or select all and delete from the current artboard.

2. Draw a square and a star similar to those shown in Figure 12.21. Make sure that they overlap.

3. Select both the square and the star and click the left-most of the Shape Mode buttons in the Pathfinder palette. This merges the two objects into one. Figure 12.22

▼

▼ shows the resulting object on the left, but on the right you see that the two separate paths still remain. (You need only one set of objects, we're using two sets so that we can show the resulting object and the paths at the same time.)

FIGURE 12.22

Because the two original paths remain, you can edit one or the other shape later without having to undo the compound shape or recreate the square and star.

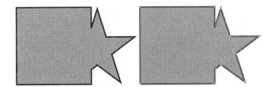

4. Undo. Now click the second button in the top row of the Pathfinder palette. This uses the front-most object as a cookie cutter, chopping away any overlap.

5. Undo. Click the third Shape Mode button. This retains only the areas of overlap, hiding the rest.

6. Undo. Click the last of the Shape Mode buttons. This is the opposite of the previous button, hiding the overlap and retaining the rest (see Figure 12.23). (This is also what you would see if you selected these two objects and used the menu command Object, Compound Path, Make.) Undo, but don't deselect or delete.

▲

FIGURE 12.23

This time it's no surprise that the original paths are maintained. However, remember that they are now merged.

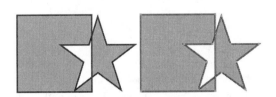

Editing Compound Shapes

With the square and the star from the previous task still selected, click the third Shape Mode button, Intersect, to retain only the area where the two shapes overlap. Select the Direct Selection tool (white arrow) from the Toolbox. Click away from the objects to deselect, and then click in the center of the visible object. The star's path should be visible.

Shift+click the left-most anchor point, at the tip of the star's arm. Now click the point again and drag it far to the left, as shown in Figure 12.24.

FIGURE 12.24
You can still edit the
original objects after
using any of the Shape
Mode buttons to create
compound shapes.

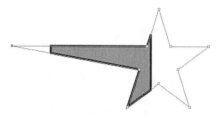

Notice in Figure 12.24 that the point has been dragged past the original left edge of the square. When the shapes overlap, the compound shape is filled and stroked. Past the edge, however, the shapes don't overlap (there's no square), so the path is unfilled and unstroked, just as it is at the right side of the star

Expanding Compound Shapes

You can remove the invisible paths if you're sure that you won't need them again to edit the compound shape. Simply select the compound shape on the artboard using the Selection tool and click the Expand button in the Pathfinder palette (see Figure 12.25).

FIGURE 12.25
Expanding a com-
pound shape actually
makes it smaller
by eliminating
unnecessary paths.

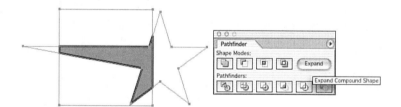

After expanding, choose Select, All or use the keyboard shortcut Command+A (Mac)/Control+A (Windows). You'll see that the only path on the artboard is that of the (formerly compound) shape. You can edit this shape normally, but can no longer use the original star and square paths.

If you know you'll not need the original shapes for editing, you can create and expand all at once by holding down the Option (Mac)/Alt (Windows) key when clicking one of the Shape Mode buttons.

Task: Discovering the Pathfinder Buttons

The buttons in the lower row of the Pathfinder palette are similar to the Shape Mode buttons, but are not live. After you use any of these buttons with a pair of shapes, the excess paths are deleted. Let's work with them.

▼ 1. Clear your artboard and create three overlapping objects. We're using a sideways triangle, a circle, and a hexagon, as shown in the upper-left corner of Figure 12.26.

FIGURE 12.26

The three objects have different fills so that we can track which colors are maintained in the resulting shape(s). The other five sets of figures are the results of Pathfinder operations. Each set is enclosed in a dashed box.

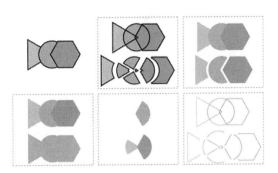

2. Select all three of your objects and click the first Pathfinder button, Divide. Overlapping paths cut each other, creating a series of objects that are grouped together. In Figure 12.26, top row middle, you can see the resulting group in the upper half of the dashed box. In the lower half of the dashed box, we have ungrouped and separated the new component pieces. The three original objects are cut into seven pieces where paths overlap. Notice that each piece has the fill of the front-most object at the place.

3. Undo. Click the second Pathfinder button, Trim. As you can see in Figure 12.26, in the dashed box in the upper-right corner, Trim has removed all hidden parts of objects and deleted the stroke. The remaining pieces retain their original fill colors. (Again, the resulting shape is shown in the top of the dashed box, and below it the individual pieces are separated.)

4. Undo. Use the third Pathfinder button, Merge. Because all three objects have different fills, Merge works the same as Trim. If, however, some overlapping objects had the same fill, those objects would be combined into one object. In Figure 12.26, the lower left dashed box, the top set of objects were merged. The objects in the bottom set were changed to the same fill before merging. You can see from the paths that the top set produced three objects grouped together, whereas the bottom set produced a single object.

5. Undo. The fourth button, Crop, uses the top-most object as a cookie cutter on any underlying objects. In Figure 12.26, in the dashed box in the middle of the bottom row, at the top, the three objects were selected and Crop was clicked. All that was

▼ retained was the area where the hexagon overlapped the circle. Below in that same

12

▼ dashed box, the circle was moved to the front before using Crop. You can see that the area of the triangle and the polygon that were underlying the circle were retained. Try it yourself by cropping, undoing, rearranging, and cropping again.

6. Undo. Use the next Pathfinder button, Outline. Outline discards fill and stroke and creates path segments, cutting each path where objects overlap. The paths have a barely visible stroke weight and fill color. In Figure 12.26, lower right, we've made the strokes a bit heavier so they show up.

7. Undo. The final Pathfinder button, Minus Back, retains only the front-most object. Any place where there is an underlying object is chopped away. Try it and see. (We didn't include this in Figure 12.26 because there really wouldn't be anything to ▲ see.)

The Pathfinder Palette Menu

The Pathfinder palette's menu, shown in Figure 12.27, has a number of important commands.

FIGURE 12.27

You access the Pathfinder palette's menu through the small triangle in the palette's upper-right corner.

- Trap: Trapping is the process of overlapping colors so that the paper doesn't show through when printed in commercial printing presses. Those monster presses, which run at very high speeds, do a great job of aligning the colors, but tiny errors can creep in. Overlapping the colors can hide the errors. Discuss trapping with your print shop before using it. (Trapping will be discussed further in Hour 21, "Printing Your Illustrations.") It is not necessary for inkjet printers.

- Repeat: This command will show you which button was last clicked and allow you to apply that Shape Mode or Pathfinder function to the currently selected objects.

- Pathfinder Options: The Pathfinder Options are shown in Figure 12.28. Redundant points are those anchor points that aren't needed after paths are combined. Unpainted artwork includes all paths that are unstroked and unfilled.

- Make Compound Shape: This command is the same as using the first Shape Mode button.

FIGURE 12.28

The default values, which are shown, are usually the most appropriate.

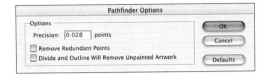

- Release Compound Shape: With a compound shape selected on the artboard, this command restores the objects to their original independence, complete with stroke and fill.

- Expand Compound Shape: You can use this command or you can click the palette's Expand button.

The Align Palette

There are a lot of places, in several hours, where the Align palette could be discussed. We'll talk about it here because by default it is nested with the Transform and Pathfinder palettes.

Align enables you to line up objects with each other or with the artboard and to distribute them by position. The palette and its menu are shown in Figure 12.29.

FIGURE 12.29

Hide/Show Options is the same as clicking the double arrow in the palette's tab.

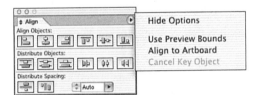

Lining Up Your Objects

The first row of buttons enables you to align selected objects vertically to the left, center, or right, and horizontally to their tops, middles, or bottoms. In Figure 12.30, the original grouping of objects is shown in the upper left. There were six other identical sets of rectangles—until we used each of the align buttons.

The buttons do a pretty good job of showing you how they work. Refer back to Figure 12.29, to the menu command Align to Artboard. When this option is selected, a checkmark will appear beside it. Objects will then be aligned to the center or edges of the artboard. (Not the page tiling area, but the artboard itself.)

FIGURE 12.30

The original positions are shown in the upper left. The sets in the top row are aligned vertically, and those in the bottom row are aligned horizontally.

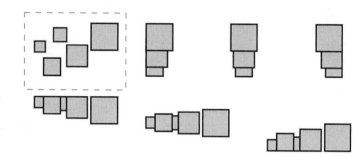

When multiple objects need to maintain their relative positions, yet need to be aligned to the artboard, group them first, align, and then ungroup.

Spreading Out Your Objects

The second line of buttons in the Align palette distributes the selected objects according to position. The objects will be evenly spread out based upon their centers or the edges that you select. You can also distribute in relationship to the artboard.

The bottom line of the Align palette enables you to determine the exact distance between objects. A key object (see the following section) must be designated. The key object serves as a base from which the other objects are distributed.

Key Objects

One of the neatest tricks in Illustrator is aligning to a key object. Normally when you align a bunch of things on the artboard, they average their positions to reach a mutually acceptable compromise position. However, you can force all the other objects to align to the key object. Select all the objects to be aligned, and then click once on the object that you want to use as the base. When you click the appropriate align button, the key object remains in place and the other objects align to it. Very cool!

The Magic of Blends

Speaking of cool, one of my absolute favorite Illustrator capabilities is blends. Blends force Illustrator to do your work for you. You create two objects; Illustrator creates a series of objects in between that blend or morph from one to the other. See the example in Figure 12.31.

Figure 12.31

The two original objects are shown to the left. Illustrator created all the intermediate objects seen on the right.

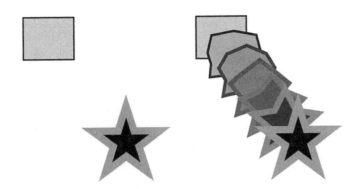

The Three Types of Blends

The menu command Object, Blend, Blend Options opens the dialog box shown in Figure 12.32. The biggest decision you'll make is which of the three types of blends you want to create.

Figure 12.32

The Spacing pop-up menu determines what type of blend you'll create. Orientation determines whether the intermediary objects will remain oriented to the top of the page (left) or to the path (right).

Illustrator will blend two objects in any of three different ways, which are shown in Figure 12.33:

- Their color will evenly transition from one to another (Smooth Color).
- A predetermined number of intermediary objects will be created (Specified Steps).
- Enough objects to fill the space between the two original objects will be created, with each new object at a predetermined distance from the previous (Specified Distance).

12

FIGURE **12.33**

From the top, the blends are Smooth Color, Specified Steps (set to 10), and Specified Distance (set to 25 points).

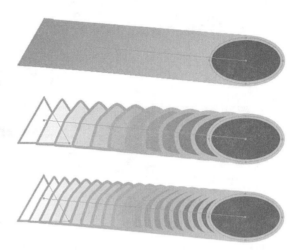

Editing Blends

Notice in Figure 12.33 that the blends are selected, yet only the paths for the original two objects show, connected by a line. Unless you expand the blend, only the two original objects can be edited. Illustrator, by the way, will update the blend to match if you change the shape or color of one of the original objects. Expanding a blend is similar to expanding a compound shape (which we discussed earlier in this hour). You create individual objects from the component pieces.

Keep in mind that once you expand a blend you can no longer edit it as a blend. It becomes a series of grouped objects and must be edited as such.

That line that you see in Figure 12.33 connecting the two original objects is called the blend's spine. Think of it as the path along which the blend travels. You can edit that path, or even replace it with another path altogether. Illustrator will always use a straight path segment as the spine. That doesn't mean that you can't do things such as those shown in Figure 12.34 once the blend has been created.

The Blend submenu, shown in Figure 12.35, enables you to replace a spine, reverse a spine, or even reverse the blend.

FIGURE **12.34**

*The original blend is
shown at the top. In
the others, the spine
has been edited or
replaced.*

FIGURE **12.35**

*The Blend submenu
gives you access to the
Blend Options and sev-
eral other capabilities.*

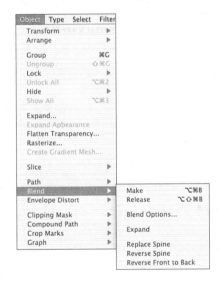

12

To replace the spine, create the new path, select it and the blend, and then use the
Replace Spine command. Reversing the spine basically flips the object perpendicular to
the spine. Reverse Front to Back flips the stacking order of the objects. Figure 12.36
shows our original blend, the results of Reverse Spine, and the results of Reverse Front
to Back.

Figure 12.36

A blend, the blend with spine reversed, and the same blend reversed front-to-back.

We've been working with two objects to create blends. Illustrator's blend command, however, can work with several objects at the same time. Keep in mind that only adjoining objects are actually blended. The blend, for example, would go from Object A to Object B, Object B to Object C, Object C to Object D, and so on. Objects A and C would never actually blend with each other.

Task: Using the Blend Tool

▼ TASK

There's an even more sophisticated way to blend in Illustrator. In addition to the Blend commands, there's a Blend tool. It enables you to control how the two objects will morph (up to a point). Let's practice.

1. Open a new document or clear the artboard.

2. Press D on the keyboard to set the fill and stroke to the basic appearance.

3. Add a five-pointed star to one corner of your artboard and a rectangle to the opposite corner.

4. Select the Blend tool from the Toolbox (see Figure 12.37), or press the keyboard shortcut W.

5. Open the Blend Options dialog box by using the menu command Object, Blend, Blend Options. Set the Spacing pop-up menu to Specified Steps and input 7 in the numeric field.

6. Click the top point of the star and then click the upper-left corner of the rectangle. (When the little square of the Blend tool's cursor is directly over the anchor point, it will be filled in and a small X will appear to the lower right of the cursor.) The blend should look similar to Figure 12.38.

▼

12

FIGURE 12.37

The Blend tool shares space with the Auto Trace tool, although they are not related.

FIGURE 12.38

The Blend tool designates which anchor points should blend into each other.

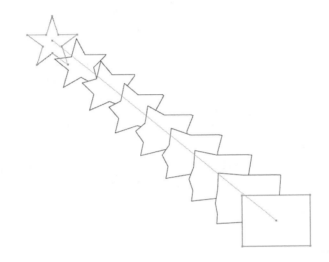

7. Undo. Click again on the upper point of the star and then on the lower-left corner of the rectangle. The blend should look similar to Figure 12.39.

FIGURE 12.39

The blend changes as the objects are rotated differently to match up the designated points.

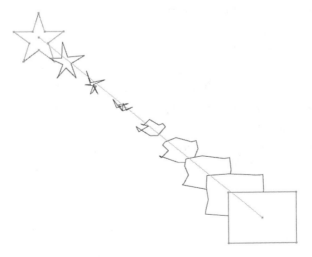

Releasing Blends

Releasing a blend creates editable objects from each of the steps that Illustrator creates for you. If you're having trouble printing an image that contains a blend, the command Object, Blend, Release might solve the problem. Releasing a blend also enables you to extract one or more steps from the blend for use elsewhere.

Summary

What an hour! You've learned an awful lot about some rather complex subjects. You've learned how to use the Transform tools and commands to alter artwork, how to create compound shapes and to use the Pathfinder palette to combine shapes, how to align and distribute objects on the artboard, and how to create blends.

Workshop

With all that new knowledge fresh in your head, we're torn. We can take it easy on you and let things settle in, or we can work hard to reinforce it all. Let's take the middle ground! A bit of a review, an easy quiz, and then some exercises to extend your understanding.

Q&A

Q Can I change the point of origin after I click with a transform tool?

A You can indeed, with all except the Reflect tool. Additional clicking moves the point of origin for the other transform tools that use it. However, a second click with the Reflect tool will establish the line of reflection and complete the transformation.

Q After you create a compound shape, that's it, right?

A No. Compound shapes are live. You can later edit the original shapes, and you can release the shape to its original shapes.

Q My system seems to slow to a crawl when I work with blends. Is this normal?

A Well, it's obviously not what any of us want, but blends can be rather complex and take a lot of the computer's horsepower. Patience is required, especially with systems that have lesser-video capabilities—the biggest slowdown is often with screen redraw.

Quiz

1. All the Transform tools are duplicated by menu commands.

    a. True

    b. False

2. Free Transform is a command that enables you to add anchor points to a path.

    a. True

    b. False

3. The Pathfinder palette enables you to reset shapes to their original fills and strokes after a Merge.

    a. True

    b. False

Quiz Answers

1. b. False. The Free Transform tool, for example, cannot be duplicated by a command.

2. b. False. Reshape is a tool that usually adds anchor points. Free Transform is a tool that does not add anchor points.

3. b. False. You can return objects to their original appearance by releasing a compound shape, but the Pathfinder commands are not reversible except with the Undo command.

Exercises

1. Draw a series of objects using the Line, Rectangle, Ellipse, and Spiral tools. Give them all the default of one-point black stroke and white fill. Select each in turn and experiment with the Twist tool. Compare the effects of the tool on an ellipse and a perfect circle.

2. Draw three rectangles of approximately the same size and fill them each with a different pattern. Use the Shear tool to try to find the proper angles to make them look like two walls and a floor.

3. Create a bunch of objects on the artboard. Open the Align palette. Practice designating a key object for alignment. (Remember that the key object doesn't move, all other objects align to it. After selecting the objects to be aligned, click once with a selection tool on the key object. Work with the Distribute Objects buttons, too. Get a feel for the difference between distributing with and without the Align to Artboard option. Get a feel for Distribute Spacing, too. (If it's not showing in the palette click the arrow in the palette's tab to cycle through the options.)

12

4. Create a star, a circle, and a square on a blank artboard. Give them different colored fills and strokes. Select them in order with the Selection tool, and then create a blend. Undo. Deselect. Select them in a different order, say, circle, star, square, and create a blend. Undo. Work with the Blend tool to designate various anchor points to blend.

PART III
Powerful Illustrator

Hour

Hour 13

Gaining Flexibility Through Layers

You've seen many times in past hours how the order you draw objects determines how they overlap and in what order they appear. Back in Hour 4, "Making Selections," you learned to use the commands under the Object, Arrange submenu to shuffle objects in the stacking order. Now you'll learn far more powerful ways to arrange and control your artwork in an illustration. In this hour, you'll learn:

- How layers work
- The Layers palette
- Creating layers and sublayers
- Rearranging layers and moving artwork between layers
- Showing, hiding, and locking layers
- Layer appearances and targeting layers
- Targeting objects on layers

Working with Layers

Theoretically, layers work like transparent sheets of plastic. You put the artwork on the layer and anyplace that there's no artwork, the lower layers show through. This is simply an extension of what we've been doing—when you create objects, anyplace there aren't objects, things behind can show through. For example, if you have two overlapping objects and the top object has a fill of None and a black stroke, the lower object shows through the middle but is hidden by the stroke.

If layers themselves were not transparent, the following artwork would not be visible. In Figure 13.1, you can see on the left what four nontransparent layers might look like. On the right, however, you see the kind of mess transparent layers allow you to create.

FIGURE **13.1**

Each object is on a separate layer. With transparent layers, they can be stacked and still be visible.

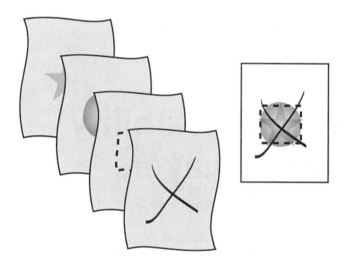

Why Layers?

If Illustrator enables us to change the stacking order of our artwork with the Object, Arrange commands, why do we need layers? Layers enable us to conveniently organize and control our artwork and, as you'll learn later in this hour, to apply appearance characteristics to entire groups of objects. Each layer can also be hidden to enable you to see other artwork better, or can be locked to prevent inadvertent changes.

Think about mapmakers, or cartographers, for just a moment. Each map has quite a few different types of symbols and artwork. You might see the land in one color and water in another. Highways, railroads, rivers, and boundaries are all different styles of lines on most maps. Cities of different sizes are represented by dots of different sizes. Terrain maps have contour lines to indicate elevation. They might also have different symbols to indicate different types of vegetation, or symbols to show where swamps and marshes are located. Each type of artwork can be isolated on a separate layer, making it easy to find and update. With the ability to hide layers, the cartographer can remove distractions and work with one category of symbols at a time.

As you create increasingly complex illustrations you'll come to love the flexibility that Illustrator's layers allow.

The Layers Palette

At the heart of this flexibility is the Layers palette, as shown in Figure 13.2. This is where you do things such as organize your artwork, show and hide and lock, apply styles, and select or even delete large numbers of objects at the same time.

Figure 13.2

The Layers palette enables you to control your artboard.

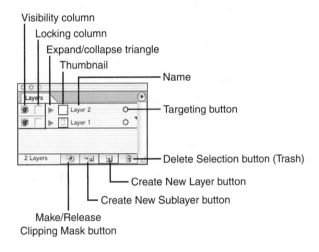

- Visibility: Clicking in this column will show or hide the content of the layer (or the specific path or group). It's also possible to have a layer show in Outline mode by Command+clicking (Mac)/Control+clicking (Windows) in this column.

- Locking: When a layer (or path or group) is locked, no changes can be made to the contents. (However, you can still delete the layer and its contents by dragging it to the trash icon in the Layers palette.)

- Expand/Collapse: Because the Layers palette can get crowded quickly, Illustrator enables you to show all the contents of a layer (or sublayer or group), or streamline the palette by just showing the major items.

- Thumbnail: The content of the layer (or sublayer or group, or a path itself) will be shown in miniature.

13

- Name: The name of the layer (or sublayer, group, or path) will be shown. Double-click to open the Layer Options and rename. (Layer Options will be discussed later in this hour.)

- Targeting Button: As you'll see throughout this hour, targeting a layer (or sublayer, group, or path) is basically the same as selecting it on the artboard. When you target a layer, you select all the artwork on the layer. (Locked items cannot be targeted.)

- Make/Release Clipping Mask Button: Clipping masks, which will be discussed in Hour 16, "Showing and Hiding with Masks," enable you to selectively reveal the contents of a layer. The topmost object on the layer is used as a mask, and any artwork beyond its path is hidden. The button creates and releases masks.

- Create New Sublayer Button: As you'll see in a few moments, Illustrator enables you to create sublayers to further organize your artwork.

- Create New Layer Button: Click to add a new layer, Option+click (Mac)/Alt+click (Windows) to add a new layer and immediately open the Layer Options dialog box.

- Delete Selection Button (Trash): Click this button to delete the active layer or sublayer (and all the contents) or a group or path. The item(s) to be deleted must be highlighted in the layers palette before you click the button.

In Figure 13.2, the current document has two layers. The triangles to the left of the layer names enable you to expand or collapse them in the palette, showing or hiding their content. Let's expand them and see what is actually on the artboard (see Figure 13.3).

FIGURE 13.3

When expanded, you can see the full content of the artboard.

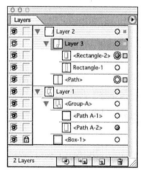

In previous hours (and most following), we use *path* to refer to an open path and *object* to refer to a closed path. The Layers palette, on the other hand, makes no differentiation—open or closed, paths are paths.

As you can see, Illustrator uses a hierarchical structure for the Layers palette. That is, items on a layer or sublayer or within a group show as indented to the right under that parent layer, sublayer, or group. We'll start by looking at the items in the palette.

Layer 2 contains a sublayer (Layer 3) and a path named <Path>. The sublayer has a pair of objects, called <Rectangle-2> and Rectangle-1. Layer 1 includes the group <Group-A>, with its two component paths, and a separate object called <Box-1>.

> By default, Illustrator will name layers and sublayers with the name Layer and the next available number. Paths and groups, in contrast, are named generically as, <Path> and <Group>, respectively. (The angle brackets are included by Illustrator.) When you rename layers, sublayers, groups, and paths you can use whatever name you like, with or without brackets. Notice, for example, Rectangle 1 in Figure 13.3. When it was renamed, brackets were not used.

Looking at your Layers palette, you can see that the layers and sublayers have shading behind their names, whereas the group and the paths do not. That enables you to instantly differentiate groups and sublayers, no matter what name they have.

Selecting Objects Using the Layers Palette

Just as you can select objects and paths by clicking them with a selection tool on the artboard, you can click them in the Layers palette to select them. Take another look at Figure 13.3. The right side of the Layers palette gives you visual feedback about what paths and groups are selected. There are four variations.

- The empty circles to the right of most items in the Layers palette in Figure 13.3 indicate that the items are not currently selected (and have not had an appearance characteristic applied).
- A filled circle, such as those next to <Rectangle-2> and <Path A-2>, indicates that an appearance characteristic has been applied.
- The empty concentric circles next to <Path> show that the object is currently selected but has not had an appearance applied to it.
- When the filled circle has a circle around it, such as <Rectangle-2>, the object is currently selected and has had an appearance characteristic applied to it.

Appearance characteristics that will cause the targeting button in the Layers palette to appear filled include effects, additional strokes or fills, and virtually anything else other than a basic fill/stroke/default transparency appearance.

13

Selecting multiple objects on the artboard is easy, just Shift+click. Likewise, you can Shift+click multiple items in the Layers palette. You can even mix and match layers, sub-layer, groups, and individual paths.

Layer Options

In addition to giving you a chance to rename your layers, you have a variety of other options in the Layer Options dialog box (see Figure 13.4)

FIGURE 13.4

Open the Layer Options dialog box for a layer either through the Layers palette menu or by double-clicking the layer in the palette.

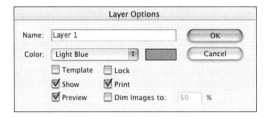

- You can assign a color for the layer from the pop-up menu or click the swatch to open the Color Picker. The layer's color is used for paths and bounding boxes (among other things) to help you identify which objects are selected on the art-board, but it has no effect on the actual color of objects on the layer.

- The Template check box makes the layer a template (as I'm sure you guessed). Templates are locked by default and are used primarily to give you a background image to trace, copy, or use as a guide.

- Unchecking the Show box is the same as clicking in the left column of the Layers palette next to the layer's name ("poking out the eyeball," so to speak). It simply hides the layer.

- When Preview is unchecked, the layer is in Outline mode. This is like using the menu command View, Outline, but it affects only the one layer instead of the whole image.

- Locking a layer prevents any changes, but the layer itself can still be deleted by dragging it to the Trash icon in the Layers palette.

- If you want a layer to be visible in the image but not print, uncheck the Print box. Non-printing layers can be used like templates to provide guides or traceable images.

- When a layer has raster images placed on it, you can make them appear dimmed out with the Dim Images checkbox and numeric field. Again, when tracing images or using them as guides, it might be helpful to have them appear more faintly on the artboard. (This is independent of reduced opacity using the Transparency palette.)

Task: Moving from Layer to Layer

Let's work with the Layers palette a little bit.

1. Open a new document in Illustrator. Make sure that the Layers palette is visible.

2. Click the New Layer button twice to create two new layers. By default these layers will be named Layer 2 and Layer 3. Notice that new layers are added above existing layers. (Just as a new object is added to the artboard above an existing object.) Your Layers palette should look similar to Figure 13.5

FIGURE **13.5**

Three empty layers should appear in the palette.

3. Press D on the keyboard to ensure that the basic appearance is active.

4. Select the Ellipse tool from the Toolbox and drag a simple circle anywhere on the artboard. In the Layers palette you should see that the active layer (Layer 3) now has a triangle next to its name, indicating that there's something on the layer. A small square appears at the right end of that line in the Layers palette, too, showing that the object is selected.

5. Click the triangle next to Layer 3 to expand that line. <Path> has been added to Layer 3 and the targeting button has the distinctive concentric circles, indicating that the path is selected on the artboard. The item named <Path> also has a square to the right (see Figure 13.6). That square should match the color of the path visible around the circle on the artboard.

FIGURE **13.6**

The object is selected on the artboard, but notice that Layer 3 is still selected in the Layers palette.

13

6. Press the Command (Mac)/Control (Windows) key and hold it down, temporarily switching to the Selection tool. The bounding box should appear around the circle, also in the color of Layer 3. Release the key.

▼ 7. In the Layers palette, click <Path> and drag it directly on top of Layer 2. A large sideways arrowhead will appear to the left of Layer 2. Release the mouse button. The Layers palette should now look like that shown in Figure 13.7. On the artboard, the color of the circle's path has automatically been updated.

FIGURE 13.7

The selection indicator square is now next to Layer 2 instead of Layer 3, and the color of the boxes now matches Layer 2's color.

8. Double–click Layer 2 in the Layers palette. In the Layer Options dialog box, change the color to Olive Green or Lavender, whichever suits your mood. Click OK. The path on the artboard and the squares for <Path> and Layer 2 in the Layers palette are automatically updated.

9. Double-click Layer 2 in the Layers palette to reopen the Layer Options dialog box. Check the Template box (see Figure 13.8) and click OK.

FIGURE 13.8

When you click Template, the layer is automatically locked, the options to Show, Preview, and Print are grayed out, and you now have the option of how dim you want placed raster images to appear on the layer.

10. In the Layers palette, Layer 2 now has a new symbol in the visibility column (far left), the name is now in *italics*, and it is locked. Because the layer is locked, <Path> is no longer selected (see Figure 13.9). (Even though the layer was automatically locked in the Layer Options dialog box, you can unlock it by clicking on
▼   the lock icon in the Layers palette. It will remain a template layer.)

FIGURE **13.9**

An object on a locked layer cannot be selected, either on the artboard or in the layers palette.

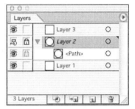

11. Make Layer 3 active and click the New Sublayer button in the Layers palette. The new sublayer appears indented below Layer 3 and takes the next available number for its name (Layer 4 in this case). Note that the new sublayer is automatically selected in the Layers palette. (Illustrator assumes that you made the sublayer because you want to use it.)

12. Drag a rectangle. Expand Layer 4 in the Layers palette. Layer 3 and Layer 4 both have squares to the right, indicating that a piece of artwork is selected somewhere within their territories. However, the two layers have different colors assigned. Although the new <Path> assumes the color of Layer 4, the sublayer does not assume the color of its parent layer (see Figure 13.10).

FIGURE **13.10**

Open the Layer Options dialog box for a layer either through the Layers palette menu or by double-clicking the layer in the palette.

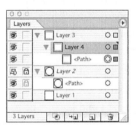

13. Drag the new <Path> item in the Layers palette from Layer 4 to Layer 3. Its selection indicator box will change color. It will no longer be indented two places to the right, appearing instead at the same hierarchical level as Layer 4. You can close this document now without saving it.

The Layers Palette Menu

The Layers palette menu shown in Figure 13.11 gives you a lot of commands with which to work.

13

Figure 13.11

Figure 13.11

Not all the options are available all the time. Many are grayed out unless one or more paths or layers are selected.

Most of them are self-explanatory. Creating new layers and sublayers can be done either with the palette's buttons or commands. You can duplicate a layer or a path by dragging it to the New Layer button. You can delete a path or layer by dragging it to the Trash icon, and so on. However, there are some pretty neat things buried here, too.

- Locate Object: In a very complicated illustration, with about a gazillion objects and paths, it might be hard to find one specific little circle or square in the Layers palette (especially if everything is named <Path>). Find the item on the artboard and select it. Use this menu command and the Layers palette will automatically expand and scroll to show you where it is.

- Merge Selected: You can Shift+click to select multiple layers. Using this command moves all the artwork on all the layers to one layer. The empty layers are then automatically deleted. A great way to neaten up the Layers palette!

- Flatten Artwork: This command puts all the artwork from all layers on a single layer. (Don't confuse this with Photoshop's Flatten layers command—all the Illustrator objects remain independent and editable.)

- Collect in New Layer: Shift+click to select multiple paths and objects on the artboard or in the Layers palette, then use this command to bring them all together on a single layer.

- Release to Layers: These commands are especially cool when creating animations. You can draw all the artwork on a single layer, then use one of these commands to move each object to a separate layer, preparing the image for frame-based animation. The difference between the two Release to Layers commands is whether or not preceding items are repeated. When you use Release to Layers (Sequence), each new layer gets one object. When you use Release to Layers (Build), all the preceding objects are included in each successive layer. Figure 13.12 shows the comparison.

FIGURE 13.12

The original is shown in the dashed box (left). You can release the five dots to individual layers using either Sequence (middle) or Build (right).

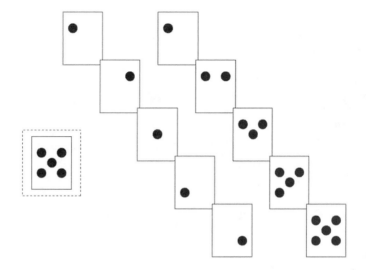

- Reverse Order: You can swap the stacking order of selected items in the Layers palette.
- Paste Remembers Layers: This option, when selected, helps you copy objects and paths. Pasting an object back into the document from the Clipboard will put it on the original layer. If the original layer can't be found, one is created. This even works when copying between documents.

Appearances and Layers

In Hour 11, "Applying Appearances and Styles," you learned that you can select an object on the artboard and apply a style or change an appearance characteristic. You can also do this through the Layers palette. Click the targeting icon for a path or object in the Layers palette and make the changes. Simple enough. Ah, but there's more! And it's better. You can target an entire layer and apply appearance characteristics to every object on it at one time.

13

Targeting a Layer

Let's say that you maintain a chart. You use this chart to track the status of four-hundred projects. When a project is in progress, it's a yellow circle. When there's a problem, it's red. When the project is ahead of schedule, it's blue. Take a look at Figure 13.13.

FIGURE 13.13

Each of the four hundred dots represents a project. With the layer Red targeted in the Layers palette, its circles are selected on the artboard.

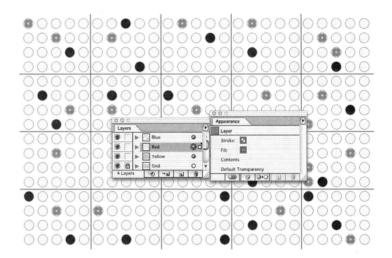

The layer Red is targeted in the Layers palette (the targeting button is a pair of circles, one filled). The Appearance palette shows that a red fill and no stroke will be applied to any object on the layer. On the artboard, each of the red circles is selected. Contrast Figure 13.13 with Figure 13.14. When an object is selected, the Appearance palette shows the individual object's characteristics, not those of the layer.

FIGURE 13.14

The red circle nearest the middle has been selected on the artboard.

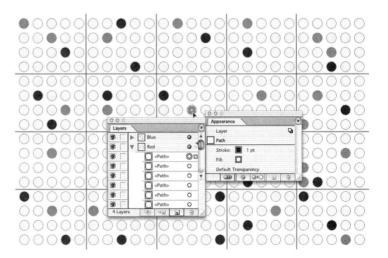

Task: Working with Targeted Layers

The best way to learn how to work with targeted layers is to actually work with them.

1. Open a new document in Illustrator. The default values are fine.

2. In the Layers palette, click twice on the New Layer button to create a pair of new layers.

3. Click the targeting icon for Layer 1 in the Layers palette. You'll see the concentric empty circles to the right of the name.

4. In the Styles palette, click the style called Caution Tape or another style.

5. Click the targeting icon for Layer 2 and select the style Bermuda.

6. Do not assign a style to Layer 3.

7. Make Layer 3 the active layer by clicking on its name in the Layers palette.

8. Press D on the keyboard to restore the basic setting, or click the little icon to the lower left of the fill and stroke icons in the Toolbox.

9. Select the Rectangle tool in the Toolbox or press M on the keyboard.

10. Drag a rectangle on Layer 3. It should have the default white fill and black one-point stroke.

11. In the Layers palette, if necessary, expand Layer 3 by clicking the triangle to the left of the layer name. Drag <Path> from Layer 3 to Layer 2. The rectangle assumes the Bermuda style.

12. Drag the rectangle to Layer 1. It now picks up the Caution Tape style. You can close this document without saving.

Task: Targeting Layers versus Targeting Objects

Illustrator gives you additional flexibility with targeting, too. When working with styles, you can create a complex object by targeting the layer or you can maintain individual objects by targeting the paths. Here's how it works.

1. Open a new document, using the RGB color mode.

2. Press D on the keyboard to restore the basic appearance.

3. Drag three overlapping rectangles, as shown in Figure 13.15.

4. Switch to the Selection tool by pressing V on the keyboard. Shift+click each of the objects on the artboard. The objects will appear within a bounding box on the artboard and will show as selected in the Layers palette (see Figure 13.16).

▼

FIGURE 13.15
Note that all three rectangles are on the same layer.

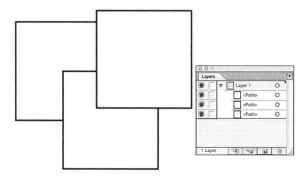

FIGURE 13.16
All three rectangles are selected.

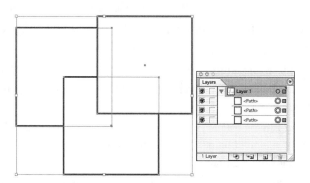

5. Using the Styles palette, apply the Patriotic Ribbon style to the three selected rectangles. Deselect the rectangles by clicking away from them on the artboard. They will appear on the artboard as three separate objects, each with the style (see Figure 13.17).

FIGURE 13.17
The thumbnails in the Layers palette also reflect the change in appearance.

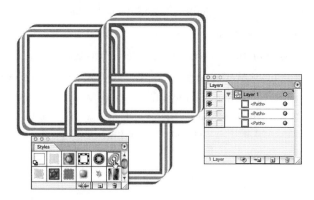

▼

▼   6. Use Command+Z (Mac)/Control+Z (Windows) to Undo.

     7. In the Layers palette, click the targeting button for Layer 1 to select the layer.

     8. Now apply the Patriotic Ribbon style by clicking on it in the Styles palette. As you can see in Figure 13.18, the rectangles are treated as a complex object and the style is applied to them as a whole. Also note in the Layers palette that the thumbnails for the individual paths show the basic appearance in their thumbnails.

FIGURE 13.18

The appearance is applied to the layer as a whole, not to the individual objects.

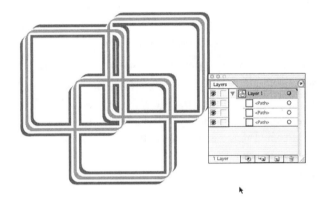

     9. Undo.

    10. Select the three rectangles on the artboard and use the menu command Object, Group; or use shortcut Command+G (Mac)/Control+G (Windows).

    11. In the Layers palette select the group by clicking on its targeting button.

    12. Apply the style Patriotic Ribbon to the group. You'll see that the results are the same as applying the style to the layer.

    13. In the Layers palette, click the New Layer button.

▲   14. In the Layers palette, drag the topmost <Path> item from Layer 1 to Layer 2. The style is left behind and the object returns to the basic appearance.

13

Summary

You've learned a lot about the power of the Layers palette in Illustrator in this hour. Not only does it enable you to organize your work, but it expands your creative capabilities through layer targeting.

Workshop

A little reinforcement is good for dams, bridges, bulkheads, and anyone completing this hour. A few review and quiz questions, and a couple of exercises to cement ideas firmly in your brain, and we'll call it quits for this one.

Q&A

Q If I move an object from one layer to another, will it change color?

A If no appearance characteristics are applied to either layer, the only color change you'll see is in the path and bounding box when the object is selected.

Q How does targeted appearance work?

A The appearance belongs to the item in the Layers palette. If the item is a path and the path is moved to another layer, the appearance goes with it. If the appearance is targeted to a layer, then any object created on or moving to the layer assumes the appearance. Likewise, any object moving from the layer to another layer leaves the appearance behind.

Q Why would I want to flatten an image?

A Some file formats don't support Illustrator layers. Putting all the artwork on one layer can prevent problems. Also, you can create on multiple layers freely, flatten the image, then release to layers to prepare for animation.

Quiz

1. When the Layers palette shows concentric hollow circles to the right of a layer's name...

    a. ...an effect has been applied to the layer.

    b. ...no effect has been applied to the layer, but you can do so now.

    c. ...one or more objects on the layer have effects applied.

    d. ...only one object of many on the layer is selected.

2. The difference between selecting an object on the artboard with the Selection tool and clicking its targeting button in the Layers palette is...

    a. ...none.

    b. ...one works, the other doesn't.

    c. ...when using the Layers palette, only effects can be applied.

    d. ...the targeting button will cause the object to be automatically deleted.

3. When you assign a color to a layer using the Layer Options dialog box, what happens?

    a. Every object on the layer uses that color as its fill

    b. Every object on the layer uses that color as its stroke

    c. The bounding boxes and edges of objects on that layer will match the color

    d. Grids and guides assigned to that layer will be that color

Quiz Answers

1. b. The inner circle indicates that no effect has yet been applied (it is hollow). The outer circle indicates that the layer is targeted.

2. a. You can select objects either way.

3. c. The layer's color is designed to help you determine what layer selected objects are on.

Exercises

1. Open a blank Illustrator document. Open the Layers palette. Start creating new layers and sublayers. Get comfortable with where a layer will be added. Don't forget to experiment with the modifier keys!

2. Create a variety of objects on various layers of an Illustrator document. Practice moving items from layer to layer and changing the stacking order within a layer using the Layers palette.

3. Open a new Illustrator document. Create several layers. Assign a style to each, using the Layers palette. Create a layer at the top and don't assign a style to it. On that layer, create a rectangle with the basic appearance (black and white). Move it from layer to layer and watch how its appearance changes. Go back to the top layer. Create a circle. Assign a style to it. Move the circle from layer to layer and watch the interaction of styles.

13

HOUR 14

Applying Advanced Typography Techniques

In Hour 10, "Adding Text," you learned all about creating text in Illustrator. You learned about the three kinds of text, and how to move text around. But there's a lot more to text than just the words themselves. In this hour, you'll learn how to work with the type—or more importantly, how to make it look good. Of course, that's the goal with anything you do, and Illustrator has the tools to make text look great.

In this hour, you'll learn all about the following:

- The Character palette
- Fonts
- The Paragraph palette
- The Tab palette
- The MM Design palette
- Multiple-master fonts

The Character Palette

You control your type (and believe me, type needs lots of controlling) by using Illustrator's Character palette (see Figure 14.1). To open the Character palette, use the Command+T (Macintosh)/Control+T (Windows) keyboard shortcut, or select Character from the Type submenu under the Window menu. In the Character palette, you specify fonts, point size, leading, and kerning. The Character palette is the central location for editing type style—how your type looks.

FIGURE 14.1

The Character palette, in all its glory, with the Multilingual Options section open.

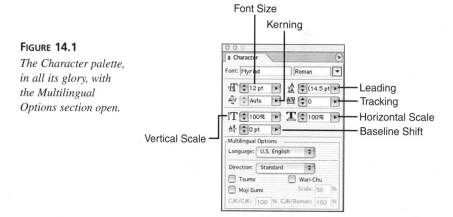

To edit text, you must select it. To do so, you can either use one of the Selection tools to select the entire text block, or you can select characters individually by

- Clicking and dragging text with the Type tool
- Clicking in the text with the Type tool and pressing the left or right arrow key on the keyboard while holding down the Shift key to select one or more letters
- Clicking in the text with the Type tool and pressing the left or right arrow key on the keyboard while holding down the Command (Mac)/Control (Windows) key to select one or more words
- Clicking in the text with the Type tool and pressing the up or down arrow key on the keyboard while holding down the Shift key to select one or more lines of type
- Clicking in the text with the Type tool and pressing the up or down arrow key on the keyboard while holding down the Shift+Command (Mac)/Shift+Control (Windows) keys to select one or more paragraphs of type

Font

NEW TERM A *font* is a style of type, usually grouped in families such as Helvetica or Times. Many different fonts are available, and a font is basically the personality of your type. Loud text such as "Caution!" might be in a fat bold font, whereas more delicate words, such as "Kiss," might be in a script italic font (see Figure 14.2).

After you choose a font, you also specify what style you want, such as Roman (normal), italic, bold, and so on.

FIGURE 14.2
Use different fonts.

Size

NEW TERM Type is traditionally measured in *points*. You can specify your type to be any size from 0.1 point (really small) up to 1296 points (really large). You can quickly enlarge or reduce your type in two-point increments by pressing Command+Shift+> (Mac)/Control+Shift+> (Windows) (that's the right angle bracket key) and Command+Shift+< (Mac)/Control+Shift+< (Windows) (the left angle bracket key), respectively. This method works regardless of how you selected the type (with the arrow keys or the Type tool).

The amount of change in point size that occurs when invoking keyboard shortcuts is determined by the setting in Preferences, Type & Auto Tracing. The default setting is 2 points.

If you need even bigger type, you can simply use the Scale tool to resize it.

14

Leading

NEW TERM *Leading* (pronounced *ledding*) is the amount of space between each baseline in a paragraph of type, and it's also measured in points. (The baseline is the invisible line that runs along the bottom of most letters, including every letter in this sentence except for g and y.) If the leading size and the point size are the same, your text has *solid leading*. A lot of space between each baseline is called *open leading*, whereas very little space is called *tight leading* (see Figure 14.3). Leading is important in determining readability. Typically, the wider your block of text, the more leading you need. You can also enable Illustrator to determine the leading, even if you change type size in a paragraph, by using the Auto option from the Leading pop-up menu in the Character palette.

FIGURE 14.3

Text with auto leading (left), open leading (center), and tight leading (right).

The term "leading" comes from the thin strips of metal that were once inserted by hand between rows of cast type. Because of the origin of the term, it is pronounced like the metal, rather than like the verb *to lead*.

The term "leading" comes from the thin strips of metal that were once inserted by hand between rows of cast type. Because of the origin of the term, it is pronounced like the metal, rather than like the verb *to lead*.

The term "leading" comes from the thin strips of metal that were once inserted by hand between rows of cast type. Because of the origin of the term, it is pronounced like the metal, rather than like the verb *to lead*.

The keyboard shortcuts for increasing and decreasing leading are Option+↓ (Mac)/Alt+↓ (Windows) and Option+↑ (Mac)/Alt+↑ (Windows), respectively.

Kerning and Tracking

NEW TERM *Kerning* is the space between two adjacent characters. *Tracking* is the amount of letter spacing (the space between individual letters) applied globally across many letters. Negative numbers mean that your kerning or tracking is tight, and the letters are closer to one another. Positive numbers mean that your kerning or tracking is loose, and the letters are farther apart from each other (see Figure 14.4).

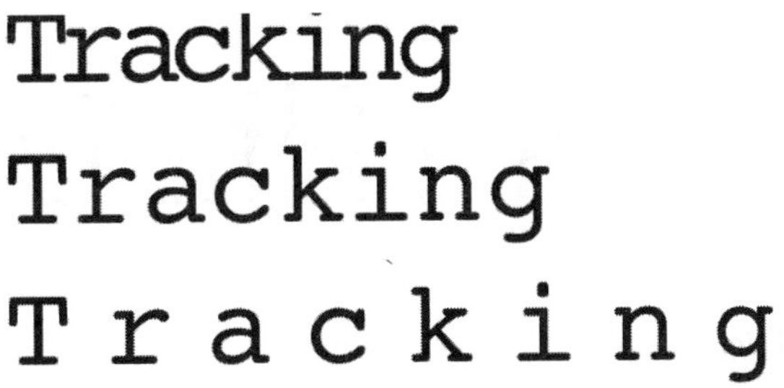

FIGURE 14.4

The top word has tight tracking, the middle word has tracking set to zero, and the bottom word has loose tracking.

Tracking

Tracking

T r a c k i n g

The keyboard shortcuts for tightening and loosening kerning or tracking are Option+← (Mac)/Alt+← (Windows) and Option+→ /Mac)/Alt+→ (Windows), respectively. If you have more than one letter selected, Illustrator automatically applies tracking. Otherwise, invoking the keyboard shortcut applies kerning.

Horizontal and Vertical Scale

Using horizontal and vertical scale, you can adjust the width and height of selected text (see Figure 14.5). Adjusting the text this way can result in type that looks squashed and distorted in unsightly ways. For true horizontal and vertical scaling, try to use multiple master typefaces, which are covered later in this hour.

FIGURE 14.5

From the left, the original letter; scaled vertically to 150% and then scaled horizontally to 150%.

Baseline Shift

All type is aligned to a baseline. You can select type and shift the baseline for that selection (see Figure 14.6). Shifting type is useful for creating superscripts or subscripts as well as creating type effects. In Illustrator, however, one of the most useful applications for baseline shift occurs when you have type on a path (see Figure 14.7). You can use baseline shift to move the type off the path, and you can give the path a stroke without detracting from the look of the type itself. Remember that when you use type on a path, the path automatically gets a fill and stroke of None. (Make sure you use the Direct Selection tool; otherwise, the type gets a stroke, too.)

14

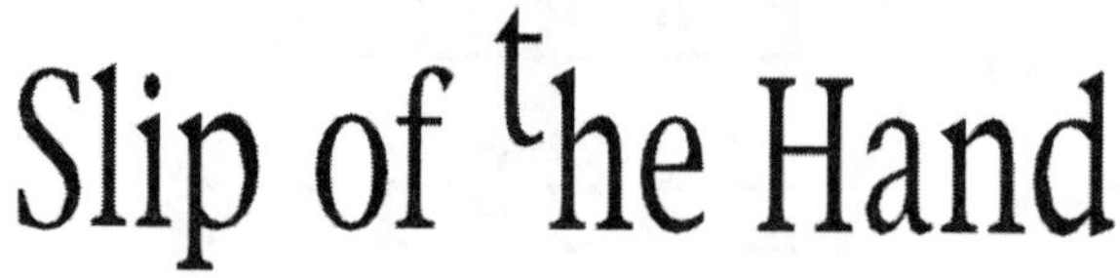

FIGURE 14.6

The "t" has a positive baseline shift.

Slip of the Hand

FIGURE 14.7

By using baseline shift to move up the type, you can create a colored stroke by using the same path the type is on, and the stroke won't interfere with the type.

The keyboard shortcuts for raising and lowering baseline shift are Option+Shift+↑ (Mac)/Alt+Shift+↑ (Windows) and Option+Shift+↓ (Mac)/Alt+Shift+↓ (Windows), respectively. The increment is set in Illustrator's preferences. By default, each time you press the shortcut key you change the baseline by 2 points.

Task: Applying a Baseline Shift

▲ TASK

I saw you sit up straight in your chair just now. Admit it, you thought that what you saw in Figure 14.7 was pretty cool. Why don't you try it now?

1. Press L to select the Ellipse tool, and then draw a circle.

2. Switch to the Type tool by pressing the T key.

3. While holding down the Option (Mac)/Alt (Windows) key, click the path of the circle at the top.

4. When you see a blinking cursor where you clicked, Illustrator is waiting for you to type something. Type Baseline Shift (or any words that may come to mind).

5. With the cursor still blinking, press Command+A (Mac)/Control+A (Windows) to select all your type.

6. Press Command+Shift+C (Mac)/Control+Shift+C (Windows) to center the text on the path. (I'll cover centering in detail later in the hour, so don't worry.)

7. Increase the type size by pressing Command+Shift+> (Mac)/Control+Shift+> (Windows) repeatedly until you achieve the size you want.

▼

8. Press Option+Shift+↑ (Mac)/Alt+Shift+↑ (Windows) repeatedly until the type is as far from the baseline as you like.

9. Press Command+Shift+A (Mac)/Control+Shift+A (Windows) to deselect everything, and then press the A key to select the Direct Selection tool.

10. To make this process easier, switch to Artwork mode by pressing Command+Y (Mac)/Control+Y (Windows). You should now be able to see the path. Using the Direct Selection tool, click the path to select it.

11. If the Stroke palette is not already open, press the F10 key to open it, and enter a weight for the stroke.

12. Switch back to Preview mode by pressing Command+Y (Mac)/Control+Y (Windows). You now have the stroked path and the type on the path, all within one object.

The Paragraph Palette

On the Paragraph palette, you specify alignment, indents, word, and letter spacing, as well as options such as autohyphenation and hanging punctuation (see Figure 14.8).

FIGURE 14.8
The Paragraph palette.

Justification

Justification actually refers to paragraph *alignment* with both margins aligned (see Figure 14.9).

FIGURE 14.9
Paragraph alignment.

FLUSH LEFT

Lorem ipsum dolor sit amet, consectetuer adipiscing elit, sed diam nonummy nibh euismod tincidunt ut laoreet dolore magna aliquam erat volutpat. Ut wisi enim ad minim veniam, quis nostrud exerci tation ullamcorper suscipit lobortis nisl ut aliquip ex ea commodo consequat. Duis autem vel eum iriure dolor in hendrerit in vulputate velit esse molestie consequat, vel illum dolore eu feugiat nulla

FLUSH RIGHT

Lorem ipsum dolor sit amet, consectetuer adipiscing elit, sed diam nonummy nibh euismod tincidunt ut laoreet dolore magna aliquam erat volutpat. Ut wisi enim ad minim veniam, quis nostrud exerci tation ullamcorper suscipit lobortis nisl ut aliquip ex ea commodo consequat. Duis autem vel eum iriure dolor in hendrerit in vulputate velit esse molestie consequat, vel illum dolore eu feugiat nulla

CENTERED

Lorem ipsum dolor sit amet, consectetuer adipiscing elit, sed diam nonummy nibh euismod tincidunt ut laoreet dolore magna aliquam erat volutpat. Ut wisi enim ad minim veniam, quis nostrud exerci tation ullamcorper suscipit lobortis nisl ut aliquip ex ea commodo consequat. Duis autem vel eum iriure dolor in hendrerit in vulputate velit esse molestie consequat, vel illum dolore eu feugiat nulla

JUSTIFIED

Lorem ipsum dolor sit amet, consectetuer adipiscing elit, sed diam nonummy nibh euismod tincidunt ut laoreet dolore magna aliquam erat volutpat. Ut wisi enim ad minim veniam, quis nostrud exerci tation ullamcorper suscipit lobortis nisl ut aliquip ex ea commodo consequat. Duis autem vel eum iriure dolor in hendrerit in vulputate velit esse molestie consequat, vel illum dolore eu feugiat nulla

FORCED JUSTIFIED

Lorem ipsum dolor sit amet, consectetuer adipiscing elit, sed diam nonummy nibh euismod tincidunt ut laoreet dolore magna aliquam erat volutpat. Ut wisi enim ad minim veniam, quis nostrud exerci tation ullamcorper suscipit lobortis nisl ut aliquip ex ea commodo consequat. Duis autem vel eum iriure dolor in hendrerit in vulputate velit esse molestie consequat, vel illum dolore eu feugiat nulla

14

You can align a paragraph of type in five different ways in Illustrator:

- Align left: Command+Shift+L (Mac)/Control+Shift+L (Windows)
- Align right: Command+Shift+R (Mac)/Control+Shift+R (Windows)
- Centered: Command+Shift+C (Mac)/Control+Shift+C (Windows)
- Justify full lines: Command+Shift+J (Mac)/Control+Shift+J (Windows)
- Justify all lines (flush left and right): Command+Shift+F (Mac)/Control+Shift+F (Windows)

You can select these options quickly by clicking the icons found at the top of the Paragraph palette (see Figure 14.10).

Figure 14.10

The alignment icons in the Paragraph palette.

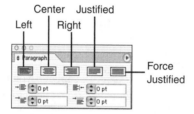

> Certain characters do not show up on your screen when you type them, such as a space, a soft or hard return, a tab, and so forth. Some page layout programs—QuarkXPress, for example—have an option called Show Invisibles, which enables you to see these characters as symbols. (They don't print, of course; you can just see them onscreen.) Illustrator can also show these characters. Simply select Show Hidden Characters from the Type menu. To hide the characters, simply select the menu item again.

Indents

NEW TERM   The three different *indent* settings on the Paragraph palette are Left Indent, First Line Indent, and Right Indent. The left and right indents affect the entire paragraph of type, whereas the first line indent affects just the first line of the paragraph. You can also use negative numbers, especially with First Line Indent, to move type outward.

Illustrator also includes a setting for space before each paragraph. Sometimes you might want to add a little bit of extra space before each paragraph to increase readability, as well as make it easier to identify where a paragraph ends and the next one begins (see Figure 14.11).

FIGURE 14.11

The different paragraph settings.

LEFT INDENT	FIRST LINE INDENT	RIGHT INDENT	SPACE BEFORE PARAGRAPH
Lorem ipsum dolor sit amet, consectetuer adipiscing elit, sed diam nonummy nibh euismod tincidunt ut laoreet dolore magna aliquam erat volutpat. Ut wisi enim ad minim veniam, quis nostrud exerci tation ullamcorper suscipit lobortis nisl ut aliquip ex ea commodo consequat. Duis autem vel eum iriure dolor in hendrerit in vulputate velit esse molestie consequat, vel	Lorem ipsum dolor sit amet, consectetuer adipiscing elit, sed diam nonummy nibh euismod tincidunt ut laoreet dolore magna aliquam erat volutpat. Ut wisi enim ad minim veniam, quis nostrud exerci tation ullamcorper suscipit lobortis nisl ut aliquip ex ea commodo consequat. Duis autem vel eum iriure dolor in hendrerit in vulputate velit esse molestie consequat, vel illum dolore	Lorem ipsum dolor sit amet, consectetuer adipiscing elit, sed diam nonummy nibh euismod tincidunt ut laoreet dolore magna aliquam erat volutpat. Ut wisi enim ad minim veniam, quis nostrud exerci tation ullamcorper suscipit lobortis nisl ut aliquip ex ea commodo consequat. Duis autem vel eum iriure dolor in hendrerit in vulputate velit esse molestie consequat, vel	Lorem ipsum dolor sit amet, consectetuer adipiscing elit, sed diam nonummy nibh euismod tincidunt ut laoreet dolore magna aliquam erat volutpat. Ut wisi enim ad minim veniam, quis nostrud exerci tation ullamcorper suscipit lobortis nisl ut aliquip ex ea commodo consequat. Duis autem vel eum iriure dolor in hendrerit in

Word and Letter Spacing

Word and Letter Spacing settings in the Paragraph palette let you control spacing between words and letters when justified type is used. These settings control when words become hyphenated or are forced to another line by specifying how far Illustrator can stretch the spacing between words and letters.

The Tab Palette

To create tabs in a paragraph, open the Tab Ruler by choosing it from the Type submenu of the Window menu (see Figure 14.12). It's a floating palette, so you can position it anywhere on the page (see Figure 14.13). To add a tab, click the ruler where you want the tab to appear. After you click, a highlighted tab arrow appears. You can now make the tab a right, center, left, or decimal tab by clicking the icons in the upper-left corner of the Tab Ruler palette (see Figure 14.14). To delete a tab, drag it off the palette (see Figure 14.15), and to change the measurement system quickly, Shift+click in the upper portion of the palette.

14

FIGURE 14.12

Choose Tab Ruler from the Type submenu.

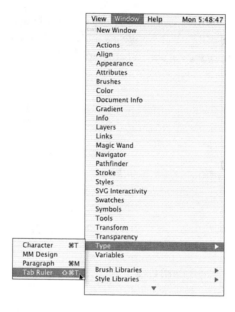

FIGURE 14.13

The Tab palette.

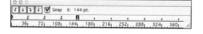

FIGURE 14.14

Clicking these icons defines the type of tab.

FIGURE 14.15

Drag a tab off the palette to delete it.

The MM Design Palette

Illustrator has full support for multiple-master typefaces. Developed by Adobe, a multiple-master typeface contains a variable width, weight, or even serif axis (see Figure 14.16). By controlling the axis, you can modify the typeface to fit your exact specifications. The MM Design palette (found with the other type palettes in the Window menu) enables you to modify multiple-master typefaces in real-time, right in Illustrator (see Figure 14.17). Simply drag the sliders to edit the typeface. You need to have a multiple-master font and have it selected to use this feature.

Figure 14.16

A multiple-master typeface can have scalable widths, weights, or other attributes that you can modify.

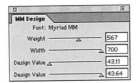

Figure 14.17

The MM Design palette.

> Although multiple-master fonts are still sold and supported by Adobe, the emphasis now is on OpenType fonts. In addition, Mac OS X does not allow you to take advantage of multiple master technology.

Converting Text to Outlines

One of the most powerful text features in Illustrator is the capability to convert type into fully editable Bézier paths. If you choose Create Outlines from the Type menu (you need to have type selected with the Selection tool when you do this), as shown in Figure 14.18, Illustrator turns the type into Bézier paths. You can then edit each letter by using the techniques you learned in previous hours (see Figure 14.19).

14

FIGURE 14.18

Choose Create Outlines from the Type menu, Command+ Shift+O (Mac)/ Control+Shift+O (Windows).

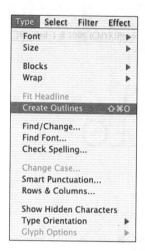

FIGURE 14.19

Edit the type that was converted to outlines.

Task: Using Type As a Mask

TASK

You can even use the type as a mask. You don't even have to convert it to outlines first—type can be used as a mask and retain its fully editable status!

1. Start by creating some art that you want to appear inside the type. I've decided to create a row of evenly spaced horizontal lines. To do the same, select the Pen tool, click once, and then, while holding down the Shift key, click again to the right or left of the first point. I've given the lines a weight of 8 points.

2. Switch to the Direct Selection tool and, while holding the Option (Mac)/Alt (Windows) key, click anywhere in the middle of the line. The line is now selected.

3. Hold the Option (Mac)/Shift+Alt (Windows) key, and click and drag the line down a bit. You have just created a copy of the line (see Figure 14.20).

4. Press Command+D (Mac)/Control+D (Windows) several times to repeat the transformation you just made in step 3. You should now have a row of lines (see Figure 14.21).

FIGURE 14.20

Using the Option (Mac)/Alt (Windows) drag function to create a duplicate.

FIGURE 14.21

A row of evenly spaced horizontal lines.

5. Because you're going to be using the lines as one unit, group them all together. After selecting them all, press Command+G (Mac)/Control+G (Windows) to create the group.

6. Using the Type tool, click away from the lines, and type a word. Make the type large, so it will be easier to see during the following steps.

7. If you want to customize the shapes, you should now select the text (Command+click for Mac, Control+click for Windows) and convert the text to outlines by pressing Command+Shift+O (Mac)/Control+Shift+O (Windows) . You can use the Direct Selection tool, or any of the other path-editing capabilities you've learned, to reshape the letters to match your concept. (Remember that you don't have to convert type to outlines to use it as a mask.)

8. A mask must be a single shape, so to use the word as a mask, you must make the word a compound path. With all the letters selected, choose Object, Compound Paths, Make, or press Command+8 (Mac)/Control+8 (Windows).

9. Position the type over the lines (see Figure 14.22). Remember, you can just press and hold the Command (Mac)/Control (Windows) key to access the Selection tool to move the word.

10. Select both the word and the lines by pressing Command+A (Mac)/Control+A (Windows) to select all.

11. To create the mask, press Command+7 (Mac)/Control+7 (Windows), or choose Object, Clipping Mask, Make. The words will now mask the lines you created (see Figure 14.23).

14

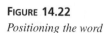

FIGURE 14.22
Positioning the word over the lines.

FIGURE 14.23
The final masked word.

You might want to convert type to outlines for two other reasons. One is that certain filters don't work on type. To run those filters, you need to convert your type to outlines first. Another reason is if you are sending your file out to another person or to a service bureau that might not have your font. Converting the type to outlines assures that it will print perfectly. When you create a logo, converting any type to outlines is always a good idea. This way, whenever you use it, you don't have to worry about fonts.

After text is converted to outlines, it cannot be turned back into text again, so you can't fix any typos. Saving a version of your file before you convert your text to outlines might be a good idea, in case you need to edit the text. In Hour 18, "Working with Filters and Live Effects," you'll learn more about creating text outlines.

Change Case

This situation happens all the time: You type something in all caps and you need it in lowercase, or vice versa. With this handy little feature, your hands are spared a few more moments from that repetitive strain injury. Simply highlight the type with the Type tool, and choose Change Case from the Type menu (see Figure 14.24). In the resulting dialog box, you can then choose how you want to change your type (see Figure 14.25).

FIGURE **14.24**
Choose Change Case from the Type menu.

FIGURE **14.25**
The Change Case dialog box.

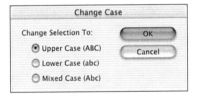

Find Font and Find/Change

You just finished an entire job, and a representative for your client calls to say his bosses loved it, but could you just change one little thing? They want all instances of the word Fred to be changed to Frederick, or maybe they want to switch one typeface for another. After you hang up the phone and slam your head into the monitor, go to the Type menu and select Find Font (see Figure 14.26). In the Find Font dialog box, you can easily change one font to another throughout the document (see Figure 14.27).

As far as changing the actual text, select Find/Change from the Type menu and, in the Find/Change dialog box (see Figure 14.28), type the word you are looking for and what it should be changed to. These functions work the same as they would in any word processing program. All happy now?

14

FIGURE **14.26**
*Select Find Font from
the Type menu.*

FIGURE **14.27**
*The Find Font dialog
box.*

FIGURE **14.28**
*The Find/Change
dialog box.*

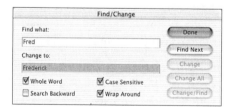

Smart Punctuation

If you want to make your type look as if it were set by an expert typographer (or just to
make it correct), use Smart Punctuation (see Figure 14.29). It replaces regular quotation
marks with the curly kind (see Figure 14.30) and inserts ligatures (on the Macintosh), em
and en dashes, ellipses, and expert fractions in your document.

FIGURE 14.29

Found in the Type menu, the Smart Punctuation feature lets you make changes to selected text or an entire document.

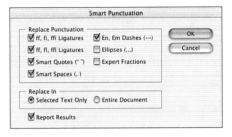

FIGURE 14.30

To the left are plain quotes, and on the right are the curly quotes from the same fonts.

Check Spelling

Illustrator also has a built-in spell checker. You can find the Check Spelling function in the Type menu (see Figure 14.31). This spell checker, shown in Figure 14.32, works just like a spell checker you would find in a word processor. It enables you to change or skip words as well as add words to the dictionary.

FIGURE 14.31

Choose Check Spelling from the Type menu.

14

FIGURE 14.32

Illustrator's Check
Spelling dialog box.

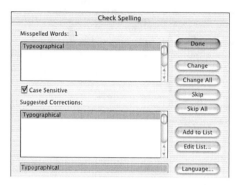

Summary

Fonts, points, leading, kerning, indents, justification: You learned all about these fancy words along with a lot of other cool stuff this hour. You learned how to use multiple-master fonts, as well as how to adjust word and letter spacing. The Change Case feature will save you hours of extra typing, and you really felt the power of Illustrator when you converted type to outlines and had the opportunity to edit the Bézier paths. By the way, converting type to paths and analyzing how the anchor points are set up is a good way to learn more about Bézier paths.

Q&A

Q Can I use multiple fonts in the same text block?

A Sure! Use the Type tool to select individual letters, words, or sentences and change the typeface in the Character palette.

Q What's the difference between leading and baseline shift?

A Leading is a paragraph attribute. That means an entire paragraph can have only one leading setting. Baseline shift enables you to adjust baseline spacing on a character basis.

Q Can I create tab leaders?

A Tab leaders are the characters that fill up the space between tabs (for example, the dots between the text and the page numbers in the Table of Contents section of this book). Unfortunately, Illustrator currently does not support tab leaders.

Q Can a paragraph have more than one indent setting?

A Yes. A single paragraph can have all three indent settings: left, right, and first line.

Quiz

1. Leading refers to
    a. Taking a few steps off first base
    b. The amount of space between baselines of type
    c. The amount of space between letters

2. Tracking refers to
    a. The amount of spacing applied across several letters
    b. Finding your FedEx package
    c. The distance a paragraph is moved inward from the left and right edges of a text block

3. Justified type means
    a. The type is aligned to the left and right of the text block.
    b. The measurement system used for measuring type.
    c. The paragraph has an indent.

4. To delete a tab setting, you
    a. Press the Delete key
    b. Shift+click the tab
    c. Drag it off the Tab palette

5. Multiple master refers to
    a. A dog with more than one owner
    b. A font technology developed by Adobe
    c. A special version of Illustrator

Quiz Answers

1. b. The term actually comes from the thin strips of lead (the metal) that were once placed between rows of type.

2. a. And the term *kerning* refers to the space between a pair of letters.

3. a. *Alignment* refers to having a straight margin on one or the other side, *justification* is having alignment on both margins.

4. c. Click directly on the tab arrow and drag it up or down, completely off the Tab Ruler, before releasing the mouse button.

14

5. b. Although multiple-master fonts never really became popular, the technology is still supported, and still *way* cool!

Exercises

1. Create several lines of area type, and practice using the keyboard shortcuts to adjust the point size, leading, kerning, and tracking.

2. Experiment using the baseline shift feature to create superscripts or subscripts as found in trademarks (™) or H_2O.

3. Create some large text in several typefaces, and convert the text to outlines. Using the Direct Selection tool, examine the paths, looking at the placement of the anchor points and the control handles. Switch to Artwork mode for easier viewing. This exercise is a good way to learn how Bézier paths work.

HOUR 15

Inserting Charts and Graphs

A picture speaks a thousand words. I'm referring, of course, to charts or graphs used to convey numerical data in a graphical way, making information easier to understand and more useful.

The advantage of using Illustrator to create graphs as opposed to a dedicated graphing program is when you create a graph in Illustrator it is made up of Illustrator-vector objects. Therefore, you can edit the graph just as you would any illustration; giving you complete control over how your graph looks. If necessary, you can then export the graph in any of Illustrator's many export formats.

In this hour, you'll learn about the following:

- Identifying the various types of graphs
- Creating a graph
- Importing and editing graph data
- Editing graph appearance
- Customizing graphs with Graph Design

Creating a Graph

Illustrator has several types of graphs you can use—nine to be exact (see Figure 15.1):

FIGURE 15.1

The many graph tools in Illustrator.

- Column: This type uses vertical bars to compare values.
- Stacked Column: The same as a Column graph except that values are stacked one on top of the other on vertical bars in this type.
- Bar: The same as a Column graph except that bars are horizontal rather than vertical.
- Stacked Bar: The same as a Stacked Column graph except that bars are horizontal, not vertical.
- Line: This type is often used to show trends over a period of time; values are plotted and connected with a line.
- Area: The same as a Line graph except that areas are filled in, indicating totals as well as trends.
- Scatter: This type is similar to a Line graph; points are plotted but not connected with any lines. This type is used to identify patterns and trends.
- Pie: This type of graph is made up of wedges, each wedge represents a portion of the whole.
- Radar: This type of graph is also called a Web graph. Radar data is presented in a circular format.

Each of these types of graphs is used to present a different kind of data. If you aren't sure which type you need, don't worry; you can switch between graph types at any time, even after you've entered data.

If you do change the type of graph later, make sure that you look at it very closely to make sure that tick marks and labels are okay. (Tick marks are explained in a few minutes.)

Task: Drawing a Graph

▼ TASK

15

In Illustrator, you begin to make a graph by defining the physical size of the graph. You do so in much the same way you draw a rectangle:

1. Select the desired Graph tool.

2. Press and drag to define a rectangle. Hold down the Option (Macintosh)/Alt (Windows) key while dragging to draw out from the center, and the Shift key constrains it to a square.

▲

Alternatively, you can just click once with the Graph tool, and Illustrator will prompt you with a window in which you can enter the dimensions of the graph numerically (see Figure 15.2).

FIGURE 15.2

You can enter graph dimensions numerically after clicking with the Graph tool.

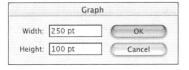

NEW TERM The next step is to give Illustrator the facts—the actual values that will be used to make the graph mean something. After it creates the bounding box for your graph, Illustrator presents you with the Graph Data window (see Figure 15.3). If you've ever used Microsoft Excel or Lotus 1-2-3, this window will look familiar to you. It is filled with rows and columns in which you enter the *graph data*.

FIGURE 15.3

The Graph Data window.

If you look in the upper-left corner of the Graph Data window, you'll see why we don't call it a palette or a dialog box. There are two little round buttons, miniature versions of those that control all of the windows, including the document windows themselves and the floating palette windows. Palettes have tabs, dialog boxes have OK and Cancel buttons. In addition, you are limited in what else you can do in Illustrator while you have your graph's data showing in the window.

Importing Graph Data

 NEW TERM Several items are placed across the top of the Graph Data window. The first is an area to input your values. Select a cell (*cells* are the boxes that actually contain the data), and then type your value. Press Tab to go to the next column; press Enter to go to the next row.

> Cells can also be navigated using the arrow keys. Additionally, unlike most data entry programs, Shift+Tab does *not* move to the previous cell, rather it is used to select multiple cells. Both Shift+Tab and Shift+Enter/Return can be used to highlight a number of contiguous cells for such purposes as copying and pasting.

You can either enter the data manually or import it from programs such as Excel or Lotus (or even from a tab-delimited text file). Notice that in the upper-right corner of the Graph Data window are six buttons. The following describes these buttons from left to right:

- Import Data: Imports data from an external file.
- Transpose: Switches columns and rows of data, no matter what the graph type.
- Switch x/y: Swaps the values of the x- and y-axes on a Scatter graph only.
- Cell Style: Sets the parameters for a selected cell (each box in the grid in the Graph Data window is a cell). You can set the number of decimal places as well as the column width (see Figure 15.4). You can also change the column width manually by grabbing a vertical line and dragging it left or right (see Figure 15.5) .

FIGURE 15.4

The Cell Style dialog box.

FIGURE 15.5

Adjusting the width of a column manually.

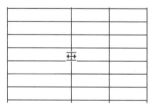

- Revert: The Revert button sets the data in the graph back to the way it was before you last clicked the Apply button.
- Apply: The Apply button applies your changes to the graph.

Before importing data from another application, make sure that numbers do not have commas. 1,234 needs to be 1234 to be recognized properly in Illustrator.

15

Editing Graph Data

What makes the graph function in Illustrator even more powerful is the capability to update the data in your graph. At any time, you can select the graph and choose Object, Graphs, Data. You are presented with the Graph Data window again, where you can update the numbers. When you click the Apply button in the Graph Data window, the graph is automatically updated with the new information.

Graph Options

After you create your graph, you can edit it to perfection. Choose Object, Graphs, Type, and you are presented with the Graph Type dialog box. You are first presented with Graph Options (see Figure 15.6). Here you can change the type of graph, even though you selected another type earlier from the Toolbox. You can also choose where to place the value axis.

FIGURE 15.6

The Graph Type dialog box.

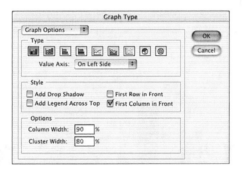

In addition to the options to add drop shadows or add a legend across the top, you can also set the column and cluster widths here (see Figure 15.7). These settings control the width and spacing of the bars or columns in a graph. Entering a number greater than 100 causes the columns to overlap and might produce very interesting effects (see Figure 15.8).

FIGURE 15.7

Setting the column and cluster widths.

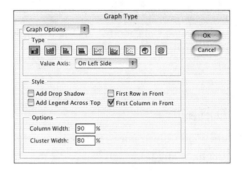

FIGURE 15.8

Graphs set with different cluster widths.

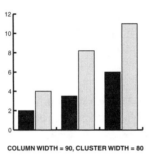

COLUMN WIDTH = 90, CLUSTER WIDTH = 80

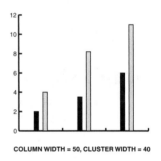

COLUMN WIDTH = 50, CLUSTER WIDTH = 40

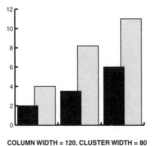

COLUMN WIDTH = 120, CLUSTER WIDTH = 80

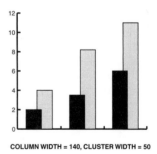

COLUMN WIDTH = 140, CLUSTER WIDTH = 50

NEW TERM In the Graph Type dialog box, you can also specify settings for the value axis and category axis. Select them from the pop-up menu at the top of the dialog box (see Figure 15.9). In the *Value Axis* panel (see Figure 15.10), you can set the length of tick marks, which are the lines along the side of the graph that help indicate the position of data (see Figure 15.11).

FIGURE 15.9

Selecting Value Axis from the pop-up menu in the Graph Type dialog box.

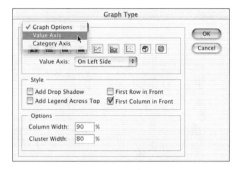

FIGURE 15.10

The Value Axis panel.

FIGURE 15.11

Choosing tick mark specifications.

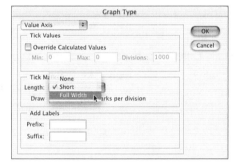

Setting tick marks at full length causes them to be drawn as lines throughout the entire graph (see Figure 15.12). You can also specify these settings for the tick marks for the Category Axis (see Figure 15.13).

FIGURE **15.12**
A graph showing tick marks across the full width.

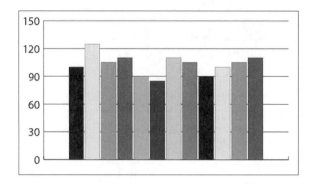

FIGURE **15.13**
The Category Axis panel.

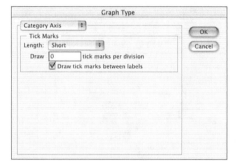

Graph Design

Illustrator includes a feature called Graph Design that enables you to use just about any vector art to display information in your graphs. Say, for example, you're doing a report on how many shooting stars are seen each year. You would ordinarily make a bar graph, but to add a visual element to your graph, wouldn't it be great if you could use stars instead of boring bars?

Task: Creating a Graph Design

▲ TASK

You can make graphs come alive using graphics to better portray the values within it. Perform the following steps to do it:

1. Define the artwork for the bars. To get started, simply draw a star, (see Figure 15.14).

2. With the art selected, choose Object, Graph, Design.

3. Define the graph design by clicking New Design. Then click the Rename button to give your graph design a name. I called mine Star (see Figure 15.15).

▼

15

FIGURE 15.14
The star will be used to represent data in the graph.

FIGURE 15.15
Define the graph design.

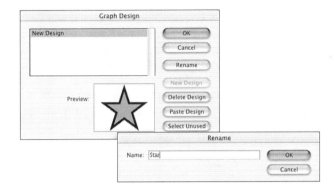

4. Create a graph. Using the Column Graph tool, I dragged a rectangle to create my graph, and when the Graph Data window opened, I used 350 and 560 for my data (see Figure 15.16). Clicking the Apply button tells Illustrator to update the graph.

FIGURE 15.16
The "ordinary" graph.

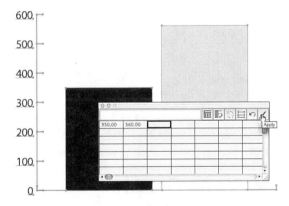

5. Close the Graph Data window. With the graph selected, choose Object, Graphs, Column.

6. In the Graph Column dialog box, select the star design and choose from the other options listed in the box. I chose a repeating column type so that the star appears for every 100 units, which I've also specified in the box. For fractions (350 and 560 do not represent full stars), I chose to have the stars chopped (see Figure 15.17); the other choice is to have them scaled.

FIGURE 15.17
The Graph Column dialog box.

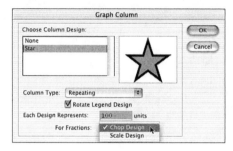

7. Click OK to see the newly designed graph (see Figure 15.18). Remember that you can always go back and tweak the design to get it just how you want it.

FIGURE 15.18
The new graph in all its starry glory.

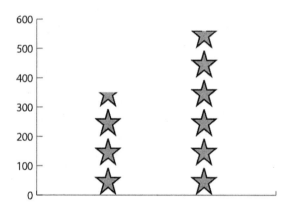

Remember that you can use patterns in your custom graph symbols, but not effects or patterns that use effects, such as the drop shadow in Blue Goo.

Ungrouping Your Graph

A graph is actually a group of many objects. You can ungroup a graph at any time, but be aware that when you do, the art loses its reference as a graph, and you no longer can make changes to it through the Graph Data and Graph Type dialog boxes. This process is just like converting type into outlines: After you change it, it becomes a different kind of object. Your best bet is to save a copy of the original graph before ungrouping so that you can go back to it if needed.

15

Of course, after you ungroup the graph, you have complete and total freedom to do whatever you please with the graph's elements. You can color them, run filters on them, and so on. Let your mind roam free, and you can create some really dynamic presentations.

Summary

Even though Illustrator is not known for its graphing capabilities, you just learned that it can hold its own when it comes to creating great-looking charts. You learned how to import graph data from other applications and how to take that data and turn it into something that makes sense.

Workshop

If you use databases to create graphs in other programs, this was probably pretty familiar. If graphing is new to you, however, you'll benefit from some review and practice.

Q&A

Q Can I apply an appearance to a graph?

A Yes, you can apply an appearance, or any other attribute, to a graph. It will be treated as a group.

Q Can a graph design contain a placed image?

A No, you can use gradients or even brushes to define artwork for a Graph design, but you cannot use placed images.

Q My data is correct but the graph isn't. Am I doing something wrong?

A Sometimes Illustrator understands data differently from other programs, such as Microsoft Excel, in the way the data is entered into the fields. Try using the Transpose and Switch X/Y functions to fix it.

Quiz

1. Illustrator has how many graph types?

    a. 5

    b. 9

    c. 7

2. A tick mark is

    a. A line that indicates a value

    b. A swollen red area on your skin from a bug bite

    c. The length of a column or bar

3. The feature used to create graphs out of vector art is called

    a. VectorGraph

    b. Graph Design

    c. Graph-O-Rama

4. The column width can be greater than 100%.

    a. True

    b. False

5. After you ungroup a graph, you can edit the data.

    a. True

    b. False

Quiz Answers

1. b. Illustrator has nine graph types: Column, Stacked Column, Bar, Stacked Bar, Line, Area, Scatter, Pie, Radar (or Web).

2. a. In a column graph, the tick marks are along the side and show the value at a particular column height. Options for tick marks are None, Short, and Full Width.

3. b. With Graph Design, you can use any symbol or object to portray the values in a graph.

4. a. True. Column widths more than 100% cause the columns to overlap.

5. b. False. After a graph is ungrouped, the data cannot be edited.

Exercises

1. After you enter data into the Graph Data window, click the Transpose Row/Column button and the Switch X/Y button to see how they affect the position of the data. Then see how clicking these buttons affects the graph itself.

2. Redo the exercise you did using the star as a graph design, but this time use a different shape, such as a circle or spiral.

3. Create a graph using one particular data type. Then switch that same graph to a different graph type and observe how the data is presented differently.

Hour 16

Showing and Hiding with Masks

Masks are used to make parts of an image invisible or to apply a translucent pattern to the selected artwork. When working with the first type, clipping masks, the artwork outside the mask is completely hidden. In the second case, opacity masks, you use a pattern as if it were a screen, reducing the opacity of part of the underlying artwork.

In Hour 12, "Utilizing Transformations and Blends," we looked at compound shapes, which you create by combining a couple of objects to produce a third shape. Clipping masks work somewhat similar to compound shapes, as you will see in this hour. In Hour 8, "Using Strokes, Fills, and Gradients," we worked with pattern fills and with gradients, which are among the most common opacity masks.

In this hour, we'll look at

- The nature of masks
- Working with clipping masks

- Working with opacity masks
- Clipping masks as layer masks

Masks and How They Work

Keep in mind that, at their heart, masks are nothing more than objects. They are paths that we use to define the visibility or opacity of other objects. Clipping masks use the masking object's path to determine what parts of underlying objects should be visible and what parts should be invisible. (You might also hear the terms *reveal* and *hide*.) Opacity masks, on the other hand, use the masking object's fill to selectively expose parts of the underlying object(s).

Before we start discussing how masks work in Illustrator, we have to make one thing clear—there is a difference between, say, a Halloween mask and a mask in Illustrator. The mask you put on your face hides your face everywhere the mask exists. In Illustrator, the masking object exists where the artwork is shown, not hidden.

The Mechanics of Clipping Masks

Clipping masks, created through the Object menu, use a path to define the visible limits of another object or objects. Masks can also be applied to layers, so that every object placed on the layer will be shown or hidden depending on its position relative to the mask. (Layer masks will be discussed at the end of this hour.)

The top object loses its fill and stroke, leaving only an invisible path. The selected objects behind are visible only within that path. Figure 16.1 shows an example.

FIGURE 16.1

The before-and-after pictures.

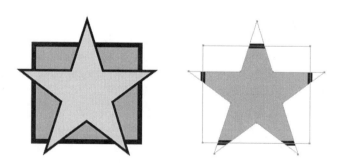

Illustrator combines the two objects so that they can be moved together without disrupting the masking. (This is not the same as grouping the objects, because the Ungroup command cannot be used. It's more like the results of using the compound shape buttons of the Pathfinder palette.) The paths of both the masked object and the masking object can still be selected with the Direct Selection or Group Selection tool and moved individually. You can also select a path and edit it by moving path segments of anchor points.

Opacity Masks in Action

16

Opacity masks, which are created with a command from the Transparency palette menu, apply the brightness or darkness of the masking object's fill to the object or objects being masked. This changes the opacity of the object being masked. When the masking object is a solid color, the effect is uniform. When the masking object is filled with a pattern or a gradient, or when a photograph is used, more complicated effects can be produced, as shown in Figure 16.2).

FIGURE 16.2

The gradient is used to determine the opacity of the pattern-filled star. Note that the solid black of the rectangle's stroke leaves the pattern completely opaque.

In Figure 16.3, the stacking order of the objects is different. On the left, the pattern-filled star is used as the opacity mask for the gradient rectangle. On the right, the rectangle was moved in front and its pattern is used as the opacity mask for the star.

FIGURE 16.3

Like clipping masks, opacity masks use the top-most object as the masking object.

Between Clipping and Opacity

Although both varieties are masks and have many things in common, clipping masks and opacity masks can be very different, too.

- Both kinds of masks are used to expose certain areas of the masked object(s).
- Both kinds of masks use the top-most object as the mask, showing and hiding the objects behind it.
- Both kinds of masks can be applied to multiple objects at the same time. (When applying an opacity mask to multiple objects, they must first be grouped.)
- Both kinds of masks can be released or removed, returning the masked objects to their original appearances.
- Clipping masks are created through the Object menu; opacity masks are created through the Transparency palette.
- Clipping masks ignore the stroke and fill of the masking object; opacity masks are created from the stroke and fill of the masking object.

Working with Clipping Masks

When you get a feel for this incredibly powerful capability, your imagination can run wild. For now, let's think about some simple (yet practical) ways to use clipping masks.

- You've placed a raster image in your illustration, for instance a picture of a city park. However, you don't need the whole photo, just a particular tree. Rather than going to Photoshop or another image editing program to crop the picture, a simple clipping mask hides the part you don't need. (See Figure 16.4.)

FIGURE 16.4

As you can tell from the visible paths, the photo on the right is still all there, just masked.

• You want a series of objects to appear as if they fill another object, without spilling over. A clipping mask trims the objects to within the shape you specify.

FIGURE 16.5

Each of the individual objects retains its own path. Each path can be edited or moved with the Direct Selection or Group Selection tool.

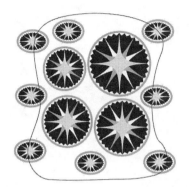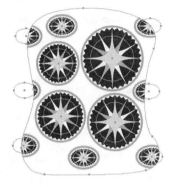

16

Task: Create a Clipping Mask

▼ TASK

Let's work a little with clipping masks, just to get a feel for their power—and how to control it.

1. Open a new document, letter size, RGB or CMYK, Landscape (sideways) orientation.

2. Create a star, a circle, and a square. Make each about one inch (72 points) in diameter or width. Give each a colored fill and a stroke.

3. Switch to the Selection tool by pressing V on the keyboard or by clicking it once in the Toolbox.

4. Hold down the Option (Mac)/Alt (Windows) key and drag copies of your objects around on the artboard. Fill it up and don't be afraid to overlap objects. Make your artboard look similar to that shown in Figure 16.6.

5. Click away from all objects with the Selection tool to deselect.

6. Press D on the keyboard to reset to the default appearance. Now, with the Fill icon in front in the Toolbox (and Color palette), click once on the None icon below. That gives you a one-point black stroke and no fill for the next object you create.

7. Make that next object a great big rectangle that covers most of your artboard, as shown in Figure 16.7.

▼

FIGURE 16.6

Clutter it up! Load your artboard with quite a few objects. Watch how the stacking order is affected when you Option+drag (Mac)/Alt+drag (Windows) objects.

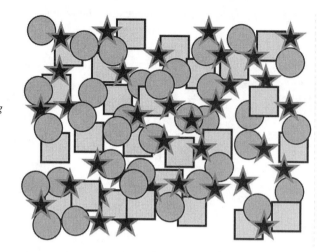

FIGURE 16.7

The rectangle will be used as the clipping mask.

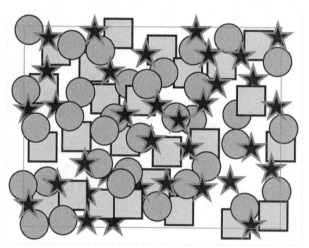

8. Use the menu command Select, All, or press Command+A (Mac)/Control+A (Windows) on the keyboard.

9. Use the menu command Object, Clipping Path, Make (see Figure 16.8). Look how the objects that were completely or partially outside the top rectangle are now hidden.

10. Undo once, using either Command+Z (Mac)/Control+Z (Windows) or the menu command Edit, Undo Make Clipping Mask.

11. Grab the Polygon tool from the Toolbox and add some polygons near the corners of the large rectangle. Give them strokes and fills that make them visible. Make sure that they extend beyond the path of that large rectangle.

FIGURE 16.8

When a clipping mask is active on the artboard, the Release command is also available.

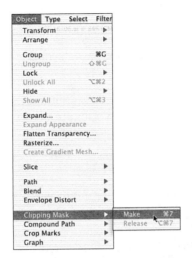

16

12. Once again, select all and create the clipping path. Surprise! The most recently drawn object is the top-most path, and therefore becomes the clipping mask. Look at Figure 16.9 and you'll know which of the polygons was created last.

FIGURE 16.9

The lower-right polygon was the last object created and was, therefore, at the top of the stacking order. Illustrator used it as the clipping mask.

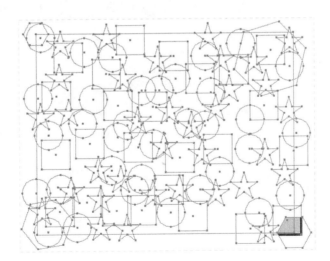

13. Undo. Select the polygons by Shift+clicking on them with the Selection tool.

14. Use the menu command Object, Arrange, Send to Back.

15. Reapply the clipping mask and see how the polygons are integrated into the mask. Keep this document open we're going to work with it some more.

Task: Edit a Clipping Mask

Okay, so clipping masks are great. But there are times when you have a clipping mask that's only semigreat. It's not quite what you wanted it to be. You don't have to start over, because the mask and the objects being masked are still editable paths. Let's look at some of the techniques.

1. We're going to continue using our masterpiece from the previous Task. Hold down Command+Shift (Mac)/Control+Shift (Windows) and press A on the keyboard. That's the keyboard shortcut for Deselect All.

2. Get the Group Selection tool from the Toolbox. Click any one of the objects being masked. Notice how it, and it alone, is selected.

3. Shift+click several more of the masked objects. Include some that are on the edge of the mask and are partially hidden (see Figure 16.10) .

FIGURE 16.10

Applying what you learned in Hour 13, "Gaining Flexibility Through Layers," you could also select members of a clipping group using the Layers palette.

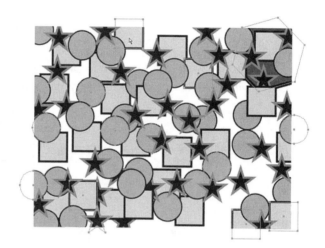

4. Delete them using the Delete (Backspace) key or the menu command Edit, Clear. Undo.

5. Deselect. Change to the Direct Selection tool.

6. Click the path (the edge) of any object that is partially hidden by the clipping mask.

7. Click any anchor point and drag to reshape the object. Undo.

8. Click with the Direct Selection tool on the clipping mask's path. Watch the cursor—it will change to indicate when you are directly over the path (see Figure 16.11). With the clipping mask selected, you can use the Direct Selection tool to

move anchor points, use the Convert Anchor Point tool to create smooth corner points, reposition the mask using the arrow keys, or, well, the list goes on and on. When the path has been selected you can edit it in just about any way you can edit any object's path.

FIGURE 16.11

With the Direct Selection tool active, a small black box appears to indicate that the cursor is directly over a path.

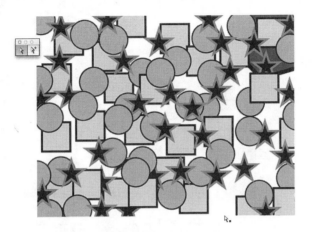

9. Keep the clipping mask's path selected and open the Stroke palette. Give the clipping mask's path a wide stroke, at least 20 points. Look closely at the stroke and where the masked objects overlap it. The stroke is actually behind the objects and the objects appear above the stroke, but only to the actual path itself. Although they overlap the stroke to the path, beyond the path the objects are masked, and therefore hidden.

10. Add a pattern fill and reduce the opacity using the Transparency palette (see Figure 16.12). Illustrator by default gives a clipping mask's path a stroke and fill of None, but that doesn't mean things have to stay that way. Although the masking object was on top when we created the clipping mask, any stroke and fill you give it will show up behind the masked objects. (Remember, too, that you can add additional strokes and fills using the Appearance palette's menu commands. We learned all that in Hour 11, "Applying Appearances and Styles.")

11. Undo to remove the fill, but retain the stroke.

12. We're going to give you a sneak peak at what we'll present in Hour 18, "Working with Filters and Live Effects," just a quick look at some of the fun that awaits you. With the clipping mask's path still selected, use the menu command Effect, Distort & Transform, Pucker & Bloat. Check the Preview box. Drag the slider a little way to the right and release the mouse button (see Figure 16.13). Drag it back past the center the other way and release the mouse button. Experiment—for just a minute

▽ or two—with the slider to see what you can do to a clipping mask. Click the Cancel button. Close the document without saving. Well, go ahead and save it if you'd like.

FIGURE 16.12

The pattern and stroke appear behind the masked objects, even though the clipping path is technically on top of the stacking order, as shown by the Layers palette.

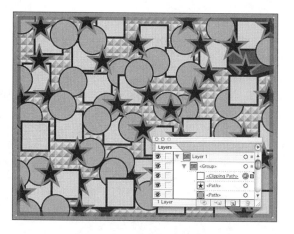

FIGURE 16.13

Because of the complexity of the group, it might take your computer a second or two to show the preview.

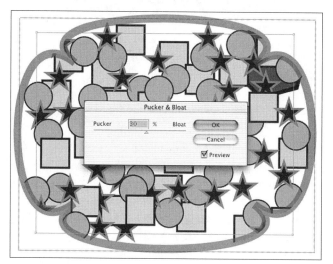

▲

Working with Opacity Masks

Like clipping masks, opacity masks use the top-most object to selectively hide and show objects below it in the stacking order. However, while clipping masks use only the upper object's path, opacity masks use the object's stroke and fill. Raster images, such as photographs, can also be used in opacity masks. (We'll talk about images constructed of pixels in Hour 19, "Working with Raster Images and Programs.")

Opacity Masks Fundamentals

The order in which objects appear on the artboard (and therefore in the Layers palette) is critical to how an image will appear. In Figure 16.14, a photograph and a gradient fill are combined in an opacity mask, with the gradient centered atop the photo.

FIGURE 16.14

To the left you see the original photo and gradient. To the right, the gradient is centered on the photo and an opacity mask is created.

16

In Figure 16.15, the stacking order was reversed and the photo was on top when the opacity mask was created. In this case, the photo's lightness and darkness were applied to the gradient as a mask.

FIGURE 16.15

The image on the right is actually the gradient fill with an opacity mask applied to it.

Remember that an opacity mask by default will show the lower object(s) where the mask is white or light, and hide where the mask is black or dark. In Figure 16.16, the photo is used as an opacity mask for the gradient (as in the previous figure), but the opacity mask is inverted. You can see this option in the Transparency palette's menu.

FIGURE 16.16

When you invert the opacity mask, the lighter areas of the masking object hide, whereas the darker areas reveal.

Remember that an opacity mask uses the lightness and darkness of both the fill and the stroke of the masking object. In Figure 16.14 we used the gradient as an opacity mask on the photo. The rectangle had a stroke of None and a simple black-white radial gradient. In Figure 16.17, we'll apply the same gradient opacity mask, but with a broad, light-colored stroke on the masking object.

FIGURE 16.17

The light-gray stroke enables the masked object to appear. A black stroke would completely hide the photo in that area (unless, of course, the opacity mask was inverted).

Task: Create an Opacity Mask

We'll practice with a pattern-filled object and a gradient. We'll also do a little reinforcement of a variety of techniques from other hours as we work.

1. Open a new Illustrator document, using the same settings used previously.

2. Click near the upper-left corner of the artboard with the Rectangle tool. In the Rectangle tool's dialog box, enter 300 pt for width and 400 pt for height. No matter what unit of measure you're using for the document, this will create a rectangle 300 points by 400 points.

3. With the rectangle still selected, press D to give it the basic fill, stroke, and opacity.

4. In the Stroke palette, change the stroke weight to 10 points.

5. Make sure that the Fill swatch is foremost in the Toolbox and the Color palette, and in the Swatches palette click the Black, White Radial gradient.

6. Press V to activate the Selection tool.

7. Press Option+Shift (Mac)/Alt+Shift (Windows) and drag the rectangle to the right side of the artboard. Option (Mac)/Alt (Windows) tells Illustrator that you want to copy as you drag, Shift ensures that the two objects are aligned.

8. In the Swatches palette, click the Pyramids pattern to apply it to the second rectangle. Your artboard should contain two objects like those shown in Figure 16.18.

FIGURE 16.18

Two rectangles, exactly the same size, and perfectly aligned. On the left is the Black, White Radial gradient fill, and on the right is the Pyramids pattern fill.

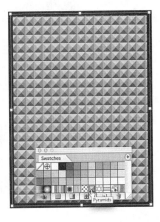

9. Use the Window menu to show the Align palette. From the Align palette's menu, select the command Align to Artboard (see Figure 16.19).

FIGURE 16.19

When aligning or distributing, Illustrator uses the artboard as a reference point.

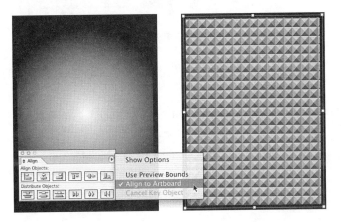

10. Select both rectangles, then click once on the Horizontal Align Center button and then on the Vertical Align Center button (see Figure 16.20).

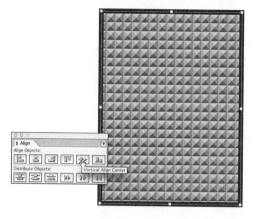

11. In the Transparency palette menu, select Make Opacity Mask (see Figure 16.21).

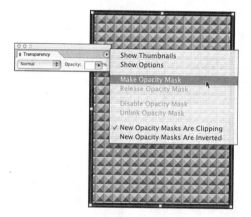

12. With the selection still active, use the Transparency palette's menu command Release Opacity Mask.

13. Open the Layers palette and click the triangle to expand Layer 1.

14. Drag the lower path (with the gradient thumbnail) above the other path and release the mouse button. This changes the stacking order (see Figure 16.22).

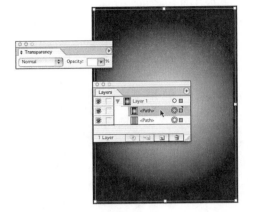

FIGURE 16.22
Although the gradient is now on top, both objects are still selected.

15. Use the Transparency palette's menu to make an opacity mask. Take a look at the result, then Undo.

16. In the Transparency palette's menu, select New Opacity Masks Are Inverted (see Figure 16.23) .

FIGURE 16.23
This option reverses the light-dark opacity. Darker areas of the masking object will now be used to reveal the underlying object(s).

17. Use the Make Opacity Mask command. Compare this mask to your memory of the previous mask. Don't close this document yet.

Task: Edit an Opacity Mask

▼ **TASK**

Editing an opacity mask is quite a bit different from editing a clipping mask. The first thing to remember is that opacity masks, unlike clipping masks, consist of a single object.

1. With the opacity mask from the previous Task selected on the artboard, click a couple of times on the Transparency palette's tab to fully expand it. (Alternatively, you can use the palette's menu command Show Options.)

2. Use the Window menu to show the Layers palette and click the triangle next to Layer 1 to expand it (see Figure 16.24).

FIGURE 16.24

The palettes might be in different locations, but the contents should be the same.

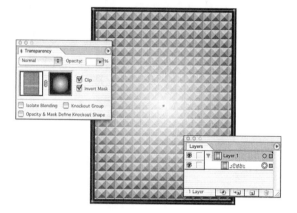

3. Compare the Layers palette in Figure 16.24 to that in Figure 16.12. Note that this has only one object on Layer 1 now, and that <Path> is underlined with a broken line. (A clipping path is underlined with a solid line.) You can now hide the Layers palette.

4. In the Transparency palette, play with the Invert check box to see how easy it is to switch the opacity mask's effect. In this case, because our two objects are the same size, the Clip option is irrelevant. However, when the gradient object was scaled to 50%, as shown in Figure 16.25, you can see one case where the Clip option would make a difference.

FIGURE 16.25

If Clip were deselected in the Transparency palette, the pattern object would not be hidden outside of the gradient opacity mask.

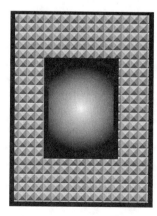
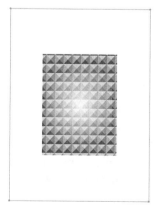

5. In the Transparency palette, click once on the little chain icon between the two thumbnails to unlink the opacity mask from the masked object (see Figure 16.26).

FIGURE 16.26

The link icon indicates that the opacity mask and the masked object will move as a unit when dragged.

16

6. Press V on the keyboard to activate the Direct Selection tool.

7. Uncheck the Clip option in the Transparency palette—here's another situation where it makes a difference.

8. In the Transparency palette, click the thumbnail to the right, the miniature of the gradient (the masking object). A heavy black line will appear around the thumbnail (see Figure 16.27) .

FIGURE 16.27

When the thick black line is around the thumbnail on the right, the mask is selected, not the object itself.

9. On the artboard, click in the center of the opacity mask and drag it toward the lower-left corner of the artboard, as shown in Figure 16.28. Observe how the gradient mask is relocated within the masked object.

FIGURE 16.28

Also take a look at how the thumbnails in the Transparency palette have been updated to show the new relationship between the objects.

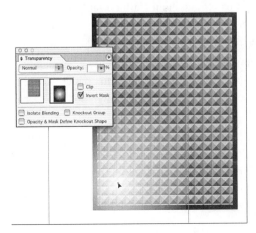

10. Now click Clip in the Transparency palette to select that option. The path of the opacity mask is now used to hide the pattern-filled object where it extends beyond the mask.

11. Press A on the keyboard to activate the Direct Selection tool. Click twice on the visible anchor point in the upper-right corner of the opacity mask, and then drag it upward and to the right (see Figure 16.29). The mask must be selected in the Transparency palette to manipulate it.

Figure 16.29

When selected, you can edit an opacity mask's path like any other path.

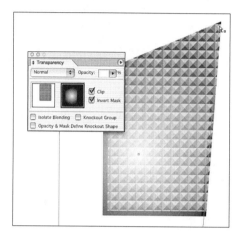

12. Undo. Now click the left-hand thumbnail in the Transparency palette to make the masked object active.

13. Press V to switch back to the Selection tool and drag the pattern-filled object to the right. Undo. Drag it to the left. Undo. Drag it in any direction. Undo. When unlinked from the mask, the object itself can be repositioned.

14. Show the Align palette. It should still be set to align objects to the artboard. With the masked object still selected, align the center both vertically and horizontally. (Actually, because you used Undo, it should not move at all.)

15. Click the thumbnail for the gradient opacity mask and align it in both directions. It should once again be directly on top of the pattern-filled object. When unlinked, not only can you edit a mask, you can align and transform it as well. Hide the Align palette.

16. In the Transparency palette, click once between the thumbnails, right where the link icon used to be. Nothing happens. Now click on the thumbnail of the masked object (on the left) and then click between the object and its mask. The link icon should reappear.

Layer Clipping Masks

There's a third type of mask in Illustrator, closely related to the clipping mask. In fact, we can consider layer-clipping masks to be nothing more than a clipping mask assigned to a layer. Rather than selecting objects and creating a clipping group, we use a path to determine what area of a layer will be visible. Any objects created on or moved to that layer will then be visible or hidden based on their position on the layer.

Task: Create a Layer Clipping Mask

Layer clipping masks are simple to create and to edit.

1. Open a new document, open the Layers palette, and draw the object that you want to use as a mask. In this case, we're using a large star (see Figure 16.30).

FIGURE 16.30

In this case, there's only one object on the layer. If multiple objects exist on a layer, the topmost becomes the clipping mask.

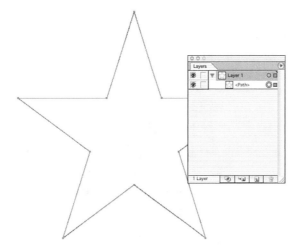

2. With the object still selected, click the Make/Release Clipping Mask button at the bottom of the Layers palette (see Figure 16.31).

3. Create a whole bunch of objects on the layer. Their visibility will be determined by their placement in relationship to the layer-clipping mask. In Figure 16.32, we've added a patchwork of rectangles. Where they don't fall within the clipping mask, they are not visible.

FIGURE **16.31**

The same button both makes and releases layer-clipping masks. It knows which to do based on whether or not a mask already exists.

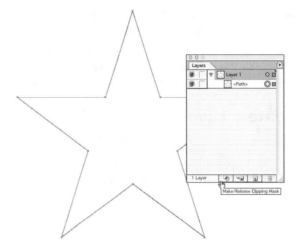

FIGURE **16.32**

In the Layers palette, the thumbnails show the shape of each of the objects. Note that the clipping path is at the bottom of the list.

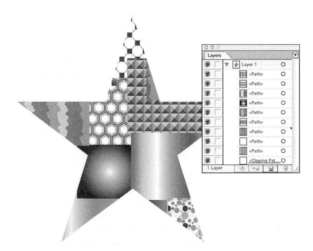

Additional Transparency Options

There are three additional check boxes at the bottom of the Transparency palette. They pertain to all objects, not just masks, but this is a great place to remind you about them.

- Isolate Blending: When checked, the blending mode of a group of objects applies only within the group. The blending mode does not apply to objects under the group on the artboard.

- Knockout Group: This option is used only with commercial CMYK (offset and flexographic) printing. Objects within a group are not printed when they fall beneath another member of the group and would not be visible. (This is discussed in more detail in Hour 21, "Printing Your Illustrations. ")
- Opacity & Mask Define Knockout Shape: Again used with commercial printing, underlying objects are not printed when they should not be visible.

Summary

This hour has shown you how you can show and hide various parts of one or more objects by using masks. In addition to blocking out entire sections of objects, you've seen how to use gradients, patterns, and even photos to create opacity masks.

Workshop

A lot of this hour has been hands-on, but we believe that practice makes perfect. The two exercises that follow will give you a couple of more-advanced ideas for the use of masks. (You may want to bookmark these pages so that you can come back after Hour 23, "Animating the Web.") And to make time for the exercises, we'll keep the quiz short, too.

Q&A

Q Can I apply more than one clipping mask to an object or layer?

A Indeed, you can have a clipping path within a clipping path. Take a look at the Layers palette in Figure 16.33. The first clipping path is the rectangle in the lower right. (You can only see the path, of course.) The second clipping path is the star (which is the top-most clipping path in the Layers palette).

FIGURE 16.33
Using multiple clipping paths means making multiple clipping groups.

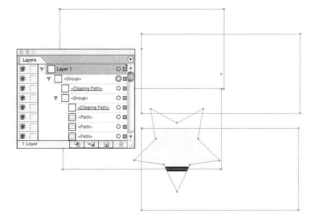

You can also create a clipping path (using the menu command Object, Clipping Path, Make) in conjunction with a layer clipping path (created using the button at the bottom of the Layers palette).

Q If I have an opacity mask applied, can I still use a clipping mask?

A Sure! Apply the opacity mask. Select or create the object that is to be used as the clipping mask (and make sure that it is above the opacity mask in the stacking order). Shift+click to select the opacity mask. Use the menu command Object, Clipping Mask, Make. You use the path of the top-most object as a clipping path for the opacity mask.

Q I seem to be having trouble outputting my clipping masks. Is there anything I can do?

A First, if the mask itself is a very complex path, you can simplify it. You can simplify the whole clipping group by selecting it and using the menu command Object, Path, Simplify. Or, you can simplify just the clipping path by selecting it with the Direct Selection tool and using the same command.

You can also rasterize the clipping group using the menu command Object, Rasterize. Consider using the Transparent Background option if there are large hidden areas.

Q Can I use type to create a clipping mask or an opacity mask?

A What a great idea! You sure can, and not only that, the type remains fully editable. To make a clipping mask, create the object to be masked. Place the type in front of it. Select both and use the menu command Object, Clipping Mask, Make. You can use the Type tools at any time to edit the text.

To make an opacity mask using text, create the object to be masked, put the type in front of it, and use the Transparency palette's command Make Opacity Mask. To edit the type, you must first unlink the mask from the masked object. Click the link icon between the thumbnails to unlink. You can then edit the text with the Type tools. (Don't forget to relink when done.)

Quiz

1. The object that becomes the clipping mask…

    a. …is the top-most selected object of the stacking order.

    b. …is the selected object highest in the Layers palette.

    c. …will get a fill and stroke of None.

    d. All of the above.

2. When using a black-to-white gradient as an opacity mask, by default the black area will do what?

    a. Expose the object or objects underneath

    b. Hide the object or objects underneath

    c. Expose only light-colored parts of the object(s) underneath

    d. Maintain the status quo

3. You've changed your mind about using a clipping mask. But you had closed and reopened the file, so Undo doesn't help. What do you do?

    a. Select all of the objects on the artboard and use the command Mask, Clipping, Delete

    b. Select the top-most opacity mask, ungroup it, invert the colors using the Color palette

    c. Select the clipping group and use the menu command Object, Clipping Mask, Release

    d. Use the Direct Selection tool to select the masking object and duplicate it

16

Quiz Answers

1. d. The selected object that's highest in the stacking order is highest on the Layers palette, too, and its fill and stroke are changed to None when it's made into a mask.

2. b. Light exposes, dark hides—by default, of course. You can reverse the effects by checking the Invert box in the Transparency palette.

3. c. However, you can use the Direct Selection tool to select the *masked* object and use Copy/Paste to duplicate it without the mask. Or, you can use the Direct Selection tool to select the masking object and delete it.

Exercises

1. Start a new document. Create a rectangle 150 pixels (or points) wide and 75 pixels (or points) high. (Remember that you can type 150 px for 150 pixels.) Give the rectangle a two-point black stroke and fill it with the Black, White Radial gradient from the Swatches palette.

Select the Type tool and open the Character palette. Make the font Arial Black, 24 point. In the Paragraph palette, make the type center aligned. Type Click Here. Give the type a 1-point black stroke and for the fill color, choose 60% gray from the Swatches palette.

Select both the type and the rectangle and use the Align palette to center align them both vertically and horizontally. Keep them both selected.

In the Transparency palette menu, choose Make Opacity Mask.

In the Layers palette, drag Layer 1 to the New Layer button to copy the layer and its content. Click the eyeball icon next to Layer 1 to hide it. Expand Layer 1 copy by clicking on the triangle, and click the targeting button to the right of <Path> to select it on the artboard. (Or, you can hide Layer 1 and use the Selection tool to select the copy of the opacity mask.)

Expand the Transparency palette and check the Invert Mask box. You now have a copy of the opacity mask on one layer and an inverted copy on the other layer.

Now, in the Layers palette, make Layer 1 visible again. Then click the eyeball icon next to Layer 1 copy, repeatedly, to show and hide the duplicate layer. Because the two opacity masks are on separate layers it will be a breeze to create an animated Web button—after you finish Hour 23, of course. (You can save this document if you'd like.)

2. Open a new document. Create a rectangle 150 pixels wide and 75 pixels high. Fill the rectangle with the color of your choice.

   Create a line of text, Arial Black, 48-point, that says Click.

   Center align the rectangle and the text, both horizontally and vertically. Keep both selected.

   Use the menu command Object, Clipping Path, Make.

   In the Layers palette, drag Layer 1 to the New Layer button to duplicate it. Hide Layer 1, but leave Layer 1 copy visible. Make sure that <Group> on Layer 1 copy is still selected.

   Use the Type tool to highlight the word Click and overtype it, replacing Click with Here.

   In the Layers palette, hide Layer 1 copy. Show Layer 1. Hide Layer 1. Show Layer 1 copy. Hide Layer 1 copy…. (The easiest way to flash between the two layers is with a series of double-clicks on the eyeballs, alternating layers.)

HOUR 17

Distorting, Warping, and Liquifying Your Artwork

You've learned just about all there is to learn about creating artwork in Illustrator. For the next couple of hours, we're going to show you how to have fun with Illustrator. (And, I suppose, you'll hear about some very productive techniques, too.)

As you've seen, one of the best things about vector art is being able to work directly with the objects' paths. Editing paths gives you virtually total control over the shape of an object. Now you'll learn some of the ways that Illustrator makes that process easy for you.

In this hour, you'll learn about

- Using the Envelope Distort commands
- Illustrator's warping commands
- Customizing distortions with your own paths
- The Liquify tools

Envelopes: Sending Your Artwork out of This World!

The new envelope distortions are among the coolest features in Illustrator. You can transform your artwork in a variety of ways, change your settings later, or even remove the distortion without affecting the original object.

◤ TASK ▼ Task: Envelope Warping

Let's get right to work! The best way to learn the basics of these capabilities is hands-on.

1. Open a new Illustrator document, landscape, RGB or CMYK, letter size.

2. Create a rectangle 225 points wide, 75 points high. Assign the Caution Tape style to it from the Styles palette.

3. Click the Fill icon in the Toolbox or the Color palette. Switch to the Swatches palette. Click the 20% Black swatch near the middle of the top row.

4. Grab the Type tool. Click anywhere in the document and type Envelopes. Using the Character palette, make the text Arial Black, 36 point. Use the Swatches palette to assign it a fill color of Yellow. Give it a one-point black stroke.

5. Use the Align palette to center the two objects both vertically and horizontally.

6. With both objects still selected, use the menu command Object, Group or the keyboard shortcut Command+G (Mac)/Control+G (Windows). Your artwork should look like that shown in Figure 17.1.

FIGURE 17.1

The type and the rectangle are grouped as a single object.

7. Use the menu command Object, Envelope Distort, Make with Warp (see Figure 17.2).

8. Click the Preview button. You'll see what the default settings can do (see Figure 17.3). And that's just the tip of the iceberg!

9. Grab the Bend slider and drag it to –50% and release the mouse button (see Figure 17.4).

FIGURE 17.2

Warp is just one of the Envelope Distort options.

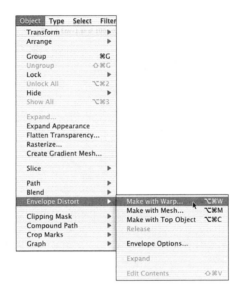

FIGURE 17.3

Illustrator leaves the Preview button unchecked by default.

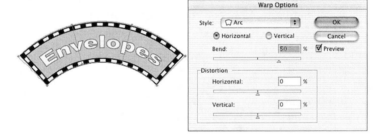

FIGURE 17.4

Most of the Warp distortions can work in either direction.

17

10. Set the three sliders to these values (all positive values, to the right on the sliders): Bend 65%, Horizontal 60%, Vertical 40%. Figure 17.5 shows how Illustrator's Warp distortions can be used to simulate 3D.

FIGURE 17.5
The object appears to be bending in three dimensions.

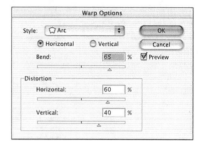

In addition to using the sliders, Illustrator enables you to change these values by typing directly in the numeric fields. You can use the Tab key (and Shift+Tab) to move from field to field. When you're in a numeric field, don't forget that you can use the up and down arrow keys to change the numbers, too.

11. Just to show you how powerful these simple sliders really are, try these settings: Bend 100%, Horizontal 0%, Vertical 50%. While the Reflect tool and command can also show you the *back* of an Illustrator object, this is far cooler! (See Figure 17.6.)

FIGURE 17.6
Illustrator's Warp distortions can even flip objects completely over.

12. Return the numeric fields to the default values of 50/0/0. Now click the Style popup menu (see Figure 17.7) and select Flag.

13. Use the pop-up menu to try the various settings. (Just take a quick look at each of them for now—there will be plenty of time to play during the end-of-hour exercises.)

14. Click the Cancel button and return the object to its original state. Don't close the document.

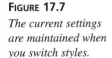

FIGURE **17.7**

FIGURE 17.7

The current settings are maintained when you switch styles.

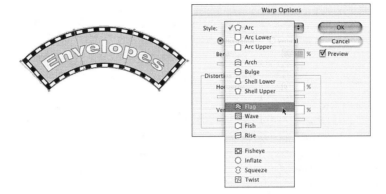

Envelope Meshes

If you watched closely, you saw that different distortions added different numbers of points to the object. Figure 17.8 shows a couple of examples.

FIGURE 17.8

To the left, Arc has been applied. On the right, we used Twist.

The original rectangles had only their four anchor points, one in each corner. As you can see, Envelope Distort has added additional points and segments. However, notice that these new points are not anchor points. They have more than two lines extending from them. Think back to Hour 8, "Using Strokes, Fills, and Gradients." These new points are comparable to those used to create gradient mesh objects; they even have the same diamond shape.

In Figure 17.9, we've applied the twist you just saw to the test object on the left. On the right, we've used the Direct Selection tool to customize the mesh by dragging mesh points and moving control points.

Illustrator makes it even easier for you to create custom envelope meshes. On your artboard, select your Caution Tape-Envelope rectangle. Use the menu command Object, Envelope Distort, Make with Mesh. This command opens the dialog box shown in Figure 17.10.

FIGURE 17.9

Modifying an envelope mesh is quite similar to editing a gradient mesh.

FIGURE 17.10

As with gradient meshes, you determine the number of rows and columns, rather than the number of mesh points.

After you click OK, the object is converted to an envelope mesh. You can now use the Direct Selection tool to modify the mesh points.

The Appearance palette (and the Layers palette) lists this object simply as an Envelope (see Figure 17.11).

FIGURE 17.11

The Envelope object consists of contents and transparency (which can be modified in the Transparency palette).

You can use the Appearance palette to add new strokes and fills, and you can even add styles from the Styles palette. Any new characteristics will conform to the envelope mesh. (Keep in mind that when you've created a mesh from multiple objects new characteristics are applied to all.

Using Custom Paths for Distortions

You can also draw a custom path to use as the basis for your envelope distortion. Make the path and make sure that it's the top-most selected object (see Figure 17.12).

Next use the command Object, Envelope Distort, Make with Top Object. The underlying object or objects will be distorted to match the custom path (see Figure 17.13).

Figure 17.12

The custom path has the basic appearance, but any object can be used.

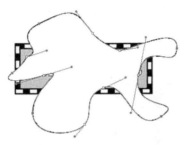

Figure 17.13

The selected objects below the custom path are distorted to match as closely as possible.

17

Options

The menu command Object, Envelope Distort, Envelope Options opens the dialog box shown in Figure 17.14.

Figure 17.14

These are Illustrator's default options.

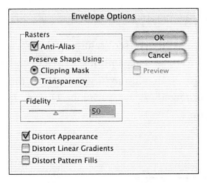

The top section of the box, Rasters, is used when an envelope object will be rasterized. Antialiasing helps preserve the appearance of smooth curves. Clipping Mask uses vector paths and provides good compatibility. Transparency can help retain shadows and glows.

Fidelity determines how precisely Illustrator will follow a path when creating the envelope object. Higher fidelity comes at the price of speed and complexity. A setting of 50 is usually adequate.

The Distort Appearance, Distort Linear Gradients, and Distort Pattern Fills options are illustrated in Figure 17.15.

FIGURE 17.15
The original object is in the upper left.

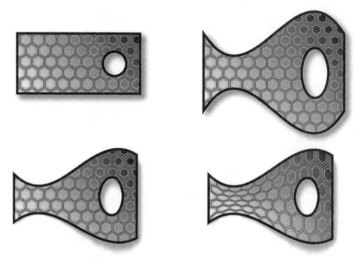

To create the object in the upper right, none of the options were checked. In the lower left, only the Distort Appearance option was selected. In the lower right, all three options were checked.

Editing the Original Path

Because envelope distortions can be reversed, returning the object to its original appearance, they can be considered to be live capabilities. (The concept of live will be explored fully next hour.) In addition, you can edit the original path without discarding the envelope distortion. The menu command Object, Envelope Distort, Edit Contents shows you the original object (see Figure 17.16).

FIGURE 17.16
These are the top two objects from the previous figure. Note that on the right, you can now see the anchor points and path segments of the original object.

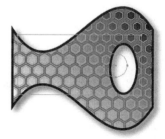

With the original path visible, you can edit it using the Direct Selection tool (and other tools). The envelope object will be automatically updated, as you can see in Figure 17.17.

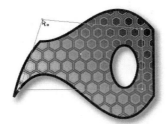

To be able to edit the envelope again, you need to use the menu command Object, Envelope Distort, Edit Envelope. (You'll find it where Edit Contents used to be.) The keyboard shortcut to toggle between these two modes is Shift+Command+V (Mac)/Shift+Control+V (Windows) .

Release and Expand

The other two commands in the Envelope Distort menu are similar, yet very different. In both cases they turn an envelope object into a regular object. Let's look at Expand first.

When an envelope object is selected on the artboard, using the Expand command converts it into a group, while retaining the current appearance and effects. If you use the Ungroup command, you'll get a regular object with the appearance characteristics of the original object. This returns the object to its original state, allowing you to edit it normally. In Figure 17.18, we've expanded one of the envelope objects and ungrouped it.

FIGURE 17.18

The Appearance palette tells the story: a normal compound path with an extra fill and a drop shadow. Just like the original object.

The difference between this expanded object and the original rectangle is only the shape of the path.

When you use the Release command, you restore the original object and you create an object from the envelope. In Figure 17.19, the release command has been used. The two objects that resulted are shown on the left. On the right, we've separated them so that you can better see their paths.

FIGURE 17.19

The original object is restored, and the envelope shape is a mesh object.

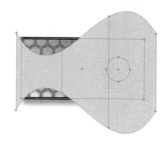
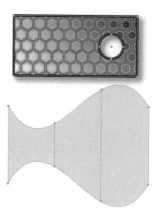

At first glance, you might wonder why the shape was saved as a mesh object, and why it wasn't simply deleted when you used the Release command. It seems that Illustrator is environmentally friendly. Rather than simply tossing that shape into the trash, it gives you the opportunity to recycle it. This is especially cool if you've spent a lot of time adjusting an envelope or need to apply the same envelope to multiple objects. It can be stored in the Symbols palette for later use!

Task: Recycling an Envelope

▼TASK

Go back to our original Caution Tape-Envelope document for this little demonstration.

1. Select the objects and if they're not grouped, group them.

2. Open the Warp Options dialog box (choose Object, Envelope Distort, Make with Warp). Select Wave. Use the following settings: Bend 32%, Horizontal 80%, Vertical 20%. You should see something similar to Figure 17.20.

3. Before you click OK, drag that Bend slider back and forth. Notice how it affects the fill, with very little change to the weight of the stroke. Another thing to keep in mind for creating Web animations.... Return Bend to 32% and click OK.

4. Activate the Direct Selection tool. Shift+click the mesh point in the upper-right corner of the rectangle, then click it again and drag outward.

▼

FIGURE **17.20**

Your results should be the same.

5. Make a number of other changes to the mesh points and control lines. Have some fun. See Figure 17.21 for an idea.

FIGURE **17.21**

The envelope object on your artboard can be drastically different, as long as it's not boring!

6. Choose Object, Envelope Distort, Release.

7. Use the Selection tool and click in an empty part of the artboard to deselect, then click the shape object to select just it.

8. In the Symbols palette, click the New Symbol button (See Figure 17.22). This adds your envelope shape as a symbol.

FIGURE **17.22**

You might have to scroll downward to find your symbol in the palette after you add it.

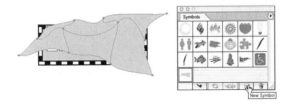

9. Select all and delete.

10. Create a couple of objects and apply various styles to them. In Figure 17.23, you can see a rectangle with the Honeycomb Silk style and a circle with Bermuda.

11. In the Symbols palette, click your newest symbol and drag a single instance of it onto each of your objects.

FIGURE 17.23
We'll apply a custom envelope to these two objects.

12. Select one of the objects and the symbol atop it, then use the menu command Object, Envelope Distort, Make with Top Object. Repeat for the other object. Your objects should take on the envelope distortion, similar to those in Figure 17.24.

FIGURE 17.24
Your results will vary, of course, depending upon your objects.

Task: Enveloping Multiple Objects

You can also use a single envelope command for numerous objects.

1. Select all and delete. Press D on the keyboard to restore the basic appearance.

2. Create a series of seven squares, each 72 points (1 inch) in width and height.

3. Open the Align palette. From the menu, choose Align to Artboard, then click the Vertical Align Center box.

4. Deselect Align to Artboard and click the Horizontal Distribute Center button. You want the artboard to look similar to Figure 17.25

FIGURE 17.25
Make sure that the boxes are spread across the artboard.

5. With all seven squares selected, choose Raindrop from the Styles palette (top row, third from left). Now in the Swatches palette, select Pyramids. You should now have objects similar to those shown in Figure 17.26.

6. Use the menu command Object, Envelope Distort, Make with Warp. Select Arc and make the settings 50/0/0. Your results should be the same as Figure 17.27.

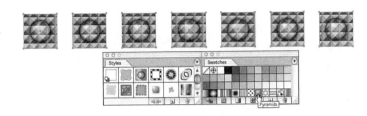

FIGURE 17.26
Depending on whether your image is RGB or CMYK, the style will be named either Raindrop CMYK or Raindrop RGB. The location should be the same.

FIGURE 17.27
Envelope distortions can use several objects, and they need not be grouped.

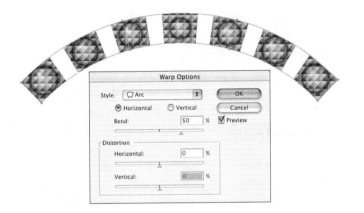

The Liquify Tools

Illustrator's Liquify tools are perhaps just as much fun as Envelope Distort. There's a major difference between the two capabilities, however. Although you can expand or release the distortions, after you use a Liquify tool, the path is permanently altered. (With an exception for the Undo command, of course.)

Getting to Know the Liquify Tools

As you'll recall from Hour 6, "Editing Bézier Curves," Illustrator has seven tools that are grouped under the term Liquify (see Figure 17.28). They've picked up the name because they melt an object's path and reform it.

FIGURE 17.28

The seven Liquify tools are found on a hidden palette below the Warp tool.

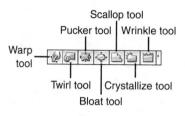

The tools all use brushes to define the area in which they work. They alter the path of an object by adding and moving anchor points.

- The Warp tool pushes and pulls on an object's path, distorting the path segments. New anchor points are created as necessary to modify the shape. To use it, click a selected object or objects and drag in the direction you want the path to go.

- The Twirl tool should not be confused with the Twist tool (one of the Transform tools). The Twirl tool does not create the smoothly regular transformations of its cousin. Rather, it is used to modify one or more path segments in a nonuniform manner. To use it, click a selected path or object and drag the cursor in a small arc or circle.

- The Pucker tool modifies a selected object or path by collapsing the sides of an object in toward each other. (It is especially useful when the brush size is large enough to enclose the entire object.) To use it drag a selected object or path.

- The Bloat tool is the counterpart of the Pucker tool. It expands the sides of an object away from each other. To use it, click a selected object and drag.

- The Scallop tool creates a series of curves along the edge of a selected object. To use it, click a selected path or object. Drag the cursor in the direction that you want the new curves to go.

- The Crystallize tool is similar to the Scallop tool, but rather than creating curves, it creates pointed segments. To use it, drag it away from the direction in which the points should go.

- The Wrinkle tool creates a series of angles along an edge, much like the Crystallize tool, but these angles are restricted to certain angles by the Liquify options.

Task: Using the Liquify Tools

The best (and most fun) way to learn these tools is to work with them.

> Be patient with the Liquify tools. It might take your monitor a couple of seconds to catch up. These tools require a lot of horsepower!

1. Select all and delete. If you don't have an open document, start a new one. Either color mode is okay, and make it Letter size, Landscape orientation.

2. Select the Star tool. Click right in the middle of your artboard, hold down the Shift key, but not Option (Mac)/Alt (Windows), and begin to drag. Press the up arrow key a couple of times if necessary to give the star seven points. Drag until you're near the top or bottom of the artboard, and then release the mouse button. You can also click in the center and enter 230/115/7 in the star dialog box.

3. Give the star a 5-point black stroke and a fill of 20% gray (from the Swatches palette).

4. Tear off the Liquify tools' hidden palette and park it in the middle of your star for easy access. Your artboard should look the same as that shown in Figure 17.29.

FIGURE 17.29

A seven-pointed star that fills the artboard.

5. Select the Warp tool and drag it up and down over the top point of the star. Drag it in small circles. Constrain your dragging to that one point of the star.

6. Let's move clockwise to the next point. Select the Twirl tool. Make several tiny circles, right around the tip of the star's second point.

7. The third point needs the third tool, Pucker. Center the circular cursor directly over the tip of the next point. Drag inward toward the center of the star, but not too far. At this point, your artboard should look similar to Figure 17.30.

FIGURE **17.30**

Each point will be treated differently.

8. Select the Bloat tool for the next point. Position the cursor so that the brush circle covers as much of the fourth point of the star as possible. Drag down and to the right, along the arm of the star.

9. Position the center of the Scallop tool directly on the star's point to the lower left. Slowly drag along the arm toward the body of the star.

10. Move to the next point. Select the Crystallize tool and do the same that you did for the previous tool. Put the center of the cursor over the tip of the star and drag inward.

11. Use the Wrinkle tool on the last point. Click and drag the cursor over the point. At the end, your star should look similar to Figure 17.31 (more or less).

FIGURE **17.31**

Seven points, seven tools, and an interesting, if not artistic, result.

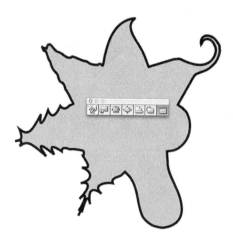

The Liquify Tool Options

Double-click the Warp tool in the Liquify tools tear-off palette to open its dialog box (see Figure 17.32).

FIGURE 17.32

Each Liquify tool has its own options, but many of them are common to all seven tools.

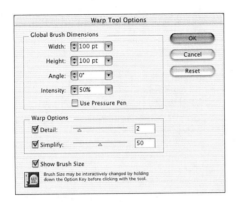

The upper half of the dialog box is the same for each of these tools. And they all use the same brushes. If you make a change to the brush here, it will be changed for all seven tools. Shaping the brush is quite similar to creating a calligraphy brush, which you learned in Hour 9, "Working with Brushes." The option Use Pressure Pen enables you to take advantage of a Wacom tablet's capabilities.

The lower part of the dialog box has several variations. The Warp, Pucker, and Bloat tools have the options shown in Figure 17.32. The Twirl tool adds the option Twirl Rate.

The Scallop and Crystallize tools share the options dialog box shown in Figure 17.33. Of the three options at the bottom of the Warp Options box, one or two must always be selected. You can modify anchor points and either of the tangent handle types or you can modify both types of tangent handles and not the anchors points. Or, of course, you can choose just one of the three.

The Wrinkle tool adds a little more complexity to the options (see Figure 17.34). You'll see that there is a little more control over the warping capability. Like the Scallop and Crystallize tools, one or two of the Brush Affects options can be selected.

During the exercises at the end of this hour you'll get some more experience with some of the Liquify tools options.

FIGURE 17.33

Two tools use these options.

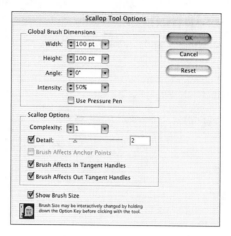

FIGURE 17.34

This is the most complex of the seven dialog boxes.

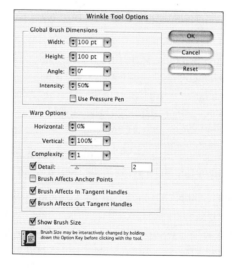

Remember that the Liquify tools add anchor points to a path. Using them can lead to very complex paths with huge numbers of anchor points. Extremely complex paths can lead to output problems when printing to a PostScript printer (such as a laser printer or an image setter). In addition to the Simplify slider in the Liquify tools options, Illustrator offers the command Object, Path, Simplify to help reduce the number of anchor points without substantially changing the appearance of a complex path. You'll learn more about this command in Hour 21, "Printing Your Illustrations."

Summary

We hope you've been inspired by what you've just learned. Not only are these capabilities powerful, they can be fun. You've seen ways that Illustrator helps you easily make very complex changes to your artwork. A command here, a drag there, and suddenly you've gone from a simple shape to an intricate object.

Workshop

Your creative juices are probably overflowing at this point. There's little doubt that you've got lots of experiments on your mind, and you're ready to start playing with these cool new capabilities. Well, hold on for just a moment or two. There are a couple of questions and a little quiz, then you can tear loose in the exercises!

Q&A

Q Can I apply multiple envelope distortions to the same object?

A No, only one can be used at a time. However, you can go back and edit the envelope distortion at any time. And when an object that has been distorted is selected, you can change the current settings with Object, Envelope Mesh, Reset with Warp, or you can use Object, Envelope Distort, Reset with Mesh. (Don't tell anyone else, but you can also use the Expand command and then apply another envelope distortion to the same object.)

Q I can't think of a time when I would want to save and reuse an envelope distortion, can you?

A Here's one: You've decided to create an illustration of dollar bills floating to earth. Each will have to be presented as 3D, bending in the wind as they drop to the ground. Spend some time getting one envelope distortion just right, save the envelope mesh as a symbol, and then apply it individually to each of the bills. Then you only need to make a few simple changes to each to randomize their appearances.

Q Why is Illustrator so slow when using the Liquify tools?

A The speed with which Liquify tools work is a function of your computer's hardware and the amount of memory available to the program. The more powerful the CPU, the faster things go. Having a good video card helps with screen redraw, and having plenty of memory gives Illustrator some relief. Remember that the program is calculating not only the paths, but also placement of new anchor points and the direction lines for each of those points.

17

Q **I can't seem to change the size of the brush for the Liquify tools while I'm working. The bracket keys won't work.**

A That's right, the bracket keys do not resize the brush for the Liquify tools. Instead, try this:

1. Select a Liquify tool from the Toolbox.
2. Select Show Brush Size in the tool's options.
3. Hold down the Option (Mac)/Alt (Windows) key.
4. Click the mouse and drag to resize the brush.
5. Add Shift to keep the brush round.
6. Drag down-right for bigger.
7. Drag down-left for smaller.

Quiz

1. You open an Illustrator document and see that the Arc envelope distortion has been applied to an object when it should have been Arch. (Okay, so you're pretty picky about this stuff.) How can you change it?

    a. Object, Envelope Distort, Release, delete the envelope mesh object, reapply the distortion.

    b. Object, Envelope Distort, Expand, then reapply the distortion.

    c. Undo, then reapply the distortion.

    d. You must delete the object and start over, distortions are forever.

2. Using the Expand command automatically rasterizes an object to which an envelope distortion has been applied.

    a. True

    b. False

3. Objects on which you use the Liquify tools can be restored to their original appearance using what technique? (Choose all that are correct.)

    a. Object, Liquify, Release

    b. Edit, Liquify, Release

    c. Edit, Undo

    d. Choose the command Remove Liquify from the Liquify palette's menu

4. Each Liquify tool's brush is...

    a. ...assigned individually through the Brushes palette.

    b. ...exactly the same, for every tool, but can be changed globally in the options settings.

    c. ...customized individually through the tool's options.

    d. ...is set permanently and cannot be changed.

Quiz Answers

1. a. Releasing and replacing is one of several ways to fix the problem.

2. b. False, the expanded object is still vector and you can still edit its path.

3. c. Undo is the only way. And remember that Undo is not an option once the document is closed.

4. b. The Liquify tools use a global brush; it is the same for all tools. However, you can double-click any of the tools to change the brush size and shape.

Exercises

1. Open a new document. Create a rectangle and assign a pattern from the Swatches palette. Work with the Envelope Distort warp commands until you're comfortable that you understand how each works and what the sliders do in combination. Experiment with the difference between subtle adjustments (between –10 and +10) and extreme adjustments (less than –75 or greater than +75). Sometimes less is more.

2. Select all and delete or open a new document. Press Command+1 (Mac)/Control+1(Windows) to zoom to 100% view. Use the Line Segment tool to create a single horizontal path that extends the width of your screen. Press D to restore the basic appearance, then change the fill to None. Hide all your palettes except for the Toolbox, and tear off the Liquify tool hidden palette. Practice with the tools, using very small circles and drags, until you can make the tools perform at your command. In particular, try these techniques:

    • Double-click the Twirl tool and uncheck the Simplify box in the options dialog box. Pick a spot on the left end of the line and drag three tiny concentric circles. Reopen the options and change Simplify to 0.2% and repeat just to the right on the line. Drag the Simplify slider to 50% and repeat a little farther down the line. On a right end of the line, drag three more tiny circles with Simplify set to 100%. Compare the number of anchor points added. (See Figure 17.35 for an example.)

FIGURE 17.35

At the top you can see the original line and markers showing where and how the Twirl tool was dragged. Below, the resulting path.

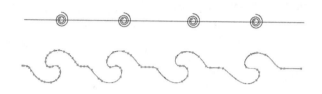

- Using another straight path segment, experiment with the difference between the Scallop and the Crystallize tools.

- Select the Pucker tool. Click a straight path segment and drag downward until the cursor's circle is no longer on the original line. Release the mouse button. Pick another section of path. Click and drag downward the same distance but don't release the mouse button until Illustrator finishes puckering the path. On a third segment, click and drag downward a little, wait, drag a little more, wait, drag some more, wait, and so on until your cursor is at the same place as the first two tests.

3. On an empty artboard, drag a five-pointed star. From the Styles palette, assign the Bermuda style to the star. Use the Bulge envelope distortion, set to Horizontal, with the settings: Bend 85%, Horizontal 0%, Vertical 70%. (These settings give sort of a "jumping jack" look to the star.) Now grab your Liquify tools and give the envelope mesh a good going-over. Experiment with how you can manipulate the envelope distortion. (Figure 17.36 shows an example.)

FIGURE 17.36

In the upper left, the original Bermuda star. In the middle, the distorted star. On the right, you can see how the Liquify tools have altered the envelope mesh.

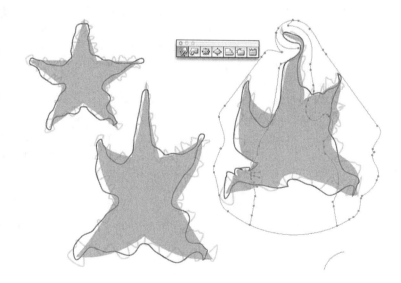

HOUR 18

Working with Filters and Live Effects

Perhaps the most important thing about vector art is Bézier curves. Without them, of course, we really wouldn't have vector capabilities. Next on the list is the ability to edit those paths to meet our requirements. Illustrator's filters and effects would perhaps be third on the list, although that's not to take away from the importance of type, of course! (Lobbyists are everywhere these days.)

In this hour, you'll learn about

- Live capabilities in Illustrator
- What filters and effects Illustrator offers
- The difference between filters and effects
- When to use effects and when to use filters

Effects and Filters in Illustrator

Illustrator's nearly 140 filters and effects enable us to create images quickly and easily. Images that otherwise would take so much time that we probably wouldn't even bother with them. Consider, for example, a simple glow. In Illustrator, we select the object on the artboard or in the Layers palette, and then use the menu command Effect, Stylize, Outer Glow. A dialog box opens, we input some numbers, we click OK. Manually, we'd have to create a series of gradients, one at a time, extending outward from the object. No big deal with a circle or rectangle, perhaps, but complex objects become a nightmare.

There are also effects and filters that work wonders with photographic images, manipulating their appearances in artistic, eccentric, and practical ways. Some of the effects and filters are for use with vector art, some for raster art, some for both, and one set is used only with scalable vector graphics (SVG). Many capabilities appear under both the Effect and Filter menus. All can be applied with just a few clicks of the mouse.

One thing that makes our Illustrator creative process really easy is the capability to radically transform the appearance of an object and be able to change our minds later. Illustrator's effects are live, meaning they can be easily changed or reversed without affecting the original object. The filters, on the other hand, are more permanent in nature. Many capabilities are available as both effects and filters.

The Live Experience

You've already seen many of Illustrator's live capabilities. You know that you can apply a style to an object and still edit the path or switch to another style with the click of a button. You know that you can create compound shapes and later release them, returning to the original objects. In Hour 16, "Showing and Hiding with Masks," you learned how to create clipping and opacity masks, and how to edit the paths of which they're made. And you learned how to remove those masks at any time. We can even add re-editable text to the list. (Imagine how much trouble it would be if you had to retype an entire paragraph because of one misspelling!)

In all these cases, Illustrator allows you to change your mind quickly and easily. Let's look at one example. In Figure 18.1, the upper-left rectangle is the original object. The three copies have a variety of effects and appearance characteristics applied. However, as you can tell from the paths, the objects themselves remain rectangles. And *that* is what live is all about.

FIGURE 18.1

Despite their radically different appearances, all four objects at their hearts remain identical rectangles.

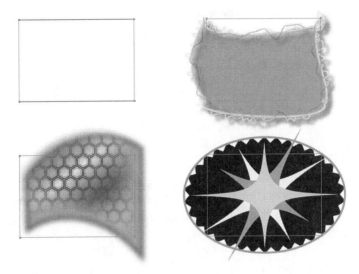

Is it Live or Is It...

Lots of things that you can do to an object or path in Illustrator are not live. For example, if you use the Direct Selection tool to drag an anchor point, and later change your mind, you must either use Undo or go back and move the point again manually. (And remember that Undo is not available after you close the file.)

You can often tell if a technique, capability, or characteristic is live by checking the Appearances palette. If it's there, you can reverse it or change it at any time. If it's not there, then it might not be live. Figure 18.2 shows some examples of liveness.

FIGURE 18.2

The characteristics listed in the Appearance palette can all be considered live.

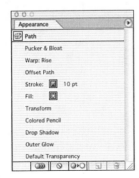

18

In the previous hour you learned about using Illustrator's envelope distortions. As you recall, you can, at any time, use the Release command to restore the object to its original appearance. Even though the Appearance palette doesn't show the envelope distortions as characteristics, because they can be released, we can consider them to be live.

On the other hand, last hour also introduced you to the Liquify tools. They cannot be considered live, because the object cannot be restored to its original appearance without the Undo command. (Or, with a heck of a lot of work, with the Direct Selection tool!)

The Effect Menu

Illustrator's Effect menu (shown in Figure 18.3) offers 18 categories with a total of more than 120 individual effects. In addition, there are three other commands at the top of the menu. The list of categories is divided into two sections. Roughly speaking, *most* of the effects at the top are designed primarily for vector art, and *most* of the effects in the lower section are mainly for raster art. Some of the lower sets of effects can be applied to vector objects, and can be highly effective with pattern-filled objects.

FIGURE 18.3

Illustrator's Effect menu has three commands at the top, then two sections of effect categories.

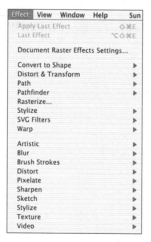

Repeating Effects

At the top of the Effect menu are two similar commands. In Figure 18.3, they are shown as Apply Last Effect and Last Effect. When you've applied an effect, the menu will show which effect was applied last (see Figure 18.4).

When you use the menu command Apply Last Effect (shown in Figure 18.4 as Apply Pucker & Bloat), the same effect, with the same settings, is applied to selected objects on the artboard. When you choose Last Effect (shown as Pucker & Bloat), the dialog box will open. Note the respective keyboard shortcuts, Shift+Command+E (Mac)/Shift+Control+E (Windows) and Option+Shift+Command+E (Mac)/Alt+Shift+Control+E (Windows). They can speed up your production even more when repeating effects.

FIGURE 18.4

In this case, the most recently applied effect was Pucker & Bloat.

Document Raster Effects Settings

The rasterization options (see Figure 18.5) might look similar to those offered in the dialog box for the menu command Object, Rasterize, but they serve a different purpose. These settings are used when an Illustrator effect requires that the artwork be rasterized. (Way back in Hour 1, "Understanding Illustrator," we talked about raster art and pixels. Rasterizing artwork changes it from objects created from paths, to a series of small, colored squares called pixels. You'll learn all about the subject in the next lesson, Hour 19, "Working with Raster Images and Programs.")

FIGURE 18.5

These settings apply to vector objects that must be rasterized for effects to be applied. Remember that as an effect, the rasterization can be reversed.

18

Effects for Vector Artwork

As mentioned earlier, many of the capabilities listed under the Effect menu are designed for use with vector artwork. Many of these effects modify paths by working with anchor points. Others use the object's path as a guideline and create a rasterized object to match (such as the glows and shadows).

Convert to Shape

Especially handy for creating objects that will automatically resize, this command often sees duty when preparing buttons for Web pages. In Figure 18.6, a second fill has been added to a type object, and using the Appearance palette to select it, the fill was converted to a rounded rectangle. When the object was duplicated and the text changed from "Next" to "Previous," the rounded rectangle automatically resized itself.

FIGURE 18.6

Convert to Shape was applied to the lower fill in the Appearance palette to put it behind the text.

Distort & Transform

These commands duplicate some of Illustrator's tools. Unlike the transform and Liquify tools, as effects the settings can be changed or removed at any time. Figure 18.7 shows how the commands work with a simple rectangle.

FIGURE 18.7

Top row: Original object, Bloat, Pucker, Roughen. Bottom row: Scribble & Tweak, Twist, Zig Zag.

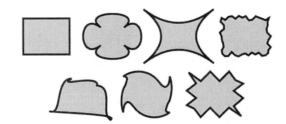

The Free Distort effect offers you a dialog box in which you move anchor points. The Transform effect's dialog box gives you numeric control, using the same dialog box we saw for the menu command Object, Transform, Transform Each. (Try this: Open the

Transform Each dialog box and position it somewhere onscreen. Click the Cancel button. Now open Effect, Distort & Transform, Transform. The dialog box appears in the same location.)

Path

The Path commands Outline Object and Outline Stroke are similar to those found under the Object, Path menu, but are effects rather than permanent changes to the object. The command Effect, Path, Offset Path creates a new path at a distance specified from the selected object (see Figure 18.8). The original object is on the left. In the center, Offset Path has enlarged the object without changing the original path. On the right, a second stroke was added in the Appearance palette and Offset Path was applied only to the new stroke.

FIGURE **18.8**

Offset Path can be applied to individual strokes using the Appearance palette.

Pathfinder

The Pathfinder effects include live versions of the 10 buttons we saw in the Pathfinder palette during Hour 12, "Using Transformations, Compound Shapes, and Blends." In addition are three print-related capabilities. Hard and soft mix and trap affect how overlapping colors will be printed by offset presses in commercial printing plants. Soft Mix and Trap will open the dialog box shown in Figure 18.9.

FIGURE **18.9**

Both the Soft Mix and Trap options are set in one dialog box.

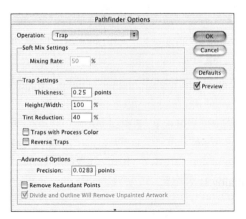

Hard and soft mix and trapping are used only with commercial printing, such as with offset and flexographic presses. Don't use these options without consulting your print shop first. You can read more about them in Hour 21, "Printing Your Illustrations."

Rasterize

This command opens the dialog box shown in Figure 18.10. The options you have for rasterization are the same as those found under the Object menu. The difference is that this command doesn't really create pixels from your object—it's simply an effect.

FIGURE **18.10**

The color model pop-up menu will offer Grayscale and Bitmap (black and white) in addition to either CMYK or RGB.

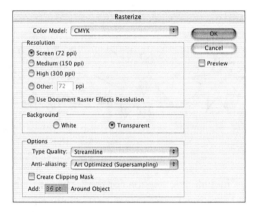

Using the Appearance palette, strokes and fills can be rasterized individually, even with different settings.

Task: Stylizing

We know that you must be chomping at the bit to play with some of these effects, so it's time for some hands-on training.

1. Open a new document in Illustrator, choose either orientation, choose either color mode, and Letter size.

2. Use the Line Segment tool to produce a horizontal line half the width of your artboard. Give it a black stroke of 5 points.

3. Use the menu command Effect, Stylize, Add Arrowheads to open the dialog box shown in Figure 18.11. Click the Preview box and take a look at the various available arrowheads. Don't forget to experiment with the Scale field, too! When you're done, click Cancel and delete the line.

FIGURE 18.11

Start and End are determined by which direction you dragged the tool.

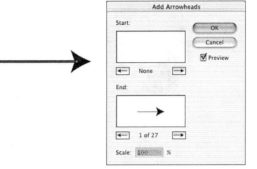

4. Select the Rectangle tool and Shift+drag a square. Give it a 5-point black stroke and a fill of None. Open Effect, Stylize, Drop Shadow and click Preview (see Figure 18.12). Click Cancel when done.

FIGURE 18.12

Don't ignore the Color option. Try using a blue shadow for an interesting effect.

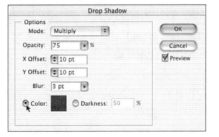

18

Be patient when applying effects, especially if you have an older or under-powered computer. It's not a good idea to interrupt the application of an effect, except by using the Stop button (when offered). You might experience delays of several seconds while performing the tasks in this section.

5. Using the Styles palette, apply the Star Burst style to your square. Use the stylize effect Feather as shown in Figure 18.13.

6. Select all and delete. Press D on the keyboard to restore your basic appearance. Shift+Option+drag (Mac)/Shift+Alt+drag (Windows) a large 5-pointed star on the left side of the artboard. Give it the Caution Tape style and then from the Swatches palette, apply the 20% Black swatch to the star's fill.

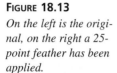

FIGURE 18.13

On the left is the original, on the right a 25-point feather has been applied.

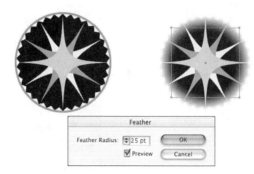

7. Open the Inner Glow dialog box. Change the Blur to 10 points and click the Preview box. After the screen updates, click the Center button. When your star has been redrawn, click Cancel.

8. Open the Outer Glow dialog box. Don't click Preview yet. First, click the color swatch and switch to a rich purple. Change the blending mode from Screen to Multiply. Make the Opacity 100% and the Blur 30 points. Now check the Preview box. Be patient and wait for the screen to redraw itself. Admire your work for a moment, then click Cancel.

9. With your star still selected on the artboard, open the Round Corners dialog box. Click Preview. Now enter 30 points in the radius field. Hit Tab to update. Change to 100 points and hit Tab. Notice that the star's original path remains intact, despite the change in appearance (see Figure 18.14) .

FIGURE 18.14

As an effect, Round Corners doesn't actually change the object's path.

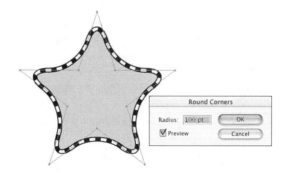

10. Select all and delete, leaving your document open for the next hands-on exercise a little later in the hour.

SVG Filters

These filters are used exclusively for preparing Scalable Vector Graphics (SVG) files for the Web. They'll be discussed in Hour 22, "Creating Web Graphics."

Warp

The Warp effects are "live" versions of the envelope distortions you learned about last hour. However, as live effects, they don't change the underlying object. In Figure 18.15, the top object is an arc created with Object, Envelope Distort, Make with Warp. Below is an arc created with Effect, Warp, Arc. Compare the paths.

FIGURE 18.15

A warp created as an effect doesn't change the underlying object. When created as an envelope distortion, the envelope mesh is applied.

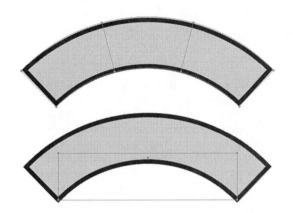

18

When warped as an effect, it's easy to use the Direct Selection tool to modify an object's path (see Figure 18.16).

FIGURE 18.16

Warped as an effect, the rectangle can be modified directly.

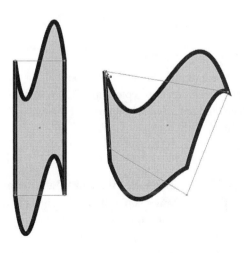

Raster Effects and Filters, for Raster and Vector Objects

You'll be learning a great deal about raster artwork in Hour 19. For now, let's simply remember that raster images, such as photos taken with a digital camera, are made up of tiny colored squares called pixels. Each pixel can be only one color. The size of the pixels determines how much detail an image can have. Larger pixels produce grainier images with less detail. Tiny pixels produce pictures that can be indistinguishable from photographic prints.

Keep in mind that the capabilities discussed here are also available for vector art and can be very effective with pattern-filled objects. They are only available under the Effect menu, and use the Document Raster Effects Settings.

 Illustrator raster effects and filters are based on plug-in filters from Adobe Photoshop. There are quite a few of them and it wouldn't be practical to explain each of them in a single hour. You could write an entire book about these filters and effects. In fact, that book has been written! Kate Binder, our dear friend and colleague (and the technical editor of this book) recently updated *Photoshop 6 Cookbook* (Silver Dollar Press). It takes a single image (of an eye) and applies most of Photoshop's filters to it to produce a series of different images. It's a great way to become familiar with the capabilities of the raster filters and effects in Adobe Illustrator 10.

Illustrator's raster effects and filters adjust the color of pixels or groups of pixels to change the appearance of the image. They are found in the lower half of the Effect and Filter menus.

Artistic

These effects and filters use digital technology to apply classic art techniques. Effects and filters from Colored Pencil to Watercolor, and Fresco to Neon Glow, give that fine-art look to placed and rasterized artwork. Figure 18.17 shows a list of the effects, as well as one of the dialog boxes.

Blur

Blur, Gaussian Blur, and Radial Blur soften the look of a raster or vector object. You won't see the full impact of these effects if your vector object is filled with a solid color. The blurs are very effective with patterns (see Figure 18.18).

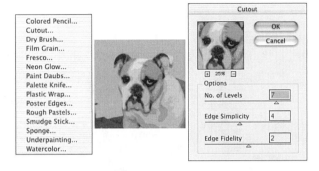

Figure 18.17
The artistic dialog boxes typically offer two or more sliders, an option or two, and a preview window.

Figure 18.18
On the left, the original object. In the center, a Gaussian blur. To the right, a motion blur using the Zoom option.

Gaussian Blur is also used to reduce *pixelization* in an image. When an image looks jagged or grainy, a Gaussian blur can smooth the edges. (Normally in these situations, you'll want to follow the blur with a Sharpen filter to reduce the blurriness in the image's details.)

Brush Strokes

Brush Strokes are another *artistic* set of effects and filters. These effects and filters simulate various—you guessed it—brush techniques. Figure 18.19 shows the Brush Strokes submenu, along with an example of Angled Strokes.

Distort

The three Distort effects/filters (listed in Figure 18.20) include two that are very similar, Glass and Ocean Ripple, which produce the appearance of clear distortion. The Diffuse Glow feature, however, works with the brightness of the image.

18

Figure 18.19

Two or three adjustment sliders are in each of the dialog boxes, along with a tiny preview window.

Accented Edges...
Angled Strokes...
Crosshatch...
Dark Strokes...
Ink Outlines...
Spatter...
Sprayed Strokes...
Sumi-e...

Figure 18.20

The Glass dialog box is more complex than the one for Ocean Ripple (shown here), but gives more control over the effect.

Diffuse Glow...
Glass...
Ocean Ripple...

Task: Pixelating

The Pixelate effects generally use a series of dots or lines to re-create the raster or vector object. It's time to experiment again! You should have an empty document still open. If not, start a new one.

1. Press D on the keyboard to restore the basic appearance. Draw a large circle and fill it with the Clown Attack swatch from the Swatches palette.

2. Use the Direct Selection tool and Option+drag (Mac)/Alt+drag (Windows) four copies of the circle to various places on the artboard. You should end up with five Clown Attack circles. (One of them will retain the original appearance for reference.)

3. Use the menu command Effect, Document Raster Effects Settings to open the dialog box. Set the Resolution to Screen (72 ppi) and click OK.

4. Select one of the circles and try Effect, Pixelate, Color Halftone. Use the default settings.

5. Select another circle and use Effect, Pixelate, Crystallize with cell size 10. (By the way, this effect is not related to the Crystallize tool you've seen in the Liquify tools.)

6. Pick a third circle and apply Mezzotint, using the Fine Dots setting.

7. The fourth circle should have the Pointillize effect applied. Experiment with the slider and see what shows up in the Preview window. Settle on Cell Size 6 before you click OK.

8. Now return to Effect, Document Raster Effects Settings. Change from 72 ppi to 300 ppi and click OK. (Be patient, this might take a quite few seconds.) Observe the difference in the appearance of the effects (see Figure 18.21). After examining the difference, you can close (don't save) this document.

FIGURE 18.21

The four outer circles to the left had the effects applied at 72 ppi. On the right, 300 ppi was used. (The circle in the center is the original on both sides.)

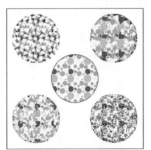 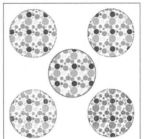

Sharpen

The Unsharp Mask effect, found in the Sharpen submenu of the Effect menu, is unintuitively named. Rather than dulling (unsharpening), it does actually sharpen an image. When applied to a photographic image, it gives the appearance of improved focus. It can also be used with Illustrator's vector patterns.

Rasterizing and then sharpening a pattern is not as effective as printing the pattern as vector art, but it might be useful when saving files in non-PostScript formats or when printing to an inkjet printer. Use it only if your patterns are not printing as sharply as you need them to print.

The Unsharp Mask capability in Illustrator is comparable to one of the most important Photoshop filters. By finding and emphasizing edges in an image, Unsharp Mask can make the picture appear more focused.

In Figure 18.22, the placed image in the upper left has been over sharpened. Notice how sharpening has emphasized the speckled background and created a halo around the dog. (Trust me on this one; that dog does *not* have a halo!) The image to the lower right has been more appropriately sharpened. By increasing the Threshold level, the background sharpening was avoided, by keeping the Amount and Radius to lower levels the halo was eliminated.

FIGURE 18.22

Sharpening is especially valuable after applying a Gaussian Blur to eliminate "noise" in an image.

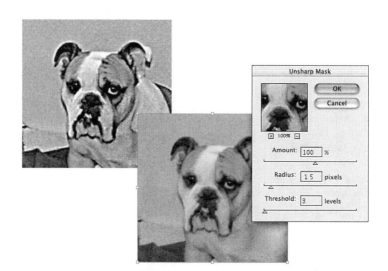

Sketch

The 14 Sketch effects/filters produce a wide variety of artistic techniques, as shown in Figure 18.23. Note that all the effects except Water Paper (the last one) produce grayscale or black-and-white images from your color images.

From left to right, top to bottom, the effects shown are Bas Relief, Chalk & Charcoal, Charcoal, Chrome, Conté Crayon, Graphic Pen, Halftone Pattern (split diagonally), Note Paper, Photocopy, Plaster, Reticulation, Stamp, Torn Edges, Water Paper. (Halftone Pattern shows Pattern Type: Dot to the upper left and Pattern Type: Circle to the lower right.)

FIGURE 18.23

Because of the radical difference in the options for Halftone Pattern, that sample is divided diagonally.

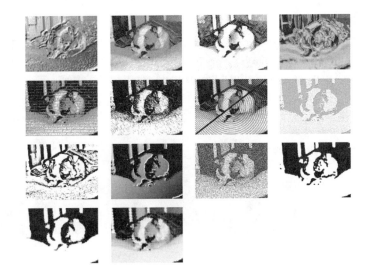

 You can often get better results with the Sketch effects and filters if you first apply a Gaussian Blur to eliminate the finest detail in an image.

18

Stylize

The only Stylize effect included with Illustrator is Glowing Edges. It finds lines of high contrast between colors and emphasizes them.

 This is an excellent spot to sneak in one of my favorite things about using Illustrator's effects with vector objects. Take a look at Figure 18.24. Notice that the effect Glowing Edges was applied to just one of the object's fills. That's right! You can apply effects to a fill (or stroke) rather than an object by using the Appearance palette. And doesn't *that* open up some rather interesting possibilities.

FIGURE 18.24

The object has three fills, but Glowing Edges has been applied to only one of them.

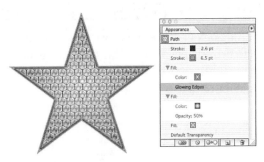

Texture

The Texture menu includes six different effects/filters. Shown in Figure 18.25, they are (from left) Craquelure, Grain, Mosaic Tiles, Patchwork, Stained Glass, and Texturizer. Each enables you to adjust the size and depth of the effect.

Video

Illustrator includes two effects/filters for use with video. De-Interlace eliminates scan lines from video captures. (Digital images of TV screens show horizontal black lines, often called scan lines. De-interlacing is a way to eliminate them.) The second video effect is NTSC Colors. It is used to prepare an image for use with North American standard broadcast television. It adjusts the image's colors to the appropriate gamut.

Quite a few effects and filters are on the market and on the Web for Illustrator use as plug-ins. Some are freeware (available for the time it takes to download them), some are shareware (a modest fee is charged, often on the honor system), and some are full-fledged commercial products. Before downloading or buying, however, make sure that the plug-in is compatible with Illustrator 10 and if you are using Mac OS X, make sure that it is carbonized.

Filters Not Offered As Effects

Illustrator's Filter menu (shown in Figure 18.26) offers 15 categories of filters, divided into two sections. Most of the filters are duplicates of the effects we've just discussed. However, Illustrator offers some commands only under the Filter menu. You'll find them in three categories.

FIGURE **18.26**

*Most of the Filter
menu should look
familiar to you from
the Effect menu.*

Colors

Adjust Colors is used to fine-tune the appearance of placed raster images, but can also be used with vector objects. With vector objects, it makes permanent changes to fills and strokes, but does not work with patterns and gradients.

The Blend commands (Blend Front to Back, Blend Horizontally, and Blend Vertically) are used with three or more vector objects. Although the Blend command under the Object menu creates new objects, this command simply mixes colors. It uses the first and last objects (front and back, left and right, top and bottom) and blends the colors of all objects in between.

The Convert commands (Convert to CMYK, Convert to Grayscale, and Convert to RGB) enable you to change colors modes for selected objects. Remember, however, that Illustrator does not enable both RGB *and* CMYK objects in a single document. (Grayscale is allowed in either.)

Inverting colors gives you the opposite color's value for the stroke and fill of vector objects. (If you're familiar with the color wheel, each color's inverse is exactly across the wheel.)

Overprint Black is used with commercial printing. Black is the darkest color, and overprinting it reduces the chance that overlapping inks will show through.

The Intensity slider enables you to make the colors of selected objects richer or paler. This is not the same as creating a tint of a color.

Create

With vector objects, only the Trim Marks option is available. Trim marks are similar to crop marks. However, instead of indicating a single area of a page, trim marks can be

18

used to identify several individual areas on the same page. When printing business cards, for example, it's common to have several cards on a single page. Trim marks can identify where the cards should be cut.

Object Mosaic creates tiles that represent your original image. Unlike the Pixelate and Texture effects/filters, these tiles are actually individual raster objects, which can be ungrouped and manipulated individually. As you can see in Figure 18.27, the Create Mosaic dialog box offers no preview.

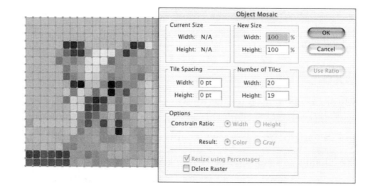

Pen & Ink

In addition to applying a hatch effect, this menu enables you to save and load sets of custom hatches. A hatch effect reproduces an object using a series of short lines. The Hatch dialog box is shown in Figure 18.28.

Filters Versus Effects

You might be wondering why Illustrator offers both effects and filters. As you know, effects are live and filters are not. That can be a great advantage if, for example, you need to fine-tune or change the look of an effect. And, normally, live is a good thing.

However, filters also have their place in the Illustrator world. For one thing, if you've got a rapidly approaching deadline and a computer that's more than a couple of weeks old, you might find yourself thinking bad thoughts every time you have to wait while an effect is reapplied. Even simply moving an object on the artboard can result in delays while the object is redrawn and the effects are reapplied. Filters, on the other hand, make changes directly to the rasterized object and what's done is done. There's no delay for reapplication. File size is generally smaller, too, with filters.

Summary

This hour has introduced you to some of the most powerful features available in computer graphics. The power of these effects and filters is matched only by the power they require from your computer! Although they take a lot of resources, they do some amazing things. The best way to find out how powerful these capabilities are is simply to play with them. (Tell your boss we said so!)

Workshop

We've put together a few questions that should clarify some of the questions you might have about effects and filters. We've kept the quiz short (but tough, we think) so that there's more play time. The exercises this hour include some rather loosely structured time to experiment with effects and filters.

Q&A

Q Other than the fact that effects are live and filters are not, and some filters don't work with vector objects, how do the individual effects/filters differ?

A They don't. If you apply an effect to a raster object with specific settings and the counterpart filter with the same settings, the result should be the same.

Q Some of the filters seem to be available sometimes but not others. What gives?

A Color mode gives. A number of filters and effects are only available for RGB images, not CMYK. Specifically, filters/effects that can be used only with RGB images include Artistic, Brush Strokes, Distort, Sketch, Stylize, Texture, and Video. Quite a list, eh?

18

Q I just applied Mezzotint effect to an object. What's the difference at this point between the menu commands Effect, Apply Mezzotint and Effect, Mezzotint?

A Effect, Apply Mezzotint will skip the dialog box and apply the filter with the last selected settings. The second command, Effect, Mezzotint, will open the dialog box and enable you to change settings. The most recently used effect will appear in the commands. And, by the way, the Effect and Filter menus are separate—the most recently used effect will not appear at the top of the Filter menu.

Q Why does the resolution of a rasterized object have such a big effect on how many of the effects and filters appear?

A The effects and filters in question work with pixels. The higher the resolution, the more pixels there are with which to work. The more pixels in the same area means that each pixel is smaller. Therefore, anything done to the pixels will appear to have finer detail.

Quiz

1. Why can't you use the command Effect, Distort & Transform, Pucker & Bloat with a raster object?

    a. The effect works only on gradient fills.

    b. Raster objects don't have anchor points and path segments to distort.

    c. What do you mean *can't*? You're not trying hard enough!

    d. You must first use the command Object, Vectorize.

2. The difference between the commands Object, Envelope Distort, Warp and Effect, Warp is…

    a …none. There are two sets of commands simply for your convenience.

    b. There is no relationship between the two commands. Envelope distortions have nothing to do with warp effects.

    c. …the former creates an envelope mesh object that can be manipulated to change the appearance of the object. The latter retains the object's original path.

    d. …using the command under the Object menu retains the vector object, whereas those under the Effect menu creates a rasterized object.

3. Using the Effect, Distort menu commands is the same as using the Distort tools from the Toolbox.

    a. True

    b. False

Quiz Answers

1. b. Select a placed raster object on the artboard and try to use the Convert Anchor Point tool on one corner. Illustrator will let you know that it's not an anchor point.

2. c. If you want to save the distortion for later use, definitely use the Object, Envelope Distort commands. If you just need a simple (*simple?*) warp, stick with the Effect menu.

3. b. False. There are no Distort tools. The Effect, Distort commands apply glows and create ripples as if the image was seen through water or glass.

Exercises

1. Open an Illustrator document, RGB, any size, and either orientation. Embed a raster image or create a pattern-filled vector object and rasterize it at 150 ppi. Option+drag (Mac)/Alt+drag (Windows) to copy the object on the artboard. Apply the filter Brush Strokes, Angled Strokes, with settings 50/15/3. Select the other copy of the object. Apply Filter, Pixelate, Crystallize with a cell size of 10. Now apply Angled Strokes with the same settings. Compare the two images. (An example is shown in Figure 18.29.)

FIGURE 18.29

To the left, Angled Strokes. To the right, Crystallize, then Angled Strokes.

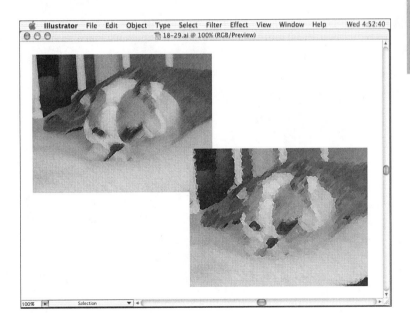

18

Experiment with other filters and effects in combination. (Remember that if you use effects you'll be able to change settings, but screen redraw can slow you down.)

2. Open a new RGB Illustrator document (or select all and delete). Embed a raster image. Apply one or more filters. Save the file as an Illustrator file, using the name <FileSize-1.ai>. Close the document. Open a new Illustrator document. Embed the same image. Apply the same changes, but this time as effects rather than filters. Use the same settings. Save the file as <FileSize-2.ai>. Close the document. In Windows Explorer or the Mac Finder, compare the file sizes. If you embedded a large, high-resolution image, the first file might be substantially smaller.

3. Open a new RGB Illustrator document (or select all and delete). Place a raster image, preferably a favorite photo. Option+drag (Mac)/Alt+Drag (Windows) to make two copies. Use the Object, Rasterize command to make one 300 ppi version, one 150 ppi version, and one 72 ppi version. Use all the time remaining in this hour to experiment with effects and filters on the three images. Watch how resolution affects the filter or effect. Try different settings in the various dialog boxes.

Part IV
Productive Illustrator

Hour

HOUR 19

Working with Raster Images and Programs

As you know, Illustrator is a vector art program. It uses Bézier curves to produce objects on the artboard. However, Illustrator also enables you to incorporate pixel-based imagery into your illustrations. And, of course, you can convert your objects to pixels by using the Rasterize command.

If you're familiar with Adobe Photoshop, you know a great deal about raster images already. If not, don't worry, we'll bring you up to speed quickly!

In this hour, you'll learn

- What makes raster images tick
- How to bring a raster image into Illustrator
- The difference between linking and embedding
- How resolution affects file size
- How to work with raster images
- About the Links palette
- Working with Photoshop

Working with Raster Images in Illustrator

A raster image can be brought into an Illustrator document several ways. A variety of pixel-based file formats can be opened directly in Illustrator, files can be added to an existing Illustrator document using the Place command; you can also copy and paste between programs.

After you've placed a raster image in Illustrator, it can be treated as if it was an object. You can move it, scale it, and even apply effects and transformations to it.

Raster Versus Vector, Reprise

In Hour 1, "Understanding Illustrator," we spent some time discussing the differences between raster and vector artwork. Here's a refresher course, with a whole lot more!

- Vector artwork is created mathematically with paths that can be filled and stroked. It can be scaled to any size without loss of sharpness. Raster artwork is created with pixels and can be resized by increasing either the size or number of pixels.

- When you rasterize vector artwork in Illustrator, you should treat it as raster artwork. It is no longer comprised of objects, but rather is a series of colored pixels.

- Pixels are tiny colored squares, and each can be only one color. An image is constructed by controlling the colors of the pixels. Each pixel is independent; there are no objects in raster art.

- *Resolution* refers to the organization of those pixels, how large or small they are and how closely packed they will be when printed.

- Resolution is measured two ways. We use *pixels per inch* (ppi) for use onscreen, for scanning, and for digital photos. We use *dots per inch* (dpi) when discussing printing. (Think of pixels as the electronic data and as dots being drops of ink.)

- Documents containing raster artwork can be RGB or CMYK. CMYK documents with embedded raster images will be larger because more color information must be stored.

- Raster art can contain subtle transitions from color-to-color, which enables for photographic-quality reproduction. Vector art can contain gradients and patterns, but it is very difficult to produce photo-quality work with vector objects.

- All raster images are rectangles, even if they don't appear to be. Pixels can be transparent, but the image is still a rectangle.

- When placed or opened in Illustrator, a raster image can be considered to be an object. This raster object can be manipulated in shape (within certain limits), but you have limited control over the content (see Figure 19.1).

FIGURE **19.1**

Manipulating the bounding box is one way to alter a placed raster image.

- Embedded raster images and rasterized vector art can result in *huge* file sizes.

- Illustrator has a variety of effects and filters that can be used with raster artwork. Some can be applied to both vector and raster art, some are raster-only.

Adding Raster Art to Illustrator

Illustrator can open a variety of file formats. Among them are several raster image formats, including BMP, GIF, JPEG, Kodak Photo CD, PICT, PCX, Pixar, PNG, Targa, TIFF, and Photoshop's native file format, which uses the filename extension .psd. Figure 19.2 shows the full list.

FIGURE **19.2**

The list is from Illustrator's Open dialog box. You'll find it as the Show pop-up menu.

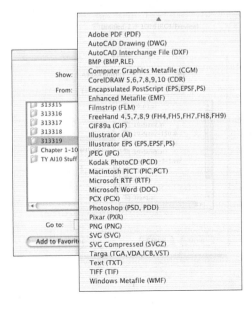

19

Remember that you don't use the Save command to create a raster file, but rather the Export command. You can export BMP, JPEG, PICT, and TIFF files among others.

Illustrator also enables you to use the Copy and Paste commands (and drag and drop) to bring in raster art from an open image editing program. (This will be discussed in greater detail later in the hour, when we talk about using Illustrator with Photoshop.)

A far more common way to open a raster file is by using Illustrator's File, Place command. Place enables you to add an image as an object in an existing Illustrator document (see Figure 19.3).

FIGURE 19.3

Illustrator's Place dialog box is very similar to the Open dialog box.

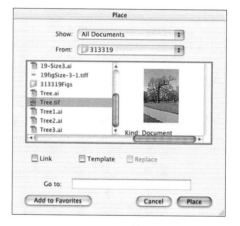

You can place files of every type that Illustrator can open, both raster and vector, with one exception—you cannot use the Place command to add an Illustrator (.ai) file to an Illustrator file.

Notice in the dialog box the check boxes for Replace, Template, and Link. Replace is only available when a placed object is selected on the artboard. It deletes an existing raster image and puts the newly selected image in its place. Any effects or appearance characteristics applied to the original placed image will be retained.

The Template option is handy for bringing in artwork that you will trace. Illustrator automatically creates a new layer below the active layer and places the artwork there. That new layer is locked and in Outline mode, just as if you had used the Layer Options dialog box to create a template layer (see Figure 19.4) .

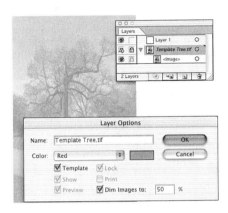

FIGURE 19.4

There is no difference between checking the Template box in the Place dialog box and checking the Template box in the Layer Options dialog box.

That third check box, Link, is far more important. It gets an entire section later in this hour.

Sources of Raster Images

Pixels are everywhere these days. Digital cameras, scanners, image collections on CDs and the Web—you can find raster images all around you. If you own a digital camera, you probably can download the images in JPEG format directly to your hard drive.

You might need a scanner to bring an image into an image-editing program, such as Photoshop, Photoshop Elements, or Photoshop LE. If so, an appropriate program likely came with the scanner. If not, the scanner's software will enable you to scan and save an image, possibly as a TIFF file.

Collections of images on CD are usually "royalty free." You've paid all you have to pay, and the images are yours to use, as you will. (Well, there usually are some restrictions, such as not reselling the images as a collection.) The pictures themselves can be in a variety of formats. Some require special plug-ins or translators to bring them into Illustrator.

Images purchased from "stock photography" collections either on the Web or on CD are usually in either JPEG or TIFF format, or both. The documentation and licensing agreement that came with the CD or is posted on the Web site will tell you about restrictions on how you can use the pictures.

Linking Versus Embedding Raster Artwork

When you place artwork, raster or vector, into an Illustrator document, the biggest decision you have to make is whether or not to check the Link box. We use the terms *linked* and *embedded* to differentiate between the two.

19

The Pros and Cons

Linked artwork actually remains separate from the Illustrator document. Illustrator puts a preview image on your screen, but does not actually include the artwork in its file. The placed image can be modified or edited outside of Illustrator and Illustrator will always look for the latest version. On the downside, if you send your Illustrator file out to be printed or otherwise distributed, you must remember to include a copy of the linked image. Also, you've got to remain in contact with that linked file. If, for example, the file is stored on a network drive, you'll not be able to update it if the drive isn't available.

Embedded artwork actually becomes part of your Illustrator document. This can dramatically increase the size of the file. (We'll show you some actual numbers a bit later in the hour.) Embedded artwork can slow down Illustrator, especially in such operations as saving files. On the plus side, when an image is embedded, you know it will be included when you send the file out and you never have to worry about it being available. Embedding also prevents the occasional problem of a linked file being "updated" to a version that you don't want.

Embedded pixel-based artwork, whether placed images or rasterized vector art, can add greatly to file sizes. You do have some control over the matter, however.

Test Case: Embedded Tree

Our original sample image is an RGB TIFF file created from a digitized photograph. (You might remember this image from Hour 16, "Showing and Hiding with Masks.") The TIFF file is 3.6 MB on disk. When opened in Illustrator, the picture is approximately 14 inches by 22 inches, which is far too large to fit on a letter-sized artboard (see Figure 19.5).

In this figure, the Document Info palette is set to show the embedded images. It shows that the photo is 1024 pixels by 1536 pixels with a non-standard resolution of just over 70 pixels per inch. When we simply save this document as an Illustrator file (.ai), the file size is approximately 7.1 MB. (Don't confuse the file size with the size of the embedded image, which is shown in the Document Info palette.)

When we scale this embedded raster image to 25%, a more useable size, and then save the image again, the file's size remains the same because the same number of pixels are being stored (see Figure 19.6).

FIGURE **19.5**

The opacity of the picture has been reduced so that you can see the artboard.

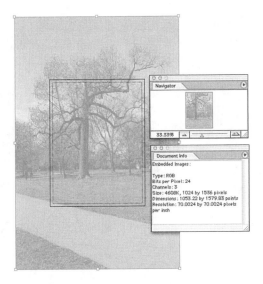

FIGURE **19.6**

The Document Info palette shows that the embedded image is still 1024×1536 pixels, but the resolution is now approximately 280 pixels per inch.

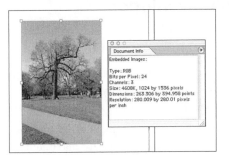

If we convert the document to CMYK color mode, the file size jumps to 9.6 MB. (CMYK documents contain four color channels, where RGB documents contain three.)

The menu command Object, Rasterize enables us to work with the embedded artwork. Using the RGB version of the Illustrator file, when we rasterize at 300 ppi, the file size increases to 8.1 MB. If, on the other hand, we reduce the resolution to 150 ppi, the document drops to 2.3 MB. There is, however, some reduction in quality, as shown in Figure 19.7.

19

Figure 19.7

At 100% zoom, the difference is indistinguishable. At 600%, however, you can see the pixelization of the lower-resolution image on the right.

Picking the Right Resolution

Here are a couple of simple rules of thumb to help you balance file size and quality issues.

- If the image is destined for the Web or other onscreen purposes, use 72 ppi. This ensures that the image will appear in a Web browser at the appropriate size. (Always check Web graphics in Illustrator at 100% zoom.)
- When the image will be printed to an inkjet printer, keep it as an RGB image and use a resolution between 150 and 225 ppi for maximum quality.
- If the image is part of a CMYK document that will be printed commercially on an offset press, the appropriate resolution for the image is 1.5 to 2 times the line screen frequency of the press, measured in lines per inch (lpi). Ask your print shop for the lpi.

The Links Palette

Illustrator's Links palette helps you keep track of linked and embedded images. In addition to telling you their status, you can get lots of handy information, and even change the status of a placed image (see Figure 19.8).

When you open a document and Illustrator can't find a linked image, you'll get the opportunity to replace it. You can use the Replace button in the box shown in Figure 19.9.

FIGURE 19.8

The palette will show different symbols for missing, modified, and embedded images. You can double-click an image's name in the Links palette to get full information.

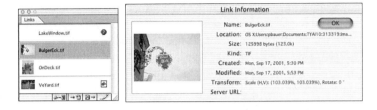

FIGURE 19.9

If you ignore the warning, the illustration will have an invisible box in place of the missing image.

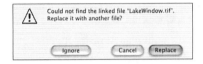

If you'd like, you can set Illustrator to automatically attempt to update any linked images that have been modified. Use Illustrator's Files & Clipboard preferences (see Figure 19.10).

FIGURE 19.10

The Update Links option is used with placed images.

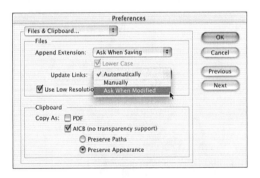

19

At the bottom of the Links palette you'll see four buttons. From the left, they are Replace Link, Go To Link, Update Link, and Edit Original. Replace Link enables you to substitute another image. When you've clicked on a link in the Links palette and use the Go To Link button, Illustrator will reposition the document in the window to center it on the placed image and the image will be selected on the artboard. Update Link will fetch the latest version of the linked image. (You don't have to wait until the file is opened again.) Edit Original opens the linked image in the program from which it comes, if available.

You might have noticed that the Replace capability seems to be everywhere in Illustrator. Yet, you might wonder how often you'll change your mind and want to put in an entirely new picture. Well, not even I change my mind like *that* very often. But, that's a very practical use for Replace. If you'll recall, placing high-resolution images into an Illustrator document can really slow things down. Instead, place low-resolution copies of all the images in the document, do your creative thing, then at the last minute replace the low-resolution versions with high-resolution versions. That's a very handy way to keep Illustrator humming along!

Working with Raster Art

Some things Illustrator lets you do with placed raster images, and some things it won't let you do.

- You can manipulate the shape of the placed image by using the raster object's bounding box (as you saw in Figure 19.1).

- The Object, Transform commands and most of the Transform tools can also be used on placed raster images (see Figure 19.11). The Twist and Reshape tools can't manipulate placed images because the raster objects don't have actual anchor points.

FIGURE 19.11
Both the Shear command and the Shear tool can be used with raster objects.

- As you learned last hour, Illustrator has a variety of effects and filters that can be applied to raster images (see Figure 19.12).

- In Hour 16 you learned how to use clipping masks and opacity masks with raster images.

- Envelope distortions are available for use with raster images.

- You can even create a gradient mesh object from a photograph, as shown in Figure 19.13.

FIGURE 19.12

Feather, Warp, Colored Pencil, Glass, Mosaic Tiles, and Radial Blur are just a few of the effects that can be applied to raster images.

FIGURE 19.13

It takes a lot of rows and columns to preserve any resemblance to the original, which means a very complex object.

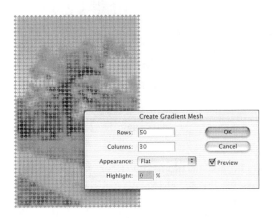

19

- Remember, too, that the Object, Rasterize command is available. In addition to changing the resolution of a placed image, you can convert a color image to grayscale, and even change a grayscale image to color. (The image won't be colorized, but a number of effects and filters require that the target object be in RGB color to work properly.)

Illustrator and Photoshop

Illustrator and its image-editing relative Photoshop work very well together. In fact, Illustrator can open and export native Photoshop (.psd) files. Remember, however, that some capabilities are not shared between the programs, and not all artwork can be moved directly back and forth.

Objects in Illustrator, Layers in Photoshop

The key concept when transferring artwork between the two programs is objects versus layers. If you bring a Photoshop image with only one layer into Illustrator, you'll have a single raster object. If each element of the Photoshop image is on a separate layer, Illustrator can create separate raster objects from them.

On the flip side, when sending artwork from Illustrator to Photoshop, you want to put each object on its own layer. In Photoshop, each object remains separate, even though rasterized.

Photoshop's Multilayered Files to Illustrator

In Figure 19.14, you can see our test Photoshop file, still in Photoshop, complete with its Layers palette.

FIGURE 19.14

The original Photoshop file has five layers, including one type layer.

When we open this Photoshop file in Illustrator, we get a dialog box asking how we want to handle the layers (see Figure 19.15). We can choose to flatten the image to a single layer (which reduces the file size and preserves its appearance), or we can retain the layers.

FIGURE 19.15

You'll see this dialog box when opening Photoshop files that haven't been flattened.

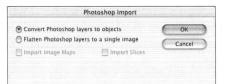

When the Photoshop files contain image maps and/or slices, you can choose to preserve those as well. (Image maps and slices are used with Web graphics. You'll learn about them in Hour 22, "Creating Web Graphics.") When we retain the Photoshop layers, the image opens in Illustrator as a multilayered document, with one raster object on each layer (see Figure 19.16).

FIGURE 19.16
The layers retain the Photoshop names, and each contains a single raster object, also with that name.

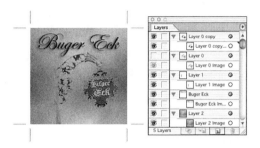

Notice that the Photoshop-type layer retains the appearance of the Photoshop layer effects (drop shadow and emboss). Unfortunately, Photoshop-type layers opened in Illustrator are rasterized, and therefore, are no longer editable type.

> Illustrator's Layers palette menu includes the commands Collect in New Layer, Merge Selected, and Flatten Artwork. If you Command+click (Mac)/Control+click (Windows) to select some or all the layers and use Collect in New Layer, the old layers become sublayers of a new layer. Merge Selected moves the objects to the new layer and deletes the old layers. Flatten Artwork doesn't require layers to be selected. It moves all objects to a single layer, then discards all other layers.

Photoshop also offers the capability to export paths to Illustrator. This can be used with paths created with Photoshop's Pen tool and the Shape tools. To export a shape layer clipping path, either double-click it in the Paths palette and give it a name to duplicate it, or make sure the shape layer is selected in the Layers palette. You then use the Photoshop menu command File, Export, Paths to Illustrator.

19

Moving Artwork from Illustrator to Photoshop

The best way to take your artwork from Illustrator to Photoshop is by exporting a copy as a .psd file. You'll have the opportunity to save layers and text, among other features (see Figure 19.17).

Remember that when opened in Photoshop 6, the vector artwork will be rasterized. Photoshop, however, preserves the Illustrator layers and sublayers (see Figure 19.18).

FIGURE **19.17**

*When exporting to
Photoshop format,
you'll see this list of
options.*

FIGURE **19.18**

*In addition to layers,
Photoshop provides
transparency for
Illustrator images
exported to Photoshop
format.*

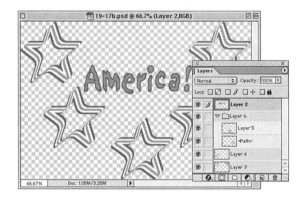

The exception to the rasterization rule is type. Make sure, however, that the type is on a separate layer. If there is any other vector object on the layer, the type will be rasterized. As you can see in Figure 19.19, some other features that can cause type to be rasterized when exporting to Photoshop format are applying an effect, using an envelope distortion, and adding a stroke. (Layer 2 has been sheared with Illustrator's Object, Transform, Shear command. It remains editable text.)

Copying and Pasting Between Illustrator and Photoshop

The Files & Clipboard preference settings govern illustrator's clipboard. It enables you to choose PDF or AICB (Adobe Illustrator Clipboard) formats. AICB further offers priority for paths or for appearance. (Photoshop prefers AICB when moving objects from Illustrator.)

FIGURE **19.19**

Each of the text lines is on a separate Illustrator layer, and some can still be edited when exported to Photoshop format (.psd).

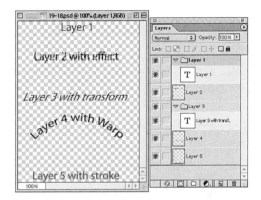

Remember that copy/paste and drag/drop do not support transparency. Nonrectangular objects or selections will include a white background. It's usually worth the extra moments to export from Illustrator as Photoshop format and to open Photoshop files.

Rasterizing Illustrator Artwork

As you've seen several times in previous hours, Illustrator enables you to create raster artwork from your vector objects. You might want to apply a filter or effect to your artwork that's not available for use with vector objects. Perhaps your artwork is destined for a raster format and you want to control the final appearance. Perhaps you need to move a gradient—or pattern-filled object to Photoshop and don't want to worry about copy/paste. There are lots of reasons you might want or need to rasterize vector objects.

You can convert the selected objects either permanently or as a reversible effect. Remember that the menu command Object, Rasterize can be reversed only with the Undo command, whereas Effect, Rasterize is live and can be reversed at any time.

Among the options you have when rasterizing are resolution, transparent or opaque background, and antialiasing. You can also add empty space around the artwork and create a clipping path (see Figure 19.20).

19

FIGURE 19.20

Whether using the Rasterize command under the Object menu or under the Effect menu, the dialog box is the same.

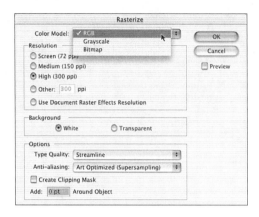

Summary

In this hour, you've seen a lot of technical stuff about working with pixel-based images. You've been exposed to moving artwork between Illustrator and Photoshop. Although it's probably not been a barrel of laughs, integrating raster images into your Illustrator documents can be one of the key factors in creating your artwork.

Workshop

Let's go through a few questions to reinforce some of the key points of this hour, then we'll work with a couple of practical exercises.

Q&A

Q How can Illustrator work with pixels—it's a vector art program!

A Raster (pixel) artwork is added to a vector illustration as an object. The object has no assigned stroke and the fill is the picture itself.

Q What happens to a raster object when a transformation, such as Shear, is applied?

A Think of it as rerasterizing the object with new dimensions. Illustrator calculates the changes to each of the pixels and redraws the image to match.

Q How can I include a linked image when sending an Illustrator file to my printer?

A The first of two steps is to make sure that the linked file is recorded along with the Illustrator document on the CD or Zip disk. Second, update the link using the Links palette to look for the image on the transfer disk.

Q Photoshop is making hash of my Illustrator artwork. What can I do to preserve the look of my objects?

A Rasterize in Illustrator, using a high resolution. That should protect the appearance when you move the artwork to Photoshop.

Quiz

1. What type of artwork retains its appearance better when enlarged?

    a Vector objects

    b. Raster images

    c. Rasterized vector artwork

    d. Vectorized raster artwork

2. Each pixel in an image containing a black-to-white gradient has how many shades of gray?

    a. If it's an RGB image, three—one for each color channel

    b. If it's a CMYK image, four—one for each color channel

    c. One

    d. 256

3. After you rasterize an object at 72 ppi it can only be used for Web graphics.

    a. True

    b. False

4. The best file format to use for vector art that will be transferred to Photoshop is what?

    a. JPEG, it can be opened by any image editor.

    b. EPS, it will maintain vector paths when opened in Photoshop.

    c. Photoshop, it can maintain layers and editable text.

    d. Illustrator, it's the only format that supports all Illustrator's features.

19

Quiz Answers

1. a. Vector artwork can be scaled with no loss of quality.

2. c. Each pixel can only be one color—always. However, the RGB or CMYK mode determines how many component colors make up that one color.

3. b. Raster images can be used for any purpose, regardless of resolution. Quality, however, might be an issue for print when working with 72 ppi images.

4. c. Photoshop. JPEG does not support vectors, layers, or transparency. EPS files are rasterized when opened in Photoshop. Illustrator files are opened as Generic PDF and rasterized.

Exercises

1. Place a raster image (embedded) into a fresh Illustrator document. Open the Document Info palette (under the Window menu). From the palette's menu, select Selection Only and Embedded Images. Take a look at all the information available to you. Now open the Links palette. Double-click your embedded image's name in the Links palette to open the Information window. (You can also open Information from the palette's menu.) Remember that you uncheck the Link box in the Place dialog box to embed an image. Also, keep in mind that you access a palette's menu by clicking on the little triangle in the palette's upper-right corner.

2. Create a large rectangle in an empty Illustrator document. Apply a pattern fill. Rasterize the object at 300 ppi, using the menu command Object, Rasterize. Save the file as <1.ai>. Go back to Object, Rasterize and rerasterize the same object at 150 ppi. Save the file as <2.ai>. Again, rasterize the object, this time at 72 ppi, and save the file as <3.ai>. Close the file and go to the Mac Finder or Windows Explorer. Compare the sizes of the three files.

3. Embed a raster image in a new Illustrator document, and use the Object, Rasterize command to make sure that the artwork is 72 ppi. (You can also rasterize some vector artwork.) Discover what you can and cannot do to raster objects by going through the menu commands. Try the Transform commands, envelope distortions, filters, and effects.

Hour **20**

Understanding File Formats and Platform Issues

You will likely spend a lot of time creating illustrations in Illustrator. But your work is not likely to spend its natural-born life just sitting on your hard drive, waiting for you to look at it. No, artwork is usually for a purpose. Maybe for the Web, maybe for print, maybe just for fun. But odds are it will need to be compatible with something, somewhere to fulfill its destiny.

Artwork that is simply for your pleasure, and will only be viewed on your computer, can stay comfortably in the Adobe Illustrator (.ai) file format. However, images that must be viewed with a Web browser must be in a format that the browser can recognize. Likewise, artwork that will be placed into a page layout document for commercial printing must meet certain file format requirements. Even outputting to your handy-dandy inkjet printer might require some format changes.

In this hour, you'll learn about

- The file formats supported by Illustrator
- Which format to choose for which work
- Identifying the best format for each particular image
- Formats you'll probably never need
- Cross-platform considerations

File Formats, What Are They?

Just as you save that Microsoft Word document, that FileMaker Pro spreadsheet, or even how you save in the middle of a game of Diablo, Illustrator's data needs to be recorded in the proper format. Someday there might be a universal file format, one that can be used for Web graphics, word-processing documents, high-end color images, spreadsheets and databases, and even games. But until then, we need to know not only which formats we *can* use for each purpose, but which formats are *best* to use in each situation.

> No matter which file format you need, it's usually a very good idea to save the original file as an Illustrator file, too. That maximizes your editing capability should you need to make changes later.

You can think of file formats as languages. Adobe Illustrator speaks, shall we say, German. Photoshop speaks Dutch. Microsoft Word speaks Italian. AutoCAD speaks Hindi. Web browsers can only read, and only in Russian and Japanese. Page layout programs can only hear English, but they can only speak Spanish. Obviously, we need some translators. Illustrator has some built-in translation capabilities. Let's continue the language analogy to show how Illustrator works with the "languages" of file formats:

- Illustrator can, for example, understand enough Dutch (Photoshop) to get by, but can't understand everything it hears. (Illustrator can open Photoshop files, but Illustrator doesn't recognize all Photoshop's capabilities.)
- Illustrator has dictionaries that enable it to understand and speak a little Italian and Hindi. (These are the plug-ins that open and save files in word processing and CAD formats.)
- Illustrator sends documents to a translation service to make copies in Russian and Japanese. (Save for Web, a program within Illustrator, can create Web graphics.)
- Illustrator studied English in school, so it can converse in that language, but it flunked Spanish. (It can save files in formats accepted for placement in page layout programs, but it can't read the actual Quark, InDesign, or PageMaker files.)

It's up to you to save your work in the best file format available. Alas, the native Illustrator format (.ai) is not visible in Web browsers, nor can you use it in QuarkXPress, the leading page layout program. (However, the latest versions of both Adobe InDesign and Adobe PageMaker support the Illustrator format through version 9 natively.)

The Difference Between Save As and Export

There are a couple of different ways to create files from Illustrator artwork. When you first save a document, the Save command opens the Save As dialog box. Later, Save will simply record changes to the disk without changing the file format, unless there is a reason it can't. (For example, if you've been working on a TIFF file and add a vector object, the Save As dialog box will open when you try to save.)

If you're working with a file format other than Illustrator's native format, you'll need to use either the Save As, Export, or Save for Web command. Save As gives you access to Illustrator's native format (.ai) , Encapsulated PostScript (.eps) , Adobe PDF (.pdf) , and the Scalable Vector Graphics (.svg and .svgz) formats. The menu command File, Export opens the way to produce a variety of formats, for Web, print, architecture/engineering (CAD) programs, and some specialty programs (see Figure 20.1). (Illustrator also offers Save for Web, which is discussed in depth in Hour 22, "Creating Web Graphics.") Save for Web enables you to create Web graphics in the JPEG, GIF, PNG, SWF, and SVG formats.

Because there is a strong connection among Illustrator (.ai), EPS (.eps), and PDF (.pdf) formats, you can consider Save As to be the vector format command. Export, on the other hand, works with all other file types and formats.

FIGURE 20.1

Illustrator's Export command gives you access to all these file formats.

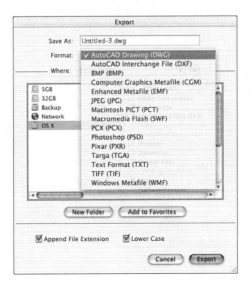

The File Format Plug-Ins and Where to Find Them

Illustrator sorts its file format plug-ins (the mini-programs that serve as translators) into three basic categories: Illustrator Formats—Standard, Illustrator Formats—Other, and Photoshop Formats (see Figure 20.2).

FIGURE 20.2

Illustrator's Plug-Ins folder holds separate folders for the three types of file format plug-ins.

By the end of this hour, you'll know pretty much which file formats you'll need and which plug-ins can be deleted.

Save and Save As, the Vector Formats

While some file formats can support clipping paths to define transparency, only a couple are actually vector file formats. Primary among them are the Illustrator format (.ai), Encapsulated PostScript (.eps) , Adobe PDF (.pdf) , and Scalable Vector Graphics (.svg and .svgz) . (The CAD formats, discussed later, also work with vectors.) These three primary file formats (and SVG) are produced through Illustrator's Save As dialog box (see Figure 20.3).

Saving in Illustrator Format: The Options

The only format that supports 100% of Illustrator's features is, not surprisingly, Illustrator's own format, which is based on PDF. It is, naturally, the default file format (.ai). In addition to Illustrator, programs that can work directly with .ai files include Adobe PageMaker, Adobe InDesign, and Adobe GoLive. Photoshop can recognize Illustrator files and open them as PDFs, and Adobe Streamline can save files in the .ai format.

When you choose Illustrator format and click OK in the Save As dialog box, you're presented with a box full of options (see Figure 20.4).

FIGURE 20.3

Four types of files can be created through the Save As dialog box. Compressed SVG (.svgz) doesn't really count as a separate format.

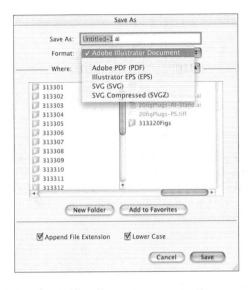

FIGURE 20.4

The Illustrator format options dialog box.

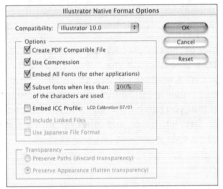

The Compatibility pop-up menu enables you to choose from versions of the native Illustrator .ai file format dating back to the Dark Ages. Well, as early as Illustrator version 3.0. If you choose a version earlier than 10, Illustrator will remind you that you'll lose some editing capabilities if you reopen the file in Illustrator 10 (see Figure 20.5).

You should choose prior versions of the Illustrator format only when sharing the file with someone (or some program) that can't handle the Illustrator 10 format.

The next option enables you to create an Adobe Acrobat-compatible file. Acrobat Reader can be found on most computers now, and its PDF format is very common for software documentation and other electronic document exchange. If this box is unchecked, the file size might be a little smaller.

20

FIGURE 20.5

Among the fun features not supported in earlier versions are symbolism and envelope distort.

You are saving this document in Adobe Illustrator 9.0 format. Saving this document in an older format may disable some editing features when the document is read back in.

Cancel   OK

If you've got a client, colleague, or friend who you want to see your Illustrator format (.ai) file, but who doesn't have the Illustrator program, tell them they can open the file in Acrobat Reader. (It's a good idea to make a copy of your file and use the command Flatten Artwork from the Layers palette menu first.)

Illustrator's compression option can substantially reduce file size. It's not unusual for this check box to reduce file size by 75%. There is no reason to uncheck the box.

The two types of file compression are lossy and lossless. Lossy compression is used by JPEG and is an option for GIF in the Save for Web dialog box. It discards image data to reduce file size. Depending on the amount of compression, the image quality can be virtually indistinguishable from the original, or so horrid that you can hardly tell what's what. Lossless compression is used in PNG, TIFF, Illustrator, and other file formats. It won't make the files as small, but no data is thrown away.

When an Illustrator image contains type, it's a good idea to embed the font. That ensures that the typeface you chose will be the typeface that others see and print. Subsetting the font will embed only the characters actually used. (Don't subset if the type might be edited on another machine—it would be a shame if that special symbol wasn't there when needed.)

If you're working in RGB and have a monitor profile active in your Color Settings dialog box, Illustrator allows you to embed the profile so that others can get an accurate look at your colors. Illustrator also enables you to embed CMYK profiles when working in that color mode.

If the file contains linked images, you can check the box to include them, or you can send them separately. (It's usually a good idea to check the box.)

The option Use Japanese File Format is only required when saving in Illustrator version 5 format or earlier, and only for Japanese format files.

The Transparency options are required only when saving to Illustrator 8 format or earlier.

Saving in EPS Format

Encapsulated PostScript (EPS) is one of the two most common graphics formats used in publishing (TIFF is the other). EPS files can be placed in every major page layout program. They can contain vector information as well as raster imagery. When saving as EPS, you have several options (see Figure 20.6).

FIGURE 20.6

The EPS options parallel the Illustrator options.

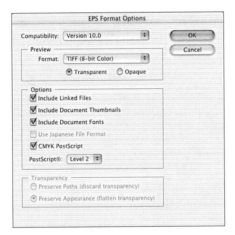

- The first choice is compatibility with Illustrator. Generally, you'll want to stick with version 10.

- It's a good idea to include a preview, especially if the image will be placed in a page layout program. TIFF (8-bit Color) enables cross-platform compatibility, and checking Transparent is a good idea if the artwork is not rectangular.

- Similar to the Illustrator format, EPS enables you to include both linked files and fonts, and if saving in earlier versions, you can elect to use the Japanese file format and choose how to handle transparency in the file.

- EPS also enables you to choose what version of the PostScript page description language to use. PostScript 2 is very common, but select PostScript 3 if your print shop uses it.

- As the tiny warning at the bottom of the window tells you, EPS will automatically flatten some effects. This preserves their appearance, but they will no longer be live.

20

- Photoshop can open EPS files, but any vector data (including type) will be rasterized.

- An EPS version of a file is likely to be substantially larger than an Illustrator version saved with compression.

Using the PDF Format

Illustrator also enables you to create actual Acrobat files (true PDF) directly. This is a great way to produce documents that can be easily shared without loss of quality or fear of incompatibility. It doesn't hurt, however, to flatten your artwork before saving as a PDF.

When you choose Save As and select the PDF format, you'll have two sets of options with which to work. The first set, General, is shown in Figure 20.7

FIGURE 20.7

The General PDF options enable you to select sets. Default, Screen Optimized, and Custom are the choices in the pop-up menu.

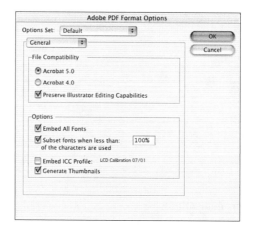

Screen Optimized automatically unchecks the boxes for Preserve Illustrator Editing Capability and Generate Thumbnails. This reduces the file size and, as you already know, that's a good idea when preparing images that need to be download via the Web.

The second set of options can also have a large impact on file size and quality. The Compression options are pictured in Figure 20.8.

Color and grayscale images can be resampled to a lower resolution if necessary, and you can choose from JPEG (lossy) or Zip (lossless) compression, or enable the PDF engine to automatically select the compression method. The Quality pop-up menu offers a choice of 8-bit color depth or 4-bit. The 4-bit option can produce substantial changes in your image's appearance, so generally stick to 8-bit.

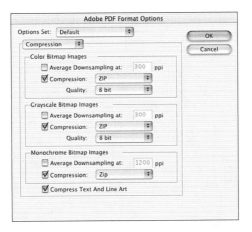

FIGURE 20.8

Illustrator's PDF Compression options offer ZIP encoding for all types of images. This is a lossless compression that will not harm the appearance of your artwork.

Monochrome (black-and-white) images should be saved at much greater resolutions because they have no shades of gray to soften curves. Zip is also a very good choice for the compression method.

Compressing text and line art reduces file size without affecting quality.

An SVG Overview

Scalable vector graphics are something relatively new in the world of Web design. SVG files can be viewed in Web browsers that have an appropriate plug-in, typically called a viewer, or that have native support for SVG. The images remain vector until they are actually downloaded to the browser, so they can be scaled and manipulated and still look great.

In Figure 20.9 you can see some of the great potential of the SVG format. Both browser windows have opened the same file. The smaller window shows a zoomed-in view. That's right—zooming in on an image in a Web browser! Notice the cursor. The familiar Hand tool enables you to move that zoomed-in image around in the window, just as you can in Illustrator. Take a look at the contextual menu, too. The grayed out commands Pause and Mute are used with animations, and the Adobe SVG Viewer has a built-in Find feature.

Not all SVG plug-ins offer the same features. When you installed Illustrator 10, you had the option of installing the SVG Viewer plug-in in any available Web browsers. You can get the latest version, as well as much more information on SVG, at www.adobe.com/svg/ at your convenience.

20

When saving as SVG, you have quite a few options from which to choose. In Figure 20.10, you can see the two dialog boxes.

Figure 20.10

SVG enables you to embed or link both fonts and images, and offers support for cascading style sheets (CSS). The encoding option is used primarily with extended fonts, including Japanese and Chinese fonts.

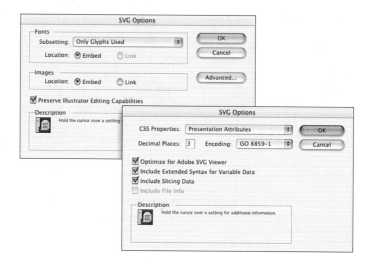

Also of note, Illustrator offers live effects for SVG and the capability to preserve Illustrator editing. (In Hour 18, "Working with Filters and Live Effects," we breezed right past Effect, SVG Filters. Those effects are used with these files and we'll talk about them in Hour 23, "Animating for the Web.")

Formats for the Web

In addition to SVG, Illustrator offers several of the more-common Web file formats. GIF and JPEG (the two main image formats for the Web) and PNG can be created using Illustrator's Save for Web feature (which is explained later in this hour). JPEG files can also be created using the Export command. SWF, which is typically used to create animations in the Flash format, can also be exported or optimized with Save for Web.

It's very important that you remember to append the file-format extension when creating graphics for the Web. Web browsers are not the smartest of programs and may not recognize an image file unless the extension is present. And, for maximum compatibility, use lowercase.

Graphical Interchange Format (.gif)

GIF is used primarily for images with large areas of solid color, such as logos and cartoons. It can be used for photographic images, but the quality of the image might suffer. GIF files can contain a maximum of 256 different colors. While that might seem like a lot, it's actually very few when you consider the number of individual shades of red in a photo of an apple. GIF can create tiny little files with very few colors. It uses lossless compression.

Joint Photographic Experts Group (.jpg)

JPEG is actually the name of the compression scheme used in JFIF (JPEG File Interchange Format), but we generally just use JPEG. As you might deduce from the name, this format is designed for use with photos. In addition to being used on the Web, you'll find it as an image-archiving format because of the great reduction in file sizes. Remember, though, that JPEG uses a lossy compression system, throwing away image data to make small files. JPEG supports both RGB and CMYK color modes, but only RGB is acceptable for the Web.

Flash (.swf)

Flash is both the name of the file format and the name of its parent program from Macromedia. You can create neat animations using vector objects and Illustrator's layers. Flash will be discussed in detail in Hour 23.

When you export a file to SWF format as an animation, Illustrator presents you with the dialog box shown in Figure 20.11.

FIGURE 20.11

Three types of files can be created.

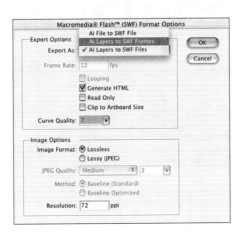

20

Export to an SWF file if you'll continue working in the Flash program, use SWF Frames to create an animation, and select AI Layers to SWF Files to create individual Flash files from each layer.

Portable Network Graphics (.png)

Developed as an alternative to JPEG and GIF, PNG comes in two flavors. To replace GIF, there's 8-bit PNG, which can have a maximum of 256 colors per file. To substitute for JPEG we have 24-bit PNG, which can handle 16.7 million colors. PNG-8 produces files comparable to GIFs, but there's no licensing fee. (GIF-compatible programs include a license to use its compression system.) PNG-24 won't produce files quite as small as JPEG, but the compression is lossless. Older Web browsers do not support PNG, but all modern browsers can show the images.

Save for Web

Perhaps the largest dialog box in the history of computers, Save for Web is perhaps better considered a program within a program (see Figure 20.12). It even generates its own preferences file! This is the state-of-the-art way to optimize Web graphics, reaching that elusive balance between image quality and download speed. Smaller files download faster, keeping your Web site's visitors happier, but shrinking files can harm appearances.

FIGURE 20.12

Save for Web enables you to create the best possible graphics files in several file formats.

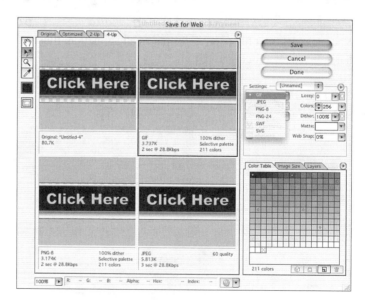

Using Save for Web

Prepare your image and save the original as an Illustrator file. (This enables you to make changes later.) Now, with the file still open, select File, Save for Web. The four tabs in the upper-left corner enable you to view the original, a preview of the image as it will appear with the current optimization settings, or you can compare two or four different variations. When working with multiple panes, click the version that you want to change and use the options to the right. When you like what you see, click the OK button, give the file a name, and pick a location.

To the far left are a few tools for use during optimization. The Slice Select tool enables you to optimize individual slices of an image. You can change the zoom factor in the lower-left corner (but it is always best to view raster Web graphics at 100% zoom). The status bar at the bottom gives you feedback on specific color information, and to the right of that is a pop-up menu that will launch any available Web browser and show you the image in its window.

Optimization Options

The beauty of Save for Web is the control it gives you over the way an image is saved. In Figure 20.13, you'll see the options available for GIF. (The PNG-8 options are comparable.) Save for Web enables you to select the number of colors that will be included in the image, right down to deleting an individual color from the Color Table. You can also specify whether or not the image will have a transparent background and how much *dithering* will be used. Dithering is the process of mixing colored pixels to make it appear as if two colors blend into each other.

FIGURE 20.13

There are some preset combinations available in the Settings pop-up menu, and you can create custom settings for each image.

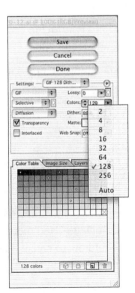

20

JPEG uses 24-bit color, so there is no Color Table available. You can choose the level of compression by selecting a Quality percentage. Therefore, the lower the quality, the smaller the file. You can also apply a slight blur to further reduce file size and even embed an ICC color profile. Save for Web's JPEG options (Figure 12.14), like others, enables you to optimize an image to a specific size. The Image Size tab enables you to specify exact pixel dimensions or a percentage of the original size. (This is separate from the quality/compression decisions you'll make in the upper half of the options.)

FIGURE 20.14

The JPEG offers very fine control over the quality of the image.

PNG-24 options in Save for Web are restricted to *interlacing* (having the image appear bit-by-bit in the Web browser), transparency, and matte color.

The SWF (Flash) options in Save for Web are almost identical to those you saw earlier for the Export command.

Save for Web also enables you to create SVG files. Again, this is comparable to using the Export command.

Task: Comparing GIF, JPEG, and PNG

Let's compare the main Web file formats and see how they handle different jobs.

1. If you haven't replaced your preference file recently, now is probably a good time to do so. That will restore all your tools, palettes, and menu commands to their factory-fresh settings. (If you're unsure about how to create a new Prefs file, check the instructions on the card that came in the front of this book.)

2. Open a new Illustrator document. Because we'll be working with Web formats, it needs to be RGB. The dimensions and orientation can be letter-size and landscape.

3. Create a square, 150 pixels (or points) by 150 pixels, give it a 5-point black stroke, and fill it with blue from the Swatches palette.

4. Option+drag (Mac)/Alt+drag (Windows) the square to copy it to the lower right, overlapping the original square. Change the fill to red.

5. Option+drag (Mac)/Alt+drag (Windows) to overlap as a third square and fill it with yellow. Your artboard should look similar to Figure 12.15.

FIGURE 20.15

Here are three solid-filled squares. Let's pretend it's our new company logo.

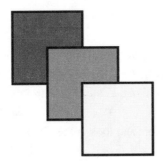

6. Open Save for Web and click the 4-Up tab to generate four versions of the image. Click the upper-right pane and use the GIF settings shown in Figure 20.16. The file size should show at approximately 2.87K at the bottom of the selected pane.

FIGURE 20.16

Even though the image has only four colors (black, yellow, red, blue), it looks best with 16 colors. That allows for smoother transitions between fills and strokes.

20

▼   7. Switch to the lower-left pane and change to JPEG, Quality 10, and check the boxes for Optimized and Progressive. The file size should be about 3.47K. Notice that the background in the pane is white rather than the checkerboard pattern that represents transparency. JPEG doesn't support transparency.

8. In the fourth pane, change the settings to PNG-8 and duplicate the settings shown in the preceding figure. The file size should be just under 2.5K.

9. Cancel. Select all and delete.

10. Create a square 400×400 pixels. Give it a 10-point black stroke and fill it with the RGB Rainbow gradient from the Swatches palette.

11. Open Save for Web again. Click in the upper-right pane. Set it to GIF, 8 colors, no dither.

12. Set the lower-left pane to GIF, 8 colors, Diffusion dither, and 100% dither.

13. Change the lower-right pane to GIF, 8 colors, and Pattern dither. (Notice that the Dither percentage slider is grayed out. You can't control the amount of Pattern or Noise dithering.)

14. Switch all three panes to 16 colors and look at the difference.

15. Now switch them all to 256 colors.

16. Switch all three panes to JPEG, upper right at High quality, lower left at Medium, and lower right at Low. Compare the file sizes and the appearance. The smallest file is virtually indistinguishable from the largest in appearance, and it's one-third the size.

17. Change the lower-left pane to PNG-24 and compare it to the JPEG High and JPEG Low panes. It should look as good as either, and the file size might even be a little smaller.

▲   18. Cancel and close, don't save.

Formats for Page Layout and Commercial Printing

Many images created in Illustrator are destined for the pages of magazines, books, newspapers, and other printed materials ranging from billboards to box tops. What these files all have in common is ink. While Web images are seen only on-screen and can therefore be reproduced in RGB color, printed materials generally need to be prepared in CMYK color. (The exception, as you know by now, is inkjet printing. Inkjet printers, except for the high-end machines, use RGB images.)

To ensure that the illustrations can be printed, they must be in appropriate formats, as well.

Page Layout Programs

If you print directly from Illustrator, you don't need to worry about page layout programs. If you use InDesign or PageMaker, you can usually stick with Illustrator's native format for your files. However, when preparing an image for QuarkXPress or another layout program, consider TIFF and EPS as your options.

Preparing for the TIFF Format

TIFF is a raster image format—your vector paths are going to be converted to pixels. For that reason, we recommend that you always keep the original artwork in Illustrator's .ai format and make a copy for conversion to TIFF.

When you choose the menu command File, Export and select TIFF as the file format, you'll see a set of rasterization and file format options (see Figure 12.17).

FIGURE 20.17

The resolution should be 1.5 to 2 times the line screen frequency (measured in lpi) at which the job will be printed.

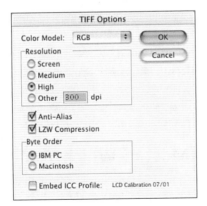

You can choose the resolution at which to rasterize the image, and you can select Anti-Alias to help prevent "jaggies" along curves. LZW compression will substantially reduce file size, and you can choose whether to encode the file for Windows or Macintosh. (When in doubt, choose IBM PC.) You also have the opportunity to embed the appropriate ICC color profile, and you can even change the image's color mode using the pop-up menu at the top of the box.

20

The "Other" File Formats

Although the vast majority of the illustrations produced with Illustrator are either for the Web or for print, quite a few other file formats are available. You might never need them, but it's nice to know they're there.

CAD Formats

Computer Aided Design (CAD) is primarily used in architecture and engineering. The files, like Illustrator's own, rely on Bézier curves to define paths. Illustrator can export two CAD formats: DWG (the native format of AutoCAD) and DXF (AutoCAD's interchange format).

> If you work with CAD files, you might need to give Illustrator a boost. CValley Software has a couple of CAD-related products, including a suite of CAD tools and an advanced import/export plug-in for CAD file formats.

Clip Art Formats

Illustrator also supports the file formats used by Microsoft Office (and other programs) for clip art. WMF (Windows Metafile) and EMF (Enhanced Metafile) are vector formats. Saving pattern-filled objects will result in the pattern being broken into its component paths. When reopened in Illustrator, solid-filled objects will be editable as objects, but patterns will be a series of paths, and gradients will be rasterized.

Specialty Formats (Most of Which You'll Never Need)

There are a few file formats with which Illustrator can work that you'll probably never need. For example, if you don't work at all with CAD, perhaps you can eliminate DWG and DXF. If you will never produce clip art, WMF and EMF probably aren't required. You can streamline your Export format menu by deleting some of the other plug-ins that you'll never need. (If you do need them some day, they can be reinstalled from the Illustrator CD.) The file format plug-ins are found in three separate folders inside the Illustrator Plug-Ins folder (see Figure 20.18).

- BMP: A raster art file format. (Photoshop Formats folder)
- CGM (Computer Graphics Metafile): This format is designed for extremely complex engineering and architectural diagrams. It is not suitable for illustrations with large amounts of text. (Illustrator Formats—Other folder)

- CorelDRAW: The proprietary format of an Illustrator competitor. If you don't exchange files with people who use it, you don't need the plug-in. (Illustrator Formats—Other folder)

- DXF: If you don't use CAD, you don't need this. (Illustrator Formats—Standard folder)

- FilmStrip: An animation format used by Adobe Premiere, among other programs. (Photoshop Formats folder)

- FreeHand: Another Illustrator competitor. Again, if you don't exchange files with someone who uses it, you don't need the plug-in. (Illustrator Formats—Other folder)

- PCX (Paintbrush): A file format of the PC Paintbrush program, Illustrator supports only version 5 completely. (Photoshop Formats folder)

- Photo CD: The Kodak Photo CD file format is sometimes found with stock art collections, and can be used for digitized versions of snapshots by your film processing lab. (Photoshop Formats folder)

- Pixar: The proprietary format developed by and for Pixar Animation Studios, the folks who brought us *Monsters, Inc.*, *Toy Story*, and *A Bug's Life*. (Photoshop Formats folder)

- Targa: A raster-image format used by several MS-DOS based programs, it is actually designed for use with hardware incorporating the Truevision video board. (Photoshop Formats folder)

FIGURE 20.18

As you'll recall from the beginning of this hour, here's where you'll find those you'll-never-need-'em plug-ins.

20

Platform Issues and What They Mean to You

Even if you work only on Macintosh or only on Windows computers you should be aware of the differences between the two operating systems, and how it affects your work in Illustrator. Virtually all the file formats discussed in this hour are cross-platform. That is, an appropriate program on either Windows or Macintosh computers can open them. Other factors and some wider issues come into play, however.

The Mac–Windows Chasm and How to Bridge It

Macintosh computers can read Windows-formatted disks natively. They don't need any special software. Windows machines, however, can't recognize a Mac disk without some help. The solution? If you work with a Mac, or exchange files with someone using a Mac, make sure that the files are always recorded on PC-formatted disks.

Filenaming is less of a concern than in the past, but it's important that filenames retain the file extension (the two or three letters to the right of the dot) when working with Windows.

Color Concerns

In addition to using two different 8-bit system palettes, Windows and Macintosh use different gamma levels. The basic system palette is not a major concern anymore, even for the Web—most Web surfers now have monitors set to display thousands if not millions of colors. (The system palettes are collections of 256 standard colors. Window and Mac computers have 216 of the 256 in common. These are referred to as the Web-safe colors. (More on that next hour.)

The gamma difference means that the screens of the different systems have different brightness levels. This can come into play with Web graphics as well.

Naming Files for the Web

When creating Web graphics it's critical that you attach the file extension so that the Web browsers can recognize the file type. It's best to use lowercase letters. That makes the filename universally recognizable. Illustrator makes it easy for you by providing a pair of options in the Save As and Export dialog boxes (see Figure 20.19).

FIGURE 20.19

Check the boxes at the bottom and leave them checked!

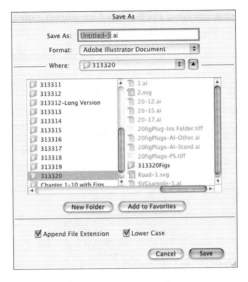

Summary

We've talked about a lot of technical stuff again this hour. But it's these little things that can make the difference between success and failure when it comes time to meet deadlines. You've not only learned a lot about the various file formats, but you've learned which to use in what circumstances.

Workshop

The quiz might be a little tougher than usual this time, but we'll make up for that with some really tough exercises, too!

Q&A

Q I work primarily with JPEGs and GIFs for the Web. Is there any reason I need to save copies of my images as Illustrator files?

A It's always a good idea to save the original of any file in the format which allows you the most opportunity for change. In the case of Illustrator, only its native format supports all its features. Because the majority of your images get rasterized, there's no other way for you to retain the capability to make changes. Also, don't forget that you might be able to save time down the road by recycling certain objects from images, something you can't do after the image is rasterized.

20

Q **I'm going to save a file as a TIFF. Can I go ahead and rasterize some parts of it at 300 ppi and other parts at 72 ppi?**

A There's no real advantage. The entire image will be rerasterized at a single resolution as part of the export process.

Q **What happens if I delete all those file-format plug-ins that you say I don't need and later it turns out that your wrong?**

A Whoa, Nelly! I suggested that there are some you *probably* don't need, but I left it up to you to decide which ones. But don't panic, you can reinstall from the Illustrator CD.

Quiz

1. Which of the following file formats supports vector type?

   a. TIFF, but only if you use the Vector TIFF format.

   b. JPEG, that's how they create the buttons on the Web.

   c. EPS, but not if the file is opened in Photoshop.

   d. GIF, that's how they create the buttons on the Web.

2. The best way to reduce the size of an Illustrator file while retaining the highest-quality artwork is

   a. Use compression in the Save/Save As dialog box.

   b. Use the Select All command, followed by the Clear command.

   c. Simplify all paths to 50%.

   d. Use Save for Web to create a JPEG, using a setting of 10.

3. The four viewing options in Save for Web are

   a. Original, JPEG, GIF, PNG, TIFF

   b. Original, 2-Up, 3-Up, 4-Up

   c. 4-Up, Optimized, 2-Up, Original

   d. 7-Up, Hands-Up, Original, Extra Crispy

4. Which of the following is a list of Web file formats?

   a. PNG-8, PNG-24, SWF-8, SWF-24

   b. GIF, JPEG, TIFF, Photoshop

   c. SVG, PNG, LZW, GIF

   d. JPEG, SWF, SVG, PNG-24

5. The Illustrator native format (.ai) can be used with all the following programs EXCEPT:

    a. Photoshop

    b. Flash

    c. GoLive

    d. InDesign

Quiz Answers

1. c. EPS supports vector type, but if you open an EPS file in Photoshop, the entire image is rasterized.

2. a. The other three choices could lead to disasters for your artwork.

3. c. Not in that order, but all four are there.

4. d. LZW is a compression scheme, not a file format; SWF comes in only one flavor, not –8 and –24; Photoshop and TIFF are not recognized by Web browsers.

5. b. Flash. The other programs can all work with Illustrator's files.

Exercises

1. Place a photograph in an Illustrator document. Open Save for Web. Try various settings for PNG-24 and JPEG to see how small you can get the file before quality goes away. See if you can get a decent-looking Web image using GIF for the photo.

2. Create an Illustrator document with lots of fancy stuff in it. Use patterns and gradients. Reduce the opacity of overlapping objects. Apply drop shadows and other Stylize effects. Use Envelope Distort. Grab the Symbol Sprayer and toss in some symbols.

   Now save the file in various versions of the Illustrator format. In the options dialog box, choose version 9, version 8, and version 6 or version 5. Reopen the files in Illustrator 10 and see what capabilities remain editable and how the appearance has changed.

3. Open a new Illustrator document. Add one square, 150 points by 150 points. Give it a 10-point black stroke and fill it with the Mediterranean Tiles pattern. Use the menu command Object, Rasterize and rasterize the square at 72 ppi. Open Save for Web and select GIF as the file format. Look at the number of colors in the Color Table. Click the Image Size tab in the lower-right corner. Look at the dimensions of the object in the Original Size section. Click Cancel. Undo.

20

Rerasterize the object, this time at 300 ppi. Return to Save for Web and look at how many more colors there are in the Color Table. Click the Image Size tab and notice the lack of change in the original size.

HOUR **21**

Printing Your Illustrations

One of the primary destinations for artwork created in Illustrator is the print shop. Even illustrations created for the Web are often printed, either for client approval or archiving. Printing, whether to the inkjet on your table or to huge commercial offset presses, can present certain problems and situations. It's best to plan from the beginning for the type of output required. For example, if the illustration will be published in a magazine, start in CMYK mode rather than converting from RGB later.

In this hour, you'll learn about

- CMYK output vs. inkjet printing
- Using crop marks, trim marks, and printer's marks
- Potential problem areas
- Overprinting and trapping
- Outputting color separations

Commercial (CMYK) Printing versus Inkjet Printing

Commercial printing presses can stand as high as my house and cost millions of dollars. They typically put each page through four (or more) separate presses, each of which applies only one color of ink. On the other hand, inkjet printers from manufactures such as Epson, Hewlett-Packard, and Canon can be small enough to fit in your briefcase and still print all four colors (or six colors) at once. But size isn't the biggest difference between them.

Commercial printing usually requires that an image be prepared in CMYK color mode, so that it can properly be printed using cyan (C), magenta (M), yellow (Y), and black (K) inks. The vast majority of inkjet printers, on the other hand, need RGB data. Even though you see CMYK inks under the hood of the printer, you still need to create in RGB color mode for inkjet output. This is because the print driver (the software that runs the printer) assumes that the colors will be RGB. The colors are automatically converted to the printer's particular CMYK space. If they're already CMYK, the colors in your image are likely to turn out muddy and dark.

There are exceptions to the "RGB for Inkjet" rule. If you fall into one of the categories, you probably know it already. Raster image processors (RIPs) are either hardware or software devices that work with your printer to produce the highest quality image possible. If you're using a software RIP, such as Epson's Stylus RIP, you can use CMYK with your printer. If you're using a high-end proofer, or a fine art printer, you likely have a RIP, too. Again, you have the option of working with CMYK.

One of the deciding factors might also be PostScript. If your color printer is PostScript capable, check the documentation to see if it prefers to work with CMYK images. Until recently, color PostScript printers were either laser printers or high-end proofers and large-format machines. Now you can find PostScript inkjet printers for under $1,700.

Most of what follows in this hour pertains only to images destined for four-color printing. It is not appropriate for most inkjet printers, and has virtually nothing to do with Web graphics. However, we encourage you to read on, even if you'll never produce a single four-color layout.

Preparing a Document for Printing

Before you send your image to the print shop, there are some things you might need to do. The various printer's marks might need to be added. You certainly should check to make sure that linked images and fonts are included. You should do some housekeeping to make sure that you don't have anything extra tagging along in the file.

Crop and Trim Marks

Crop marks indicate where the page should be cut. They are especially important when you've designed artwork that contains *bleeds*. Bleeds are areas where the ink goes past the edge of the printed page to make sure that no unwanted white spaces appears. In these cases, the crop marks are the only thing that tells the print shop where to cut. Trim marks, which we mentioned in Hour 18, "Working with Filters and Live Effects," are used to show multiple places where a page needs to be cut. (If you recall, we used the example of printing multiple business cards on a single page.) Trim marks differ from crop marks in a couple of important ways. There can be only one set of crop marks, but you can have many trim marks. In Illustrator, the crop marks' appearance cannot be edited, but trim marks can be whatever width and color you choose. An Illustrator document can have both trim marks and a set of crop marks.

> Don't use crop and trim marks (or printer's marks) if the illustration is to be placed into a page layout file. The page layout document will have crop marks for its page, which are more important than crop marks for an image placed on the page. The exception would be a situation in which someone receiving the image will crop it and then place it into another document.

Task: Setting Crop and Trim Marks

▼ TASK

We'll simulate a page of business cards to show how trim and crop marks are prepared.

1. Start with a fresh Illustrator document. Make it CMYK (of course, because we're practicing for print), letter size, portrait orientation.

2. Near the top center of the artboard, create a rectangle, 252 points wide and 144 points high. (That's 3.5 inches by 2 inches.) Fill it with 20% black from the Swatches palette. Duplicate it down the artboard twice.

3. Use the Align palette to make sure that all the copies align vertically as shown in Figure 21.1.

▼

21

FIGURE 21.1

Three "business cards" on a single sheet of paper.

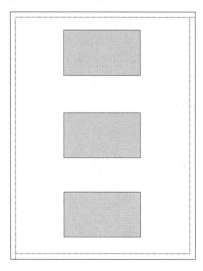

4. Select the top card and use the menu command Filter, Create, Trim Marks.

5. Select the next card and use the keyboard shortcut Command+E (Mac)/Control+E (Windows) to duplicate the filter. Repeat for the third card (see Figure 21.2).

FIGURE 21.2

Three cards, three sets of trim marks.

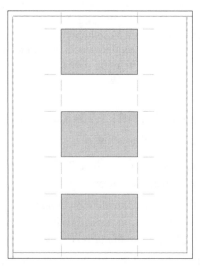

6. Select all and delete.

7. Click with the Rectangle tool somewhere near the upper-left corner of the artboard and create a shape 500-points wide and 700-points tall. Fill it with the pattern of

▼   your choice. If necessary, reposition the rectangle so that it's entirely within the
     page tiling.

8. Drag another rectangle, somewhat smaller than the original, and position it inside
   the first. Press D on the keyboard to return the rectangle to the basic appearance. In
   Figure 21.3, we've colored and reduced the opacity of the second rectangle so that
   it shows more clearly.

Figure **21.3**

*The first rectangle sim-
ulates a bleed, with
artwork extending past
the edge of the page.
The second rectangle
represents the actual
cut size of the page.*

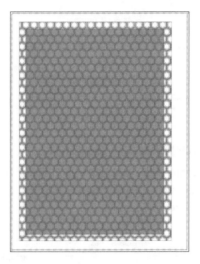

9. With the second rectangle still selected, use the menu command Object, Crop
   Marks, Make. The rectangle is replaced by the crop marks. Open the Layers palette
   and expand Layer 1. Notice that the crop marks do not appear as a path.

10. Select all and delete. The original rectangle disappears, but the crop marks remain.

11. Use the menu command Object, Crop Marks, Release, and before you delete this
    rectangle, observe that it no longer has a stroke or fill. Now delete the rectangle,
▲   leaving you with an empty artboard once again.

Printer's Marks

The printer's marks include registration targets and variations called star targets, calibration bars, and labels for the particular separation or printing plate. (Separations are discussed later in the hour.) The registration marks help the printer align the printing plates
so that the inks are placed exactly on the paper. The calibration bars help the printer
maintain the color values.

Printer's marks are added by using a check box in the Separations Setup dialog box (see
Figure 21.4).

21

FIGURE 21.4

You can see the printer's marks in the preview window. The check box is directly below.

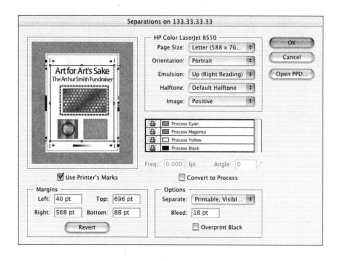

Specifying the Rasterization Settings

File, Document Setup opens a three-pane window, which you might remember from your earliest Illustrator hours. The third pane, Transparency (see Figure 21.5), controls how much of an image will be rasterized on output.

FIGURE 21.5

These settings can help solve output problems.

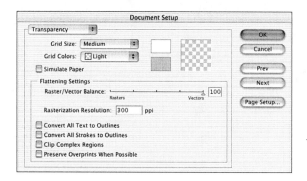

The Flattening Settings slider has five settings. Dragging the slider to the left makes it easier to output your artwork because more of it gets rasterized. That, however, can result in reduced quality. Generally you'll want to use the default settings (shown) unless and until you have output problems.

Easy Ways to Avoid Output Problems

Illustrations can be very complicated documents. The more complicated the document, the more probable it is that output problems will occur. There are some things you can do (and avoid) to help prevent problems.

Slim the File

Putting your documents on a diet is another simple way to eliminate a few potential problems. Strip away all the unused brushes, swatches, symbols, and styles. Each of these palettes has a command called Select All Unused (see Figure 21.6). Use that command, followed by the palette menu's Delete command. This removes the various unnecessary items from the palette and from your document. The savings in file size can be more than 100K.

FIGURE 21.6

The related palettes have similar commands.

Don't be afraid to delete the swatches, brushes, styles, and symbols. The contents are part of the startup document, and the palettes will be back to normal with the next document you start. If you edit one of these documents sometime down the road and find that you need a specific brush that was deleted, don't worry! Each of the palettes can be restored using the appropriate Library command under the Window menu.

> Illustrator includes an Action that will do most of this housekeeping for you. You'll learn about Actions in Hour 24, "Maximizing Efficiency with Automation."

21

Clean Up the Artboard

Use the menu command Object, Path, Clean Up followed by the Delete (Mac)/ Backspace (Windows) key. This can rid your document of a variety of potentially problematic junk (see Figure 21.7).

FIGURE 21.7

A complicated illustration can collect a bunch of random points and empty paths.

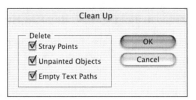

Rasterize Effects, Blends, Gradients, and Transparency

Blends and gradients can create big headaches for some printers. Consider, if you will, a smooth color blend that can produce more than 250 intermediate objects. And, if the objects were complex to begin with, well, you get the picture.

You can cut down on the complexity of a blend by specifying the number of steps. You can also rasterize blends, gradients, and gradient mesh objects to make them easier to print.

Overlapping transparency, especially with multiple blending modes, can lead to problems, too. You especially want to be careful when using transparency in an EPS file. Again, rasterization can be the solution.

Some of the effects and filters can produce unbearably complex objects. The Pen and Ink filters, for example, can produce objects with enough anchor points to choke the most powerful of imagesetters. Here's the secret—if it takes a long time for Illustrator to create, or a long time to draw onscreen, consider rasterizing.

Convert Large Type to Outlines

Changing headline type to paths can sometimes solve a printing problem. You can use the command Type, Create Outlines. As you can see in Figure 21.8, the paths do an excellent job of reproducing the original type.

Splitting Long Paths

One of the most common problems in outputting vectors to a PostScript printer or imagesetter is complexity. A path with too many anchor points can choke the memory right out of an imagesetter. (Imagesetters are high-resolution laser printers that create the separations used to produce printing plates. We'll discuss separations in just a few minutes.)

Illustrator can create paths from any type, but save it for very large text or you might create more problems than you can solve.

If you're getting an error message, make a copy of the file as a backup. Open the Document Setup dialog box (under the File menu) and switch to the Printing & Export pane (see figure 21.9). Check the box for Split Long Paths. Try again to output the image.

Splitting long paths can reduce the strain on an imagesetter's memory.

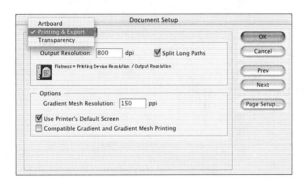

Don't Forget to Include Linked Images and Fonts!

If you've linked any images to your Illustrator document, or if you're using some unusual font, you'll have to remember to send a full package to your printer or service bureau. You can double-check to make sure that you've got everything by using the Document Info palette. From the palette's menu, remember to deselect Selection so that you get data from the entire document.

21

Producing Color Separations

Printing presses apply ink to the page one color at a time. Each of those inks is applied using a separate press, with all four presses (or more) working together. Each press handles one ink; putting it on the page according to the *printing plate*. The plate is what actually transfers ink to paper. A plate is typically created either directly from the computer, using a procedure called (ingeniously) direct-to-plate, or it's created using a *film separation*.

A film separation is a piece of film comprising a grayscale representation of the image, showing where one ink should be placed, and how much ink should be placed there. Your printer or service bureau typically generates the separations, one for each color. They can be produced directly from Illustrator, if you have a very high-resolution PostScript printer or imagesetter.

The Separations Setup Dialog Box

You saw this dialog box just a little while ago, when we discussed printer's marks. Rather than flipping back to that image, refer to Figure 21.10.

FIGURE 21.10

Another look at what seems to be a very complex dialog box.

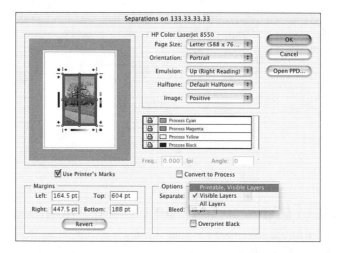

Other than the preview, this dialog box breaks down into four areas. Below the preview are margin settings. These will be generated automatically for you, based on your crop marks. If you haven't added crop marks, they will be generated based on the outer-most artwork. Be warned, however, that it's based on path position, not the outside of any strokes. Take the time to make crop marks. You can adjust the margins if you feel the need. The great big Revert button is there because a lot of folks discover that it's not necessarily a good thing to mess with the margins.

In the upper-right section of the dialog box are printer-specific options. Your print shop will let you know if you have to flip the separations (the emulsion setting) or change the halftone setting.

Immediately below you'll find a list of the four process colors (CMYK) and any spot colors being used in the image. You can click the little printer icon next to a color to hide it, which tells Illustrator not to generate a separation for that color. This can come in handy if you need to generate, for example, only the black separation and a separation for a spot color. There's no need to waste film on the other three process colors. The line-screen frequency (measured in lpi) and the screen angle should be changed *only* if instructed to do so by the print shop. Convert to Process is available for spot colors that you want to be simulated using the four process colors. (Printing four colors is much less expensive than adding a fifth run for the spot color.)

The last section of the Separations Setup dialog box enables you to create the separations based on all the layers in the document, just the visible layers, or the visible/printable layers. Bleed, as mentioned earlier in this hour, is the extension of color past the crop marks so that the print is sure to go all the way to the edge of the page. The last option is to overprint black. Because black is the darkest, most opaque ink, printing it on top keeps things looking neat and clean.

Trapping to Compensate for Misregistration

> In the following paragraphs we discuss the process called trapping. Do *not* attempt to trap any image without speaking first with your printer or service bureau. If you don't trap according to the press's tolerances, you can end up with a huge mess, and some quite large expenses for retrapping the image professionally. Always talk to the printer or service bureau first.

Trapping is the process—no, the science—no, the *art* of making sure that the printed page doesn't show tiny lines and slivers of paper where two colors didn't quite match up. On the computer screen, the artwork will always align perfectly. When printing to your inkjet printer, which applies all four (or six) inks in one pass, artwork should also align properly. But those giant printing presses are a different story!

I mentioned earlier in the hour that the paper actually passes through four presses, one after another. Paper can stretch a little, the printing plates can shift just a hair, and humidity can even affect whether or not the four inks are placed perfectly. When the inks don't hit the page just right, we might see *misregistration*. This is typically visible as a tiny slice of white paper showing between two colors (see Figure 21.11).

21

FIGURE 21.11

FIGURE 21.11

On the left, the two squares are perfectly registered. On the right, you can see a tiny problem with misregistration.

In the example in Figure 21.11, the original artwork might have been created with a large square and a small square. But that's not how it will print. To keep the colors as true as possible, sometimes hidden areas don't print. If the press put down ink under the smaller square, it could affect that object's color. Instead, the upper object knocks out the lower object. And that's one of the reasons we need to consider trapping.

The menu command Effect, Pathfinder, Trap opens the dialog box that enables you to set trapping specifications (see Figure 21.12).

FIGURE 21.12

In addition to trapping, the Pathfinder Options enable you to specify soft mix settings. Soft mix is actually superceded by Illustrator's transparency capabilities to a large degree.

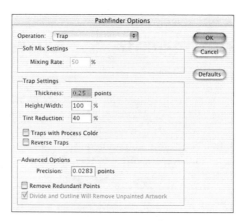

In the dialog box you can set the specifications that you got from your print shop or service bureau. Again, we would like to note that you should always speak with your printer or service bureau before using Illustrator's trapping capability.

A Note About Proofing

Proofing is checking a document to make sure that everything is right. Typically, at the end of the game, just before we print, we've checked everything we can. It's then time to verify that the colors that will be printed are correct.

Illustrator's View menu offers the Proof Colors command. It even allows you to soft proof (proof on a monitor) according to your selected CMYK color profile. This is all well and good and a nice convenience, but a word of warning. Even a perfectly calibrated monitor is no guarantee that you're seeing what the printing press will produce. Hard proofs, especially laminates, are the best way to go when color is critical.

Summary

Producing perfectly printed output is half science, half art, and maybe a pinch or two of magic and luck. The best way to ensure the best output is to find a good print shop, establish (and maintain) a good relationship, and communicate. We've addressed a number of the subjects about which you'll have to communicate to get perfect output. You've now got the background to ask the right questions.

Workshop

There's a whole lot to this subject of printing. In fact, perhaps that's why we have specialists in the field! Put on your thinking cap, because we've got some tough stuff to close this hour.

Q&A

Q Why can't my inkjet printer print CMYK—those are the inks I buy!

A The printer's software, the print driver, is written to convert RGB data to CMYK for the printer. There are not many people buying inkjet printers who have access to software that's CMYK-capable. Illustrator, Photoshop, and some of the competing products can produce CMYK images. However, not even Photoshop Elements or Photoshop LE work in the print color space.

Q Okay, so I'm preparing my images in RGB. But my inkjet printer won't print them. It just stops. I even tried rasterizing my image. What else can I do?

A The file may be too large for the printer to handle. Try reducing the resolution. Most inkjet printers will produce maximum quality at resolutions between 150 and 225 ppi. You'll have to experiment to see where yours is within that range.

Q I called my printer, as you suggested, and asked about CMYK setup and trapping and several other issues. I got a great big "I dunno" from somebody in the office. They do good work, and I don't want to change to another print shop, what should I do?

21

A Try calling and scheduling an appointment with the chief pressman (or woman) to discuss your questions and concerns. If you have a sales representative, that might be the channel through which to set things up.

Quiz

1. You've got a CMYK image with three spot colors. How many separations are required?

   a. Seven, unless you check Convert to Process for one or more spot colors

   b. Never more than four

   c. Just one for each spot color, CMYK is handled automatically

   d. Images with spot colors don't require separations

2. Your type was printing funny, so you converted it to outlines. Now the imagesetter is giving you a limitcheck error. What to do?

   a. Hope that you saved a copy of the image in its original state

   b. Don't convert small type to outlines

   c. Go back to the original file and make sure to embed the fonts

   d. All of the above

3. Which statement is true about crop marks and trim marks?

   a. You can have multiple sets of crop marks on a page, but you can only trim one rectangle.

   b. Trim marks can be any color, but you can't change the width of crop marks.

   c. Crop marks are permanent, whereas trim marks can be removed.

   d. Trim marks are nonprinting, whereas crop marks print.

Quiz Answers

1. a. Each spot color and each process color will normally produce a separation.

2. d. Yet another good reason to save a backup copy.

3. b. Tricky wording on the answer, those statements are not really parallel.

Exercises

1. If you have an inkjet printer, open or create an elaborate and beautiful piece of art. Print it as RGB. Make a copy of the image and convert the color mode to CMYK. Print again. Compare the two.

2. Create a CMYK illustration that uses several spot colors. Using a laser printer or an imagesetter (output to paper, not film), produce separations for all channels.

Now open Separations Setup and check Convert to Process for the spot channels and reprint the separations. Compare the CMYK separations.

3. Create a document that includes some very large type. Copy the type by Option+dragging (Mac)/Alt+dragging (Windows) with the Selection tool. Convert the copy to outlines. Use the command Object, Path, Simplify. See how great a reduction you can make in the number of anchor points without harming the appearance of the type.

Hour **22**

Creating Web Graphics

It seems that we're all either creating Web graphics or will be someday. The World Wide Web is becoming part of every aspect of computer graphics. Even long-standing prepress professionals are sometimes being called upon to produce a graphic or two for the company Web site.

In this hour, you'll learn about

- The basic concepts of Web graphics
- Controlling color on the Web
- Producing basic Web images
- Slicing Web graphics
- Creating image maps

Web Graphic Basic Training

Graphics created for the World Wide Web are, first and foremost, graphics. There are certain rules to which they must adhere, but they are just graphics.

File Formats for the Web

Both vector and raster file formats exist on the Web, but the vast majority of images in the Internet are pixels (raster-based). The vector formats, including Flash and SVG, can still be considered specialty formats, because not all Web browsers support them. (Hour 20, "Understanding File Formats and Platform Issues" discussed the various formats in depth, and introduced Illustrator's Save for Web feature.)

You can use both vector and raster images in your Illustrator artwork, but remember that the vector objects will be rasterized when saved as GIF, JPEG, or PNG, the three main graphics formats. It's also important that your documents be RGB. Web browsers don't recognize CMYK images.

The restrictions on file formats are a by-product of the computer language used on the Web, HTML (Hypertext Markup Language). This is the code that Web browsers read. It's an agreed-upon standard that ensures various programs and hardware all work together.

Web Color

As you know, Web graphics must be RGB. But controlling color on the Web is not an easy thing. When you send an image to your printer, you can adjust various settings so that it looks the same on paper as it does onscreen. You don't have such control with the Web. For example, the site's visitors probably haven't calibrated their monitors. The colors they see could all have a red tint, or a hideous green look, or they might be too light or too dark, or...well, you get the picture (so to speak).

You'll hear talk of Web-safe colors, and in fact we discussed the concept in Hour 7, "Understanding and Applying Color." These are the 216-basic colors that are common to both the Windows system palette and the Macintosh system palette. If you need to have a color look consistent to all visitors to your site, this is the place to start. However, keep in mind that the vast majority of the monitors surfing the Web are improperly calibrated—the visitor might not see what you want her to see.

Web-safe colors were far more important a few years ago when it was common for computers to use 8-bit color. 8-bit color shows only 256 colors, as you might recall from our earlier discussions of GIF and PNG-8 files. When only 256 colors are available, subtle transitions from color-to-color can be lost. Gradients, for example, no longer seamlessly flow from one color to the next. Instead, you end up with stripes or blocks of color. Figure 22.1 uses Save for Web to show a comparison of a gradient using a full range of colors and a gradient using the Web-safe palette.

FIGURE 22.1

On the left is a smooth gradient. On the right, the same gradient as it would appear using the Web-safe palette.

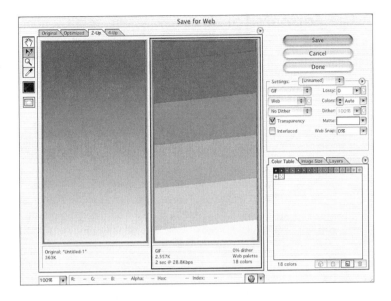

You might recall that Save for Web offers dithering when working with 8-bit color (GIF and PNG-8). That can greatly improve the look of gradients and other color transitions (see Figure 22.2).

FIGURE 22.2

On the left is the undithered 8-bit gradient. On the right, diffusion dithering has been added.

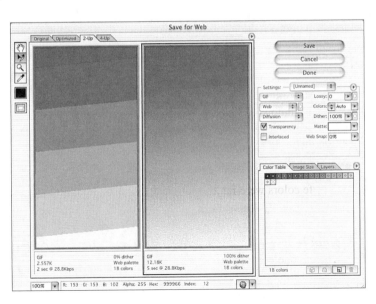

These days, almost all the visitors to your Web site will be using monitors that can display a much wider range of colors, so the concept of Web-safe is far less important. You can feel free to design and produce Web graphics in as many colors as you want, secure in the knowledge that no two monitors will be displaying them exactly the same—but hopefully many will at least be close.

> Don't be confused by the discussion of 8-bit color and thousands of colors, of Web-safe colors and GIF's 256-color limitation. You can design a graphic in thousands of colors, reduce it to GIF's 256-color maximum, and still have a fine-looking image. If, for example, the artwork uses a wide variety of shades of blue, but virtually no other colors, GIF can use 256 shades of blue in its color table. Using the Web-safe palette, on the other hand, would restrict the image to about 45 shades of blue—the hues that appear among the 216 Web-safe colors.

To view the Web-safe colors, use the menu command Window, Swatch Libraries, Web. A floating palette with swatches of the 216 colors will appear (see Figure 22.3) .

FIGURE 22.3

To see all the swatches, drag the lower-right corner of the palette.

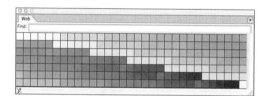

Web Graphic Image Sizes

One concept that's difficult for many to understand is that there's no such thing as resolution on the Web. You'll hear that Web graphics must be 72 ppi to display properly. Forget about it! Instead, think only in terms of how much space the image should occupy on the Web page, therefore, measure it only in pixels. Consider how many pixels wide and how many pixels high you want the image to be. Resolution is for printing pixels, not for measuring Web graphics.

Task (Optional): Debunk the Web Resolution Myth

Here's a little exercise that should solidify in your mind the fact that there's no resolution on the Web. Because you're working with Adobe Illustrator 10, you obviously have a modern operating system, either Windows or Macintosh, and some hardware that's less that a decade old. We'll assume that your equipment includes a monitor with variable resolution.

You might want to read all the way through this Task before beginning; just to make sure that you're comfortable with what it's asking you to do.

1. Open a new document in Illustrator, RGB, any size and orientation.

2. Use the pop-up zoom menu in the lower-left corner of the window to set the zoom to 100%. Alternatively, you can use the keyboard shortcut Command+1 (Mac)/Control+1 (Windows)—that's the number one, not the letter L.

3. Click once with the Rectangle tool. In the dialog box enter a width and height of 72 px, which at the print resolution of 72 ppi, creates a 1×1-inch box.

4. Using your computer's system software, you can discover how an inch isn't always an inch (see Figure 22.4).

   Macintosh OS 9: Under the Apple menu, go to Control Panels, Monitors. In the lower right, switch to a higher or lower resolution setting. The screen will resize. If you're presented with a warning box, click OK.

   Macintosh OS X: Under the Apple menu, open System Preferences. Click Displays. Change the resolution to a higher or lower setting. Close the dialog box.

   Windows: From the Start menu, choose Settings, Control Panel. Double-click the Display Properties control panel and, in the dialog box, click the Settings tab. Drag the Screen Area slider to the right or left to change the resolution. Close the dialog box.

FIGURE 22.4

The different operating systems have different monitor controls.

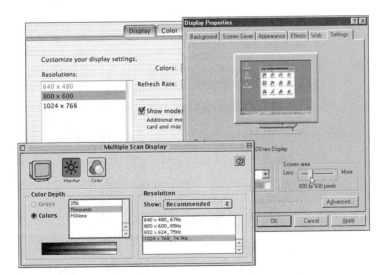

▼ 5. After you've changed the resolution of your monitor, take another look at the square. It's no longer the same size. If it was 72 pixels at 72 ppi and therefore one inch in size before, then it can't be one inch now. Or, if it's one inch now, it couldn't have been one inch before. With monitors of differing sizes and resolutions, there is no such thing as 72 pixels per *inch* because there's no such thing as a standardized *inch*.

▲ 6. Reverse Step 4 to return your monitor to its usual setting (if desired).

Web Graphic File Sizes

Another key concept to remember when preparing graphics for the Web is "smaller is better." Not the physical dimensions of the image on screen, but rather the file size. Smaller files download faster across telephone and cable-Internet connections, so they appear more quickly on screen. This keeps your Web site's visitors happy. Nobody likes to wait for images to load.

As you saw when we introduced Save for Web in Hour 20, you have lots of tools available to help you compromise between file quality and file size.

A Few Terms to Learn

Some terms used with Web graphics might be unfamiliar to you. It's a good idea to get a head start on them now, although some will be explained in greater depth during the hour.

- Image Map: An image map is a Web image that contains hotspots that can be used as links. An image map is an area of an image, a hotspot that can be used as a link. A single image can have multiple image maps.

- Link: A link is an image, hotspot, or piece of text on a Web page that can redirect your browser to another location. When the viewer clicks on a link, the Web browser searches for and loads the page indicated by the link.

- Optimize: Optimization is the process of minimizing file size while protecting image quality. There is a fine line between "small file" and "pretty image." The goal is to have the smallest file possible without compromising image quality. Small files download faster and speed Web visits.

- Slice: A single image can be divided into two or more pieces. This gives the appearance of a faster download for the visitor, allows for multiple links, and enables you to prepare each piece separately for the best quality.

- URL: Uniform Resource Locator. This is a Web address. Most start with `http://` (although some now start with `https://`). This introductory string of characters should be used when creating links to pages outside your Web site.

Task: Preparing to Create Web Graphics

Before we get rolling here, let's get set up properly. There are a few things we need to do:

1. If you haven't recently, go ahead and replace your Preferences file. If you don't remember how, or have any doubts, check the instructions on the reference card that came in the front of this book.

2. After you restart Illustrator, open Preferences, Units & Undo. Set the General pop-up menu to Pixels, set Stroke to Pixels, and leave Type set to Points (see Figure 22.5).

FIGURE 22.5

Change the units to more Web-friendly settings.

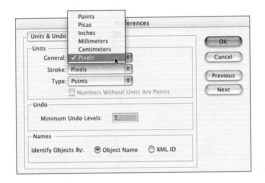

3. Switch to the Guides & Grid preferences. Change the Gridline Every setting to every 50 px with 5 subdivisions. This puts a subdivision every 10 pixels, rather than the default of every eight pixels. Click OK.

4. Open a new document. Make sure that the color mode is set to RGB. For page size, choose 800×600 (see Figure 22.6).

FIGURE 22.6

The three page sizes just below Custom are pixel dimensions for two popular Web page sizes and a standard Web banner size.

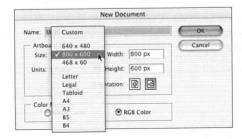

5. From the View menu, choose Hide Page Tiling (see Figure 22.7). Because we won't be printing, we don't really care about the page size.

FIGURE 22.7

Page tiling reflects the Page Setup choice for your printer. It doesn't have any bearing on Web graphics.

6. Also from the View menu, choose Actual Size. This zooms the artboard to 100%. Because, with the exception of SVG images, Web browsers always show graphics at 100% zoom, that's generally how you should work. This doesn't mean that you can't zoom in to check a detail or an alignment, but it does mean that you should always evaluate your graphics at 100% zoom.

7. Pop right back to the View menu and select Pixel Preview. Unless you're creating SWF or SVG files, your artwork will be pixels in the end. You might as well get an accurate view of how the image will look later. (Again, you can turn this off for some work, but turn it back on to evaluate the image.)

8. Use the menu command Edit, Color Settings choose Web Graphics Defaults from the Settings pop-up menu. You can leave the RGB Working Space set to the default RGB, although it is a very limited gamut, and is Windows-centric. With this setup, you can use the View, Proof Setup and View, Proof Colors commands to evaluate how your artwork will look on Windows or Macintosh monitors.

Basic Web Images

Now that Illustrator is arranged to best suit your current needs, let's make some basic Web page interface items.

Task: Creating a Web Button

TASK ▼

Virtually every Web page needs buttons with which to get around in the site. Here are a couple of techniques.

1. If you don't have an Illustrator document open, start a new one. Remember to make it RGB!

2. Click once with the Ellipse tool and create a circle 100 pixels by 100 pixels.

3. From the Styles palette, apply Blue Goo.

4. Open the Appearance palette. Drag the effect Drop Shadow to the palette's Trash icon to get rid of it.

5. Click the Stroke in the Appearance palette. Using the Stroke and Color palettes, change it from None to 8 pixels and a dark blue.

6. From the Appearance palette's menu, choose Add New Stroke. Make this stroke white and 2 pixels in width. You should have something similar to that shown in Figure 22.8.

FIGURE 22.8

The Appearance palette gives us lots of flexibility in creation.

7. Type the word Home using Helvetica Bold (or a similar sans serif font), size 27 points, and use the Character palette to increase the height to 175% and decrease the width to 90%.

8. Use the menu command Effect, Warp, Bulge. In the dialog box, click Horizontal and move the slider to 33%. Click OK.

9. Reopen the very same dialog box and this time click the button for Vertical. Again, move the slider to 33%. Your button should look similar to that in Figure 22.9.

FIGURE 22.9

Applying the Bulge effect a second time allows us to warp both horizontally and vertically.

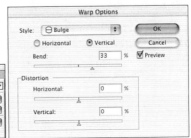

10. Use Save for Web to create a GIF file. Check the box for Transparency. (If you don't check the box, your image will have a white rectangle around it.) Experiment with the number of colors and with/without diffusion dither (at both 50% and 100%, using the Dither slider). Try to find the combination of Color Table and Dither settings that gives you the best-looking button without exceeding 4K in file size. 64 colors and 50% Diffusion Dither is a good compromise. Click the Save button and name the file home_001.gif. Save just the image, not the HTML. This GIF button can now be added to any Web page.

> When creating Web graphics, to ensure maximum file compatibility, always use only small letters, numbers, and the underscore character (_) in file-names. Never forget to add the three-letter file type extension.

11. Back in your Illustrator document, open the Layers palette and drag Layer 1 to the New Layer button at the bottom of the palette. That duplicates the layer and its contents. Click the eyeball to the left of Layer 1 to hide it.

12. Click the word Home. In the Appearance palette, drag both of the Warp, Bulge items to the trash to delete them. The text should now be normal again.

13. Drag Layer 1 copy to the New Button layer to duplicate it. Hide Layer 1 copy and work on Layer 1 copy 2.

14. Select the type and apply Bulge horizontally and vertically using a –33 setting. (The negative settings are to the left of the slider's middle point.) Your button and Layers palette should look similar to those in Figure 22.10.

FIGURE 22.10

Three layers, three versions of the button.

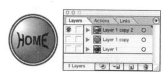

15. Save this file as an Adobe Illustrator file, using the name home_002.ai.

If you've got Adobe Photoshop (version 6 or 5.5), you can use ImageReady to create a *rollover* GIF button from these three layers. Adobe LiveMotion can also create rollovers. Rollovers use layers to change the appearance of the button when the cursor is over it or clicks it.

Although Illustrator enables you to create shadows and glows, these types of effects are not easily replicated on a Web page. They rely on variable opacity, being able to see what's behind the effect. GIF supports transparency, but only with clipping masks—a pixel is either visible or invisible. JPEG doesn't work with transparency at all. The easiest way to handle it is to re-create the Web page's background in Illustrator and include the part of it that falls behind the shadow or glow.

Slicing Web Graphics

Rather than making a bunch of little graphics and lining them up just right—and praying that the Web browsers keep them lined up—you can create a single graphic and *slice* it into pieces.

Why We Slice

The three major reasons to slice an image are to speed download, to optimize different parts of the image with different settings, and to create multiple links.

We're all familiar with Web buttons similar to the one we just created—click it and it takes you someplace. These *links*, as they are called, enable us to navigate from page to page within a Web site, and even enable the Web designer to connect a particular page with a page from a different Web site.

Links can be buttons or text, they can also be easily identifiable, such as the ones shown in Figure 22.11, or hidden and available only to those who stumble across them or know their location on the page.

FIGURE **22.11**

Some Web page links are easy to spot.

For more information, visit: WWW.adobe.com

Previous Home Next

www.mordy.com

Slicing is extremely valuable when you have to put multiple links close together. Rather than trusting the Web browser to show the different images in the right positions, slicing enables us to use a single image for multiple links.

Slicing also enables us to optimize different parts of a single image differently. Consider a graphic that contains areas of solid color, which would best be optimized as a GIF, and areas with gradients or photos, which would best be optimized as JPEG. Slicing the graphic enables you to optimize each part separately.

Task: Creating and Slicing a Banner

We'll create a single graphic that's sliced and ready to become an entire series of links.

1. Open a new RGB document in Illustrator using the 468×60 pixel size from the pop-up menu in the New dialog box. Use the menu command View, Hide Page Tiling.

2. Command+1(Mac)/Control+1 (Windows) sets the zoom to 100%. (And now you can see how tiny that banner will really be.)

3. Select the Rectangle tool and click in the upper-left corner of the artboard. Enter the dimensions 468×60 pixels. You want the rectangle to fill the artboard. Click OK.

4. Just in case you missed the exact corner, use the Align palette to align the rectangle to the vertical and horizontal center of the artboard. (Remember that you must select Align to Artboard from the Align palette menu.)

5. Give the rectangle a stroke of None and a fill of pale blue from the Swatches palette.

6. In the Layers palette, click in the second column next to Layer 1 to lock it, then click the New Layer button. This prevents you from accidentally moving the background rectangle.

7. On the new layer, create a star with Radius 1: 25 pixels, Radius 2: 10 pixels, Points: 5, stroke of None, and filled with the Nova gradient from the Swatches palette. We'll use this gradient in lieu of a pretty photo of Mordy's face.

8. With the gradient star still selected, use the Align palette to center it to the artboard vertically, and align it to the artboard's left edge.

9. Press the right arrow key five times. That moves the star inward five pixels from the edge of the artboard. Your artboard should now look similar to that shown in Figure 22.12.

FIGURE 22.12

The two objects are on separate layers.

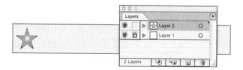

10. Add another new layer, and lock Layer 2.

11. Add some black text to this layer. I used Arial Bold Italic at 40 points, with a height of 100% and a width of 150%. Type Mordy's Place.

12. Add a one-pixel white stroke.

22

13. Use the menu command Effect, Stylize, Drop Shadow. Change the X Offset to 5 pixels, the Y Offset to 2 pixels, and the Blur to 3 pixels.

14. Use the menu command Effect, Warp, Flag, set Horizontal, 30%.

15. Let's make the type raggedy and jagged, just to test our optimization skills. Use the menu command Effect, Distort & Transform, Roughen. Add just a little, perhaps Size 4, Relative, Detail 10/in, and select Corner points. Your image should look a lot like Figure 22.13.

FIGURE 22.13

It doesn't have to be exact, but you want to make sure that your type and effects don't extend out of the artboard.

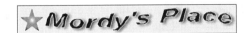

16. In the General Preferences, which you can open with Command+K (Mac)/Control+K (Windows), click the box labeled Use Preview Bounds. Notice the change in the bounding box around your type.

17. Press V to switch to the Selection tool. If necessary, press the left or right arrow keys to reposition your type so that its bounding box is exactly even with the right point of the gradient star.

18. With the type still selected, use the menu command Object, Slice, Create from Selection. Suddenly and without warning, you should see a couple of boxes with numbers appear on the artboard. (If not, use the menu command View, Show Slices.) Zoom to 400% by holding down the Command (Mac)/Control (Windows) key and hitting the + key four times. Use the Hand tool to reposition the artboard in the window so that you can see the entire left end, as shown in Figure 22.14.

FIGURE 22.14

You can ignore the right half of the artwork for now, all the action is at this end.

> User-defined and automatic are the two types of slices. When you tell Illustrator where to make a slice, the slice is created and stays that way unless you change it. When Illustrator automatically creates slices to fill the rest of the image, they are updated automatically as necessary to compensate for changes in the user-defined slices.

19. In the Layers palette, unlock Layer 1 and Layer 2.

20. Use the Selection tool to select the gradient star on the artboard, or simply click the targeting icon to the right of Layer 2 in the Layers palette.

21. Use the menu command Object, Slice, Create from Selection. Several more little slice boxes show up, giving you a total of five (see Figure 22.15).

FIGURE 22.15
If you have six slices, you probably didn't have the type bounding box perfectly aligned with the gradient star before creating the first slice. No problem!

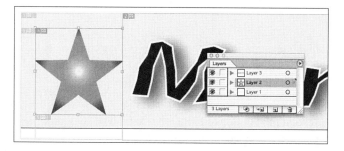

22. Save this file as an Adobe Illustrator file to protect your work, but don't close it.

> You can also create user-defined slices by dragging with the Slice tool.

If you're ever not happy with your slices, you have a couple of options. You can select the object in question on the artboard and use the menu command Object, Slice, Delete All. Or, you can open the Layers palette and drag a user-defined slice to the Trash and delete it.

Task: Optimizing Individual Slices

Now that we've created slices, let's optimize them individually.

1. Choose File, Save for Web. If you're not in 4-Up view, click that tab. Normally, with artwork that is so much wider than it is tall, Illustrator will show the four optimization windows horizontally instead of two-by-two.

2. In the upper-left corner of the window, choose the Slice Select tool. In the second preview pane from the top of the window, click Slice #2, the type slice. Choose JPEG, low quality.

3. In the third pane, choose JPEG, high quality for the type slice.

4. In the bottom pane, choose GIF, Selective, Diffusion dither at 100%, 32 colors, Web Snap 0%.

5. Decide which of the options gives you the best quality for the size. Or, of course, you can choose your own settings. Whichever you choose, that pane of the window becomes the copy of the image that you want to save. For this example, we'll choose the bottom pane.

6. Use the Slice Selection tool and click the gradient star slice. Experiment with optimization settings until you get a good balance between appearance and file size. Use those settings for that slice in the bottom pane. We'll use JPEG, Medium, Blur: 1, progressive.

7. In the target pane, the bottom for this example, click one of the auto slices. Because it should be one solid color, choose GIF, Colors: 2. The rest of the auto slices will be updated, too.

8. Click the Save button. In the dialog box, choose HTML and Images from the Format pop-up menu, give it a name, and pick a location. Make sure that All Slices is showing at the bottom of the window. Click Save.

To use this sliced image with your Web page design tool, such as Adobe GoLive or Macromedia Freehand, add the HTML to the page's source code and make sure that the images are available according to the procedures for that program.

Task: Assigning URLs to Slices and Creating Image Maps

Optimizing slices individually is great, especially if you have a single photo in the middle of a sea of solid color. The other major uses for slices are to create multiple links from a single image and to expedite downloading. If your Mordy's Place banner is not open, find it and bring it back for more!

1. Activate the Slice Select tool from the Toolbox. You'll find it under the Slice tool, just above the Hand tool.

2. On the artboard, click the type slice, which is slice #2 unless you have extra slices. We'll make that a link to Mordy's home page.

3. Use the menu command Object, Slice, Slice Options. In the Slice Options dialog box, in the URL field, type:

    `http://www.mordy.com`

4. Click OK. You've just turned the type slice into a link. When this image is open in a Web browser, clicking on the slice will take the visitor to Mordy's Web site.

5. Next, let's create an *image map* hotspot. An image map hotspot is much like one created via a slice, but it doesn't have to be rectangular. Think of it as a "hotspot" on the image, rather than a separate slice of the image. In this instance, we'll use the star, so select it with the Selection tool (not the Slice Select tool) or select it in the Layers palette.

6. Use the menu command Window, Attributes to open the Attributes palette. Click the tab a couple of times to fully expand it, if necessary.

7. In the Image Map pop-up menu, choose Polygon (see Figure 22.16). In the URL field, type:

    `http://www.mordy.com/personal_4.html`

    That creates a link to a page on Mordy's Web site that features pictures of his family. (He welcomes your visit at your earliest convenience.)

FIGURE 22.16
The Attributes palette is fully expanded.

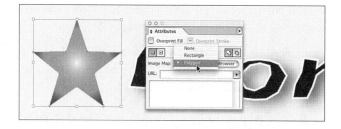

8. Use the keyboard shortcut Shift+Command+A (Mac)/Shift+Control+A (Windows) to deselect all. You can check to see if the URL assignment remained by reselecting the star. The Web address should appear in the Attributes palette again.

When you use an image map set to Polygon, the visitor must click within the object to activate the link. When it's set to Rectangle, the visitor must only click within the bounding box-sized area around the object.

Final Note: Creating Web Pages

Adobe Illustrator creates Web graphics, not Web pages. You'll want to use it in conjunction with a Web design tool, such as Adobe GoLive or Macromedia FreeHand (or, in a pinch, Microsoft FrontPage). Those are programs that actually create the pages we see when we cruise the Web. Illustrator is designed to put the pretty pictures on the pages, not to write the HTML code that produces the pages themselves.

Each of the major Web design tools functions a bit differently. We won't try to tell you how to use them. (If you've got a Web design program, you either know how to use it already, or you have the user guide at hand.)

Summary

You're not quite ready to quit your day job and hang out your shingle as a Web designer. But you're on your way! In this hour you've learned how to create basic Web graphics, slice them, link them, create image maps, optimize, and even how to prepare images that can be turned into rollover buttons using Adobe ImageReady or LiveMotion.

Workshop

Creating Web graphics is just like creating any other graphics. The differences are in how you save them and in such Web-related capabilities as slicing and linking. We'll reinforce a few key concepts and take it easy on the exercises this hour.

Q&A

Q What are the differences between slices and image maps?

A Slices actually create individual graphic files, which may or may not be linked to a URL. Image maps are hotspots on images that serve as links.

Q Can you put an image map inside a slice?

A Sure! Make certain, however, that the slice is not a link. If there's a URL assigned to both the slice and an image map within the slice, one or the other or both will not function properly. If the slice itself is not a link, there's no problem creating an image map within.

Q Illustrator is creating dozens and dozens of auto slices when I try to slice my image. What's going on?

A Be careful when slicing. Remember that the entire image will be divided into rectangles. Sometimes it makes sense to create a slightly larger slice to avoid forcing Illustrator to make lots of little slices between your user-defined slices.

22

Quiz

1. Web graphics should be in RGB color mode (or grayscale) because

    a. Web browsers cannot see CMYK JPEG files.

    b. GIF and PNG files can only be RGB.

    c. The World Wide Web is not reproduced using cyan, magenta, yellow, and black inks.

    d. All of the above.

2. When using a gradient in a Web graphic, save the file as

    a. TIFF, it reproduces gradients the best.

    b. EPS, it can contain clipping paths.

    c. GIF, it can reproduce subtle shades of a color.

    d. JPEG, it handles color transitions better than GIF.

3. You've created a round, red button for use on the Web. It has to be placed on a blue background. To avoid a white rectangle around the button, save it as

    a. TIFF, it reproduces circles the best.

    b. EPS, it can contain clipping paths.

    c. GIF, it can reproduce transparency.

    d. JPEG, it handles color transitions better than GIF.

Quiz Answers

1. d. The Web is a monitor-based medium, and its file formats are RGB. CMYK is used only with commercial printing presses.

2. d. JPEG is best suited for any Web image with subtle color transitions, including gradients and photos. TIFF and EPS images are not visible to a Web browser.

3. c. And make sure to check the Transparency button in the Save for Web dialog box.

Exercises

1. Get onto the Internet and go to some of your favorite sites. Take a look at their graphics—how they're designed, what type of fonts they use, whether they use slices, and so on.

2. Go to http://www.mordy.com/illustrator.html. Click the links at the bottom of the page to visit each of the areas. Don't miss the third step-by-step tutorial for a neat trick on making Web buttons.

3. Open a new Illustrator document. Create a rectangle. Apply the Blue Goo style.

With the rectangle selected, open the Attributes palette. From the Image Map pop-up menu, select Rectangle. Assign the URL `http://www.adobe.com`, and then des-elect the rectangle. In the Save for Web dialog box, optimize the rectangle as a GIF file with 32 colors. (We're not too concerned about the appearance.) Save the HTML file and the image to a location that you'll remember for at least a few min-utes. (Or, like me, you can write it down.) Don't forget the name either. Open your Web browser. Use its File, Open command to open the HTML file. Your rectangle should appear in the browser window. Move the cursor onto the rectangle and click once. It will take you to Adobe's Web site. Be pleased. Be very pleased.

22

HOUR 23

Animating the Web

Animations, the moving pictures of the Web, are just one of the advanced Web features we'll discuss this hour. Illustrator provides support for a number of capabilities beyond making simple graphics for your Web pages.

In this hour, you'll learn about

- Creating Flash animations
- Working with symbols for the Web
- Working with scalable vector graphics
- Cascading style sheets (CSS) in Illustrator

Animations for the Web

Animation is a series of frames, presented one after another to give the illusion of motion, much like a motion picture in the theater. When you look at the actual movie film, it's a series of individual still images, which are played back at roughly 30 frames per second. (Animations on the Web are typically 8 or 12 frames per second.) The Internet also supports video and *streaming video*, which are not the same as animation. Streaming video is digital video that plays on your screen while it downloads from the Web.

Animations consist of a series of frames stored as a single file. Rather than a movie or video, think of them more along the lines of a cartoon. Illustrator can produce simple animations using the Flash (.swf) file format. The actual Flash program from Macromedia and Adobe's LiveMotion can create enhanced Flash files, using sound and interactivity. Illustrator can export files that can be used in Flash, as well as Flash animations.

Adobe's LiveMotion also creates advanced Web graphics called *compositions*. Although LiveMotion has its own native file format (.liv) , you can use the program's Place command to add .swf files, as well as virtually any file format Illustrator can export and, most importantly, native Illustrator files, too!

Task: Preparing a Flash Animation

TASK ▼

It's time to roll up our sleeves and create our first animation. We'll start with a file we created during Hour 22, "Creating Web Graphics," the file we saved as home_002.ai.

1. Open home_002.ai in Illustrator. When we last saw this file, it had three layers, each with a copy of the button, and each copy had different warping for the type. In Figure 23.1, the Layers palette rows have been enlarged (using the palette menu command, Palette Options) so that you can see the difference among the layers.

FIGURE 23.1

We developed this three-layer button in Hour 22.

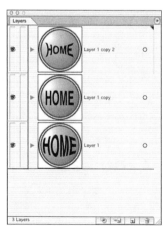

2. Drag Layer 1 copy to the New Layer button at the bottom of the palette to duplicate it. Move the new layer, Layer 1 copy 3, to the top of the Layers palette (see Figure 23.2).

▼

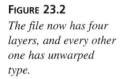

FIGURE 23.2

The file now has four layers, and every other one has unwarped type.

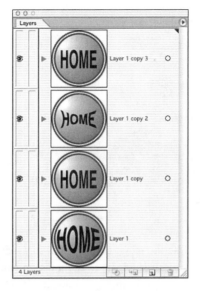

3. Use Illustrator's menu command File, Export and select Macromedia Flash (.swf) as the file format (see Figure 23.3). Remember to append the file extension, and make it lowercase. Name the file home_003.swf. Pick an easily accessible location on your hard drive, perhaps in a new folder.

FIGURE 23.3

SWF files are exported, not saved, from Illustrator.

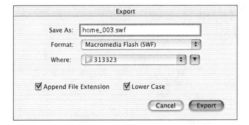

4. In the Flash options dialog box, choose Export As: AI Layers to SWF Frames, keep the default 12 frames per second (fps), check the boxes for Looping and Generate HTML, and retain the rest of the default settings (see Figure 23.4).

 Using AI File to SWF File or AI Layers to SWF Files creates a file that you can use in Flash or LiveMotion, but cannot be used as-is on the Web. To create animations directly from Illustrator, you must select AI Layers to SWF Frames.

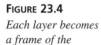

FIGURE 23.4

Each layer becomes a frame of the animation.

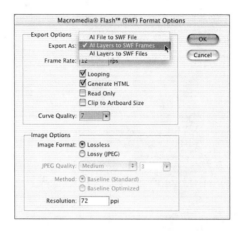

5. Open your Web browser. Use the menu command, File, Open File (or the comparable command for your browser). Navigate to the location where you saved your animation. Open the file home_003.html, not home_003.swf. In Figure 23.5, we've opened three browser windows to show the animation in action.

FIGURE 23.5

The flashing button at work!

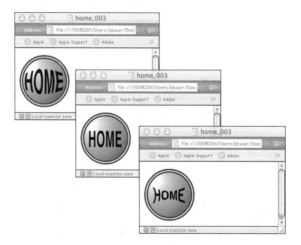

Congratulations! Your coolest Illustrator accomplishment so far! Go ahead, take a moment to show it to friends and colleagues and family. You can even e-mail it, as long as you remember to include both the HTML and the SWF files.

If you open the SWF file (that is, if your browser is equipped with the appropriate plug-in and *can* open the file directly), it will fill the browser window. Opening the HTML file shows the animation at the size at which it was designed.

Incorporating Symbols into Flash Animations

Flash files can take advantage of Illustrator's symbol capabilities. When you use symbols in your artwork, Flash creates a link from the original symbol to all the *instances* of the symbol in the artwork. The instances, or actual appearances of the graphic, are stored simply as place markers on the artboard. The actual graphic is only stored once in the file (in Flash's symbol library). This reduces file size, often considerably. (To refresh your memory about symbols, go back to Hour 3, "Creating Objects.")

Exporting Images for Animated GIFs

Although Illustrator cannot create animated GIFs, it can do everything short of producing the actual file. Just like Flash animations, animated GIFs are layer-based. You put each frame on a separate layer and either save the file as an Illustrator (.ai) file for use with LiveMotion or export it as a Photoshop (.psd) file for use with ImageReady.

Since the introduction of Photoshop 5.5 in 1999, Photoshop has shipped with a free version of Adobe ImageReady (a program sold separately prior to Photoshop version 5.5). It is a very capable program, used exclusively for creating Web graphics.

Task: Animate Using Blends and Release to Layers

Here's where we show you how to create complex-looking animations in just a few simple steps.

1. Open a new Illustrator document, 800×600 pixels, RGB (of course, because this is a Web animation). Use View, Hide Page Tiling to get rid of the unnecessary lines. Press Command+1 (Mac)/Control+1 (Windows) to zoom to 100% view.

2. In the upper-left corner, create a square 75 pixels×75 pixels, give it a black stroke 2 pixels wide, and use the Swatches palette to fill it with light blue.

▼   3. Add a couple of little circles to represent eyes and use the Arc tool to give the face
           a frown (see Figure 23.6). The mouth should have a stroke, but no fill. Select all
           the components and group them, using the menu command Object, Group or the
           keyboard shortcut Command+G (Mac)/Control+G (Windows).

FIGURE 23.6

*Create something like
this little masterpiece.*

4. In the center of your artboard, create a circle about 150 pixels×150 pixels, give it a
    black stroke 5-pixels wide, and fill it with yellow from the Swatches palette. Make
    this one a smiley face (see Figure 23.7). Again, make sure that the mouth is
    unfilled. Select all the components and group them.

FIGURE 23.7

Things are looking up!

5. Open the Blend Options dialog box with the command Object, Blend, Blend
    Options. Switch to Specified Steps and input 10 in the numeric field (see Figure
    23.8).

6. Select both of your groups, because they should be the only things on your art-
    board at this point, you can use Command+A (Mac)/Control+A (Windows) to
    select all. Use the menu command, Object, Blend, Make. Your artboard should
▼   look similar to Figure 23.9.

FIGURE 23.8

With Illustrator's 10 intermediate steps, we'll have a total of 12 objects.

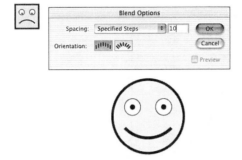

FIGURE 23.9

Illustrator has saved us a ton of time by making the transitional objects.

7. With the blend selected, use the menu command, Object, Blend, Expand.

> If Illustrator adds an unwanted fill when creating a blend, you can use the Group Selection tool to select the individual objects and change their fills to None.

8. Use the menu command Object, Ungroup or the shortcut Shift+Command+G (Mac)/Shift+Control+G (Windows). Only do this once—you want to ungroup the blend, not the faces! Each of the faces will be a separate group on Layer 1 (see Figure 23.10).

9. With everything selected on the artboard, choose the menu command, Release to Layers (Sequence) from the layers palette menu. Your Layers palette should look similar to that in Figure 23.11.

FIGURE **23.10**

The Layers palette now has 12 groups on one layer.

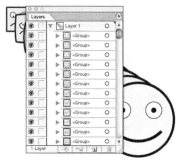

FIGURE **23.11**

Each group has been moved to its own sub-layer of Layer 1.

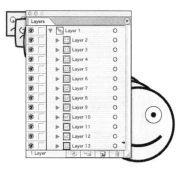

10. In the Layers palette, click the first sublayer (Layer 2) and Shift+click the bottom sublayer (Layer 13). Drag them above Layer 1, promoting them from sublayer to layer. Layer 1 will then be empty and should be deleted (see Figure 23.12).

FIGURE **23.12**

The layers are all now real layers at the top level, not sublayers. The now-empty Layer 1 has been deleted.

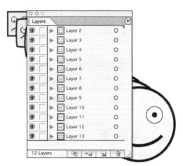

11. Now that each of the faces is on a layer instead of a sublayer, we can export to SWF to create the animation. Use File, Export, choose SWF as the file type, and name the file smiley.swf. Save it in an appropriate location.

12. In the options box, make sure to select AI Layers to SWF Frames, check Loop, and change the frame rate to 5 fps. Keep the Illustrator file open.

13. Open the animation in your Web browser. (Remember to open smiley.html, not smiley.swf.)

    That's great and all, but the animation doesn't really have impact because it moves through the motions too quickly. Let's remedy that.

14. Return to the Illustrator file. In the Layers palette, make several copies of Layer 2 (the last frame), keeping them at the top of the Layers palette. Next, make several copies of Layer 13 (the first frame), keeping them at the bottom of the palette. You can drag a layer to the New Layer button at the bottom of the palette to duplicate it, or you can highlight it and use the Layers palette menu command Duplicate Layer.

15. After you have five or so copies of both the first and the last frames export to SWF again, and name the file smiley_1.swf. Leave all the options the same. Open smiley_1.html in your browser. Adding the layer copies produces additional, identical frames, making the animation appear to pause on that frame.

> You don't need to duplicate frames when finishing an animation in LiveMotion—you'll be able to specify frame duration. Likewise, if you prepare frames for ImageReady to create animated GIFs, you won't need these filler frames.

Releasing in Sequence and Creating Builds

Illustrator offers two Release to Layers commands. Release to Layers (Sequence) puts one object on each layer. Release to Layers (Build) puts one object on the first layer, then the first and second objects on the second layer, the first three on the third layer, and so on.

When the layers are exported to frames, it makes a very big difference! Figure 23.13 has a graphic representation of sequence and build as they would appear on layers and in frames.

FIGURE 23.13

Building from frame to frame can also be referred to as type-writer style.

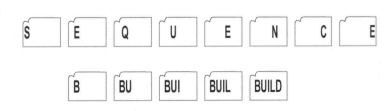

Scalable Vector Graphics (SVG)

Scalable Vector Graphics are hailed by some as the format of the future. SVG might do for Web graphics what PDF did for electronic documents. That is, become the standard and put near-perfection within reach of all. As you learned in Hour 20, "Understanding File Formats and Platform Issues," you can zoom in on SVG images in the browser window, and even play sounds and animations.

With Illustrator, you can save virtually any image as an SVG image. You also have at your command some tools to make creating artwork specifically for SVG even easier.

Using SVG Filters

When you use effects especially designed for SVG, you ensure the quality of your images. Regular stylized effects and filters must be rasterized with the artwork, but SVG effects are not rasterized until the image is downloaded to the browser. That enables the SVG plug-in to determine the size of the image before the effect is applied, rather than having to resize an effect.

To apply an SVG filter to an object selected on the artboard, use the menu command Effect, SVG Filters, Apply SVG Filter (see Figure 23.14). (Yes, even though these are effects, the menu says "filter.") Alternatively, if you know which effect you want, you can select it directly from the submenu.

FIGURE 23.14

Available effects are listed in the dialog box.

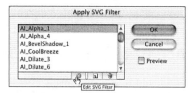

Notice the button that enables you to edit the effect. You don't need to know much XML, the language of SVG, to change an effect. As you can see in Figure 23.15, the difference between Shadow_1 and Shadow_2 is a few numbers.

FIGURE 23.15

To make an even more dramatic drop shadow, increase the stdDeviation and Offset values, then save with a new name.

```
                    Edit SVG Filter

<filter id="AI_Shadow_1" filterUnits="objectBoundingBox">
  <feGaussianBlur in="SourceAlpha" result="blur" stdDeviation="2"></
feGaussianBlur>
  <feOffset in="blur" result="offsetBlurredAlpha" dy="4" dx="4"></feOffset>
  <feMerge>
    <feMergeNode in="offsetBlurredAlpha"></feMergeNode>
    <feMergeNode in="SourceGraphic"></feMergeNode>
  </feMerge>
</filter>

                    Edit SVG Filter

<filter y="-15%" x="-15%" width="140%" height="130%" id="AI_Shadow_2"
filterUnits="objectBoundingBox">
  <feGaussianBlur in="SourceAlpha" result="blur" stdDeviation="6"></
feGaussianBlur>
  <feOffset in="blur" result="offsetBlurredAlpha" dy="8" dx="8"></feOffset>
  <feMerge>
    <feMergeNode in="offsetBlurredAlpha"></feMergeNode>
    <feMergeNode in="SourceGraphic"></feMergeNode>
  </feMerge>
</filter>
```

Task: Exploring the SVG Filters

Let's get a feel for what kinds of effects we can apply to our SVG images.

1. Open a new Illustrator document, 800×600 pixels, RGB.

2. Create a very large rectangle, large enough to fill the artboard, and fill it with pale yellow from the Swatches palette.

3. Create a 4×4 grid of rectangles, each 150 pixels wide and 100 pixels high. Give them each a 5-pixel black stroke and fill with Light Blue from the Swatches palette. (Hint: Create one rectangle and use Transform, Move three times, clicking the Copy button, to make the first row. After that, select all and Option+drag (Mac)/Alt+drag (Windows) to make the other three rows.)

4. Apply one SVG effect to each of the rectangles, skipping PixelPlay_1 and PixelPlay_2. (They can't be properly displayed in Illustrator.) Your collection should look more or less like the rectangles in Figure 23.16.

Saving SVG Files

When saving files in SVG format (remember that you use Save As rather than Export) you have a couple of dialog boxes with options (see Figure 23.17).

Font subsetting can reduce file size, as can linking images. However, embedding images ensures that the file will be viewable. Preserve Illustrator Editing Capabilities enables you to reopen the SVG file in Illustrator to make changes. Otherwise you'll need to retain the original .ai file.

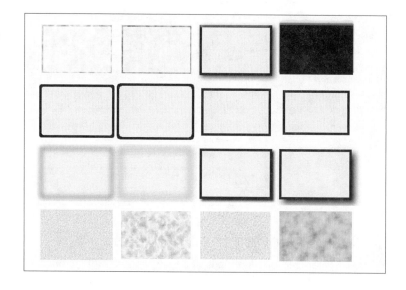

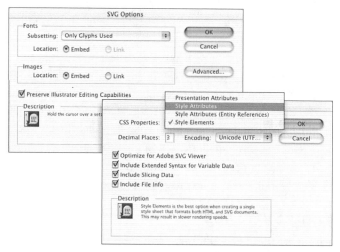

In the Advanced SVG Options dialog box, you've got some choices about how you want
to work with cascading styles sheets (when used), and font encoding. Style Attributes is
the more widely compatible way to save SVG files, although the individual files might
be somewhat larger than other options.

The SVG Interactivity Palette

If you've got skill with JavaScripting, you can add interactivity to your SVG images. JavaScripts, which can be thought of as miniprograms, can be executed when any of a number of actions take place in the Web browser window. The actions are called events, and you can load JavaScripts using the SVG Interactivity palette's menu commands (see Figure 23.18) .

FIGURE 23.18

Clicking the Add button, and then the Choose button, enables you to browse your drives looking for appropriate JavaScripts.

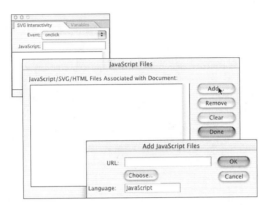

23

Cascading Style Sheets (CSS) from Illustrator

Cascading style sheets (CSS) are advanced Web features that enable you to, among other things, present different views of the same page, based on the browser in use, and even the default language of the browser. CSS enables designers to specify text formatting and position text or objects in floating boxes on a Web page.

Illustrator uses layers to define the CSS properties. Only layers will be considered for CSS, not the sublayers. (Sublayers should be used to organize artwork in a document, leaving the top-level layers for CSS.) For example, Layer 1 might have Layer 2 and Layer 3 as sublayers. Layer 1 could be the English version of a Web page. Layer 4 might have sublayers Layer 5 and Layer 6, and be a French version of the same page. Meanwhile, Layer 7, with sublayers Layer 8 and Layer 9, could be the Spanish version. All three versions of the Web page can be contained in one document using CSS.

To write the HTML that actually creates the CSS, use Save for Web. In the lower-right corner of the Save for Web dialog box, click the Layers tab (see Figure 23.19).

When you click the Save button, you'll see the Output Settings dialog box (see Figure 23.20). In the HTML pane, click the button Generate CSS.

FIGURE **23.19**

This is where CSS layers are defined. Remember that only top-level layers can be used, not sublayers.

FIGURE **23.20**

If Generate CSS is not selected, the cascading style sheets will not be created.

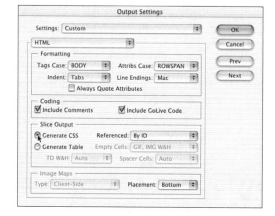

Once you've generated the HTML and images, you can use your Web design tool, such as GoLive, to actually create the Web pages.

Summary

We certainly covered a lot of ground this hour! I'm not sure that Illustrator has anything more fun than creating animations. Well, except maybe for the thrill of entering graph data, cell by cell. Okay, maybe not. In addition to the excitement of animation, we looked at some rather advanced Web concepts. SVG's JavaScript and cascading style sheets will probably take some outside learning before you can effectively implement them in Illustrator. But now you know that they're there, and have seen how to get to them.

Workshop

Creating animations will be the focus of this workshop, because that's the aspect of this hour most likely to be immediately useful. (But watch out for a sneaky question or two on other subjects.) We'll keep it to a pair of exercises so that you have time to experiment on your own, too.

Q&A

23

Q I created my artwork on a single layer, and then used Release to Layers and saved my SWF animation. But much to my surprise, it plays backward! What can I do?

A The frames play in order of the layers from which they are created. And as you recall, the first layers, the oldest ones, are at the bottom of the Layers palette. Therefore, when you get ready to create an animation, look at the layers from the bottom of the Layers palette to the top. Backward? No problem! The Layers palette menu offers the command Reverse Order. In the palette, select the layers that need to be flipped by clicking on the first and Shift+clicking on the last, and then use Reverse Order.

Q What's the difference between a Flash animation and an animated GIF?

A The most important difference for us is that Illustrator can create Flash animations and it cannot create animated GIFs. If you have ImageReady or LiveMotion, though, you might want to consider the animated GIF format. Here are some of the considerations (in no particular order):

- Although virtually all Web browsers in use today support Flash, there might still be a few out there that don't.

- With animated GIFs, you've got frame-by-frame control over the timing, as well as *tweening* (the movement of an object from frame to frame) that Illustrator doesn't offer. (The Flash program and LiveMotion can do lots of neat things to SWF files that Illustrator can't do, however.)

- Animated GIFs can be used as a button's rollover state, which can be very, very cool!

- GIFs are rasterized; SWF files remain vector art.

- Animated GIF file sizes can be much larger. A GIF animation of our smiley file is almost three times as large as the SWF version.

Q I'd like to use SVG images on my Web site, but I'm afraid that my visitors won't be able to see them. Is there anything I can do?

A I'd suggest putting a link from your from page to www.adobe.com/svg/, and a notice that folks who don't know if they have SVG-support should pop by, test their browsers, and get the latest version of the Adobe SVG Viewer. Adobe even offers a logo that you can put on your page and use as a link to the SVG Viewer download page. You can find out more at www.adobe.com/svg/svglogosinstructions.html.

Quiz

1. SVG stands for

   a. Something Very Good

   b. Somewhat Variable Graphics

   c. Specialized View Graphics

   d. Scalable Vector Graphics

2. SWF is the file format for

   a. Flash animations as created in Illustrator

   b. Scalable Width Format

   c. Animated GIF when created in Flash

   d. Animated GIF when created in Illustrator

3. What command places each object on a separate layer, all by itself?

   a. Release to Layers (Build)

   b. Release to Layers (Individual)

   c. Release to Layers (Sequence)

   d. Object, Separate to Individual Layers

4. Flash animations can be created in Illustrator using

   a. Save for Web and Export

   b. Save for Web and Save As

   c. Export only

   d. Save As only

   e. Save for Web only

Quiz Answers

1. d. Although answer (a) also sounds pretty accurate.

2. a. Illustrator does not create animated GIF files.

3. c. Release to Layers (Sequence) puts each object on a layer alone, whereas (Build) adds objects cumulatively.

4. a. The Save for Web dialog box and the menu command File, Export can both be used to produce Flash files from Illustrator.

Exercises

1. Create a couple of different objects in a fresh Illustrator document. Create a specified steps blend. (Don't forget that you have to use Blend Options and then Blend, Make to actually execute the blend.) Release to layers and create an animation. Play the animation in your Web browser.

2. Remembering that you can't blend Warp effects, but that you *can* blend envelope distortions, create four stars and spread them out in your artboard. Apply Arc Lower to the first and third, and apply Arc Upper to the second and fourth. Using Specified Steps, set to five, blend them in order, 1 to 2, 2 to 3, 3 to 4. Expand all the blends and release to layers. Create an animation and watch the star "flap its wings" around your page. (See Figure 23.21 for an example.)

FIGURE 23.21
You can build on this concept to create many types of bird-like objects.

HOUR **24**

Maximizing Efficiency with Automation

I can't say that we've taught you everything there is to know about creating in Illustrator, but I can say that you've certainly learned the basics! Just think, a few short hours ago, you were a raw beginner, and now you're at least up to intermediate. Congratulations!

There's one more area that we think you need to know before we can "graduate" you. Although we've tossed in a bunch of tips and shortcuts throughout the hours, we want to show you one of Illustrator's power features that can really speed up your work. Although some of these capabilities are designed for production work, others can be integrated into any workflow, even the most free-form creative process. We'll also show you one of Illustrator's newest power features, dynamic data-driven graphics.

In this hour, you'll learn about

- The power of Illustrator's Actions
- An introduction to dynamic data-driven graphics
- A reminder about customizing the Illustrator interface

Ready! Set! Action!

Actions are little tiny programs that execute Illustrator commands for you. They can be prerecorded to do most any repetitive task. They can also be used when precision is of the utmost importance.

Similar to Microsoft Office macros and Macintosh AppleScripting in theory; you record a series of steps and play them back later to execute them on one or more files. And, best of all, you don't need to know any programming languages at all! None! Really!

Illustrator's Actions Palette

If you've used Actions in Photoshop, this palette should look very familiar (see Figure 24.1). Illustrator, by default, loads a set of Actions, some of which are shown here.

FIGURE 24.1

The contents of your Actions palette will differ.

The structure of the palette is similar to that of the Layers palette—you click triangles to expand and shrink entries in the palette. Actions are saved in sets. The individual Actions have steps. Some steps have settings. All these levels can be shown or hidden by clicking triangles.

Across the bottom of the palette you'll see some buttons. The first three use symbols, which might be familiar from your VCR, are Stop, Record, and Play. Next you've got the New Set and New Action buttons and, as usual, the Trash icon. The buttons are duplicated in the palette's menu.

To the left of the Action names and steps are two columns. A checkmark in the first column means that the particular step of the Action will run. You can uncheck any step of any Action to skip it when the Action is run.

The second column is called the *modal* column. When a step does something that can open a dialog box, there will be either an icon in this column or an empty box. If there's not even a box, then that step doesn't have a dialog box. When the icon is showing, the dialog box will appear and the Action will stop for you to enter some info or make some changes. When the icon is missing, the Action will play with whatever settings were recorded for that step.

Take note of the palette's menu command, Button Mode. When in Button Mode, you'll see just the names of the various Actions, and you'll be able to play them with a single click. Keep in mind that the Actions will play with the latest choices for which steps to run and modal controls, and because you're in Button Mode, you'll not see those choices (see Figure 24.2) .

FIGURE 24.2

Although Button Mode offers convenience, it also hides the individual steps of an Action—and whether or not those steps are checked to play or will be skipped.

Task: Playing Back an Action

One of my favorites among Illustrator's default Actions is Style/Brush/Swatch Cleanup. It's a smart idea to run this Action when finalizing a file.

1. Open an existing Illustrator document or create a new document and add a variety of artwork. Save the file (under a new name if it's a file you want to save). In the Mac Finder or Windows Explorer, check the file size. Keep the file open.

2. In the Actions palette, click once on Style/Brush/Swatch Cleanup. (It should be in the Default Actions folder, but it's not likely to be at the top.)

3. With the Action highlighted, either click the Play button at the bottom of the palette or use the palette's menu command Play.

4. When asked whether you want to delete selected styles, swatches, and brushes, click OK.

5. When the Action is finished, take a look at your Brushes, Swatches, and Styles palettes. They will contain only the contents that the image actually uses.

6. Save the file. Take another look at it in the Finder or Windows Explorer. Compare the new size. It could be as much as 100K smaller.

Task: Recording a Custom Action

The true power of Actions comes from recording your own. If there's a task you perform regularly, record an Action to handle it for you.

1. Click the New Set button and give your set a name.

2. Click the New Action button. Name the Action Final Step and assign it to Shift+F9 (unless you already use that function key combination). (The color pop-up menu allows you to color-coordinate your Actions. The colors are used when the palette is in Button Mode.) Click the Record button (see Figure 24.3).

FIGURE 24.3

The New Action dialog box enables you to select a hot key and assign a color.

3. The Action is now recording every step you take in Illustrator. Use the menu command Select, Object, Stray Points. This makes a selection of any anchor points lying around the artboard that aren't part of a path. (It's amazing how many can accumulate on a busy artboard.)

4. Press the Delete (Mac)/Backspace (Windows) key.

5. In the Actions palette, click once on the Action Style/Brush/Swatch Cleanup.

6. Click the Play button at the bottom of the Actions palette. Click OK when asked if you want to delete the various elements.

7. When the Action is done playing, click the Stop button at the bottom of the Actions palette. Your Actions palette should be similar to that shown in Figure 24.4.

FIGURE 24.4

A simple, yet effective new Action.

This Action is a good way to finish any project. In addition to cleaning up the palettes, it rids the artboard (and the image) of any random anchor points that could lead to output problems. (It also shows that you can record an Action within an Action.)

24

Insert Menu Item

The Actions palette menu offers you a way to include in an Action various menu commands. While recording an Action, you can use the palette menu command Insert Menu Item. With the dialog box open, mouse to the menu command that you want to add and select it. Close the dialog box by clicking OK, then continue recording the Action.

Batch Mode

The Actions palette also offers a command called Batch (see Figure 24.5). This powerful feature enables you to play an Action on a whole folder full of files. You can play the Action and then save and close the images, or make copies in a different folder, even with a new name.

The Batch command is very handy for preparing similar images for the Web, using recorded optimization settings, as well as for various prepress production chores. Batch is also a great reason to know that you can record Actions within Actions. You can record a single Action that actually runs several Actions. And, if you play that new Action back with Batch, you've effectively run numerous Actions on numerous files with the click of a single button!

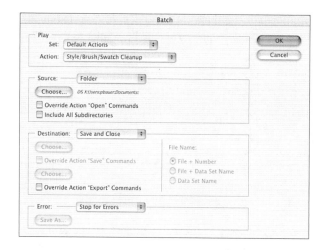

FIGURE 24.5

The Batch dialog box enables you to run Actions on folders of images or data sets, which are used with dynamic data-driven graphics.

Dynamic Data-Driven Graphics for the Web

Dynamic data-driven graphics —the name seems so cryptic! Let's break it down and tear it apart. Dynamic means that the graphics will change. Most of our artwork is static. After we create it, that's it. Dynamic graphics can be altered and in this case, it can be done automatically. Data-driven indicates that the dynamic part will be governed by a collection of information. And graphics, well, it's a little late in the game to be explaining *that* term!

When we put it back together, we're talking about graphics that can be changed automatically based on a database. The database will store images (or other elements, including graph data and text). The graphics will be updated from that stockpile of data. Dynamic data-driven graphics can be used in both print and Web environments. Let's look at one possible scenario.

Dynamic Data-Driven Graphics in Action

First, let's define the roles. The Web designer (us) is responsible for the looks and the graphics. The Web developer (typically someone else) is responsible for the mechanics and the programming. The two jobs need to work together, but they require separate sets of skills and knowledge.

Now, for some terms that might be more comprehensible—as the illustrator, we create a template. The Web developer integrates that template into the Web site. The template is updated from a database so that the Web page's content can be changed to fit a certain need or situation.

As an example, we'll use a Web site for a women's clothing store. The plan is this—when a shopper first visits the site she (or he) fills out a profile. Sizes, preferences, tastes, preferred price range, favorite designers, and so on. On future visits, the Web page will greet the shopper by name, and make several recommendations.

Our job is to design a Web page that holds slots into which images will be loaded from the database of product pictures. The page will also hold a text variable so that the shopper is greeted by name. We don't have to worry about how the Web site will read the shopper's *cookie*, how images will be selected, or even how the images will load into the page. We only need to be concerned with establishing the *template* for the page.

When the shopper visits the site, the page shows a couple of appropriate blouses, a skirt or pair of slacks, a handbag or other accessory, and a pair of shoes or boots.

We provide the template, complete with the dynamic data-driven graphics capabilities; the Web developer coordinates the access to the database; the shoppers spend lots more money; the company becomes more profitable; the developer gets a big bonus, and we…we design more templates.

24

Who They're for and When to Use Them

Dynamic data-driven graphics are targeted toward the big, powerful Web sites that handle lots and lots of visitors. That doesn't mean, however, that they can't be integrated into anyone's Web site. It takes a little knowledge of XML (Extensible Markup Language, one of the languages of the Web), and access to an ODBC-compliant data source. And, of course, a talented Adobe Illustrator expert, ready to create the template.

One of the keys to dynamic data-driven graphics is the database. It should be ODBC-compliant. That's Open Database Connectivity. It might sound scary and over-our-heads, but if you've got FileMaker Pro, Microsoft Excel or Access, you're in business! FoxPro, dBASE, Oracle, IBM DB2, and SQL are other names and acronyms that fit the bill.

The Mechanics of Dynamic Data-Driven Graphics

A variety of terms are associated with this new technology that are probably unfamiliar to you.

- Template: The template is the graphic Web page, incorporating all the various elements. It holds images and text that will remain the same, and the images, text, and data that will change. It is, at heart, simply an Illustrator illustration.

- Variable: Variables are the parts of the template that will change. You identify a variable in the Variables palette (which we'll discuss in a few minutes). Text strings, linked images, graph data, and even the visibility of objects can be identified as variables.

- Data Set: A data set consists of one or more variables and the associated items that can be used in the variables, the data itself.

- Data Source: The data source is the database from which the variables are filled.

- Binding: The Web design tool, such as Adobe GoLive, is used to bind a variable to the data source. (This is not done in Illustrator.) Scripts or image servers can be used.

- Dynamic/Static: Dynamic objects can change, these are the variables. Static objects will remain unchanged, because they are the remainders of the template.

A typical development process might go something like this: The Web team gets together and decides that it wants to (and can) implement this exciting new technology. A basic plan is sketched out. The developer creates some sample data sets and perhaps writes XML code to create the actual variables. The sample data sets and variables are passed to the designer. The designer creates the template, using the sample data sets to make sure that everything will appear in the correct positions and relationships. The designer passes the completed template to the developer. The developer then uses programming knowledge (and perhaps some mystical powers) to bind the template's variables to the database.

The Variables Palette

The primary tool of dynamic data-driven graphics in Illustrator is the Variables palette (see Figure 24.6).

FIGURE 24.6

Dynamic data-driven graphics are coordinated through the Variables palette.

You use the palette to identify variables and associate objects in the template with a variable. In Figure 24.7, a rough idea of a template is starting to take shape. Each of the image boxes (which must be linked images, not vector objects or embedded images) is a variable. When operational, the Web page will show a photograph of the appropriate product in the designated spot. There's also a text variable. The shopper's name will be retrieved from a database and displayed as a personalized greeting.

FIGURE 24.7

Variables can be text, linked images, graph data, or an object's visibility.

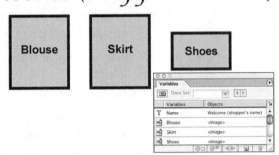

You can add a variable without associating any object or text to it by clicking the New Variable button at the bottom of the palette. If you hold down the Option (Mac)/Alt (Windows) key while clicking, the Variable Options dialog box will automatically open (see Figure 24.8).

FIGURE 24.8

You can open the options for any variable at any time by double-clicking it in the Variables palette.

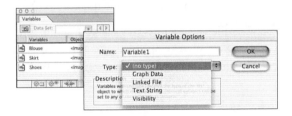

To associate a linked image, graph, or text with a variable, select it on the Artboard, select the appropriate variable in the Variables palette, and click the Make Object Dynamic button at the bottom of the Variables palette, the left-most button. The variable must be set to the appropriate type or not have a specific type assigned. Text must be point type, not area type, or type on a path.

From the designer's perspective, dynamic data-driven graphics at first seems pretty difficult. However, when we chop out the developer's part of the work, we're simply creating the template for a Web page in Illustrator and clicking a few buttons in the Variables palette. It's up to the developer to coordinate with the database and bind the variables using GoLive or an image server.

A Look Back at Customizing Illustrator

Way, way back in Hour 2, "Setting Up Illustrator," I talked about customizing Illustrator's keyboard shortcuts. I believe I said something along the lines of "At the end of Hour 24, you'll probably have a pretty good idea of how you want to set your preferences, what options make most sense for you." Well, we're almost there, just about at the end of Hour 24. You probably know a *lot* more about what options work best for you.

- You know that if you're going to be doing Web work, pixels is probably the unit of measure you want as the default.
- You know that if you'll be doing mostly prepress work you'll want to stick with CMYK color mode.
- You know that there are some commands and tools that you'll be using regularly, commands and tools that should have custom keyboard shortcuts assigned.
- There are probably some custom styles and swatches in the back of your mind, just waiting to be created.
- Think back to the discussion of startup files. Time to plan what you want and don't want in them, which swatches, brushes, styles. You should also know by know what page size and orientation is going to be typical for you, another thing that can be set in the startup files to save you some time.

Take some time soon, while Illustrator is fresh in your mind, to jot a few notes about customization. Creating your own keyboard shortcuts and startup files can save you minutes per document, which can add up to hours pretty quickly if you use Illustrator regularly.

Summary

Mordy and I would like to congratulate you on finishing the book. But, although the 24 hours are over, your education never ends. We all continue to learn and grow as we gain experience with Illustrator. Check out www.mordy.com for some additional tips and tricks and tutorials. And when you're ready for a great big, heavy-duty reference book to keep you company while you work with Illustrator, pick up a copy of my *Special Edition Using Adobe Illustrator 10*. It's got the answers to your questions, and a whole lot more.

Thanks for sharing these 24 hours with us!

Pete Bauer & Mordy Golding

Workshop

A couple of easy questions, and one final exercise to cap it all off!

Q&A

Q Is everything in Illustrator recordable in an Action?

A No, not everything. Almost all the creative process is recordable, but interface-related activities, such as showing and hiding palettes, are not. Nor are some of the document-level operations, such as the Page Setup and Document Setup commands, or Illustrator-level things like the Preferences.

Q Can I share Actions with friends and colleagues?

A Yes, you can. Select the appropriate set of Actions and use the palette's Save Actions command. If you just want to share one Action, create a new set and copy the Action into it, then save. You can send the saved Action to anyone using a comparable version of Illustrator. (It's best to add the file extension .aia, by the way.) The person on the receiving end uses the Actions palette command Load Actions to add the set to the palette.

Q I want to use dynamic data-driven graphics on my personal Web site. Will Illustrator create the pages for me?

A Illustrator will create the *templates* for you. You will have to build the Web site in a real Web design program, such as Adobe GoLive.

Quiz

1. Illustrator's Batch command is found where?

    a. File, Automate, Batch

    b. File, Scripts, Batch

    c. The Actions palette menu

    d. An Actions palette button

2. The modal column of the Actions palette is designed to…

    a. …enable you to use the Type tool in an Action.

    b. …give you the option of using settings recorded in a dialog box or open the dialog box for new settings.

    c. …let you determine whether a particular step of an Action will run or not.

    d. …prevent error messages from stopping Actions while running unattended overnight.

3. With dynamic data-driven graphics, a variable is used to do what?

    a Identify a part of an illustration that is dynamic.

    b. Insert images, text, or data from a database.

    c. Make a Web page flexible in content.

    d. All of the above.

Quiz Answers

1. c. (It's Photoshop's Batch command that's under File, Automate.)

2. b. It's used with commands and tools that have dialog boxes.

3. d. Variables are the core of dynamic data-driven graphics.

Exercises

1. Close your book. Close your eyes. Breath in deeply. Let it out slowly. Get a great big grin on your face and shout "Hurrah!" It's time to celebrate a job well done!

INDEX

C